Mathematics

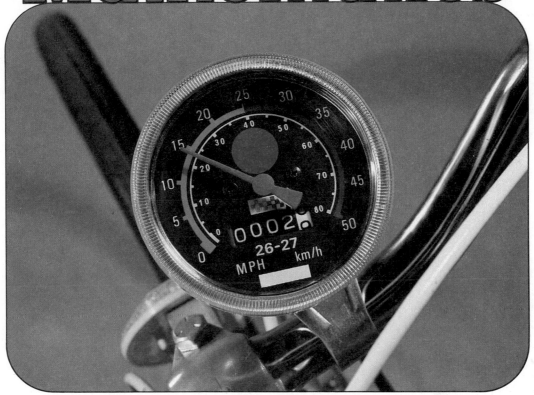

Coordinating Author   Ernest R. Duncan

Authors   W.G. Quast
William L. Cole
Thelma M. Sparks
Mary Ann Haubner

Houghton Mifflin Company   BOSTON
Atlanta   Dallas   Geneva, Ill.   Hopewell, N.J.   Palo Alto   Toronto

Authors

Ernest R. Duncan
Rutgers University
New Brunswick, New Jersey

W.G. Quast
Slippery Rock State College
Slippery Rock, Pennsylvania

William L. Cole
Michigan State University
Lansing, Michigan

Thelma M. Sparks
Anne Arundel County Schools
Annapolis, Maryland

Mary Ann Haubner
Mount Saint Joseph College
Cincinnati, Ohio

Editorial Advisor

Charles E. Allen
Los Angeles City Schools
Los Angeles, California

Andrew Gleason
Harvard University
Cambridge, Massachusetts

Teacher Consultants

Laura Grounsell
Instructional Consultant
Rockdale County Schools
Conyers, Georgia

Miguel Salazar
Teacher and Department Chairman
Morey Junior High School
Denver, Colorado

ISBN: 0-395-35839-6
CDEFGHIJ-D-93210/8987654

Contents

4 Geometry and Measurement

5 Number Theory and Developing Fractions

6 Addition and Subtraction of Fractions

10 Percents

11 Percent Applications

12 Probability and Statistics

13 Geometry and Measurement

14 Integers

Applying Your Skills

Something Special

Numeration and Measurement

1

What units of measure would you use to measure this sculpture?

Whole Numbers

How many one-dollar bills do you think there are in use at one time in the United States? Recently there were 3,339,756,324. Let's look at that number in the place value chart below.

Billions			Millions			Thousands					
hundreds	tens	ones	hundreds	tens	ones	hundreds	tens	ones	hundreds	tens	ones
		3	3	3	9	7	5	6	3	2	4

The digit 5 is in the ten thousands' place. It has a value of 50,000, or $5 \times 10,000$. We read the number shown above as *three billion, three hundred thirty-nine million, seven hundred fifty-six thousand, three hundred twenty-four*.

Standard form: 3,339,756,324

Expanded form: 3,000,000,000 + 300,000,000 + 30,000,000 + 9,000,000 + 700,000 + 50,000 + 6000 + 300 + 20 + 4

Exercises

Complete.

1. 32 = 30 + ▓

2. 127 = 100 + ▓ + 7

3. 1075 = ▓ + 70 + 5

4. 2400 = 2000 + ▓

5. 189 = ▓ hundred 89

6. 1680 = 1 thousand, ▓ hundred 80

7. 12,500 = ▓ thousand, 5 hundred

8. 30,490 = 30 thousand, ▓ hundred 90

Write the value of the underlined digit.

9. 18<u>5</u>6

10. 21,49<u>7</u>

11. 50<u>9</u>,686

12. 1,<u>4</u>09,028

13. 12,008,<u>5</u>29

14. 247,5<u>1</u>9,003

15. 1,<u>4</u>87,765,998

16. <u>2</u>47,890,456

Write the standard form.

17. 6 hundred 9

18. 4 thousand, 6 hundred

19. 5 million, 4 thousand

20. 16 billion, 480 thousand

21. 127 billion, 12 thousand

22. 147 million, 301 thousand, 430

23. 300 + 40 + 8

24. 5000 + 800 + 60 + 1

25. 30,000 + 7000 + 800 + 40 + 1

26. 700,000 + 2000 + 900 + 70 + 6

Write in expanded form.

27. 756   **28.** 1290   **29.** 3092   **30.** 81,200   **31.** 500,731

32. 1,000,200   **33.** 788,000   **34.** 42,976   **35.** 2,380,000   **36.** 3,298,577

Using Large Numbers

News reports and tables often use a combination of numbers and words for large numbers. For example, we may write 4,580,000,000 as *4,580 million*.

Write these numbers in standard form.

37. 1,865 million   **38.** 28,619 million   **39.** 305,610 million

★ **40.** The chart shows the amount of money spent on recreation in the United States in one year in millions of dollars. Write each amount in standard form.

Spending for Personal Recreation (millions of dollars)	
Books and maps	5,975
Toys and sports equipment	30,630
Radio and T.V receivers, and musical instruments	21,036
Admission to movie theaters	4,339
Magazines, newspapers, and sheet music	10,384
Flowers, seed and potted plants	5,329
Radio and TV repair	1,948
Admission to spectator sports	2,059
Other	18,346
Total spending for personal recreation	101,046

Decimals

Our number system is based on tens. If you split something into ten
equal pieces, each piece is a **tenth** of the whole. If you split something
into a hundred equal pieces, each piece is a **hundredth** of the whole.

a unit

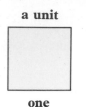

one

10 pieces

△ **a tenth**

100 pieces

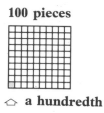

△ **a hundredth**

In the chart below, notice that the decimal point separates the whole
number from the tenths and hundredths.

hundreds	tens	ones	.	tenths	hundredths
		0	.	1		⬦ 0.1 ⬦ 1 tenth
		0	.	0	1	⬦ 0.01 ⬦ 1 hundredth
		4	.	3		⬦ 4.3 ⬦ 4 and 3 tenths
		9	.	9	5	⬦ 9.95 ⬦ 9 and 95 hundredths

> The word *"and"*
> marks the position
> of the decimal point.

Sometimes a number like 4.3 is read as *4 point 3.*

Exercises

Complete.

1. 0.7 = ▩ tenths

2. 0.3 = ▩ tenths

3. 2.6 = ▩ and ▩ tenths

4. 5.4 = ▩ and ▩ tenths

5. 0.04 = ▩ hundredths

6. 0.02 = ▩ hundredths

7. 0.09 = ▩ hundredths

8. 0.14 = ▩ hundredths

9. 6.05 = ▩ and ▩ hundredths

10. 4.42 = ▩ and ▩ hundredths

Write as a decimal.

11. 4 tenths

12. 8 tenths

13. 5 tenths

14. 2 and 9 tenths

15. 4 and 2 tenths

16. 7 and 3 tenths

17. 4 hundredths

18. 36 hundredths

19. 50 hundredths

20. 3 and 21 hundredths

21. 2 and 30 hundredths

22. 7 and 42 hundredths

23. 5 and 7 hundredths

24. 10 and 8 hundredths

25. 14 and 1 hundredth

Write in words.

26. 0.2

27. 0.7

28. 0.8

29. 0.03

30. 0.05

31. 0.66

32. 2.1

33. 8.4

34. 3.06

35. 5.26

Writing Checks

When you write a check, there are two places for writing the amount of money. You write the amount once with digits and once with words. The amount in words usually shows the cents as hundredths of a dollar written as a fraction.

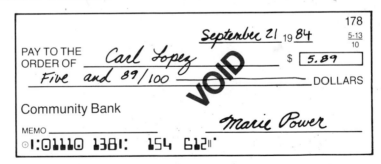

It is customary to write zero cents as shown below.

$ 52.00

Fifty-two and no/100 ———————— DOLLARS

Write the amount of money in words as you would write it on a check.

36. $13.02

37. $24.00

38. $7.98

39. $12.00

40. $49.98

41. Why do we write the amount of money on a check in two ways?

1

Decimals and Place Value

A calculator can multiply two numbers in thousandths of a second.
The place-value chart below includes **thousandths** and **millionths**.

ones	.	tenths	hundredths	thousandths	ten-thousandths	hundred-thousandths	millionths
2	.	3	5	8			
0	.	0	0	1	5		
0	.	0	0	0	1	7	2

▷ 2 and 358 thousandths
▷ 15 ten-thousandths
▷ 172 millionths

Sometimes we read a number like 2.358 as *two point three five eight*.
The expanded form shows the value of each digit.

Standard form		Expanded form
2.358	=	2 + 0.3 + 0.05 + 0.008

Writing extra zeros after the last digit in the decimal does not change
the value of the number.

$$2.358 = 2.3580 = 2.358000$$

Exercises

Complete.

1. 0.002 = ▨ thousandths

2. 0.06 = ▨ hundredths

3. 0.0217 = ▨ ten-thousandths

4. 0.000356 = ▨ millionths

5. 0.28 = 0.2 + 0.0▨

6. 0.029 = 0.02 + 0.00▨

7. 0.42 = 0.▨ + 0.02

8. 0.042 = 0.0▨ + 0.002

9. 6.103 = 6 + 0.1 + 0.00▨

10. 4.017 = ▨ + 0.01 + 0.007

Write the decimal in standard form.

11. 263 thousandths

12. 8 millionths

13. 6 and 503 thousandths

14. 28 and 78 ten-thousandths

15. 0.01 + 0.009

16. 0.6 + 0.03 + 0.002

17. 1 + 0.03 + 0.009

18. 47 + 0.9 + 0.008

Write the expanded form.

19. 2.9

20. 8.36

21. 1.08

22. 3.758

23. 6.0027

24. 9.0876

25. 2.4879

26. 5.3027

Are the decimals equal? Write *Yes* or *No*.

27. 0.15; 0.150

28. 0.2; 0.02

29. 10.3; 1.03

30. 3.5; 3.500

31. 0.290; 0.29000

32. 1.07; 1.70

Splitting Seconds

The time it takes a computer to do a calculation may be measured in **milliseconds**, **microseconds**, or **nanoseconds**.

1 millisecond = 0.001 second
1 microsecond = 0.000 001 second
1 nanosecond = 0.000 000 001 second

Complete.

EXAMPLE   0.029 s = 29 milliseconds

★ **33.** 0.008 s = ▨ milliseconds

★ **34.** 0.087 s = ▨ milliseconds

★ **35.** 0.000 004 s = ▨ microseconds

★ **36.** 0.000 016 s = ▨ microseconds

★ **37.** 0.000 000 112 s = ▨ nanoseconds

★ **38.** 0.000 987 s = ▨ nanoseconds

★ **39.** 0.000 001 520 s = ▨ microseconds

★ **40.** 0.005 400 s = ▨ milliseconds

Comparing Whole Numbers

Hello, Dolly! and *My Fair Lady* were two very popular musicals on Broadway. Let's compare the number of performances.

Hello, Dolly!   2 8 4 4 performances
My Fair Lady   2 7 1 7 performances

The thousands are the same. ——⏋⏋—— 8 hundreds is more than 7 hundreds.

2844 **is greater than** 2717, or 2717 **is less than** 2844

2844 > 2717   2717 < 2844

The chart lists the plays in order, according to the number of performances, from greatest to least.

2844 > 2717   and   2717 > 2329

Play	Performances
Hello, Dolly!	2844
My Fair Lady	2717
Man of La Mancha	2329

If two whole numbers have a different number of digits, the number with more digits is the greater.

107 > 58
3 digits   2 digits

Exercises

Complete. Write < or > .

1.   5 > 3
     25 ▨ 23
    250 ▨ 230

2.   4 ▨ 7
   400 ▨ 700
  1400 ▨ 1700

3.   6 ▨ 8
   60 ▨ 80
  560 ▨ 580

4.   9 ▨ 4
  189 ▨ 184
1891 ▨ 1841

Compare the numbers. Write < or > .

5. 75 ▨ 53

6. 31 ▨ 39

7. 37 ▨ 432

8. 746 ▨ 647

9. 615 ▨ 61

10. 4328 ▨ 4319

11. 1892 ▨ 968

12. 987 ▨ 6042

13. 12,729 ▨ 12,725

14. 73,048 ▨ 72,965

15. 857,200 ▨ 857,203

16. 6,475,289 ▨ 986,794

17. 2,374,589 ▨ 2,383,107

18. 439,286 ▨ 9,482,970

19. 53,274,860 ▨ 3,274,859

List the numbers in order from least to greatest.

20. 26; 39; 18

21. 128; 82; 91

22. 102; 99; 201

List the numbers in order from greatest to least.

23. 41; 39; 108

24. 4003; 561; 75

25. 311; 6004; 1234

Tickets, Please!

★ **26.** We can list events by the order in which they happened. This is called **chronological order**. The earliest event is listed first.

List the dance groups in chronological order by the year they were founded.

Dance Group	Year Founded
Australian Ballet	1962
Ballet Nacional de Cuba	1948
Bolshoi Ballet	1820
Dance Theater of Harlem	1969
Dutch National Ballet	1961
Paris Opera Ballet	1671
Pilobolus Dance Theater	1971
Twyla Tharp Foundation	1965

★ **27.** A special exhibit of the treasures of King Tut toured museums several years ago. The attendance figures at the exhibit are shown below.

List the attendance figures in order from greatest to least.

King Tut Exhibit	
Place	**Attendance**
Washington, D.C.	832,853
Chicago	1,349,724
New Orleans	870,855
Los Angeles	1,250,629
Seattle	1,293,203
New York	1,267,000
San Francisco	1,360,000

The digits on the cards can be arranged to form 24 different numbers. List these numbers in order from least to greatest.

Comparing Decimals

Two friends are comparing their batting averages. Who has the greater batting average?

Batting Averages

Juan   0 . 3 2 5
Willie   0 . 3 2 7

The tenths and the hundredths are the same.

7 thousandths is greater than 5 thousandths

0.327 > 0.325,   or   0.325 < 0.327

Willie has the greater batting average.

Sometimes, before you compare two decimals, it helps to write zeros after the last digit of a decimal. To compare 0.5 and 0.53, think of 0.5 as 0.50.

0.50 < 0.53 so 0.5 < 0.53

Exercises

Compare the numbers. Write < or > .

1. 0.4 ▦ 0.9

2. 0.5 ▦ 0.19

3. 1.36 ▦ 1.28

4. 0.278 ▦ 0.269

5. 5.18 ▦ 5.173

6. 8.965 ▦ 12.64

7. 1.2 ▦ 1.02

8. 0.26 ▦ 0.026

9. 0.406 ▦ 0.46

10. 904 ▦ 904.2

11. 6.52 ▦ 6.523

12. 0.3796 ▦ 0.3788

13. 0.9 ▦ 1.14

14. 56.311 ▦ 56.31111

15. 3.75 ▦ 3.705

16. 0.005 ▦ 0.01

17. 0.204 ▦ 0.024

18. 0.0089 ▦ 0.01

19. Arrange the numbers in order from greatest to least.

Batting Averages

Cahaly	0.310	Cawley	0.309
Caffin	0.289	Chang	0.298
Callahan	0.275	Cortez	0.319
Calderelli	0.304	Coleman	0.328
Curran	0.321		

What's on the Tube?

Use the chart to answer the questions.

Number of People Viewing Prime Time TV (in millions)

Monday	92.06
Tuesday	86.68
Wednesday	87.67
Thursday	83.89
Friday	84.69
Saturday	86.77
Sunday	104.70

20. On which night do the most people watch TV during prime time?

21. On which night do the fewest people watch TV during prime time?

22. List the number of viewers in order from greatest to least.

★ **23.** Write in standard form the number of people watching prime time TV each night.

Checkpoint A

Write the standard form. (*pages 10–11*)

1. 8 hundred 9

2. 6 thousand, 7 hundred 50

3. 20,000 + 6000 + 700 + 8

4. 70,000,000 + 3,000,000 + 80

Write as a decimal. (*pages 12–13*)

5. 8 tenths

6. 72 hundredths

7. 3 and 5 tenths

8. 9 and 4 hundredths

Write in standard form. (*pages 14–15*)

9. 875 thousandths

10. 82 millionths

11. 3 + 0.2 + 0.009

12. 12 + 0.08 + 0.0006

Compare the numbers. Write $<$ or $>$. (*pages 16–17*)

13. 548 ▓ 571

14. 6782 ▓ 6780

15. 62,728 ▓ 62,579

16. 42,752,000 ▓ 45,976,892

Arrange the numbers in order from greatest to least. (*pages 18–19*)

17. Average Number Hits per Game

Minsk	1.68	Marjan	0.93
Margolis	1.94	Mannheim	1.34

Extra practice on page 420

Rounding Whole Numbers

A reporter making her report after a concert says, *A record 15,000 people attended the concert.*

Actually, there were 14,854 people at the concert. The reporter rounded the number to the nearest thousand.

Here is how you round 14,854 to different places.

Number	Round to the nearest	Digit to the right	Is it 5 or more?	Round
14,854	ten	4	no	down to 14,850
14,854	hundred	5	yes	up to 14,900
14,854	thousand	8	yes	up to 15,000

Exercises

Round the number by completing the chart.

	Number	Round to the nearest	Digit to the right	Is it 5 or more?	Round
1.	162	ten	2	no	down to ?
2.	3865	ten	5	yes	?
3.	583	hundred	8	?	?
4.	2447	hundred	?	?	?
5.	8462	thousand	?	?	?
6.	19,699	thousand	?	?	?
7.	2,899,763	million	?	?	?
8.	164,092,622	million	?	?	?

Round to the nearest ten.

9. 34   **10.** 315   **11.** 709   **12.** 6388   **13.** 4861

14. 9649   **15.** 1304   **16.** 2996   **17.** 27,752   **18.** 99,999

Round to the nearest hundred.

19. 182   **20.** 609   **21.** 951   **22.** 7248   **23.** 3550

24. 8825   **25.** 12,062   **26.** 14,968   **27.** 200,856   **28.** 99,999

Round to the nearest thousand.

29. 4178   **30.** 7502   **31.** 8268   **32.** 14,257   **33.** 20,855

34. 39,904   **35.** 563,399   **36.** 845,571   **37.** 1,578,469   **38.** 999,999

Special Report

Suppose you are a TV reporter preparing a special report on communications. Write a headline for each fact, using numbers rounded to the nearest million.

39. An estimated 210,715,349,000 phone calls are made in a year.

40. The number of homes having one or more TV sets is 76,347,500.

41. There are 162,076,774 telephones in use.

42. The number of radios manufactured in one year was 12,497,850.

Calculator Corner

Suppose the pattern at the right is continued.
1. How many letters will be in the J row?
2. Which row will have 32,768 letters?

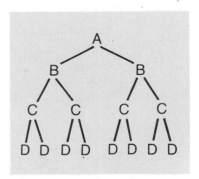

Rounding Decimals

Scientists estimate that the distance of a new star from Earth is 4.572 light years. A newspaper article says the star is about 5 light years away.

4.572 was rounded to 5.

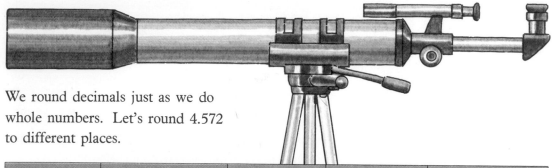

We round decimals just as we do whole numbers. Let's round 4.572 to different places.

Number	Round to the nearest	Digit to the right	Is it 5 or more?	Round
4.572	whole number	5	yes	up to 5
4.572	tenth	7	yes	up to 4.6
4.572	hundredth	2	no	down to 4.57

Exercises

Round the number by completing the chart.

	Number	Round to the nearest	Digit to the right	Is it 5 or more?	Round
1.	7.3	whole number	3	no	down to ?
2.	0.67	whole number	6	yes	?
3.	4.72	tenth	2	?	?
4.	9.35	tenth	?	?	?
5.	81.479	tenth	?	?	?
6.	7.087	hundredth	?	?	?
7.	0.0536	hundredth	?	?	?
8.	0.5219	thousandth	?	?	?
9.	0.6184	thousandth	?	?	?

Round to the nearest whole number.

10. 5.7   **11.** 2.3   **12.** 4.6   **13.** 7.9   **14.** 0.5

15. 14.6   **16.** 21.35   **17.** 8.62   **18.** 9.56   **19.** 41.61

Round to the nearest tenth.

20. 0.62   **21.** 0.41   **22.** 1.35   **23.** 0.64   **24.** 0.29

25. 0.321   **26.** 7.456   **27.** 0.672   **28.** 0.407   **29.** 0.091

Round to the nearest hundredth.

30. 0.416   **31.** 0.835   **32.** 0.651   **33.** 0.211   **34.** 0.724

35. 0.3842   **36.** 0.7161   **37.** 0.4339   **38.** 0.6067   **39.** 0.4013

Round to the nearest thousandth.

40. 0.2114   **41.** 0.8635   **42.** 0.0117   **43.** 0.3672   **44.** 0.2134

45. 1.2681   **46.** 6.4139   **47.** 1.7204   **48.** 1.6713   **49.** 8.0107

The chart gives the distance of each planet from the sun in millions of kilometers.

50. Make a similar chart showing the distances rounded to the nearest million. Do *not* write in standard form.

EXAMPLE   78.8 million km = 79 million km

51. Write the distance of each planet from the sun, using a number in standard form.

EXAMPLE   78.8 million km = 78,800,000 km

Distance From Sun (millions of kilometers)			
Mercury	57.9	Saturn	1426.1
Venus	108.1	Uranus	2869.1
Earth	149.5	Neptune	4495.6
Mars	227.8	Pluto	5898.9
Jupiter	777.8		

Measuring Length

Like our number system, the metric system of measurement is based on the number ten. The ruler shows **centimeters (cm)** and **millimeters (mm).** A centimeter is divided into ten millimeters.

$$10 \text{ mm} = 1 \text{ cm} \qquad 1 \text{ mm} = 0.1 \text{ cm}$$

Film for cameras is often measured in millimeters. At the right is a picture of 35 mm film.

All measurements are approximations. We can measure the width of the film to the nearest centimeter or to the nearest millimeter.

> To the nearest centimeter: 4 cm
> To the nearest millimeter: 35 mm

The more **precise** measurement is 35 mm because a millimeter is a smaller unit than a centimeter.

The width of the film may also be given to the nearest tenth of a centimeter.

$$1 \text{ mm} = 0.1 \text{ cm} \quad \text{so} \quad 35 \text{ mm} = 3.5 \text{ cm}$$

Exercises

Measure the line segment to the nearest centimeter.

1. _____   **2.** _____

3. _____

Measure the line segment to the nearest millimeter.

4. _____   **5.** _____

6. _____

Measure the line segment to the nearest tenth of a centimeter.

7. _____   **8.** _____

Measure the length to
the nearest centimeter.

10.

9. **11.**

Measure the length to
the nearest millimeter.

13.

12. **14.**

15. **16.** **17.** **18.**

Measure the line segment to the nearest tenth of a centimeter.

19. _____ **20.** _____

21. _____ **22.** _____

Tape Gaps

When measured to the nearest
centimeter both tape segments are 3 cm
long. Both segments are between
2.5 cm and 3.5 cm long.

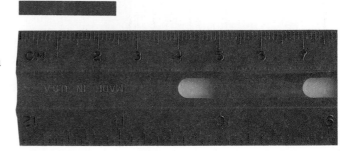

Complete.

23. A tape segment is between 8.5 cm and 9.5 cm long. Its length to
the nearest centimeter is ▨ cm.

24. A tape segment is between 16.5 cm and 17.5 cm long. Its length
to the nearest centimeter is ▨ cm.

★ **25.** The length of a tape segment to the nearest centimeter is 7 cm. It
must be no shorter than ▨.5 cm. It must be shorter than 7.▨ cm.

★ **26.** Is it possible for two segments to have measurements of 6 cm, to
the nearest centimeter, and still not be equal? Explain.

Metric Units of Length

The basic unit of length in the metric system is the **meter (m).**
A meter is about the distance from a doorknob to the floor.

We use centimeters and millimeters to measure shorter lengths. Here
are some examples.

Statement		Example
A millimeter (mm) is a tenth of a centimeter.	1 mm = 0.1 cm 10 mm = 1 cm	27 mm = 2.7 cm 38 mm = 3.8 cm
A centimeter (cm) is a hundredth of a meter.	1 cm = 0.01 m 100 cm = 1 m	265 cm = 2.65 m 341 cm = 3.41 m
A millimeter (mm) is also a thousandth of a meter.	1 mm = 0.001 m 1000 mm = 1 m	3572 mm = 3.572 m 5627 mm = 5.627 m

A **kilometer (km)** is used to measure long distances. A kilometer is
1000 m. That's about as long as 10 football fields. It takes about 12
minutes to walk a kilometer at a normal walking speed.

$$1 \text{ km} = 1000 \text{ m} \qquad 4.5 \text{ km} = 4500 \text{ m}$$
so
$$1 \text{ m} = 0.001 \text{ km} \qquad 478 \text{ m} = 0.478 \text{ km}$$

Exercises

Choose the best estimate. Write *a*, *b*, or *c*.

1. The length of a camera
   a. 14 mm   **b.** 14 cm   **c.** 14 m

2. The width of a shoelace
   a. 4 mm   **b.** 4 cm   **c.** 4 m

3. The length of a basketball court
   a. 26 mm   **b.** 26 cm   **c.** 26 m

4. The length of a large parking lot
   a. 0.1 cm   **b.** 0.1 m   **c.** 0.1 km

Complete.

5. 1 m = 100 cm
   2 m = ▢ cm
   5 m = ▢ cm
   12 m = ▢ cm

6. 100 cm = 1 m
   500 cm = ▢ m
   50 cm = 0.▢ m
   5 cm = 0.▢ m

7. 0.1 cm = 1 mm
   0.8 cm = ▢ mm
   8.0 cm = ▢ mm
   80.0 cm = ▢ mm

Complete.

8. 600 cm = ▢ m

9. 8000 cm = ▢ m

10. 5 m = ▢ cm

11. 7 m = ▢ cm

12. 40 mm = ▢ cm

13. 90 mm = ▢ cm

14. 7 cm = ▢ m

15. 4 km = ▢ m

16. 6000 m = ▢ km

17. 9 m = ▢ cm

18. 250 mm = ▢ cm

19. 60 m = ▢ cm

Other Metric Units of Length

The commonly used metric units of length are the meter, the kilometer, the centimeter, and the millimeter. The chart shows other units and how they are related.

kilometer km 1000 m	hectometer hm 100 m	dekameter dam 10 m	meter m 1 m	decimeter dm 0.1 m	centimeter cm 0.01 m	millimeter mm 0.001 m

Notice that each unit is 10 times the unit to its right.

Copy and complete.

20. 17 km = ▢ hm = ▢ dam = ▢ m

21. 3000 mm = ▢ cm = ▢ dm = ▢ m

22. 800,000 cm = ▢ dm = ▢ m = ▢ dam = ▢ hm = ▢ km

23. 62 hm = ▢ dam = ▢ m = ▢ dm = ▢ cm = ▢ mm

24. 5 m = ▢ dm = ▢ cm = ▢ mm

Metric Units of Capacity

In the metric system the **liter (L)** is used for measuring capacity.
A liter of orange juice will fill about 4 cups.

The amount of space contained in a cube with all edges 1 cm long is
a **cubic centimeter**.

A cubic centimeter holds 1 milliliter (mL). We use the milliliter to measure small amounts.

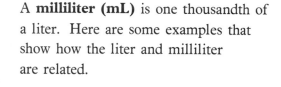

A **milliliter (mL)** is one thousandth of a liter. Here are some examples that show how the liter and milliliter are related.

1 mL = 0.001 L   so   250 mL = 0.25 L

1 L = 1000 mL   so   5.7 L = 5700 mL

Exercises

Choose the best estimate. Write *a*, *b*, or *c*.

1. The capacity of a tea kettle
   a. 20 mL   **b.** 360 mL   **c.** 2 L

2. The capacity of a gasoline can
   a. 400 mL   **b.** 800 mL   **c.** 10 L

3. The capacity of a juice glass
   a. 200 mL   **b.** 10 L   **c.** 70 L

4. The capacity of a swimming pool
   a. 1200 mL   **b.** 120 L   **c.** 120,000 L

Complete.

5. 1 L = 1000 mL
   3 L = ▢ mL
   8 L = ▢ mL
   13 L = ▢ mL

6. 1 L = 1000 mL
   25 L = ▢ mL
   2.5 L = ▢ mL
   0.25 L = ▢ mL

7. 1 mL = 0.001 L
   3 mL = ▢ L
   30 mL = ▢ L
   300 mL = ▢ L

8. 4 L = ▢ mL

9. 2000 mL = ▢ L

10. 50,000 mL = ▢ L

11. 17 L = ▢ mL

12. 23 L = ▢ mL

13. 69,000 mL = ▢ L

14. 7000 mL = ▢ L

15. 38,000 mL = ▢ L

16. 7 L = ▢ mL

Other Metric Units of Capacity

The chart shows other metric units of capacity and how they are related. Only the liter and milliliter are commonly used.

kiloliter kL	hectoliter hL	dekaliter daL	liter L	deciliter dL	centiliter cL	milliliter mL
1000 L	100 L	10 L	1 L	0.1 L	0.01 L	0.001 L

Notice that each unit is 10 times the unit to its right.

Complete.

17. 35 L = ▢ dL = ▢ cL = ▢ mL

18. 35,000 L = ▢ daL = ▢ hL = ▢ kL

19. 27 kL = ▢ hL = ▢ daL = ▢ L

20. 8 L = ▢ dL = ▢ cL = ▢ mL

21. How many milliliters are contained in a cubic meter?

Decimopolis, a small island country, has a clock based on ten. There are ten hours of daylight, and ten hours of night. Draw a clock face as it would look in Decimopolis. The times that follow are as they would appear on a regular clock. Show on a diagram how they would appear on a Decimopolis clock.

6 A.M.   12 Noon   6 P.M.   12 Midnight

Metric Units of Mass

In the metric system, mass is measured in **grams (g)**, **milligrams (mg)**, and **kilograms (kg)**. The picture below shows some common objects and their approximate masses.

about 750 g

about 1 kg

500 mg

The examples in the chart show how these units of mass are related.

Statement		Example
A milligram (mg) is a thousandth of a gram.	1 mg = 0.001 g 1000 mg = 1 g	250 mg = 0.25 g 3200 mg = 3.2 g
A kilogram (kg) is a thousand grams.	1 kg = 1000 g 0.001 kg = 1 g	1.75 kg = 1750 g 0.846 kg = 846 g

A milliliter of water has a mass of about 1 g.
So a liter of water has a mass of about 1 kg.

Exercises

Choose the best estimate. Write *a*, *b*, or *c*.

1. The mass of a pair of track shoes
   a. 10 g   **b.** 100 g   **c.** 1 kg

2. The mass of a paper clip
   a. 1 g   **b.** 100 g   **c.** 500 g

3. The mass of a 13-year-old person
   a. 4000 g   **b.** 4 kg   **c.** 40 kg

4. The mass of a box of oatmeal
   a. 40 g   **b.** 400 g   **c.** 4 kg

Complete.

5. 1 kg = 1000 g
   6 kg = ▢ g
   9 kg = ▢ g
   14 kg = ▢ g

6. 1 g   = 0.001 kg
   7 g   = ▢ kg
   700 g = ▢ kg
   7000 g = ▢ kg

7. 1 mg = 0.001 g
   5 mg = ▢ g
   50 mg = ▢ g
   500 mg = ▢ g

Complete.

8. 5 kg = ▢ g   **9.** 17,000 g = ▢ kg

10. 74 kg = ▢ g   **11.** 2000 g = ▢ kg

12. 7 kg = ▢ g   **13.** 7000 mg = ▢ g

14. 8 g = ▢ mg   **15.** 3g = ▢ mg

16. 6 kg = ▢ g   **17.** 8000 g = ▢ kg

How Strong Are You?

A cubic centimeter of water has a mass of about 1 g.

★ **18.** What is the mass of the water in an aquarium whose volume is a cubic meter?

★ **19.** Do you think you could lift an aquarium filled with a cubic meter of water?

Checkpoint B

Round to the place underlined. (*pages 20–21*)

   1. 4̲76   **2.** 78̲21

   3. 14̲,508   **4.** 356,̲479

Round to the place underlined. (*pages 22–23*)

   5. 6̲.54   **6.** 0.3̲26

   7. 0.64̲72   **8.** 4.296̲3

Measure to the nearest centimeter. (*pages 24–25*)

   9. _____

   10. _____

Measure to the nearest millimeter. (*pages 24–25*)

   11. _____

   12. _____

Complete. (*pages 26–27*)

13. 3 m = ▢ cm   **14.** 2 km = ▢ m

15. 400 cm = ▢ m

16. 4000 mm = ▢ m

Complete. (*pages 28–29*)

17. 2 L = ▢ mL

18. 8000 mL = ▢ L

Complete. (*pages 30–31*)

19. 6 kg = ▢ g   **20.** 3 g = ▢ mg

Extra practice on page 420   **31**

Problem Solving · A FOUR-STEP PLAN

Which car was faster?

1	**Understand the problem.**	What are the facts? What do you need to know?	Car 14: 2 min 3.50 s Car 23: 2 min 1.41 s Which car was faster?
2	**Make a plan.**	What do you do to solve the problems?	Compare the times.
3	**Do the work.**	Show the work.	2 min 3.50 s > 2 min 1.41 s
4	**Interpret the answer.**	Is the answer reasonable? Does it answer the question?	Car 23 is faster. Yes, it answers the question and is reasonable.

Here are some plans you may use to solve problems.

Compare Numbers (C)   Order Numbers (O)   Round Numbers (R)   Measure (M)

Write *C, O, R,* or *M* to describe your plan. Then solve.

1. Car 23 finished the race in 1 hr 42 min 15 s. Car 14 took 1 hr 41 min 35 sec. Which was faster?

2. Car 17 finished the race in 1 hr 40 min 25 s. Car 15 took 1 hr 39 min 28 s; and Car 11 took 1 hr 41 min 17 s. In what order did they finish?

3. The average speed for Car 23 was 164.7 miles per hour. State the speed for Car 23 to the nearest mile per hour.

4. A space in a scrap book is 10 cm long and 5 cm high. Will the picture at the top of the page fit in that space?

Use the facts and the plan to write a question for the problem. Then solve the problem.

FACTS	PLAN
5. The fastest lap time for Car 61 was 2 min 2.9 s. The fastest lap time for Car 51 was 2 min 3.3 s.	Compare the numbers.
6. There were 312 drivers and mechanics on the field for the big race.	Round to the nearest hundred.
7. There were 194,647 spectators in the grandstand.	Round to thousands.
8. This drawing shows Car 23 and Paul's car.	Measure and compare.

9. The total race time for Car 45 was 1 hr 39 min 17 s. Car 16 took 1 hr 39 min 48 s. Car 13 took 1 hr 51 min.	Order the numbers.
10. Car 61 used 419 L of fuel, and Car 19 used 406 L.	Compare the numbers.

Solve.

11. The Green family drove their car 24,608 km in a year. About how many thousand kilometers was this?

12. In a diagram a race track is 10 cm wide. If 1 cm in the diagram represents 1 m, what is the actual width of the track?

★ **13.** Car 54 traveled 27 times around the track in the same amount of time that it took Car 18 to go around the track 19 times. Which car was faster?

10 cm

Unit Review

Write the standard form.

1. 17 thousand, 8 hundred

2. 5 million, 2 thousand, 47

3. 5000 + 600 + 70 + 2

4. 60,000 + 900 + 20 + 4

5. 478 thousandths

6. 9 and 5 ten-thousandths

7. 0.8 + 0.09 + 0.001

8. 27 + 0.3 + 0.0004

Use the information from the chart.

Geographic Statistics of the Mountain States		
State	Total Area (km²)	Mean Elevation (km)
Arizona (AZ)	295,024	1.251
Colorado (CO)	270,000	2.074
Idaho (ID)	216,413	1.525
Montana (MT)	381,087	1.037
Nevada (NV)	286,299	1.678
New Mexico (NM)	315,115	1.739
Utah (UT)	219,932	1.861
Wyoming (WY)	253,597	2.044

List the states in order from greatest to least.

9. by total area

10. by mean elevation

Round each total area to the place indicated.

11. hundred thousands

12. thousands

Round each mean elevation to the place indicated.

13. whole numbers

14. hundredths

Match each measure at the left with the equivalent measure at the right.

15. 675 mg   **A.** 6.75 km

16. 675 m   **B.** 0.675 L

17. 675 mL   **C.** 0.675 g

18. 6750 m   **D.** 67,500 cm

19. 675 g   **E.** 6.75 L

20. 6750 mL   **F.** 6.75 m

21. 675 cm   **G.** 67,500 mm

22. 6750 cm   **H.** 0.675 kg

Write *compare*, *order*, or *round* to describe your plan. Then solve.

23. Of Nevada's total area, 1686 km² is water and 284,613 km² is land. Is there more water or land area in Nevada?

Write the standard form. (*pages 10–11*)

1. 3 hundred 20

2. 485 billion, 209 thousand, 50

3. 20,000 + 500 + 20 + 2

4. 700,000,000 + 5,000,000 + 3000 + 6

Write the decimal in standard form. (*pages 12–15*)

5. 65 hundredths

6. 3 and 2 tenths

7. 62 thousandths

8. 1 + 0.08 + 0.007

9. 0.7 + 0.008

10. 3 + 0.06 + 0.0004

Compare the numbers. Write < or > . (*pages 16–19*)

11. 283 ▪ 47

12. 538 ▪ 540

13. 13,806 ▪ 13,799

14. 1.4 ▪ 1.36

15. 0.208 ▪ 0.211

16. 0.826 ▪ 0.0954

Round the number to the place underlined. (*pages 20–21*)

17. 48<u>7</u>5

18. 14,<u>9</u>85

19. 686,<u>4</u>28

20. <u>9</u>.58

21. 0.7<u>4</u>9

What is the length of the ticket?
(*pages 22–23*)

22. to the nearest cm

23. to the nearest mm

Complete. (*pages 24–31*)

24. 6 cm = ▪ mm

25. 3000 m = ▪ km

26. 400 cm = ▪ m

27. 800 mg = ▪ g

28. 6 L = ▪ mL

29. 28 L = ▪ mL

Write *compare, order,* or *round* to describe the plan for solving the problem. Then solve. (*pages 32–33*)

30. In one day 126 children and 54 adults visited Maple Rock State Park. Were there more children, or more adults?

31. A total of 565,842 visitors used the park in one year. About how many thousand visitors used the park that year?

Temperature

In the metric system, temperature is measured in degrees Celsius. The thermometer shows some approximate temperatures. A cold temperature, such as ten degrees below zero, is written −10°C.

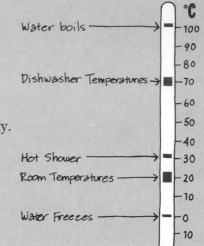

Water boils → 100
90
80
Dishwasher Temperatures → 70
60
50
40
Hot Shower → 30
Room Temperatures → 20
10
Water Freezes → 0
10
Freezer Temperatures → 20
30
40

Choose the more likely temperature for each activity. Write *a* or *b*.

1. Swimming outside   **a.** 30°C   **b.** 10°C

2. Playing baseball   **a.** 75°C   **b.** 19°C

3. Skiing   **a.** 19°C   **b.** −5°C

4. Planting   **a.** 20°C   **b.** 0°C

Draw a thermometer like the one at the right. Show each temperature on your thermometer.

5. The average temperature at the surface of the Antarctic Ocean is −2°C.

6. The hottest temperature ever recorded on Earth was 58°C at Al'Aziziyah, Libya.

7. Dallol, Ethiopia, is the hottest place on Earth. Its average annual temperature is 34.4°C.

8. The coldest place on Earth is Polus Nedostupnosti in Antarctica. The average annual temperature there is −57.8°C.

9. Vostok, Antarctica, holds the record for the coldest temperature ever recorded on Earth, −88.3°C.

10. The coldest temperature recorded in North America was −58.3°C at Floeberg Bay, Ellesmere Island, Canada.

11. Outside of Antarctica, the coldest recorded temperature was −71.1°C at Oymyakon, Siberia, USSR.

The chart shows the record high and low temperatures for seven cities.

| Record Temperatures of Selected Cities (Rounded to the nearest degree Celsius) | | | | | |
City	High	Low	City	High	Low
Atlanta, Georgia	39	−19	Phoenix, Arizona	48	−8
Burlington, Vermont	38	−34	Reno, Nevada	40	−27
Honolulu, Hawaii	33	12	Seattle, Washington	37	−18
Juneau, Alaska	32	−30			

Use the chart and the thermometer to answer the question.

12. Which city has the highest record temperature?

13. Which city has the lowest record temperature?

14. Use the chart to list the cities in order from warmest to coldest.

15. Use the chart to list the cities in order from coldest to warmest.

You can use a scale on a thermometer to find the change in temperature.

EXAMPLE Find the difference between 12°C and −6°C.

There are 18° between 12°C and −6°C on the thermometer. The difference in temperature is 18 degrees.

Find the difference between the two temperatures.

16. between 34° and 16°

17. between −8° and 0°

18. between −4° and −12°

19. between −3° and 4°

Use the chart above to find the difference between the Record High and Record Low temperature for each city.

20. Atlanta, Georgia   **21.** Burlington, Vermont   **22.** Seattle, Washington

23. Juneau, Alaska   **24.** Phoenix, Arizona   **25.** Reno, Nevada

26. In which city is the difference between record high and record low temperatures the least?

Maintaining Skills

Match.

1. 3 million, 358 thousand, 45

2. 527 thousand

3. 4,050,607

4. 527 ten thousandths

5. 5 and 27 hundredths

6. 52.506

A. 4,000,000 + 50,000 + 600 + 7

B. 5.27

C. 3,358,045

D. 0.0527

E. 52 and 506 thousandths

F. 527,000

Round the price of the car to the nearest thousand. Write *C, M,* or *L* to show on which board the key belongs.

7.

8. 10,728

9. 7099

10.

11. 50,050

12. 5643

13.

14. 5085

15. 5510

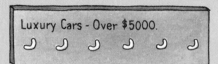

Compact Cars - Less than $5000.

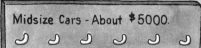

Midsize Cars - About $5000.

Luxury Cars - Over $5000.

Complete.

16. 4 L = ▓ mL

17. 90,000 mL = ▓ L

18. 73 g = ▓ mg

19. 750,000 mg = ▓ g

20. 3 km = ▓ m

21. 27,000 mm = ▓ m

Complete. Write < or > .

22. 93 ▓ 98

23. 173 ▓ 171

24. 68,420 ▓ 68,429

25. 38.301 ▓ 38.310

26. 0.007 ▓ 0.070

27. 63.681 ▓ 63.861

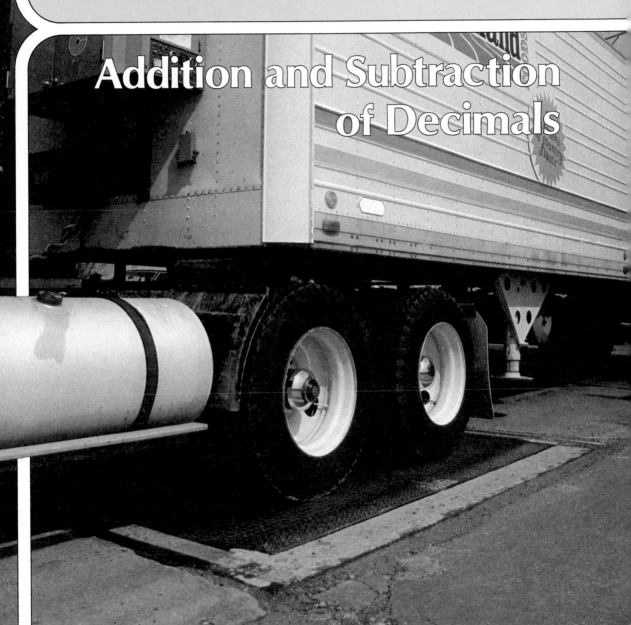

The truck has a total weight of 24.76 tons. The weight on the cab's front axle is 4.13 tons. The weight on the trailer's axles is 9.58 tons. How much weight is on the cab's rear axles?

Addition and Subtraction of Decimals

Addition and Subtraction Equations

An **equation** tells us that two numbers or quantities are equal.
For example, *3 + 6 is equal to 9* may be written as an
equation.

$$3 + 6 = 9$$

Sometimes a letter is used instead of a number. A letter used in this
way is called a **variable**.

$$n + 2 = 10$$
$$\uparrow$$
variable

The equation $n + 2 = 10$ is a short way of saying *A number plus 2
equals 10*. Let's solve $n + 2 = 10$.

$$n + 2 = 10$$
Try 7: 7 + 2 = 10 False
Try 8: 8 + 2 = 10 True

When we replace n by 8, we form a true equation. The number 8 is
called a **solution** of $n + 2 = 10$.

You can solve simple addition and subtraction equations by thinking of
the number facts.

Solve 7 + a = 15.
  7 + 8 = 15 < You know this fact.
  So, a = 8.
  The solution is 8.

Solve b − 4 = 2.
  6 − 4 = 2 < You know this fact.
  So, b = 6.
  The solution is 6.

Exercises

True or False? Write *T* or *F*.

1. 9 − 5 = 4   **2.** 14 − 9 = 3   **3.** 26 − 9 = 35

4. 17 + 9 = 25   **5.** 12 − 4 = 8   **6.** 9 + 6 = 15

Write *Yes* or *No*.

7. $h - 3 = 12$ Is 9 a solution?

8. $a - 5 = 4$ Is 1 a solution?

9. $p + 3 = 11$ Is 8 a solution?

10. $7 + n = 12$ Is 5 a solution?

11. $5 - m = 4$ Is 9 a solution?

12. $9 + b = 17$ Is 8 a solution?

Is 3 a solution of the equation? Write *Yes* or *No*.

13. $14 - p = 11$

14. $y + 17 = 20$

15. $8 - x = 3$

16. $h + 5 = 8$

17. $9 - r = 12$

18. $z + 24 = 21$

Is 5 a solution of the equation? Write *Yes* or *No*.

19. $n + 5 = 13$

20. $7 + p = 13$

21. $18 + x = 23$

22. $r + 3 = 8$

23. $8 - f = 11$

24. $n + 24 = 29$

Solve the equation.

25. $4 + 6 = m$

26. $8 - 2 = n$

27. $5 + 3 = p$

28. $x + 5 = 11$

29. $u - 2 = 12$

30. $8 + w = 15$

31. $30 + y = 50$

32. $d + 4 = 12$

33. $10 - z = 4$

Who Wins?

34. The numbers on the grid indicate moves in a game of Tick Tack Toe. The moves of each player are given by the solutions of the equations. Copy the grid and solve each equation. Mark X or O on the solution to see who wins.

First Player (X)
$a - 2 = 9$
$6 + 1 = b$
$0 + 8 = c$
$d + 1 = 5$
$e + 2 = 17$

Second Player (O)
$f + 4 = 7$
$15 - g = 9$
$12 - h = 2$
$6 - j = 5$

★ **35.** Write a set of equations whose solutions are the numbers on this Tick Tack Toe grid.

Properties of Addition

Here are some properties of addition. When parentheses are used, the addition inside the parentheses is done first.

Commutative Property

The order in which numbers are added does not affect the sum.

$$3 + 4 = 7 \qquad 4 + 3 = 7$$

Associative Property

The way in which numbers are grouped does not affect the sum.

$$(3 + 4) + 5 = 7 + 5 = 12 \qquad 3 + (4 + 5) = 3 + 9 = 12$$

Zero Property

The sum of zero and any other number is that number.

$$0 + 4 = 4 \qquad 4 + 0 = 4$$

ANNUAL 'ANYTHING YOU CAN CATCH' DERBY
0 fish + 1 shoe = 1 shoe + 0 fish
(3 salmon + 4 bass) + 5 trout = 3 salmon + (4 bass + 5 trout)

Exercises

Add to complete.

1. $3 + 4 = $ ▨
$\quad 4 + 3 = $ ▨

2. $7 + 2 = $ ▨
$\quad 2 + 7 = $ ▨

3. $5 + 9 = $ ▨
$\quad 9 + 5 = $ ▨

4. $7 + 6 = $ ▨
$\quad 6 + 7 = $ ▨

5. $(3 + 4) + 5 = $ ▨ $ + 5 = $ ▨
$\quad 3 + (4 + 5) = 3 + $ ▨ $ = $ ▨

6. $6 + (2 + 7) = 6 + $ ▨ $ = $ ▨
$\quad (6 + 2) + 7 = $ ▨ $ + 7 = $ ▨

Complete to show the Commutative Property.

7. $3 + 2 = 2 + $ ▨

8. $12 + 5 = $ ▨ $ + 12$

9. $1 + 5 = 5 + $ ▨

10. $8 + 6 = $ ▨ $ + 8$

11. $9 + 2 = 2 + $ ▨

12. $1 + a = $ ▨ $ + 1$

Complete to show the Associative Property.

13. $4 + (1 + 2) = (4 + 1) +$ ▨

14. $7 + (8 + 2) = (7 +$ ▨ $) + 2$

15. $6 + (3 + y) = ($ ▨ $+ 3) + y$

16. $(n + 4) + 3 = n + ($ ▨ $+$ ▨ $)$

Complete to show the Zero Property.

17. $0 + 3 =$ ▨

18. $8 + 0 =$ ▨

19. $5 + 0 =$ ▨ $+ 5 =$ ▨

Name the property illustrated.

20. $6 + 7 = 7 + 6$

21. $8 + 0 = 8$

22. $(5 + 2) + 1 = 5 + (2 + 1)$

23. $8 + 2 = 2 + 8$

24. $8 + 9 = 9 + 8$

25. $4 + (3 + 2) = (3 + 2) + 4$

26. $0 + y = y$

27. $5 + a = a + 5$

28. $(b + 1) + 6 = b + (1 + 6)$

29. The object pictured is something you see and touch every day. Can you tell what it is?

The numbers in the answer are the solutions to the equations that follow. Replace each solution with the variable that it matches.

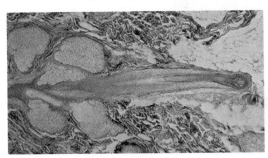

Answer:

$\underset{\text{(15)}}{\quad} \underset{\text{(1)}}{\quad} \underset{\text{(5)}}{\quad} \underset{\text{(3)}}{\quad} \underset{\text{(14)}}{\quad} \qquad \underset{\text{(15)}}{\quad} \underset{\text{(3)}}{\quad} \underset{\text{(6)}}{\quad} \underset{\text{(4)}}{\quad}$

$3 + 0 = a$

$0 + 14 = n$

$h + 3 = 3 + 15$

$6 + u = 1 + 6$

$(7 + 3) + 6 = 7 + (3 + i)$

$3 + (4 + 9) = (3 + r) + 9$

$9 + 5 = m + 9$

Missing Letters

Complete the equation to state the property.

> **EXAMPLE** Commutative Property:
> $a + b = b + a$

30. Zero Property: $a + 0 = 0 +$ ▨ $=$ ▨

31. Associative Property:
$(a + b) + c =$ ▨ $+ ($ ▨ $+$ ▨ $)$

★ **32.** A subtraction property with zero:
$a - 0 =$ ▨

★ **33.** Is subtraction commutative?

Addition of Whole Numbers

To add numbers greater than 10, add the ones, then the tens, and so on. Regroup as needed.

$$
\begin{array}{r} 1 \\ 879 \\ 247 \\ + \ 93 \\ \hline 9 \end{array}
\qquad
\begin{array}{r} 21 \\ 879 \\ 247 \\ + \ 93 \\ \hline 19 \end{array}
\qquad
\begin{array}{r} 21 \\ 879 \\ 247 \\ + \ 93 \\ \hline 1219 \end{array}
$$

Exercises

Add.

1.
$\begin{array}{r} 25 \\ + \ 4 \\ \hline \end{array}$
$\begin{array}{r} 25 \\ + \ 5 \\ \hline \end{array}$
$\begin{array}{r} 25 \\ + \ 6 \\ \hline \end{array}$
$\begin{array}{r} 25 \\ + \ 7 \\ \hline \end{array}$
2.
$\begin{array}{r} 34 \\ +22 \\ \hline \end{array}$
$\begin{array}{r} 34 \\ +23 \\ \hline \end{array}$
$\begin{array}{r} 34 \\ +24 \\ \hline \end{array}$
$\begin{array}{r} 34 \\ +25 \\ \hline \end{array}$

3.
$\begin{array}{r} 15 \\ + \ 9 \\ \hline \end{array}$
$\begin{array}{r} 15 \\ +39 \\ \hline \end{array}$
$\begin{array}{r} 15 \\ +89 \\ \hline \end{array}$
$\begin{array}{r} 15 \\ +99 \\ \hline \end{array}$
4.
$\begin{array}{r} 38 \\ +18 \\ \hline \end{array}$
$\begin{array}{r} 38 \\ +68 \\ \hline \end{array}$
$\begin{array}{r} 38 \\ +98 \\ \hline \end{array}$
$\begin{array}{r} 38 \\ +108 \\ \hline \end{array}$

5.
$\begin{array}{r} 54 \\ +38 \\ \hline \end{array}$
6.
$\begin{array}{r} 72 \\ +28 \\ \hline \end{array}$
7.
$\begin{array}{r} 364 \\ + \ 59 \\ \hline \end{array}$
8.
$\begin{array}{r} 738 \\ + \ 75 \\ \hline \end{array}$
9.
$\begin{array}{r} 365 \\ + \ 35 \\ \hline \end{array}$

10.
$\begin{array}{r} 598 \\ +598 \\ \hline \end{array}$
11.
$\begin{array}{r} 721 \\ +389 \\ \hline \end{array}$
12.
$\begin{array}{r} 642 \\ +985 \\ \hline \end{array}$
13.
$\begin{array}{r} 259 \\ +607 \\ \hline \end{array}$
14.
$\begin{array}{r} 493 \\ +228 \\ \hline \end{array}$

15.
$\begin{array}{r} 7607 \\ +3958 \\ \hline \end{array}$
16.
$\begin{array}{r} 6372 \\ +1209 \\ \hline \end{array}$
17.
$\begin{array}{r} 8640 \\ +2827 \\ \hline \end{array}$
18.
$\begin{array}{r} 2645 \\ +7688 \\ \hline \end{array}$
19.
$\begin{array}{r} 9276 \\ +9716 \\ \hline \end{array}$

20.
$\begin{array}{r} 72 \\ 83 \\ 94 \\ +45 \\ \hline \end{array}$
21.
$\begin{array}{r} 3 \\ 25 \\ 8 \\ +23 \\ \hline \end{array}$
22.
$\begin{array}{r} 141 \\ 74 \\ 288 \\ +366 \\ \hline \end{array}$
23.
$\begin{array}{r} 2790 \\ 74 \\ 9602 \\ +1829 \\ \hline \end{array}$
24.
$\begin{array}{r} 2091 \\ 895 \\ 93 \\ +1498 \\ \hline \end{array}$

25.
$\begin{array}{r} 38{,}421 \\ 7{,}646 \\ +10{,}871 \\ \hline \end{array}$
26.
$\begin{array}{r} 82{,}602 \\ 178{,}257 \\ +684{,}141 \\ \hline \end{array}$
27.
$\begin{array}{r} 86{,}859 \\ 572{,}770 \\ 8{,}661 \\ +674{,}952 \\ \hline \end{array}$
28.
$\begin{array}{r} 584{,}612 \\ 39{,}837 \\ 765{,}349 \\ + \ 94{,}601 \\ \hline \end{array}$

Add.

29. 81 + 1005 + 19 **30.** 214 + 43 + 786 + 57 **31.** 8 + 14 + 92 + 6 + 5

32. 26 + 142 + 74 **33.** 961 + 240 + 39 **34.** 9824 + 607 + 493 + 1026

35. 494 + 52 + 106 **36.** 86 + 12 + 14 + 13 **37.** 1021 + 985 + 19 + 75

Patterns in Addition

Benjamin Franklin enjoyed finding number patterns. This square
array of numbers was created by him.

52	61	4	13	20	29	36	45
14	3	62	51	46	35	30	19
53	60	5	12	21	28	37	44
11	6	59	54	43	38	27	22
55	58	7	10	23	26	39	42
9	8	57	56	41	40	25	24
50	63	2	15	18	31	34	47
16	1	64	49	48	33	32	17

38. Find the sum of the numbers in each row.

39. Find the sum of the numbers in each column.

40. Find the sum of the numbers in each diagonal.

41. In a magic square the sum of the numbers in each row, column
and diagonal is the same. Is this a magic square?

42. Find the sum of the four numbers in the green square. Try
other squares like this. Do you get the same sum?

★ **43.** Discover a pattern for the red square. Is the pattern true for
other similar squares?

★ **44.** Find the sum of the numbers in the eight blue squares. Can you
find other V-shaped patterns of numbers that have the same sum?

Addition of Decimals

Take a look at the daily jogging record on the note pad. To find the total distance for Monday through Wednesday, you add.

To add decimals, first line up the decimal points.

Add as you do whole numbers. Write the decimal point in the answer.

$$
\begin{array}{r}
3.8 \\
2.7 \\
+5.0 \\
\end{array}
$$

$$
\begin{array}{r}
3.8 \\
2.7 \\
+5.0 \\
\hline
11.5 \\
\end{array}
$$

The total distance for Monday through Wednesday is 11.5 km.

Sometimes it helps to write zeros after the decimal point so that all addends have the same number of decimal places. Here's an example.

$$12 + 8.4 + 1.78 = ?$$

$$
\begin{array}{r}
12. \\
8.4 \\
+ \ 1.78 \\
\end{array}
$$

$$
\begin{array}{r}
12.00 \\
8.40 \\
+ \ 1.78 \\
\hline
22.18 \\
\end{array}
$$

Exercises

Add.

1.
$$
\begin{array}{r}
9 \\
+6 \\
\hline
\end{array}
\qquad
\begin{array}{r}
0.9 \\
+0.6 \\
\hline
\end{array}
\qquad
\begin{array}{r}
0.09 \\
+0.06 \\
\hline
\end{array}
$$

2.
$$
\begin{array}{r}
15 \\
+48 \\
\hline
\end{array}
\qquad
\begin{array}{r}
1.5 \\
+4.8 \\
\hline
\end{array}
\qquad
\begin{array}{r}
0.15 \\
+0.48 \\
\hline
\end{array}
$$

3.
$$
\begin{array}{r}
139 \\
+668 \\
\hline
\end{array}
\qquad
\begin{array}{r}
13.9 \\
+66.8 \\
\hline
\end{array}
\qquad
\begin{array}{r}
1.39 \\
+6.68 \\
\hline
\end{array}
$$

4.
$$
\begin{array}{r}
8.4 \\
+23.71 \\
\hline
\end{array}
\qquad
\begin{array}{r}
0.84 \\
+2.371 \\
\hline
\end{array}
\qquad
\begin{array}{r}
0.084 \\
+0.2371 \\
\hline
\end{array}
$$

5.
$$
\begin{array}{r}
1.24 \\
+3.79 \\
\hline
\end{array}
$$

6.
$$
\begin{array}{r}
\$6.35 \\
+ \ 0.62 \\
\hline
\end{array}
$$

7.
$$
\begin{array}{r}
\$9.27 \\
+ \ 0.30 \\
\hline
\end{array}
$$

8.
$$
\begin{array}{r}
6.414 \\
+7.89 \\
\hline
\end{array}
$$

9.
$$
\begin{array}{r}
16.37 \\
+ \ 4.263 \\
\hline
\end{array}
$$

10.
$$
\begin{array}{r}
\$3.45 \\
0.62 \\
+ \ 5.10 \\
\hline
\end{array}
$$

11.
$$
\begin{array}{r}
6.7 \\
9.0 \\
+4.34 \\
\hline
\end{array}
$$

12.
$$
\begin{array}{r}
\$8.26 \\
0.30 \\
+ \ 0.21 \\
\hline
\end{array}
$$

13.
$$
\begin{array}{r}
6.23 \\
0.004 \\
+0.6 \\
\hline
\end{array}
$$

14.
$$
\begin{array}{r}
9.721 \\
0.3 \\
+0.544 \\
\hline
\end{array}
$$

Rewrite in columns. Then add.

15. 7.1 + 0.4 + 3.5

16. 0.6 + 2.43 + 0.33

17. $3.90 + $.04 + $5.20

18. $.76 + $.50 + $.01

19. 3.21 + 12.4 + 8.7

20. 25.66 + 0.46 + 0.022

Add mentally in the easiest way possible.

21. $.25 + $.68 + $.75

22. $2.50 + $6.88 + $2.50

23. 6.98 + 1.75 + 0.02 + 0.25

24. 20.75 + 99.99 + 100.01 + 8.25

Jog your Mind

25. Find the total of Marie's jogging distances for the week.

Record of Jogging	
Mon.	3.8 km
Tues.	2.7 km
Wed.	5.0 km
Fri.	4.7 km
Sat.	5.8 km

26. Find the total cost of Marie's jogging clothes.

Cost of Jogging Clothes	
Shoes	$26.95
Sweat suit	22.49
3 pr socks	6.75
Sweatbands	5.00
Total	

★ **27.** Marie is planning to run in the Jogathon. Her sponsors agree to pay her a certain amount for each kilometer she runs. How much will Marie collect for each kilometer? How much will Marie collect if she runs 8 km?

Jogathon Sponsor Sheet		
Sponsor	Amount per km	Amount for 8 km
I. Cramer	$.25	?
P. Sargeant	.35	?
C. Marston	.15	?
Total	?	?

Bus fare is 50¢. What is the greatest amount of money you can have in coins and yet not have exact change for the bus? Name the coins.

Take a Break

Subtraction of Whole Numbers

Last year 782 people worked on Project Clean-Up. This year there are
946 workers. How many more people are working on the project this year?

To find the increase, you subtract.

$$\begin{array}{r} 946 \\ -782 \\ \hline 4 \end{array} \qquad \begin{array}{r} {}^{8\,14} \\ 9\!\!\!/46 \\ -782 \\ \hline 64 \end{array} \qquad \begin{array}{r} {}^{8\,14} \\ 9\!\!\!/46 \\ -782 \\ \hline 164 \end{array}$$

There were 164 more workers this year. Because addition
and subtraction are opposite operations, you may check a
subtraction by adding.

$$\begin{array}{r} 164 \\ +782 \\ \hline 946 \end{array}$$

Exercises

Subtract.

1. $\begin{array}{r} 29 \\ -14 \\ \hline \end{array}$ $\begin{array}{r} 30 \\ -14 \\ \hline \end{array}$ $\begin{array}{r} 31 \\ -14 \\ \hline \end{array}$
2. $\begin{array}{r} 64 \\ -23 \\ \hline \end{array}$ $\begin{array}{r} 64 \\ -24 \\ \hline \end{array}$ $\begin{array}{r} 64 \\ -25 \\ \hline \end{array}$

3. $\begin{array}{r} 154 \\ -53 \\ \hline \end{array}$ $\begin{array}{r} 153 \\ -53 \\ \hline \end{array}$ $\begin{array}{r} 152 \\ -53 \\ \hline \end{array}$
4. $\begin{array}{r} 632 \\ -31 \\ \hline \end{array}$ $\begin{array}{r} 632 \\ -32 \\ \hline \end{array}$ $\begin{array}{r} 632 \\ -33 \\ \hline \end{array}$

Subtract and check.

5. $\begin{array}{r} 59 \\ -28 \\ \hline \end{array}$
6. $\begin{array}{r} 83 \\ -37 \\ \hline \end{array}$
7. $\begin{array}{r} 46 \\ -38 \\ \hline \end{array}$
8. $\begin{array}{r} 71 \\ -56 \\ \hline \end{array}$
9. $\begin{array}{r} 81 \\ -9 \\ \hline \end{array}$

10. $\begin{array}{r} 437 \\ -285 \\ \hline \end{array}$
11. $\begin{array}{r} 620 \\ -190 \\ \hline \end{array}$
12. $\begin{array}{r} 807 \\ -29 \\ \hline \end{array}$
13. $\begin{array}{r} 637 \\ -85 \\ \hline \end{array}$
14. $\begin{array}{r} 866 \\ -98 \\ \hline \end{array}$

15. $\begin{array}{r} 6370 \\ -2850 \\ \hline \end{array}$
16. $\begin{array}{r} 6376 \\ -2851 \\ \hline \end{array}$
17. $\begin{array}{r} 4268 \\ -1949 \\ \hline \end{array}$
18. $\begin{array}{r} 3275 \\ -497 \\ \hline \end{array}$
19. $\begin{array}{r} 9084 \\ -187 \\ \hline \end{array}$

20. 529 − 368
21. 844 − 378
22. 5241 − 133

23. 8706 − 762
24. 15,284 − 8576
25. 63,802 − 19,455

Use the chart at the right. What is the difference in cost?

26. between Monday and Tuesday

27. between Wednesday and Thursday

28. between Tuesday and Friday

29. between Monday and Thursday

30. between Monday and Wednesday

Project Clean-Up Daily Costs	
Monday	$250
Tuesday	$385
Wednesday	$270
Thursday	$835
Friday	$704

Complete.

31. $a = 5$; $b = 4$
$a + b = $ ▮
$a - b = $ ▮

32. $c = 13$; $d = 8$
$c + d = $ ▮
$c - d = $ ▮

33. $e = 100$; $f = 55$
$e + f = $ ▮
$e - f = $ ▮

Magic Squares

A magic square is a square array of numbers in which each row, column, and diagonal has the same sum. Complete the magic square by writing a number for the letter.

34. a **35.** b **36.** c **40.** g **41.** h **42.** i **43.** j

37. d **38.** e **39.** f **44.** k **45.** m **46.** n **47.** p

29	36	13	30	27
35	17	39	f	28
16	d	25	e	34
22	c	31	33	b
33	30	27	14	a

68	96	4	32	h
j	20	28	56	i
k	24	52	m	83
40	g	76	84	12
44	72	p	n	36

Subtraction of Decimals

Mark's hobby is building model ships.
If he cuts off 0.48 m from a dowel 1.50 m
long, how much of the dowel remains?

We need to subtract. First we must line
up the decimal points.

$$
\begin{array}{r}
\overset{4\ 10}{1.\cancel{5}\cancel{0}} \\
-\ 0.48 \\
\hline
\end{array}
\qquad
\begin{array}{r}
\overset{4\ 10}{1.\cancel{5}\cancel{0}} \\
-\ 0.48 \\
\hline
1.02
\end{array}
$$

Mark will have 1.02 m of the dowel left.

To subtract two numbers with a different number of decimal places, it
helps to write extra zeros.

$$
\begin{array}{r}
6.12 \\
-0.898 \\
\hline
\end{array}
\qquad
\begin{array}{r}
6.120 \\
-0.898 \\
\hline
5.222
\end{array}
$$

Exercises

Write the answer with the decimal point in the correct place.

1.
$$
\begin{array}{r} 8 \\ -5 \\ \hline 3 \end{array}
\qquad
\begin{array}{r} 0.8 \\ -0.5 \\ \hline 03 \end{array}
\qquad
\begin{array}{r} 0.08 \\ -0.05 \\ \hline 003 \end{array}
$$

2.
$$
\begin{array}{r} 52 \\ -39 \\ \hline 13 \end{array}
\qquad
\begin{array}{r} 5.2 \\ -3.9 \\ \hline 13 \end{array}
\qquad
\begin{array}{r} 0.52 \\ -0.39 \\ \hline 013 \end{array}
$$

3.
$$
\begin{array}{r} 745 \\ -187 \\ \hline 558 \end{array}
\qquad
\begin{array}{r} 74.5 \\ -18.7 \\ \hline 558 \end{array}
\qquad
\begin{array}{r} 7.45 \\ -1.87 \\ \hline 558 \end{array}
$$

4.
$$
\begin{array}{r} 601 \\ -\ 83 \\ \hline 518 \end{array}
\qquad
\begin{array}{r} 60.1 \\ -\ 8.3 \\ \hline 518 \end{array}
\qquad
\begin{array}{r} 6.01 \\ -0.83 \\ \hline 518 \end{array}
$$

Complete.

5.
$$
\begin{array}{r} 0.4 \\ -0.2 \\ \hline 0.\blacksquare \end{array}
$$

6.
$$
\begin{array}{r} 1.08 \\ -0.95 \\ \hline \blacksquare.\blacksquare 3 \end{array}
$$

7.
$$
\begin{array}{r} 0.75 \\ -0.65 \\ \hline 0.\blacksquare\blacksquare \end{array}
$$

8.
$$
\begin{array}{r} 0.0030 \\ -0.0015 \\ \hline 0.00\blacksquare\blacksquare \end{array}
$$

9.
$$
\begin{array}{r} 0.080 \\ -0.075 \\ \hline 0.0\blacksquare\blacksquare \end{array}
$$

Subtract.

10. $3.48
− 1.19

11. $2.73
− 1.08

12. 5.2
− 3.47

13. 0.834
− 0.271

14. 12.307
− 9.284

15. 6.028
− 6.014

16. 6.2 − 4.8

17. 0.96 − 0.37

18. 8.4 − 2.73

19. 21.9 − 4.66

20. 9.62 − 0.5

21. 7.8 − 6.2

Using Subtraction

22. Mark has saved $12.39. He spends $6.79 for a new model. How much does he have left?

23. A model car costs $9.29. A model boat costs $8.95. How much less is the cost of the model boat?

24. Mark bought model paint for $2.29, glue for $.89, and a paint brush for $1.49. How much change did he get from $5?

★ **25.** The directions say that a model can be assembled in less than 8 hours (h). Mark spent 1.50 h on Monday, 0.75 h on Tuesday, 2.30 h on Wednesday, and 2.25 h on Thursday. Did Mark complete the project within the 8 hours? How many minutes did he have to spare?

Checkpoint A

Solve the equation. (*pages 40–41*)

1. $3 + n = 11$

2. $15 − x = 9$

3. $6 + p = 9$

4. $r − 3 = 7$

Name the property illustrated. (*pages 42–43*)

5. $12 + 0 = 12$

6. $8 + 9 = 9 + 8$

7. $7 + (6 + 4) = (7 + 6) + 4$

Add. (*pages 44–45*)

8. 6248
5781
+4728

9. 748
839
271
+542

Add. (*pages 46–47*)

10. 8.35
+2.08

11. 0.328
+0.498

12. $13.98 + $5.30 + $21.16

13. 8.09 + 9 + 2.1

Subtract. (*pages 48–49*)

14. 670
−358

15. 5726
−3818

Subtract. (*pages 50–51*)

16. 5.026
−2.852

17. 12.71
− 8.921

18. 21.4 − 8.9

19. $9.47 − $8.02

Extra practice on page 422

Subtraction With Zeros

A parking garage has a capacity of 4000 cars. If 2846 cars are parked, how many empty spaces are there?

Before we subtract, we must regroup 400 tens as 399 tens and 10 ones.

```
  3 9 9 10          3 9 9 10
   4 0 0 0           4 0 0 0
 − 2 8 4 6         − 2 8 4 6
 ─────────         ─────────
                     1 1 5 4
```

There are 1154 empty spaces.

Exercises

Complete the subtraction.

```
      6 10             7 10              3 9 10            2 9 10            5 9 10
1.    7 0      2.      8 0      3.       4 0 0    4.       3 0 0    5.       6 0 0
    − 5 6            − 6 2            − 1 9 2           − 2 5 9           − 4 8 7
```

Subtract.

```
6.    400      7.    500      8.    300      9.    700      10.   600
    − 234          − 386          − 184          − 265          − 237


11.   300      12.   800      13.   600      14.   800      15.   500
    − 261          − 536          − 409          − 608          − 302


16.   2.04     17.   80.1     18.   9.01     19.   0.6001
    − 1.36         − 46.6         − 3.27         − 0.0359


20.   4.007    21.   90.00    22.   6.000    23.   0.5000
    − 1.238        − 12.48        − 3.049        − 0.1566
```

24. 500 − 54   **25.** 300 − 172   **26.** 4000 − 398

27. 900 − 258   **28.** 1000 − 198   **29.** 5000 − 1362

30. $20 − $11.97   **31.** $10 − $2.39   **32.** $100 − $91.23

33. $50 − $27.68   **34.** $90 − $61.57   **35.** $500 − $129.41

Complete.

36.
```
   ▊14
 + 3▊▊
 ─────
  610
```

37.
```
   ▊32
 + 7▊▊
 ─────
 1216
```

38.
```
  26▊
 + ▊3
 ─────
 1100
```

39.
```
  6 ▊8 9
 + 2 34
 ───────
 70,235
```

40.
```
   64▊
 − ▊3
 ─────
  12
```

41.
```
  12▊▊
 − ▊42
 ─────
  419
```

42.
```
   94▊
 − 6▊3
 ─────
   59
```

43.
```
  260▊
 − 1▊47
 ─────
  ▊3
```

Another Way

You have been taught to subtract two numbers by regrouping. Some people use a different method. To subtract 72 − 24 using the "method of equal additions," you add 10 ones to 72 and 1 ten to 24. Study these examples.

EXAMPLE A   72 − 24 = ?

EXAMPLE B   604 − 383 = ?

Add 10 ones. ⟶ 12
```
        7 ⁄2
```
Add 1 ten. ⟶ 3
```
      − ⁄2 4
      ─────
        4 8
```

Add 10 tens. ⟶ 10
```
        6 ⊘ 4            6 ⊘ 4
```
Add 1 hundred. ⟶ 4   4
```
      − ⁄3 8 3        − ⁄3 8 3
      ─────          ─────
            1          2 2 1
```

Subtract, using this other method.

44.
```
   60
 − 28
```

45.
```
   82
 − 19
```

46.
```
  309
 − 126
```

47.
```
  847
 − 252
```

48.
```
  525
 − 189
```

Chain Adding and Subtracting

We often add or subtract in a chain. We start with the first number and add or subtract the other numbers in order one at a time.

$$27 + 28 - 17 - 19 + 36 = 55$$

$27 + 28 = 55$	$55 - 17 = 38$	$38 - 19 = 19$	$19 + 36 = 55$

Chain adding and subtracting are used to keep checkbook records up to date. The **balance** in a checkbook is the amount of money in the checking account.

NUMBER OF TRANSACTION	DATE	DESCRIPTION OF TRANSACTION	AMOUNT OF PAYMENT OR WITHDRAWAL (−)	√	OTHER DEBITS	AMOUNT OF DEPOSIT OR INTEREST (+)	BALANCE FORWARD
		PLEASE BE SURE TO DEDUCT CHARGES THAT AFFECT YOUR ACCOUNT	SUBTRACTIONS			ADDITIONS	120 34
129	9/30	The Sound Shop	12 98				107 36
	10/1	Deposit				34 80	142 16
130	10/1	Cycle Shop	110 36				31 80
131	10/2	The Hair Cut	12 50				19 30

The amount of each check is subtracted from the previous balance. The amount of each deposit is added to the previous balance. The balance column shows the new balance after each check or deposit.

$$\$120.34 - \$12.98 + \$34.80 - \$110.36 - \$12.50 = \$19.30$$

Exercises

Complete.

1. $49 + 50 = $ ▨
   $49 + 50 - 16 = $ ▨
   $49 + 50 - 16 + 24 = $ ▨

2. $71 - 24 = $ ▨
   $71 - 24 - 17 = $ ▨
   $71 - 24 - 17 + 38 = $ ▨

3. $1.2 + 3.4 = $ ▨
   $1.2 + 3.4 - 2 = $ ▨
   $1.2 + 3.4 - 2 + 5 = $ ▨

4. $4.7 - 0.75 = $ ▨
   $4.7 - 0.75 + 6.5 = $ ▨
   $4.7 - 0.75 + 6.5 - 1.2 = $ ▨

Write the final answer.

5. $17 - 8 + 12 - 14 + 23$ **6.** $81 - 27 - 41 + 26 + 37$

7. $0.70 - 0.34 + 0.86 + 0.95$ **8.** $1.35 + 2.637 - 0.496 + 3.04$

9. $\$14.28 - \$3.99 - \$1.49 - \$7.65$ **10.** $\$6.50 - \$2.79 + \$12.85 - \$8.49$

11. $156 + 2384 - 978 - 654$ **12.** $8694 - 5278 + 10{,}797 - 6706$

Do the work in the parentheses first. Write the final answer.

13. $(244 - 38) + 29 - 63 + (27 - 9)$ **14.** $244 - (38 + 29) - (63 + 27) - 9$

15. $(244 - 38 + 29) - (63 + 27 - 9)$ **16.** $244 - (38 + 29 - 63 + 27 - 9)$

17. $244 - (38 + 29 - 63) + (27 - 9)$ **18.** $244 - 38 + 29 - 63 + 27 - 9$

Checks and Balances

Copy and enter the balance after each check or deposit.

19.

DEPOSITS (Add)		✓	CHECKS (Subtract)		BALANCE	
BALANCE FORWARDED →					96	82
			7	45	?	
			6	21	?	
25	08				?	
			14	95	?	
			9	98	?	

20.

DEPOSITS (Add)		✓	CHECKS (Subtract)		BALANCE	
BALANCE FORWARDED →					157	08
14	62				?	
			12	95	?	
			64	07	?	
32	96				?	
			52	70	?	

Calculator Corner

What would you feel if your teacher said, "No homework tonight?" To find out, enter these additions and subtractions in your calculator. Then turn the calculator upside down.

$14586 - 2934 + 89573 - 72468 + 50409 - 23988 = ?$

Estimating Sums and Differences

Suppose you have $30 to spend at the End-of-Summer Clearance Sale.
Do you have enough money to buy all the items shown? Estimate
the total.

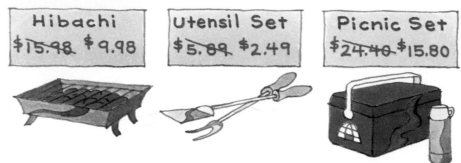

To estimate sums and differences, you round
the numbers and then add or subtract.

Round the numbers.　　　Add.

$$
\begin{array}{rcl}
\$\ 9.98 & \longrightarrow & \$10 \\
\$\ 2.49 & \longrightarrow & \$\ 2 \\
\$15.80 & \longrightarrow & +\$16 \\
\hline
 & & \$28
\end{array}
$$

The estimate shows that you
probably do have enough money.

Of course you may round numbers to any place you wish. Sometimes
it's easy just to round all numbers to the highest place of the smallest
number.

Here's an example.

$$
\begin{array}{r}
52,840 \\
-\ 8,446 \\
\end{array}
$$
Smaller number.

Round to the thousands'
place. Then subtract.

$$
\begin{array}{r}
53,000 \\
-\ 8,000 \\
\hline
45,000
\end{array}
$$

Exercises

Round each number to the nearest whole number. Estimate the sum or difference.

1.　　3.89
　　　　−3.47

2.　　$7.24
　　　　−　3.65

3.　　0.238
　　　　+0.547

4. $12.45
　　　3.89
　　+　8.04

56

Round to the nearest tenth. Estimate the sum or difference.

5.   12.085
  − 4.817

6. $16.58
  + 28.07

7.   1.879
  − 1.489

8.   3.062
    10.59
  + 1.8

Round to the highest place of the smaller number. Estimate the sum or difference.

9.   679
  − 185

10.   4928
  + 2516

11.   325,749
  + 962,201

12.   3,520,835
  − 1,587,248

Round to the place specified. Estimate the sum or difference.

13. nearest thousand: 1852 + 2035   nearest hundred: 1852 + 2035

14. nearest ten: 152.8 − 79.3   nearest whole number: 152.8 − 79.3

15. nearest hundred: $259.68 − $102.98   nearest whole number: $259.68 − $102.98

16. nearest tenth: 1.882 + 5.093   nearest hundredth: 1.882 + 5.093

17. nearest whole number: 3.59 + 1.82   nearest tenth: 3.59 + 1.82

Using Estimates

Estimating can help you catch errors you may make when using a calculator. Estimate these sums and differences. Use the estimate to decide if the answer is reasonable. Answer *Yes* or *No*.

18. 242 + 389
 1081

19. 72.8 − 3.4
 38.8

20. 24.5 + 79.1
 1036

21. 9.37 − 1.09
 8.28

22. 359 + 86
 1245

23. 786 − 45.5
 740.5

24. 1059 + 986
 2045

25. 62.1 − 4.09
 58.01

26. 34 + 102 + 68 + 79
 283

27. $110.98 + $72.49 + $35.89
 189.36

★ **28.** $4.98 + $18.62 + $42.36 − $3.98 − $21.49 + $52.36 + $18.79 − $14.07 *176.55*

★ **29.** In Exercises 18-28 above, for each unreasonable answer, find the mistake that was made in using the calculator. You may wish to use a calculator for this.

Adding and Subtracting Measurements

To add and subtract some measurements you may need to regroup.
To do this, you need to know how the units of measure are related.

U.S. Customary Units

Length
12 inches (in.) = 1 foot (ft)
3 feet = 1 yard (yd)
36 inches = 1 yard
1760 yards = 1 mile (mi)
5280 feet = 1 mile

Capacity (Liquid)
8 ounces (oz) = 1 cup (c)
2 cups = 1 pint (pt)
2 pints = 1 quart (qt)
4 quarts = 1 gallon (gal)

Weight
16 ounces (oz) = 1 pound (lb)
2000 pounds = 1 ton (t)

Time
60 seconds (s) = 1 minute (min)
60 minutes = 1 hour (h)
24 hours = 1 day (d)

These two examples use the fact that 12 in. equal 1 ft.

$$
\begin{array}{r}
3 \text{ ft} \quad 6 \text{ in.} \\
+\,1 \text{ ft} \quad 8 \text{ in.} \\
\hline
4 \text{ ft } 14 \text{ in.} = 5 \text{ ft } 2 \text{ in.}
\end{array}
$$

$$
\begin{array}{r}
\overset{2}{\cancel{3}} \text{ ft} \; \overset{18}{\cancel{6}} \text{ in.} \\
-\,1 \text{ ft} \quad 8 \text{ in.} \\
\hline
1 \text{ ft } 10 \text{ in.}
\end{array}
$$

Exercises

Complete.

1. 2 ft 14 in. = 3 ft ▢ in.

2. 2 lb 3 oz = 1 lb ▢ oz

3. 4 qt 3 pt = 5 qt ▢ pt

4. 4 yd 1 ft = 3 yd ▢ ft

5. 4 min 83 s = ▢ min 23 s

6. 4 gal 2 qt = 3 gal ▢ qt

Add or subtract. Regroup if necessary.

7.
$$\begin{array}{r} 1\text{ c }3\text{ oz} \\ +2\text{ c }4\text{ oz} \\ \hline \end{array}$$

8.
$$\begin{array}{r} 4\text{ min }12\text{ s} \\ +3\text{ min }38\text{ s} \\ \hline \end{array}$$

9.
$$\begin{array}{r} 4\text{ ft }9\text{ in.} \\ +2\text{ ft }4\text{ in.} \\ \hline \end{array}$$

10.
$$\begin{array}{r} 16\text{ lb }8\text{ oz} \\ -\ 9\text{ lb }5\text{ oz} \\ \hline \end{array}$$

11.
$$\begin{array}{r} 6\text{ yd }1\text{ ft} \\ +4\text{ yd }2\text{ ft} \\ \hline \end{array}$$

12.
$$\begin{array}{r} 6\text{ lb }\ 8\text{ oz} \\ -3\text{ lb }10\text{ oz} \\ \hline \end{array}$$

13.
$$\begin{array}{r} 5\text{ qt }1\text{ pt} \\ +3\text{ qt }1\text{ pt} \\ \hline \end{array}$$

14.
$$\begin{array}{r} 9\text{ ft }2\text{ in.} \\ -4\text{ ft }8\text{ in.} \\ \hline \end{array}$$

Flight Plans

15. Mr. Owens had two bags. One bag weighed 48 lb 10 oz. The other weighed 47 lb 12 oz. What was the total weight?

16. When the plane left Chicago, there were 12 gal of juice on board. The flight attendants served 8 qt on the way to Kansas City. How much juice was left for the return flight?

17. The flight from Cedar City to Moorestown takes 5 h 20 min including a 45 min stop in Metro. The flight from Metro to Moorestown takes 1 h 50 min. How long is the flight from Cedar City to Metro?

★ **18.** Flight 489 leaves Chicago at 11:45 A.M. and arrives in Kansas City at 1:04 P.M. How long does the flight take?

Checkpoint B

Subtract. (*pages 52–53*)

1.
$$\begin{array}{r} 700 \\ -359 \\ \hline \end{array}$$

2.
$$\begin{array}{r} 500 \\ -407 \\ \hline \end{array}$$

3.
$$\begin{array}{r} 9.00 \\ -3.69 \\ \hline \end{array}$$

4.
$$\begin{array}{r} 2.003 \\ -1.658 \\ \hline \end{array}$$

Find the answer. (*pages 54–55*)

5. $92 - 63 + 57$

6. $1.35 + 1.706 - 0.49$

7. $\$12.48 - \$2.98 + \$13.45$

8. $3,728 - 1886 + 10,576$

Round to the place specified. Estimate the sum or difference. (*pages 56–57*)

9. thousand: $2059 + 3642$

10. hundred: $15,342 - 4,589$

11. tenth: $9.92 + 0.86 + 0.51$

12. ten: $525 + 634 + 86$

13. hundredth: $1.059 + 0.023$

Add or subtract. (*pages 58–59*)

14.
$$\begin{array}{r} 3\text{ ft }\ 8\text{ in.} \\ +4\text{ ft }10\text{ in.} \\ \hline \end{array}$$

15.
$$\begin{array}{r} 3\text{ lb} \\ -1\text{ lb }8\text{ oz} \\ \hline \end{array}$$

Extra practice on page 422

Problem Solving · CHOOSING INFORMATION

1	Understand
2	Plan
3	Work
4	Answer

Paul Novak works at The Sports Place.
A customer asks him, *What is the sale
price for this pack? The tag is missing.*

Backpacks are on sale for $5 less than
the regular price. He needs to find the
sale price of the green pack.

Paul often uses a catalog to find
information. The catalog has more
information than he needs.

> **FREE SPIRIT PACK AND FRAME**
> fits youth from 150 cm to adult 200 cm.
> Measures 50 cm high × 36 cm wide ×
> 20 cm deep.
> **60A5621**-Green (7.2 kg). **$48.98**
> **60A5622**-Navy (7.2 kg) **$48.98**

First Paul finds the regular price.
Then he subtracts $5 to find the
sale price.

Catalog Price:	$48.98
$5 Off:	− 5.00
Sale Price:	$43.98

Use the catalog description to answer the question. If there is not
enough information, write *Missing Fact.*

1. What is the catalog number for the green pack?

2. How much longer will the packs be on sale?

3. How high is the Free Spirit pack and frame?

4. What is the tax on the Free Spirit pack and frame?

5. Will the Free Spirit pack and frame fit a person 180 cm tall?

6. When the pack is empty, will the Free Spirit pack and frame be
   less than 10 kg?

4-PIECE RAFT OUTFIT includes raft, 2 oars, pump.
60A53470 . . . . only **$44.99**

INFLATABLE RAFT can hold up to 140 kg. Wood-grain look.
60A53472A — (48 kg). **$19.99**

FOOT PUMP has 120-cm hose.
60A53473 — (7.5 kg). **$14.99**

PAIR RAFT OARS for small inflatable boats. 110-cm aluminum shaft.
60A53471 — (5.2 kg) pr. **$12.99**

Solve. If there is not enough information, describe the facts you need in order to solve the problem.

7. There is a sales tax of $2.25 on the raft outfit. How much must a customer pay in all to buy the raft outfit?

8. How much does it cost to buy the raft, pump, and two oars separately instead of buying the outfit?

9. How much can you save by buying the raft outfit instead of buying the 4 pieces separately?

10. The Sports Place will put the raft outfit on sale in October. How much can you save by buying the raft outfit at the sale price?

11. The raft outfit is sometimes packaged for shipping in a 1.2 kg box. What is the total mass of the raft outfit and box?

12. How much will it cost to ship the raft outfit to Helena, Montana?

Three friends, Carlo, Jan, and Kim, decide to buy the raft outfit together.

13. Carlo can pay $18 and Kim can pay $13.50. Jan says she will pay the rest. How much will Jan pay? How much change will she receive from a $20-bill?

★ 14. Carlo, Jan and Kim want to know how many of them can go out in the raft at the same time. Will the raft hold all three friends? Which of the friends may safely go out in the raft together?
Carlo: 67 kg   Jan: 79 kg   Kim: 56 kg

Solve the equation.

1. $5 + m = 14$ **2.** $11 - r = 7$ **3.** $12 - 9 = j$

Name the property illustrated.

4. $0 + 8 = 8$ **5.** $4 + 9 = 9 + 4$ **6.** $(5 + 7) + 8 = 5 + (7 + 8)$

Add or subtract.

7.
```
  6951
+ 8829
```

8.
```
    46
   327
     5
+ 1401
```

9.
```
  $6.95
+ 2.77
```

10.
```
  0.872
  1.9
+ 4.06
```

11. $814 + 392$ **12.** $12.5 + 9.7$ **13.** $6.75 + 0.4$ **14.** $1.007 + 3.4$

15.
```
  9846
- 2917
```

16.
```
  $15.25
-  12.97
```

17.
```
   4.6
- 1.19
```

18.
```
  6000
- 1225
```

19. $6825 - 6797$ **20.** $18.7 - 9.9$ **21.** $14.8 - 5.66$ **22.** $7.31 - 2.05$

23. $\$36.75 - \$25.00 - \$8.99 + \$5.75$ **24.** $74 - (35 + 16) - 8 + 12$

Round to the specified place. Estimate the sum or difference.

25. nearest hundred: $922 + 481$ **26.** nearest thousand: $9728 - 3601$

27. nearest tenth: $4.153 - 2.09$ **28.** nearest whole number: $8.71 + 5.09$

Add or subtract.

29.
```
   3 ft  4 in.
- 1 ft 10 in.
```

30.
```
  2 c 4 oz
+ 1 c 6 oz
```

31.
```
  2 min 30 s
+ 5 min 45 s
```

Find the facts you need in the shop window. Then solve.

32. What is the total cost of a basket and a tire pump?

33. If you already have $7.50, how much more money do you need to buy a speedometer?

BICYCLE SHOP
Basket $5.99
Speedometer $12.99
Tire Pump $7.49

Solve the equation. (*pages 40–41*)

1. $4 + a = 9$ **2.** $14 - b = 6$ **3.** $9 - c = 3$

Name the properties illustrated. (*pages 42–43*)

4. $4 + 9 = 9 + 4$ **5.** $(3 + 4) + 2 = 3 + (4 + 2)$ **6.** $8 + 0 = 8$

Add or subtract. (*pages 44–55*)

7. 6483 $+2219$	**8.** 5047 -1852	**9.** 7163 $-\ \ 257$	**10.** 7000 -6294	**11.** 329 48 5276 $+\ \ \ \ 2$

12. $5.48 $+\ \ 4.76$	**13.** 0.876 $+0.7257$	**14.** 0.724 -0.056	**15.** 3.75 -2.197	**16.** 1.0004 -0.3095

17. $18 + 7 - 12 + 9 - 3$ **18.** $\$1.86 + \$2.74 - \$2.43 + \$1.50$

Round to the place specified. Estimate the sum or difference. (*pages 56–57*)

19. nearest thousand: $2761 + 3598$ **20.** nearest ten: $472 - 58$

21. nearest whole number: $63.8 - 26.5$ **22.** nearest tenth: $7.83 + 2.16 + 0.118$

Add or subtract. (*pages 58–59*)

23. 5 min 25 s $+3$ min 52 s	**24.** 16 lb 2 oz -12 lb 8 oz	**25.** 3 ft 8 in. $+2$ ft 10 in.	**26.** 5 qt 1 pt -4 qt 3 pt

Use facts from the chart to solve. (*pages 60–61*)

27. How much faster was the record in 1975 than in 1875?

28. Between which two years was there the greater difference: 1875 and 1911 or 1945 and 1975?

World Records — One-Mile Run		
Year	**Runner**	**Time (in seconds)**
1875	Slade	264.5
1911	Jones	255.4
1945	Haegg	241.4
1975	Walker	229.4

Other Numeral Systems

Many ancient societies developed their own system for writing numbers long before our system was invented. Most of these systems did not use the idea of place value. An example is this system used by the ancient Egyptians.

EGYPTIAN SYSTEM NUMERATION							
Egyptian Numeral	I	∩	ℓ	⚱	∫	⚐	𓀀
Standard Form	1	10	100	1000	10,000	100,000	1,000,000

The Egyptians wrote numbers by using combinations of these symbols. Usually the symbols needed were written in order from the greatest to the least value. Here is an example.

Standard Form   **Egyptian Numeral**

$$356 \longrightarrow \begin{array}{l} 3 \text{ hundreds} \\ 5 \text{ tens} \\ 6 \text{ ones} \end{array} \longrightarrow \ell\ell\ell \quad \cap\cap\cap \text{ III} \\ \cap\cap \text{ III}$$

This is called an *additive system* because the values of the symbols used are added.

Write the standard form.

1. ∩∩∩∩ ∩∩∩ III

2. ℓℓℓ ∩∩∩ IIII   ℓℓℓ ∩ IIII

3. ⚱ ℓℓℓ ℓℓ ∩∩ III II

4. ∫∫ ⚱⚱⚱

5. ⚐ ∫∫∫ ⚱ ℓℓ ℓ I

6. 𓀀 ⚐⚐ ℓℓ III ℓℓ II

Write the Egyptian Numeral.

7. 37   **8.** 528   **9.** 2374   **10.** 40,361   **11.** 1,201,405

Another additive system that did not use place value is this one invented by the ancient Romans.

ROMAN SYSTEM OF NUMERATION			
Roman Numeral	Standard Form	Roman Numeral	Standard Form
I	1	$\overline{\text{V}}$	5000
V	5	$\overline{\text{X}}$	10,000
X	10	$\overline{\text{L}}$	50,000
L	50	$\overline{\text{C}}$	100,000
C	100	$\overline{\text{D}}$	500,000
D	500	$\overline{\text{M}}$	1,000,000
M	1000		

Standard Form   **Roman Numeral**

$$356 \longrightarrow \begin{array}{l} 3 \text{ hundreds} \\ 5 \text{ tens} \\ 6 \text{ ones} \end{array} \longrightarrow \text{CCCLVI}$$

The earliest Romans wrote 4 as IIII. A *subtractive* feature was added to the system at a later time. Here are some examples.

IV	IX	CD	CM
$5 - 1 = 4$	$10 - 1 = 9$	$500 - 100 = 400$	$1000 - 100 = 900$

Notice that the position of the symbols in relation to one another is important. For example, VI represents 6, but IV represents 4.

Write the standard form.

12. XXXII   **13.** LXXVIII   **14.** LXIV   **15.** MMDCCXIV

16. $\overline{\text{V}}$DLV   **17.** $\overline{\text{X}}$CDXXII   **18.** $\overline{\text{DC}}$XXLVII   **19.** $\overline{\text{MCL}}$CCCI

Write the Roman numeral.

20. 36   **21.** 88   **22.** 643   **23.** 1492

24. 3955   **25.** 20,916   **26.** 420,569   **27.** 1,530,004

Add or subtract.

1. 82,955
    + 67,109

2. 65,824
    + 3,791

3. 822
    143
    + 309

4.   7
     3041
       25
    + 374

5. $24.29
    + 17.98

6. 6.155
    + 1.9

7. 4.9
    6.2
    + 7.8

8. 3.014
    0.5
    9
    + 4.38

9. 4229
    − 1344

10. 86,344
    −   929

11. 4001
    − 1298

12. 50,000
    − 9,479

13. $47.09
    − 15.98

14. 6.79
    − 1.8

15. 38.1
    − 6.27

16. 12.006
    − 0.198

You play this game by tossing balls at the target. Your score is the total of the numbers written in the rings where the balls have landed. Two or more balls might land in the same ring.

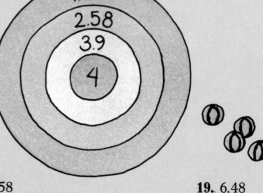

If you toss *two* balls, where would they have to land in order to get each of these scores?

17. 3.587

18. 6.58

19. 6.48

20. 8

21. 5.16

22. 2.014

If you toss *three* balls, where would they have to land in order to get each of these scores?

23. 7.587

24. 11.9

25. 6.014

Multiplication and Division of Decimals

A 40x microscope lens enlarges the image of an object so that the object's width appears to be 40 times larger. How wide would a cell with a diameter of 0.635 mm appear when seen through a 40x lens?

Multiplication and Division Equations

You know that the equation $2 \times n = 10$ can be solved by finding the value of n that makes the equation true.

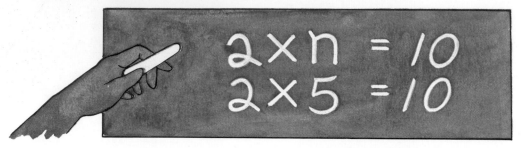

You can use your knowledge of basic facts to help you solve many equations.

$$28 \div x = 4$$
28 divided by what number is 4?
$$28 \div 7 = 4$$
$$\text{so, } x = 7$$

$$6 \times p = 24$$
6 times what number is 24?
$$6 \times 4 = 24$$
$$\text{so, } p = 4$$

Exercises

True or False? Write *T* or *F*.

1. $8 \times 3 = 24$

2. $45 \div 5 = 8$

3. $6 \times 9 = 72$

4. $5 \times 6 = 30$

5. $32 \div 4 = 8$

6. $48 \div 4 = 12$

Is 3 the solution of the equation? Write *Yes* or *No.*

7. $5 \times a = 15$

8. $b \times 6 = 21$

9. $7 \times c = 21$

10. $30 \div d = 10$

11. $e \div 3 = 0$

12. $27 \div f = 9$

Solve the equation.

13. $8 \times g = 24$

14. $h \times 5 = 20$

15. $j \times 6 = 48$

16. $k \times 9 = 36$

17. $7 \times m = 63$

18. $8 \times p = 80$

19. $18 \div q = 9$

20. $25 \div r = 5$

21. $42 \div u = 6$

22. $v \div 6 = 2$

23. $w \div 3 = 4$

24. $x \div 3 = 6$

Solve the equation.

25. $4 \times 6 = d$ **26.** $y \times 2 = 18$ **27.** $z \times 4 = 32$

28. $25 \div 5 = h$ **29.** $k \div 5 = 3$ **30.** $p \div 7 = 8$

31. $t \div 1 = 3$ **32.** $m \times 6 = 42$ **33.** $w \div 4 = 0$

34. $j \div 2 = 2$ **35.** $z \div 9 = 8$ **36.** $4 \times q = 16$

Did you know that some calculators have been around for centuries?
To name the calculators described, first find the solutions of the
equations below. Then replace each number in the answer with the
variable that it matches.

$a \times 3 = 21$ $b \div 2 = 6$ $4 \times c = 0$ $15 \div e = 3$

$16 \div 4 = f$ $7 \times 9 = g$ $15 \div i = 5$ $n \times 6 = 36$

$r \div 4 = 8$ $s \times 2 = 30$ $8 \times u = 16$

37. The earliest calculator: *Answer* (4)   (3)   (6)   (63)   (5)   (32)   (15)

38. A calculator made of rods and beads: *Answer* (7)   (12)   (7)   (0)   (2)   (15)

39. The first fully electronic computer: *Answer* (5)   (6)   (3)   (7)   (0)

Repeating Numbers

You may think of multiplication as repeated addition.

$$3 \times 5 \longrightarrow 5 + 5 + 5 = 15 \longrightarrow 3 \times 5 = 15$$

You may also think of division as repeated subtraction.

$$15 \div 5 \longrightarrow 15 - 5 - 5 - 5 = 0 \longrightarrow 15 \div 5 = 3$$

Use these ideas to solve the equation.

40. $a + a + a = 12$ **41.** $b + b + b + b + b = 30$

42. $24 - c - c - c = 0$ **43.** $35 - d - d - d - d - d = 0$

★ **44.** $26 - g - g - g - g = 2$ ★ **45.** $78 - h - h - h - h - h - h = 6$

Properties of Multiplication

Here are some properties of multiplication.

Commutative Property

If the order of the factors is changed, the product is the same.

$$3 \times 8 = 24 \quad \text{and} \quad 8 \times 3 = 24, \quad \text{so} \quad 3 \times 8 = 8 \times 3$$

Associative Property

If the grouping of the factors is changed, the product is the same.

$$(3 \times 2) \times 4 = 6 \times 4 = 24 \quad \text{and} \quad 3 \times (2 \times 4) = 3 \times 8 = 24$$
$$\text{so, } (3 \times 2) \times 4 = 3 \times (2 \times 4)$$

Identity Property

The product of 1 and any other number is that number.

$$1 \times 5 = 5 \qquad\qquad 6 \times 1 = 6$$

Distributive Property

The product of a factor and a sum is equal to the sum of the products.

$$3 \times (1 + 5) = 3 \times 6 = 18 \quad \text{and} \quad (3 \times 1) + (3 \times 5) = 3 + 15 = 18$$
$$\text{so, } 3 \times (1 + 5) = (3 \times 1) + (3 \times 5)$$

Zero Property

The product of 0 and any other number is 0.

$$0 \times 2 = 0 \qquad\qquad 3 \times 0 = 0$$

Exercises

Name the property.

1. $8 \times 1 = 8$

2. $(5 \times 7) + (5 \times 2) = 5 \times (7 + 2)$

3. $5 \times (30 + 4) = (5 \times 30) + (5 \times 4)$

4. $2 \times (4 \times 5) = (2 \times 4) \times 5$

5. $21 \times 50 = 50 \times 21$

6. $(4 \times 6) \times 7 = 4 \times (6 \times 7)$

Use the properties to solve the equation.

7. $6 \times (3 + y) = (6 \times 3) + (6 \times 4)$

8. $7 \times m = 2 \times 7$

9. $(4 \times 2) \times 3 = p \times (2 \times 3)$

10. $(5 + 3) \times 4 = (5 \times d) + (3 \times 4)$

11. $5 \times (1 + 2) = (5 \times 1) + (5 \times d)$

12. $n \times 8 = 0$

13. $(5 \times 1) + (5 \times 3) = 5 \times (1 + g)$

14. $(3 + 2) \times f = (3 \times 6) + (2 \times f)$

15. $(2 \times 1) \times 4 = c \times (1 \times 4)$

16. $b \times 1 = 7$

17. $8 \times (d + 5) = 32 + 40$

18. $g \times (4 \times 5) = 12 \times 5$

19. $h \times 9 = 9 \times 6$

20. $k \times 4 = 4 \times 8$

Remember Remainders

You may check a division by multiplying. A remainder is added to the product. Study the example at the right.

EXAMPLE

$$8)\overline{22} \;\; \substack{2 \text{ R6}} \longrightarrow \begin{array}{r} 2 \\ \times 8 \\ \hline 16 \end{array} \begin{array}{r} 16 \\ + 6 \\ \hline 22 \end{array}$$

Do the division. Check the answer by multiplying.

21. $35 \div 6$ 　　　**22.** $71 \div 10$ 　　　**23.** $34 \div 5$ 　　　**24.** $47 \div 9$

25. Andrew Jackson was President of the United States from 1829 to 1837. He was nicknamed "Old Hickory" because his troops in the War of 1812 felt he was as tough as hickory wood. He was the ▩ th president.

To complete the sentence, do these divisions. Use the remainder from each problem as the divisor of the next problem. The last quotient completes the sentence.

$69 \div 8 = 8 \text{ R}a$
$\quad 49 \div a = \blacksquare \text{ R}b$
$\quad\quad 31 \div b = \blacksquare \text{ R}c$
$\quad\quad\quad 21 \div c = \blacksquare$

Andrew Jackson was the ▩ th President.

★ **26.** When you divide by 6, what are the only possible remainders you can get? Show examples.

Order of Operations

Does $4 \times (3 + 8) - 2$ equal 42? Or does it equal 18? If you do the addition first, you get 42. If you multiply 4 times 3 first, you get 18.

The order of operations is important. Here are the steps we usually follow to simplify problems that use more than one operation.

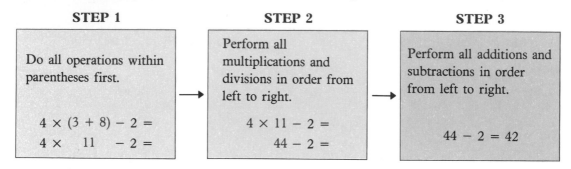

STEP 1	STEP 2	STEP 3
Do all operations within parentheses first. $4 \times (3 + 8) - 2 =$ $4 \times \quad 11 \quad - 2 =$	Perform all multiplications and divisions in order from left to right. $4 \times 11 - 2 =$ $44 - 2 =$	Perform all additions and subtractions in order from left to right. $44 - 2 = 42$

So the answer to $4 \times (3 + 8) - 2$ is 42.
Here is another example:

$$
\begin{aligned}
12 \times (4 + 1) \div 3 - 2 &= 12 \times 5 \div 3 - 2 \\
&= 60 \div 3 - 2 \\
&= 20 - 2 \\
&= 18
\end{aligned}
$$

Exercises

Complete.

1. $3 + 4 = $ ▓
$6 \times (3 + 4) = $ ▓
$6 \times (3 + 4) - 2 = $ ▓

2. $8 - 4 = $ ▓
$(8 - 4) \div 2 = $ ▓
$(8 - 4) \div 2 + 1 = $ ▓

3. $6 - 2 = $ ▓
$(6 - 2) \times 5 = $ ▓
$7 + (6 - 2) \times 5 = $ ▓

Choose the correct answer. Answer *a, b,* or *c.*

4. $2 \times 6 - 4$
   a. 4   **b.** 8   **c.** 3

5. $16 \div 4 + 4 \times 3$
   a. 6   **b.** 16   **c.** 24

6. $(20 - 4) \div 2 + 6$
   a. 2   **b.** 14   **c.** 16

7. $7 + (40 + 16) \div 8 - 1$
   a. 9   **b.** 13   **c.** 48

8. $24 \div 3 - 2 \times 4 + 4$
   a. 4   **b.** 28   **c.** 9

9. $(16 - 9) + (15 - 9 \div 3) - 2$
   a. 7   **b.** 13   **c.** 17

Simplify.

10. $(2 + 1) \times 3$ **11.** $(5 - 1) \div 2$ **12.** $3 \times (3 + 4) - 2$

13. $5 + (2 + 2) \times 3$ **14.** $6 + 2 \times (1 + 4)$ **15.** $(8 - 1) \times (7 + 1)$

16. $3 + 2 \times 8 - 4 \times 2$ **17.** $8 \div (2 + 2) - 1$ **18.** $3 \times (4 + 2) - 2 \times 5$

19. $9 \times (2 + 6 - 4) \div 2$ **20.** $(24 + 18) \div 6$ **21.** $9 \times 4 \div 4 + 2$

22. $(3 \times 7 + 3) \div 3$ **23.** $40 \div 5 + 3 - 11$ **24.** $9 \times (2 + 3 + 4) - 21$

25. $24 \div 3 + 5 \times 2$ **26.** $24 \div (3 + 5) \times 2$ **27.** $24 \div 3 + (5 \times 2)$

Calculator Keys

Many calculators do not have keys for parentheses. You need to know the right order to enter the problem.

Here's an example.

Steps on the Calculator

$4 \times (5 + 1) \longrightarrow$ 5 ⊞ 1 ⊠ 4 ⊟ 24

Match the exercise with the steps that give the correct way to enter the problem into the calculator. Write *A, B, C,* or *D.*

28. $3 \times 2 + 4$ **A.** 2 ⊞ 4 ⊠ 3   **32.** $8 \div 4 - 2 + 6$ **A.** 8 ⊟ 4 ⊠ 2 ⊞ 6

29. $3 \times 2 - 4$ **B.** 3 ⊠ 2 ⊞ 4   **33.** $(8 + 4 - 2) \times 6$ **B.** 4 ⊟ 2 ⊠ 6 ⊞ 8

30. $(3 + 2) \times 4$ **C.** 3 ⊞ 2 ⊠ 4   **34.** $(8 - 4) \times 2 + 6$ **C.** 8 ⊞ 4 ⊟ 2 ⊠ 6

31. $3 \times (2 + 4)$ **D.** 3 ⊠ 2 ⊟ 4   **35.** $8 + (4 - 2) \times 6$ **D.** 8 ⊟ 4 ⊟ 2 ⊞ 6

Rewrite the problem using parentheses to show the correct order of the operations.

★ **36.** 12 ⊞ 4 ⊟ 2 ⊞ 3 ⊟ 2

★ **37.** 12 ⊞ 4 ⊟ 2 ⊟ 3 ⊟ 2

★ **38.** 12 ⊟ 4 ⊞ 2 ⊠ 3 ⊟ 2

★ **39.** 12 ⊟ 4 ⊟ 2 ⊠ 3 ⊞ 2

Multiplication of Whole Numbers

A circus plans 6 performances a week for 28 weeks. How many performances is that in all?

To find the answer, you could add 6 twenty-eight times. It's easier to multiply. Multiply the ones.

$$\begin{array}{r} 4 \\ 28 \\ \times 6 \\ \hline 8 \end{array}$$

Multiply the tens. Add the 4 tens.

$$\begin{array}{r} 4 \\ 28 \\ \times 6 \\ \hline 168 \end{array}$$

The circus plans to give 168 performances.

Here's how to multiply 367 by 45.

First, multiply 367 by 5.

$$\begin{array}{r} 367 \\ \times 45 \\ \hline 1835 \end{array}$$

Next, multiply 367 by 40.

$$\begin{array}{r} 367 \\ \times 45 \\ \hline 1835 \\ 14680 \end{array}$$

Then add.

$$\begin{array}{r} 367 \\ \times 45 \\ \hline 1835 \\ 14680 \\ \hline 16515 \end{array}$$

Exercises

Multiply. Look for patterns.

1.
$$\begin{array}{r} 43 \\ \times 3 \end{array} \quad \begin{array}{r} 44 \\ \times 3 \end{array} \quad \begin{array}{r} 45 \\ \times 3 \end{array}$$

2.
$$\begin{array}{r} 681 \\ \times 5 \end{array} \quad \begin{array}{r} 682 \\ \times 5 \end{array} \quad \begin{array}{r} 683 \\ \times 5 \end{array}$$

3.
$$\begin{array}{r} 560 \\ \times 10 \end{array} \quad \begin{array}{r} 560 \\ \times 11 \end{array} \quad \begin{array}{r} 560 \\ \times 12 \end{array}$$

Multiply.

| 4. | 34 ×2 | 5. | 172 ×9 | 6. | 237 ×7 | 7. | 4087 ×6 | 8. | 9296 ×8 |

| 9. | 47 ×26 | 10. | 59 ×28 | 11. | 295 ×37 | 12. | 724 ×46 | 13. | 827 ×91 |

| 14. | 2792 ×59 | 15. | 54072 ×28 | 16. | 87568 ×37 | 17. | 2537 ×126 | 18. | 96884 ×306 |

| 19. | 2137 ×126 | 20. | 3763 ×244 | 21. | 9784 ×306 | 22. | 1926 ×409 | 23. | 7934 ×254 |

What is $a \times b$?

24. $a = 32$; $b = 192$

25. $a = 213$; $b = 503$

26. $a = 13$; $b = 1492$

27. $a = 121$; $b = 3941$

28. $a = 7$; $b = 918$

29. $a = 6$; $b = 746$

Cat Act

30. How would you describe the greatest cat act in the world?
    To find out, multiply, then arrange in order from least to greatest.

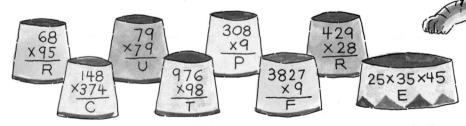

68 ×95 R

148 ×374 C

79 ×79 U

976 ×98 T

308 ×9 P

3827 ×9 F

429 ×28 R

25×35×45 E

What signs will make this a true statement?

1 ▨ 2 ▨ 3 ▨ 4 ▨ 5 ▨ 6 ▨ 7 ▨ 8 ▨ 9 = 100

Take a Break

Multiplication of Decimals

help

What is one tenth of one tenth of a dollar? $0.1 \times 0.1 = ?$

0.1 of $\$1 = 10$ cents $= \$.10$

0.1 of $\$.10 = 1$ cent $= \$.01$

So, 0.1 of 0.1 of a dollar is $\$.01$. $0.1 \times 0.1 = 0.01$

Here's how to multiply 2.31 by 1.4.

First, multiply as you do whole numbers.

$$
\begin{array}{r}
231 \\
\times 14 \\
\hline
924 \\
2310 \\
\hline
3234
\end{array}
$$

Then place the decimal point in the product.

$$
\begin{array}{r}
2.31 \quad \longleftarrow \text{2 decimal places} \\
\times 1.4 \quad \longleftarrow \text{1 decimal place} \\
\hline
924 \\
2310 \\
\hline
3.234 \quad \longleftarrow \text{3 decimal places}
\end{array}
$$

The number of decimal places in the product is the sum of the number of decimal places in the factors.

Exercises

Write the product with the decimal point in the correct place.

1.
$$
\begin{array}{r} 3.6 \\ \times 4 \\ \hline 144 \end{array}
\qquad
\begin{array}{r} 0.36 \\ \times 4 \\ \hline 144 \end{array}
\qquad
\begin{array}{r} 0.036 \\ \times 4 \\ \hline 144 \end{array}
$$

2.
$$
\begin{array}{r} 5.3 \\ \times 2.7 \\ \hline 1431 \end{array}
\qquad
\begin{array}{r} 0.53 \\ \times 2.7 \\ \hline 1431 \end{array}
\qquad
\begin{array}{r} 0.53 \\ \times 0.27 \\ \hline 1431 \end{array}
$$

Multiply.

3. 0.04 $\times 8$	**4.** 1.36 $\times 4$	**5.** 2.08 $\times 7$	**6.** 0.007 $\times 2$	**7.** 0.043 $\times 5$
8. 2.8 $\times 0.7$	**9.** 5.7 $\times 0.9$	**10.** 2.7 $\times 3.4$	**11.** 8.4 $\times 3.3$	**12.** 2.5 $\times 0.8$
13. $12.30 $\times 0.6$	**14.** 6.208 $\times 4.2$	**15.** 1.64 $\times 1.20$	**16.** 9.81 $\times 0.4$	**17.** 20.123 $\times 0.45$
18. 0.04 $\times 0.2$	**19.** $1.20 $\times 0.7$	**20.** 0.0042 $\times .061$	**21.** 0.39 $\times 0.008$	**22.** 0.086 $\times 3.9$

23. 1.2×30.8

24. 0.02×9.89

25. 0.65×3.74

26. 15.6×3

27. 12.15×1.35

28. 7.28×1.4

Computing Wages

The wages for many jobs are found by multiplying the number of hours worked by an hourly rate of pay.

$$\text{Hours Worked} \times \text{Hourly Rate} = \text{Wages}$$

What are the wages?

29. 16.5 hours at $4.20 per hour

30. 14.75 hours at $5.60 per hour

31. 22.25 hours at $3.76 per hour

32. 19.5 hours at $4.60 per hour

Solve.

33. Clare worked 6.25 h on Monday, 5.5 h on Wednesday, and 4.75 h on Friday. She earns $3.80 an hour. How much did she earn?

★ **34.** Dennis earns $4.80 per hour if he works 40 h or less. When Dennis works more than 40 h in one week, his hourly rate for the number of hours over 40 is 1.5 times his regular rate. What are his wages for 48 h?

Exponents

The expression 7^2 means 7×7. The number 7 is called the **base.**
The number 2 is called the **exponent.**

$$7^2 = 7 \times 7 \qquad 6^3 = 6 \times 6 \times 6 \qquad 3^4 = 3 \times 3 \times 3 \times 3$$
$$= 49 \qquad\qquad = 216 \qquad\qquad\quad = 81$$

We read 7^2 as *7 to the second power* or *7 squared.* We read 6^3 as *6 to the third power* or *6 cubed.*

A number with an exponent of 1 is the number itself. An exponent greater than 1 tells us how many times the base is used as a factor.

The powers of 10 form an interesting pattern. Notice that the exponent is equal to the number of zeros in the product.

$$10^1 = 10 \qquad\qquad\qquad\qquad = 10$$
$$10^2 = 10 \times 10 \qquad\qquad\qquad = 100$$
$$10^3 = 10 \times 10 \times 10 \qquad\qquad = 1000$$
$$10^4 = 10 \times 10 \times 10 \times 10 = 10,000$$

Exercises

Complete.

1. $3 \times 3 = 3^{\square}$
   $3 \times 3 \times 3 = 3^{\square}$
   $3 \times 3 \times 3 \times 3 = 3^{\square}$

2. $5 \times 5 \times 5 = 5^{\square}$
   $5 \times 5 \times 5 \times 5 = 5^{\square}$
   $5 \times 5 \times 5 \times 5 \times 5 = 5^{\square}$

3. $8 = 2 \times 2 \times 2 = 2^{\square}$

4. $81 = 9 \times 9 = 9^{\square}$

5. $64 = 4 \times 4 \times 4 = 4^{\square}$

6. $625 = 5 \times 5 \times 5 \times 5 = 5^{\square}$

Write the number using exponents.

7. 6×6

8. $2 \times 2 \times 2$

9. $4 \times 4 \times 4 \times 4$

10. $7 \times 7 \times 7$

11. 7×7

12. $9 \times 9 \times 9$

13. $10 \times 10 \times 10 \times 10$

14. $20 \times 20 \times 20$

15. $3 \times 3 \times 3 \times 3$

Write the number in standard form.

16. 2^2 **17.** 4^2 **18.** 2^3

19. 1^3 **20.** 5^2 **21.** 2^5

22. 4^3 **23.** 2^4 **24.** 5^3

25. 10^2 **26.** 10^3 **27.** 10^4

28. 10^5 **29.** 10^6 **30.** 10^7

Write the number using the exponent 2.

31. 9   **32.** 49   **33.** 100

34. 25   **35.** 10,000   **36.** 64

37. 16   **38.** 81   **39.** 36

Place Value and Exponents

Our place value system is based on powers of 10. Exponents can be used to write numbers in expanded form.

$$849 = 800 + 40 + 9$$
$$= (8 \times 100) + (4 \times 10) + 9$$
$$= (8 \times 10^2) + (4 \times 10^1) + 9$$

Write in expanded form using exponents.

40. 748   **41.** 8315

42. 37,218   **43.** 465,297

44. 4027   **45.** 80,775

46. 5,286,785   **47.** 86,000,000

48. 25,403,800   **49.** 142,000,000

50. 473,206,750   **51.** 1,000,000,000

Checkpoint A

Solve. (*pages 68–69*)

1. $7 \times 5 = a$ **2.** $54 \div 6 = b$

3. $c \div 3 = 9$ **4.** $8 \times d = 56$

Solve the equation. (*pages 70–71*)

5. $8 \times e = 3 \times 8$ **6.** $f \times 1 = 9$

7. $6 \times (3 \times n) = (6 \times 3) \times 4$

8. $5 \times (4 + 3) = (m \times 4) + (m \times 3)$

Simplify. (*pages 72–73*)

9. $12 \div 2 + 3 \times 5$

10. $16 \div (4 + 4) + 5 \times 8$

Multiply. (*pages 74–75*)

11. 5784   **12.** 852
    $\times 6$ $\times 16$

13. 1725   **14.** 187
    $\times 23$ $\times 224$

Multiply. (*pages 76–77*)

15. 3.8   **16.** 9.87
    $\times 0.5$ $\times 2.48$

17. 26.03   **18.** 62.84
    $\times 0.8$ $\times 3.07$

Write the number in standard form. (*pages 78–79*)

19. 2^4 **20.** 10^3

21. 1^5 **22.** 12^2

Extra practice on page 424   **79**

Division of Whole Numbers

Each stage of a division has the same four steps. You repeat these steps as often as necessary to complete the division. Let's divide 112 by 6.

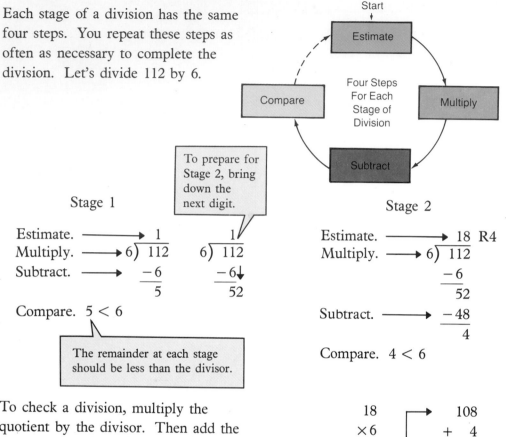

Start

Estimate

Four Steps For Each Stage of Division

Compare

Multiply

Subtract

To prepare for Stage 2, bring down the next digit.

Stage 1

Estimate. ⟶ 1
Multiply. ⟶ 6) 112
Subtract. ⟶ $\underline{-6}$
                 5

Compare. 5 < 6

1
6) 112
$\underline{-6↓}$
52

The remainder at each stage should be less than the divisor.

Stage 2

Estimate. ⟶ 18 R4
Multiply. ⟶ 6) 112
                $\underline{-6}$
                  52
Subtract. ⟶ $\underline{-48}$
                   4

Compare. 4 < 6

To check a division, multiply the quotient by the divisor. Then add the remainder. The answer should equal the dividend.

18   108
×6   +   4
108   112

Exercises

Divide.

1. 4)8   4)86   4)868

2. 6)54   6)540   6)542

3. 9)89   9)894   9)8943

4. 8)52   8)520   8)527

Divide and check.

5. 6)744   **6.** 3)861   **7.** 7)896   **8.** 4)936   **9.** 5)137

10. 7)649   **11.** 9)395   **12.** 4)383   **13.** 8)933   **14.** 2)175

80

15. $3\overline{)8946}$ **16.** $7\overline{)3472}$ **17.** $8\overline{)7184}$ **18.** $6\overline{)3571}$ **19.** $3\overline{)1562}$

20. $8\overline{)6457}$ **21.** $4\overline{)2435}$ **22.** $6\overline{)3667}$ **23.** $8\overline{)4063}$ **24.** $9\overline{)8107}$

25. $5\overline{)37291}$ **26.** $6\overline{)68403}$ **27.** $3\overline{)27152}$ **28.** $9\overline{)60235}$ **29.** $7\overline{)80742}$

What is $a \div b$?

30. $a = 280; b = 4$ **31.** $a = 381; b = 3$ **32.** $a = 572; b = 4$

33. $a = 784; b = 7$ **34.** $a = 648; b = 8$ **35.** $a = 738; b = 6$

Short Cut Division

Here is a short cut for dividing by a number less than 10. The little numbers show the remainders in the stages.

$$7\overline{)8_164} \quad\quad 7\overline{)8_16_24} \quad\quad 7\overline{)8_16_24}$$
$$1 \quad\quad\quad 1\,2 \quad\quad\quad 1\,2\,3\ \text{R}3$$

Divide, using the short cut.

36. $6\overline{)825}$ **37.** $3\overline{)119}$ **38.** $7\overline{)416}$

The Pep Club at Barton High decides to make 240 pompoms to sell at a victory rally.

39. If 5 members volunteer to make pompoms, how many pompoms must each person make?

★ **40.** If 7 members volunteer to make pompoms, how many pompoms must each person make? How many persons must make 1 extra pompom?

There are only two numbers that do not have 0 as any digit and whose product is 1 million. What are they?

Take a Break

Division of Whole Numbers

An airline kitchen has prepared 2750 dinners to be served to passengers. Each plane seats 182 people. How many flights may be served? How many extra dinners are there?

To answer we must divide 2750 by 182. To estimate, round the numbers first and then divide. Sometimes the estimate may be too large or too small.

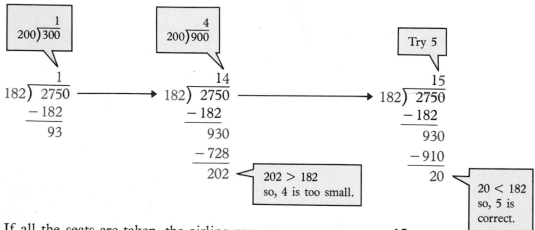

$$\frac{1}{200) \overline{300}}$$

$$\frac{4}{200) \overline{900}}$$

Try 5

$$\begin{array}{r} 1 \\ 182) \overline{2750} \\ -182 \\ \hline 93 \end{array}$$

$$\begin{array}{r} 14 \\ 182) \overline{2750} \\ -182 \\ \hline 930 \\ -728 \\ \hline 202 \end{array}$$

202 > 182 so, 4 is too small.

$$\begin{array}{r} 15 \\ 182) \overline{2750} \\ -182 \\ \hline 930 \\ -910 \\ \hline 20 \end{array}$$

20 < 182 so, 5 is correct.

If all the seats are taken, the airline may serve passengers on 15 flights. There are 20 extra dinners.

Exercises

Divide.

1. $40) \overline{91}$
$37) \overline{91}$
$37) \overline{914}$

2. $50) \overline{512}$
$48) \overline{512}$
$48) \overline{5120}$

3. $300) \overline{327}$
$300) \overline{3270}$
$300) \overline{32700}$

4. $20) \overline{2237}$
$21) \overline{2237}$
$22) \overline{2237}$

Divide and check.

5. $29\overline{)362}$　　6. $28\overline{)947}$　　7. $57\overline{)738}$　　8. $38\overline{)809}$

9. $27\overline{)1503}$　　10. $48\overline{)3576}$　　11. $24\overline{)7826}$　　12. $45\overline{)3481}$

13. $68\overline{)38754}$　　14. $19\overline{)7328}$　　15. $27\overline{)28159}$　　16. $29\overline{)16214}$

17. $278\overline{)658}$　　18. $278\overline{)910}$　　19. $342\overline{)4723}$　　20. $518\overline{)7645}$

21. $167\overline{)29357}$　　22. $172\overline{)80758}$　　23. $452\overline{)63714}$　　24. $531\overline{)85279}$

25. $667 \div 23$　　26. $1296 \div 72$　　27. $1802 \div 154$

28. $2047 \div 89$　　29. $3560 \div 712$　　30. $1256 \div 344$

Averages

The average of three numbers is found by adding the numbers and dividing the sum by 3. To average 5 numbers, add and divide by 5.

What is the average?

31. 17; 45; 85　　32. 145; 43; 67; 97　　33. 206; 341; 83; 349; 201

34. Air Speed Airlines carried a total of 1025 passengers from Porter to Montvale in 5 days. What is the average number per day?

★ 35. Airwaves Airlines served 25,536 meals to passengers in 2 weeks. What is the average number of meals per week? If business continues at the same rate, about how many meals will be served in one year?

On the first step of the division Barnie underestimated part of the quotient. Can you explain how he corrected his work without starting over again?

$$
\begin{array}{r}
4 \\
\cancel{3}8 \\
158\overline{)7684} \\
-474 \\
\hline
294 \\
-158 \\
\hline
1364 \\
-1264 \\
\hline
100
\end{array}
$$

Take a Break

Division of Decimals

A taxicab traveled 19.2 km in a series of 8 short trips. Each trip was about the same distance. About how long was each trip?

To divide a decimal by a whole number, first place the decimal point in the quotient. Then divide as you do whole numbers.

$$8 \overline{)19.2} \longrightarrow \begin{array}{r} 2.4 \\ 8 \overline{)19.2} \\ -16\downarrow \\ \hline 3\,2 \\ -3\,2 \\ \hline \end{array}$$

Each trip was about 2.4 km.

Study these examples. Notice that some quotients may require zeros.

$$\begin{array}{r} 0.04 \\ 6 \overline{)0.288} \\ -24 \\ \hline 4 \end{array} \longrightarrow \begin{array}{r} 0.048 \\ 6 \overline{)0.288} \\ -24 \\ \hline 48 \\ -48 \\ \hline \end{array} \qquad \begin{array}{r} 1.0 \\ 48 \overline{)49.92} \\ -48 \\ \hline 1\,9 \end{array} \longrightarrow \begin{array}{r} 1.04 \\ 48 \overline{)49.92} \\ -48 \\ \hline 1\,92 \\ -1\,92 \\ \hline \end{array}$$

Exercises

Write the quotient. Insert the decimal point and any needed zeros.

1. $\overset{8}{2 \overline{)1.6}}$

2. $\overset{12}{7 \overline{)0.084}}$

3. $\overset{7}{7 \overline{)0.049}}$

4. $\overset{1}{9 \overline{)0.009}}$

5. $\overset{7}{14 \overline{)9.8}}$

6. $\overset{5}{47 \overline{)2.35}}$

7. $\overset{13}{21 \overline{)0.273}}$

8. $\overset{2\,6}{37 \overline{)96.2}}$

9. $3 \overline{)27}$
   $3 \overline{)2.7}$
   $3 \overline{)0.27}$
   $3 \overline{)0.027}$

10. $61 \overline{)244}$
    $61 \overline{)2.44}$
    $61 \overline{)0.244}$
    $61 \overline{)0.0244}$

11. $24 \overline{)312}$
    $24 \overline{)31.2}$
    $24 \overline{)3.12}$
    $24 \overline{)0.312}$

Divide.

12. $3\overline{)1.5}$ **13.** $6\overline{)0.72}$ **14.** $5\overline{)2.55}$ **15.** $2\overline{)0.632}$ **16.** $5\overline{)0.60}$

17. $7\overline{)6.216}$ **18.** $4\overline{)9.132}$ **19.** $9\overline{)81.54}$ **20.** $5\overline{)23.645}$ **21.** $8\overline{)8.40}$

22. $39\overline{)31.2}$ **23.** $75\overline{)45.0}$ **24.** $52\overline{)4.68}$ **25.** $21\overline{)48.3}$ **26.** $37\overline{)0.962}$

27. $56\overline{)1.176}$ **28.** $47\overline{)1.457}$ **29.** $49\overline{)11.27}$ **30.** $65\overline{)162.5}$ **31.** $63\overline{)0.441}$

Going Ahead

You may extend a division to as many decimal places as you wish. To do this you write extra zeros after the last digit in the decimal. In the example, the quotient is found to three decimal places, that is, to the thousandths' place. Then the quotient is rounded to the nearest hundredth.

$$7.5 \div 9 \longrightarrow 9\overline{)7.500}^{\,0.833}$$

The quotient is 0.83, to the nearest hundredth.

Divide to the thousandths' place. Round to the hundredths' place.

32. $23.6 \div 3$ **33.** $85.26 \div 8$ **34.** $1.3 \div 6$ **35.** $17.7 \div 9$

Divide to the ten-thousandths' place. Round to the thousandths' place.

36. $24.1 \div 7$ **37.** $32.7 \div 7$ **38.** $69.31 \div 4$ **39.** $40 \div 3$

40. $7 \div 9$ **41.** $51.4 \div 12$ **42.** $45 \div 32$ **43.** $187.3 \div 24$

Calculator Corner

Use a calculator to do the division. Check the answer by multiplying.

$1.3 \div 8$ $527.48 \div 3290$ $9.4315 \div 68$
$12.48 \div 144$

Why do the quotients found on a calculator not always check?

Multiplying and Dividing by Powers of 10

Multiplying or dividing by powers of 10 is quite easy. Look at these examples. Do you see a pattern?

$$\begin{array}{r} 7.23 \\ \times\,10 \\ \hline 72.30 \end{array} \qquad \begin{array}{r} 7.23 \\ \times\,100 \\ \hline 723.00 \end{array} \qquad \begin{array}{r} 4.27 \\ 10\overline{)42.70} \end{array} \qquad \begin{array}{r} 0.427 \\ 100\overline{)42.700} \end{array}$$

When you divide by	The decimal point moves	Example
10	one place to the left	$42.7 \div 10 = 4.27$
100	two places to the left	$42.7 \div 100 = 0.427$
1000	three places to the left	$042.7 \div 1000 = 0.0427$

When you multiply by	The decimal point moves	Example
10	one place to the right	$7.23 \times 10 = 72.3$
100	two places to the right	$7.23 \times 100 = 723$
1000	three places to the right	$7.230 \times 1000 = 7230$

The decimal point moves to the right when you multiply, and to the left when you divide. Add zeros when necessary.

Exercises

Write the answer with the decimal point in the correct place.

1. $3 \times 10 = 30$
$3.7 \times 10 = 370$
$0.37 \times 10 = 370$

2. $7 \times 100 = 700$
$7.6 \times 100 = 7600$
$7.63 \times 100 = 76300$

3. $8 \times 1000 = 8000$
$8.3 \times 1000 = 83000$
$8.314 \times 1000 = 8314000$

4. $20 \div 10 = 2$
$26 \div 10 = 26$
$2.6 \div 10 = 26$

5. $400 \div 100 = 4$
$458 \div 100 = 458$
$4587 \div 100 = 4587$

6. $8000 \div 1000 = 8$
$8351 \div 1000 = 8351$
$835.1 \div 1000 = 8351$

Multiply by 10.

7. 7.4   **8.** 3.91   **9.** 6.2   **10.** 0.5   **11.** 9.06   **12.** 0.04

Multiply by 100.

13. 5.31   **14.** 0.76   **15.** 3.54   **16.** 7.2   **17.** 0.4   **18.** 0.3

Multiply by 1000.

19. 0.7214   **20.** 3.62   **21.** 804   **22.** 0.065   **23.** 3.1   **24.** 622

Divide.

25. 28.4 ÷ 10   **26.** 6.5 ÷ 10   **27.** 2163 ÷ 100   **28.** 8.4 ÷ 100

29. 0.6 ÷ 10   **30.** 1351 ÷ 1000   **31.** 86.2 ÷ 100   **32.** 84.6 ÷ 1000

MONTREAL 75 Km.

The Metric System

To convert from one metric unit to another, you multiply or divide by a power of 10. It's easy if you just move the decimal point.

$$1 \text{ cm} = 10 \text{ mm}$$
$$2.9 \text{ cm} = 29 \text{ mm}$$

$$1000 \text{ g} = 1 \text{ kg}$$
$$500 \text{ g} = 0.5 \text{ kg}$$

Complete.

33. 3.84 cm = ▢ mm   **34.** 9.1 kg = ▢ g   **35.** 1.8 m = ▢ cm

36. 52 mm = ▢ cm   **37.** 128 g = ▢ kg   **38.** 286 cm = ▢ m

★ **39.** Sometimes when you use the metric system you may wish to multiply or divide by 0.001. Describe a shortcut for multiplying or dividing by 0.001.

> 1 mm = 0.001 m
> 1 g = 0.001 kg
> 1 mL = 0.001 L

Division by Decimals

In a division, if you multiply both numbers by 10, the quotient remains the same. This is also true if you multiply both numbers by 100, or 1000, or any power of 10.

$$9 \overline{)27} = 3 \qquad 90 \overline{)270} = 3 \qquad 900 \overline{)2700} = 3 \qquad 9000 \overline{)27{,}000} = 3$$

You may use this idea to write a decimal divisor as a whole number before you divide. You simply multiply both numbers by a power of 10 that will result in a whole number divisor.

$$8.2 \overline{)43.46} \qquad 0.25 \overline{)4.275} \qquad 0.094 \overline{)20.68}$$

Multiply by 10. Divide.   Multiply by 100. Divide.   Multiply by 1000. Divide.

$$82 \overline{)434.6} \qquad 25 \overline{)427.5} \qquad 94 \overline{)20{,}680.}$$

```
        5.3              17.1             220
82) 434.6        25) 427.5        94) 20,680
   -410↓            - 25↓            - 18 8↓
    24 6             177              1 88
   -24 6            -175↓            -1 88
                      2 5
                    - 2 5
```

Exercises

Complete.

1. $0.3 \overline{)4.8} \longrightarrow \blacksquare \overline{)48}$

2. $0.5 \overline{)26.15} \longrightarrow 5 \overline{)\blacksquare}$

3. $0.32 \overline{)8.96} \longrightarrow 32 \overline{)\blacksquare}$

4. $0.29 \overline{)667} \longrightarrow \blacksquare \overline{)66700}$

5. $0.035 \overline{)0.14} \longrightarrow 35 \overline{)\blacksquare}$

6. $0.106 \overline{)0.2862} \longrightarrow \blacksquare \overline{)286.2}$

Divide.

7. $0.6\overline{)8.4}$　　　**8.** $0.7\overline{)4.354}$　　　**9.** $0.6\overline{)638.496}$　　　**10.** $1.6\overline{)4.48}$

11. $7.5\overline{)26.25}$　　　**12.** $0.09\overline{)3.6}$　　　**13.** $0.38\overline{)0.950}$　　　**14.** $0.073\overline{)0.365}$

15. $0.12\overline{)0.156}$　　　**16.** $0.31\overline{)207.7}$　　　**17.** $0.12\overline{)2.508}$　　　**18.** $8.9\overline{)514.42}$

19. $0.109\overline{)0.1526}$　　　**20.** $6.3\overline{)279.09}$　　　**21.** $0.074\overline{)2.22}$　　　**22.** $0.26\overline{)8.164}$

23. $0.09\overline{)1.53}$　　　**24.** $0.012\overline{)5.52}$　　　**25.** $9.3\overline{)722.61}$　　　**26.** $0.123\overline{)0.1722}$

Applications

Solve.

27. On the highway, a car used 31.8 L of gasoline to travel 445.2 km. About how far did the car travel on each liter of gasoline?

28. Guard rails are put along a section of a highway 192.5 m long. The posts are 3.5 m apart. After the work crew installs the first post, how many additional posts must they install?

★ **29.** Emergency call boxes are put along a highway at intervals of 4.5 km. The highway is 180 km long. How many call boxes are there if there is a call box at each end?

★ **30.** A bridge is 493 m long. At every 4.25 m there is a joint that allows the bridge to expand in hot weather. Not counting the beginning and end of the bridge, how many joints are there?

Estimating Products and Quotients

There were 8789 fans at a ball game. They were seated in 6 sections. Each person paid $3 to get in. About how much money was collected? About how many people were in each section?

To estimate products and quotients, round the numbers before you multiply or divide. Let's round 8789 to the nearest thousand.

8789   ⇨   9000
×3   ×3
                27,000

$6\overline{)8789}$ ⇨ $6\overline{)9000}$ = 1500

About $27,000 was collected.

About 1500 fans were in each section.

You could round 8789 to 8800, the nearest hundred. The arithmetic is not quite as easy, but the estimate is closer to the exact answer.

$3 \times 9000 = 27,000$

Nearest thousand

$3 \times 8800 = 26,400$

Nearest hundred

$3 \times 8789 = 26,367$

Exact answer

Exercises

Round. Choose the best estimate.
Write *a*, *b*, or *c*.

1. 8×72
  a. 500   **b.** 560   **c.** 600

2. 28×87
  a. 2700   **b.** 3000   **c.** 3200

3. 426×362
  a. 140,000   **b.** 160,000   **c.** 170,000

4. 2.75×32.568
  a. 60   **b.** 90   **c.** 120

5. $846 \div 24$
  a. 30   **b.** 40   **c.** 50

6. $26,532 \div 35$
  a. 650   **b.** 750   **c.** 850

7. $73,584 \div 159$
  a. 35   **b.** 350   **c.** 3500

8. $23.69 \div 3.81$
  a. 6   **b.** 7   **c.** 8

Round each number to its highest place value. Then estimate the answer.

EXAMPLE   243 ÷ 18 ≈ 200 ÷ 20, or 10

9. 38 × 52

10. 23 × 45

11. 7 × 766

12. 1.8 × 6348

13. 36 × 7.689

14. 8 × 18,473

15. 552 ÷ 18

16. 674 ÷ 23

17. 268.7 ÷ 63

18. 358.6 ÷ 1.8

19. 2584 ÷ 63

20. 72 ÷ 1.9

21. 61,485 ÷ 286

22. 49,826 ÷ 532

Using Estimates

An estimate can help you check the placement of the decimal point in an answer.

Does 2865.8 ÷ 4.6 equal 6.23, 62.3, or 623?

$$\text{Estimate: } 3000 ÷ 5 = 600$$
$$\text{So, } 2865.8 ÷ 4.6 = 623.$$

Use estimation to place the decimal point.

23. 38.6 × 1.5 = 579

24. 1.34 ÷ 2.5 = 536

25. 6.45 × 8.7 = 56115

26. 48 × 0.098 = 4704

27. 157.52 ÷ 8.95 = 176

28. 0.6 × 2.4 = 144

Checkpoint B

Divide. (*pages 80–81*)

1. 5⟌378

2. 8⟌4286

3. 6⟌3625

4. 7⟌94281

Divide. (*pages 82–83*)

5. 27⟌384

6. 52⟌4786

Divide. (*pages 82–83*)

7. 352⟌8721

8. 726⟌5047

Divide. (*pages 84–85*)

9. 7⟌6.23

10. 4⟌9.26

11. 45⟌3.735

12. 68⟌326.4

Multiply or divide. (*pages 86–87*)

13. 7.4 × 100

14. 0.583 × 100

15. 72 ÷ 10

16. 8.34 ÷ 100

Divide. (*pages 88–89*)

17. 0.12⟌0.474

18. 0.9⟌1.422

19. 0.07⟌1.386

20. 1.48⟌3.33

Estimate the product or quotient. (*pages 90–91*)

21. 37 × 62

22. 2684 × 47

23. 5872 ÷ 34

24. 54,786 ÷ 98

Extra practice on page 424   **91**

Problem Solving · PROBLEM FORMULATION

1	Understand
2	Plan
3	Work
4	Answer

A ticket agent does this arithmetic on a calculator.

$$4.5 \boxed{\times} \; 12 \boxed{=} \; 54$$

Then he tells a customer, "That will be $54."
What question did the customer ask?

TICKETS
Adults $4.50
Students $3.00

You know the facts, the arithmetic, and the answer. One possible question is "What is the cost of 12 adults' tickets?"

Use the facts in the sign above and the arithmetic shown. What is a possible question? What is the answer?

1. $3 \boxed{\times} 4 \boxed{=} 12$

2. $4.5 \boxed{+} 3 \boxed{=} 7.5$

3. $4.5 \boxed{-} 3 \boxed{=} 1.5$

4. $5 \boxed{-} 4.5 \boxed{=} 0.5$

5. $36 \boxed{\div} 4.5 \boxed{=} 8$

6. $5 \boxed{-} 3 \boxed{=} 2$

Write the facts and the answer to complete the problem.

7. Question: How many more home fans than visitors were there?
   Arithmetic: $2657 - 1125 = 1532$

8. Question: What is the cost of 5 tickets to the skating show?
   Arithmetic: $5 \times 8.50 = 42.50$

Use the facts to write a problem, then solve.

9. Paavo threw the javelin 45.72 m. Sven threw it 47.08 m.

10. Reserved seats at the ball game cost $8.25. General admission is $2.75.

11. The winner of the race completed the first stage in 15 min 42 s, the second stage in 19 min 23 s, and the third stage in 18 min 5 s.

12. Tickets to the tennis match cost $6.50 each. You buy 15 tickets.

13. The fastest time for the swim was 54 min 16 s. The slowest time was 61 min 12 s.

14. A cross-country bike race is run in 3 stages. The first is 14.5 km long. The second is 21.3 km long, and the third is 19.8 km long.

15. There were 2346 fans at the ball game. They paid an average of $4.25 for admission.

★ 16. Sandra jogs 3.5 mi each day. In one week, she spent 2 h 55 min jogging.

★ 17. At a tennis match the total receipts were $142,609, and the total costs were $53,296. The club that staged the match kept $20,000. The 4 players in the match shared the rest.

Solve the equation.

1. $36 = 4 \times n$ **2.** $45 \div u = 9$ **3.** $7 = p \div 1$

4. $k \times 1 = 9$ **5.** $4 \times p = 7 \times 4$ **6.** $7 \times (3 + a) = (7 \times 3) + (7 \times 5)$

Simplify.

7. $2 + 3 \times 5$ **8.** $4 \times (2 + 1) - 1$ **9.** $5 + 1 \times 7 - 4 \div 2$

Start at the center. Multiply or divide out to the rim of the wheel.
For example, Exercise 10 is 28×9.

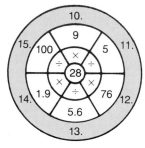
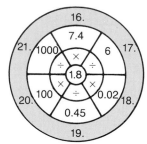

Write the number in standard form.

22. 6^2 **23.** 2^4 **24.** 1^7 **25.** 10^3

Round each number to its highest place value.
Then estimate the answer.

26. 46×12 **27.** 0.9×22.5 **28.** $6.002 \div 1.8$

Use the facts to write a problem.
Then solve.

29. A ten-speed bicycle costs $120.
Maria and Elise together have
saved $35. Their parents have
promised to give them two dollars
for every one dollar that they save.

Solve the equation. (*pages 68–71*)

1. $3 \times b = 27$ **2.** $c \div 5 = 8$ **3.** $9 = 54 \div e$

4. $6 \times 8 = n \times 6$ **5.** $3 \times y = 0$ **6.** $5 \times (j \times 4) = (5 \times 2) \times 4$

Simplify. (*pages 72–73*)

7. $3 \times 2 + 3 \times 4$ **8.** $3 + 4 \times (2 + 4) \div 8$ **9.** $8 \times (5 - 3) + 27 \div 3$

Multiply. (*pages 74–77*)

10. $\begin{array}{r} 3294 \\ \times 8 \\ \hline \end{array}$ **11.** $\begin{array}{r} 76 \\ \times 94 \\ \hline \end{array}$ **12.** $\begin{array}{r} 108 \\ \times 27 \\ \hline \end{array}$ **13.** $\begin{array}{r} 3652 \\ \times 203 \\ \hline \end{array}$

14. $\begin{array}{r} 3.7 \\ \times 8.2 \\ \hline \end{array}$ **15.** $\begin{array}{r} 412 \\ \times 0.05 \\ \hline \end{array}$ **16.** $\begin{array}{r} 0.038 \\ \times 2.3 \\ \hline \end{array}$ **17.** $\begin{array}{r} 2.065 \\ \times 0.20 \\ \hline \end{array}$

Write the number in standard form. (*pages 78–79*)

18. 2^4 **19.** 10^2 **20.** 1^5 **21.** 5^4

Multiply or divide. (*pages 80–89*)

22. $4\overline{)983}$ **23.** $24\overline{)8631}$ **24.** $125\overline{)14285}$

25. $5\overline{)6.25}$ **26.** $9\overline{)2.826}$ **27.** $54\overline{)3.024}$

28. 8.2×100 **29.** $6.3 \div 10$ **30.** 0.06×1000

31. $0.2\overline{)2.4}$ **32.** $0.15\overline{)0.033}$ **33.** $0.038\overline{)0.9671}$

Round each number to its highest place. Then estimate the answer. (*pages 90–91*)

34. 48×73 **35.** 0.7×3229 **36.** $9.64 \div 5.3$

Use the facts to write a problem. Then solve. (*pages 92–93*)

37. It costs $8.50 an hour for four players to rent a tennis court. A can of tennis balls costs $3.50.

What Is a Computer?

The times we live in have been called the Computer Age. We do not all need to be computer experts but we do need to know something about computers to be effective citizens.

A computer is made up of several parts, as shown here.

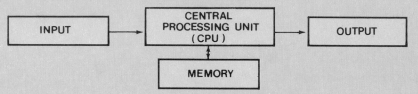

To work with a computer, we must be able to communicate with it. This is done with input and output devices.

Input: You can give a computer information and instructions with a keyboard (like a typewriter), game controls, punched cards, cassette tapes, magnetic disks and light pens.

Output: The computer can give you information on a TV screen, a printer, or a plotter (for drawing graphs).

The computer can store data and instructions in its **memory.** This information can be recalled later if it's needed for solving a problem.

The **central processing unit** (CPU) is where the computer actually does the job that it has been given. The CPU receives directions from input. It gets any data needed from memory. Then it processes the data as instructed. The results, or answers, are supplied to the person using the computer on an output device.

The way a computer works is actually very much like the way you would solve an arithmetic problem.

Input: You are given a problem by your teacher.
CPU: You analyze the problem, and decide what skill you need to use.
Memory: You recall the arithmetic facts you need.
CPU: You figure out the answer.
Output: You write the answer on your paper.

A computer can answer questions in seconds that would take us years to answer ourselves. Remember, though, that a computer must be told what to do and how to do it. Computers are also used for doing jobs that would be too boring for a person, but computers do not get bored. Also, the huge memory capacity of computers adds to their usefulness.

Identify each item as an input or an output device.

1. TV screen
2. keyboard
3. punched cards
4. game controls
5. printer
6. cassette tape
7. plotter
8. light pen
9. spoken words

State whether each activity is associated with input, CPU, memory, or output.

10. The computer looks up your checkbook balance from last month.

11. Your new balance is shown on your TV monitor.

12. You type in this month's checks and deposits.

13. A list of checks and deposits is printed for you.

14. You enter a program on a disk that you bought from a computer store.

15. The word "Overdrawn" is shown on the TV screen.

16. The computer figures your new balance after every check or deposit.

17. This month's transactions are stored to be used next month.

18. The amount you will pay for the number of checks used is figured.

Maintaining Skills

Add or subtract.

1. 25,842
   + 17,909

2. 503
   8
   + 7724

3. 65,363
   − 7,228

4. 20,001
   − 14,437

5. 6.803
   + 17.939

6. 2.9
   + 0.546

7. $14.25
   − 7.47

8. 8.2
   − 1.335

9. 5 ft 2 in.
   + 2 ft 11 in.

10. 3 qt 1 pt
    + 4 qt 1 pt

11. 5 h 30 min
    + 5 h 55 min

12. 6 lb 4 oz
    − 2 lb 13 oz

13. 8 yd 1 ft
    − 2 yd 2 ft

14. 15 min
    − 6 min 15 s

What is the tallest monument in the world?

To learn the answer, find each measure on the ruler below. Then replace the measure with the letter that it matches.

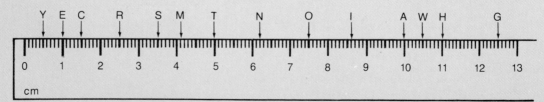

15. ___(5 cm)___ ___(110 mm)___ ___(0.01 m)___

16. ___(125 mm)___ ___(10 cm)___ ___(0.05 m)___ ___(10 mm)___ ___(10.5 cm)___ ___(100 mm)___ ___(5 mm)___

17. ___(0.1 m)___ ___(2.5 cm)___ ___(0.015 m)___ ___(0.11 m)___

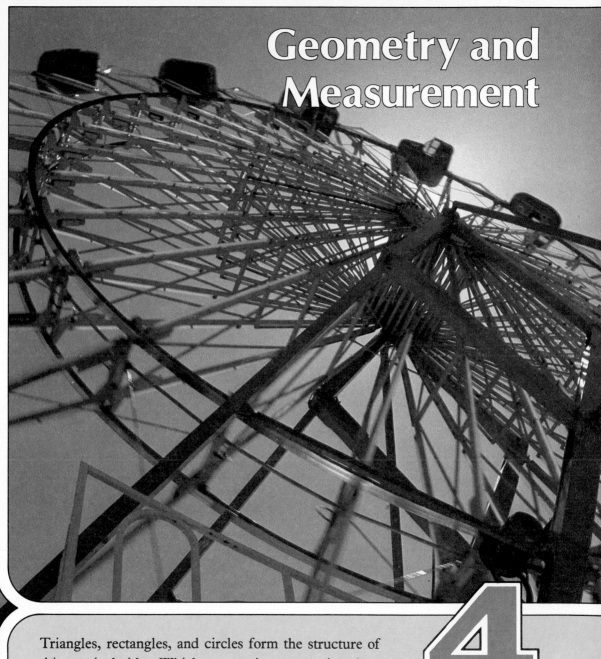

Geometry and Measurement

Triangles, rectangles, and circles form the structure of this carnival ride. Which geometric construction do you think does the most to prevent the structure from bending out of shape?

4

Basic Ideas of Geometry

A **point** shows an exact location. We use a capital letter to name a point.

Point P

A **line** is a set of points that extends without end in two opposite directions.

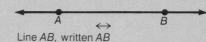
Line AB, written $\overleftrightarrow{AB}$

A **ray** is part of a line. It has one endpoint. The endpoint is named first.

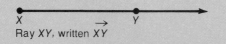
Ray XY, written $\overrightarrow{XY}$

A **line segment** is also part of a line. It has two endpoints.

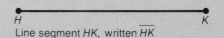
Line segment HK, written $\overline{HK}$

An **angle** is two rays that have the same endpoint. The endpoint is called the **vertex** of the angle. The rays are called the **sides.**

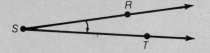
Angle RST, written ∠RST, ∠TSR or ∠S

Two lines that cross each other are called **intersecting lines.** Two lines in a plane that do not intersect are **parallel.**

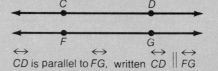
$\overleftrightarrow{CD}$ is parallel to $\overleftrightarrow{FG}$, written $\overleftrightarrow{CD} \parallel \overleftrightarrow{FG}$

A **plane** is the set of points on a flat surface that extends without end.

Plane M

Exercises

Name the figure using the letters shown.

1.
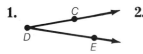

2.

3.

4.

Use the figure below.

5. Name a pair of parallel lines.

6. Name two pairs of intersecting lines.

7. Name seven line segments.

8. Name four angles.

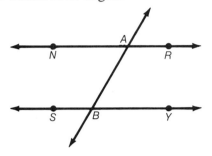

True or False? Write *T* or *F.*

9. A line has an endpoint.

10. A line segment has two endpoints.

11. A ray has no endpoints.

12. A line is part of a line segment.

13. Parallel lines intersect.

14. ∠*CAT* is another name for ∠*TAC.*

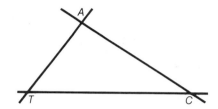

Find examples in your classroom that suggest each figure.

EXAMPLE A plane: the ceiling

15. an angle   **16.** a line segment   **17.** two intersecting lines

Vertical Angles

Vertical angles are formed by two intersecting lines.
Sometimes we use numbers to name angles.

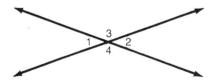

∠1 and ∠2 are vertical angles, so are ∠3 and ∠4.

Use a number to name the angle in the drawing.

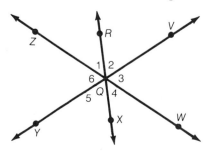

18. ∠*RQV*   **19.** ∠*VQW*

20. ∠*WQX*   **21.** ∠*XQY*

22. Name 3 pairs of vertical angles.

★ **23.** Two other names for ∠5 are ∠*XQY* and ∠*YQX.* Why wouldn't ∠*Q* be a good name for ∠5?

Measuring Angles

To measure an angle, we use a protractor. The unit of measure is called a **degree.** Most protractors show degree measure up to 180 degrees (180°). Let's measure $\angle ACB$.

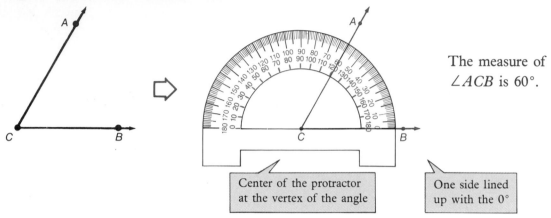

The measure of $\angle ACB$ is 60°.

Center of the protractor at the vertex of the angle

One side lined up with the 0°

We will write the fact that the measure of $\angle ACB$ is 60° as $\angle ACB = 60°$.

Here's how to draw $\angle XYZ$ with a measure of 55° using the inner scale of the protractor.

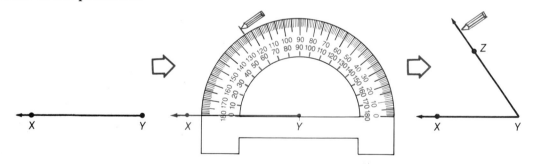

Exercises

What is the measure of the angle?

1. $\angle AOB$ 2. $\angle EOD$

3. $\angle AOC$ 4. $\angle EOC$

5. $\angle AOD$ 6. $\angle EOB$

7. $\angle AOE$ 8. $\angle BOC$

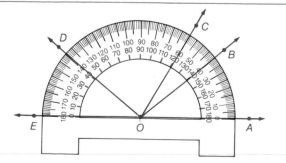

Use a protractor. What is the measure of the angle?

9. **10.** **11.**

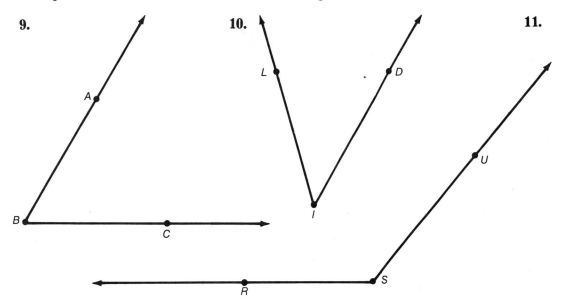

Use a protractor to draw the angle.

12. $\angle DEF = 90°$ **13.** $\angle COB - 35°$ **14.** $\angle FAT = 120°$

15. $\angle LMN = 155°$ **16.** $\angle RUN = 15°$ **17.** $\angle TAB = 72°$

18. $\angle NER = 138°$ **19.** $\angle SUM = 4°$ **20.** $\angle PQS = 180°$

Congruent Angles

Angles with the same measure are **congruent.** We say $\angle PFC$ is congruent to $\angle DOT$. We write $\angle PFC \cong \angle DOT$.

Name an angle congruent to the given angle.

21. $\angle AOB$ **22.** $\angle FOE$ **23.** $\angle COD$

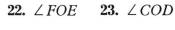

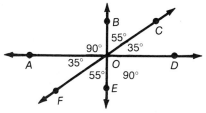

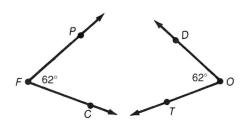

★ **24.** Draw a triangle. Measure the angles. What do you notice about the measures of the angles?

Kinds of Angles

An angle with a measure of 90° is called a **right angle.** The sides of a right angle are **perpendicular.**

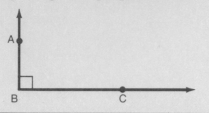

$\overrightarrow{BA}$ is perpendicular to $\overrightarrow{BC}$

$$\overrightarrow{BA} \perp \overrightarrow{BC}$$

An **acute angle** has a measure greater than 0° and less than 90°.

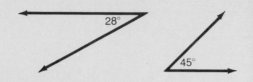

An **obtuse angle** has a measure greater than 90° and less than 180°.

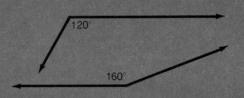

If the sum of the measures of two angles is 90°, the angles are **complementary.**

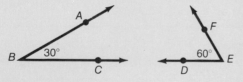

∠ABC and ∠DEF are complementary.

If the sum of the measures of two angles is 180°, the angles are **supplementary.**

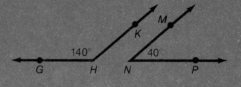

∠GHK and ∠MNP are supplementary.

Exercises

Write *right, acute,* or *obtuse* to tell which kind of angle is shown.

1.

2.

3.

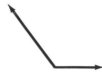

4.

Tell whether the angles are *complementary, supplementary,* or *neither.*

5. 42°, 48°   **6.** 80°, 90°   **7.** 10°, 80°   **8.** 100°, 28°

9. 125°, 55°   **10.** 1°, 89°   **11.** 45°, 45°   **12.** 90°, 90°

Write the measure of a complementary angle.

13. 30°   **14.** 20°   **15.** 80°   **16.** 89°   **17.** 15°

Write the measure of a supplementary angle.

18. 100°   **19.** 120°   **20.** 40°   **21.** 4°   **22.** 90°

Are the sides of the angle perpendicular? Write *Yes* or *No.*

23.   **24.**   **25.**   **26.**

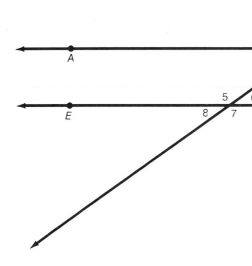

Special Angles

In the figure below, $\overleftrightarrow{AD} \parallel \overleftrightarrow{EH}$.

27. Measure the angles.

28. Name the acute angles.

29. Name the obtuse angles.

★ **30.** Name 4 pairs of congruent angles.

★ **31.** Name 4 pairs of supplementary angles.

Polygons

A **polygon** is a plane figure formed by
joining three or more nonintersecting
line segments at their endpoints.

Some polygons have special names
according to the number of sides.

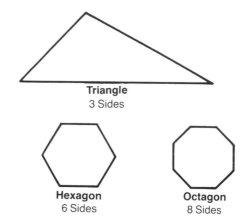

Triangle
3 Sides

Quadrilateral
4 Sides

Pentagon
5 Sides

Hexagon
6 Sides

Octagon
8 Sides

You learned that two angles that have the same measure are
congruent angles. Two line segments that have the same
length are called **congruent line segments.**

$\overline{XY} \cong \overline{WZ}$

A **regular polygon** is a polygon in which all sides are congruent and
all angles are congruent. We often mark congruent sides and
congruent angles alike.

Exercises

Name the polygon according to the number of its sides.

1. 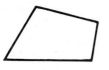 2.  3.   4.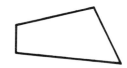

5.  6.   7. 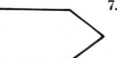 8.

The polygon is a regular polygon. Write the measures of all its sides, and all its angles.

9.
12

10.
8
120°

11.
7
60°

12.
12 in.
135°

Polygons and Diagonals

A line segment that joins two vertexes of a polygon and is not a side of the polygon is called a **diagonal.**

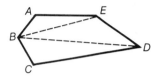

Draw the polygon and all the diagonals from one vertex. Complete the chart.

	Polygon	Number of sides	Number of diagonals from one vertex
13.	Triangle	?	?
14.	Quadrilateral	?	?
15.	?	5	?
16.	?	6	?
17.	Heptagon	7	?
18.	?	8	?

★ **19.** How many diagonals from one vertex will there be in a polygon with 100 sides?

How many times during a day are the hands of a clock perpendicular?

Take a Break

Triangles

Triangles are often used in construction because they form rigid structures.

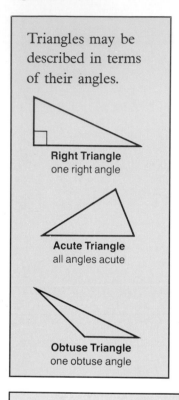

Triangles may be described in terms of their angles.

Right Triangle
one right angle

Acute Triangle
all angles acute

Obtuse Triangle
one obtuse angle

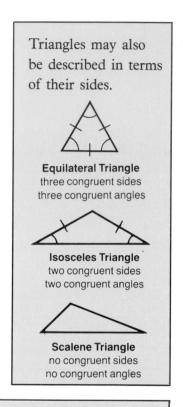

Triangles may also be described in terms of their sides.

Equilateral Triangle
three congruent sides
three congruent angles

Isosceles Triangle
two congruent sides
two congruent angles

Scalene Triangle
no congruent sides
no congruent angles

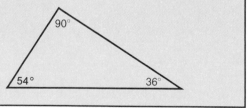

The angles of a triangle have a special property. The sum of their measures is always 180°.

90°
54°   36°

Exercises

Tell whether the triangle is *acute, right,* or *obtuse.*

1. **2.**  **3.** 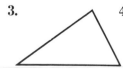 **4.**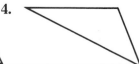

Tell whether the triangle is *scalene, isosceles,* or *equilateral.*

5. **6.**  **7.** 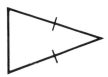 **8.**

What is the measure of the third angle of the triangle?

9. 85°, 30°   **10.** 45°, 30°   **11.** 90°, 45°   **12.** 60°, 60°

13. 126°, 31°   **14.** 96°, 38°   **15.** 72°, 39°   **16.** 103°, 33°

List all the terms that describe the triangle. Write *a, b, c, d, e,* or *f.*

a. acute   **b.** obtuse   **c.** right   **d.** scalene   **e.** isosceles   **f.** equilateral

17.   **18.**   **19.**    **20.**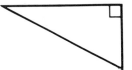

Sketch a triangle to fit the description. Mark equal parts alike.

21. scalene   **22.** obtuse isosceles   **23.** right isosceles

24. acute   **25.** equilateral   **26.** isosceles, but not equilateral

More about Polygons

Drawing a diagonal divides a quadrilateral into two triangles.
The sum of the measures of ∠1, ∠2, and ∠3 is 180°.
The sum of the measures of ∠4, ∠5, and ∠6 is 180°.
The sum of the measures of the angles of the quadrilateral is
180° + 180°, or 360°.

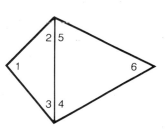

What is the sum of the measures of the angles of the polygon?

27. a pentagon   **28.** a hexagon   **29.** an octagon

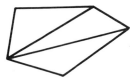      

★ **30.** a polygon with 100 sides

Quadrilaterals

A **trapezoid** is a quadrilateral with only one pair of parallel sides.

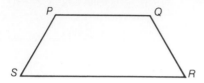

Trapezoid PQRS

$$\overline{PQ} \parallel \overline{SR}$$

A **parallelogram** (▱) is a quadrilateral whose opposite sides are parallel.

Parallelogram ABCD (▱ABCD)

$$\overline{AB} \parallel \overline{DC} \text{ and } \overline{AD} \parallel \overline{BC}$$

Here are some important properties of parallelograms.

1. Opposite sides are parallel.
2. Opposite sides are congruent.
3. Opposite angles are congruent.

Some parallelograms have special names.

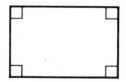

Rectangle
A parallelogram with four right angles

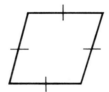

Rhombus
A parallelogram with four congruent sides

Square
A rectangle with four congruent sides

Exercises

Name all the quadrilaterals that have the property. Write *a, b, c, d,* or *e.*

a. trapezoid   **b.** parallelogram   **c.** rectangle   **d.** rhombus   **e.** square

1. All opposite sides are parallel.

2. Opposite sides are congruent.

3. Opposite angles are congruent.

4. All sides are congruent.

5. There are four right angles.

6. Only two sides are parallel.

Copy the figure. Label the length of each line segment and the measure of each angle.

7. Quadrilateral *ACEF* is a parallelogram. Quadrilateral *BCDG* is a rhombus.

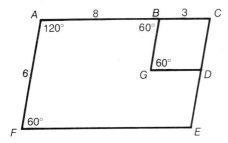

Is the statement always true, sometimes true, or never true? Write *A*, *S*, or *N*.

8. A square is a parallelogram.

9. A parallelogram is a trapezoid.

10. A rectangle is a square.

11. A rhombus is a quadrilateral.

In Other Words

The word **equilateral** means equal sides. The word **equiangular** means equal angles.

Name the quadrilateral.

12. an equilateral quadrilateral

13. an equiangular quadrilateral

14. a quadrilateral that is both equilateral and equiangular

15. a regular quadrilateral

Checkpoint A

True or False? Write *T* or *F*. (*pages 100–101*)

1. A line has one endpoint.

2. Parallel lines intersect.

3. A ray has one endpoint.

4. A line segment is part of a line.

Use a protractor to draw the angle. (*pages 102–103*)

5. ∠*PAC* = 90°   **6.** ∠*MAN* = 153°

7. ∠*TUL* = 64°

Tell whether the angle is *acute, right,* or *obtuse.* (*pages 104–105*)

8. 93°   **9.** 10°   **10.** 90°

Write the measures of all the sides and all the angles of the regular polygon. (*pages 106–107*)

11.   **12.**

What is the measure of the third angle of the triangle? (*pages 108–109*)

13. 84°, 29°   **14.** 130°, 41°

15. 90°, 45°   **16.** 60°, 60°

Name each parallelogram. (*pages 110–111*)

17. 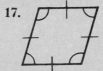   **18.**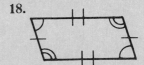

Extra practice on page 426   **111**

Perimeter

Suppose you have a piece of molding 300 cm long. Is it long enough to make a picture frame 75 cm long by 60 cm wide?

You need to know the distance around the rectangle. The distance around a polygon is called the **perimeter.** To find the perimeter of a polygon, add the lengths of all the sides.

Perimeter = 75 + 75 + 60 + 60 = 270

The perimeter of the frame must be 270 cm. So the molding is long enough to make the frame.

A **formula** is a short way of stating a rule. We can write a formula for the perimeter of a rectangle. The length and width of a rectangle are often called the **base** and **height.**

$$Perimeter = (2 \times base) + (2 \times height)$$
$$P = (2 \times b) + (2 \times h)$$

To use a formula, simply replace the letters in the formula with the numbers you know. Then do the arithmetic. Here's an example.

$b = 4$
$h = 5$

$$P = (2 \times b) + (2 \times h)$$
$$P = (2 \times 4) + (2 \times 5)$$
$$= 8 + 10$$
$$= 18 \text{ (cm)}$$

Exercises

What is the perimeter?

1.

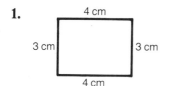

2.

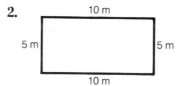

3.

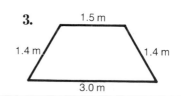

What is the perimeter?

4.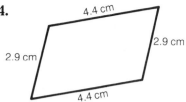

5.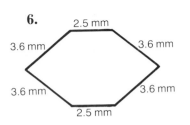

6.

What is the perimeter of the rectangle? Use the formula.

7. $b = 6$ cm; $h = 8$ cm

8. $b = 70$ m; $h = 52$ m

9. $b = 82.1$ mm; $h = 90$ mm

10. $b = 8.5$ m; $h = 0.2$ m

Each object below has a rectangular shape. What is the perimeter?

11. Rug, 3.4 m by 2.1 m

12. Picture, 25 cm by 15 cm

13. Table top, 82 cm by 40 cm

14. Mirror, 38 cm by 38 cm

15. Wall panel, 2.6 m by 1.3 m

16. Chair seat, 35 cm by 35 cm

Writing Formulas

The sides of a square all have the same length. We can use this fact to write a formula for the perimeter of a square.

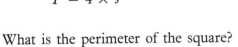

Perimeter = 4 × length of a side

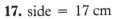
$$P = 4 \times s$$

What is the perimeter of the square?

17. side = 17 cm

18. side = 25 cm

19. side = 2.38 cm

Write a formula for the perimeter of the polygon.

20. a regular hexagon

21. a regular octagon

22. a regular pentagon

★ **23.** Maura uses the formula $P = (2 \times b) + (2 \times h)$ for the perimeter of a rectangle. Laura uses the formula $P = 2 \times (b + h)$. Will they both get the same answer? Why? Name the property.

Circles and Circumference

A **circle** is the set of all the points in a plane that are the same distance from a particular point in the plane. The point is called the **center** of the circle.

A **radius** is a line segment that joins the center and a point on the circle. A **diameter** is a line segment that joins two points on the circle and that contains the center. The distance around the circle is called the **circumference.**

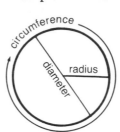

We will use the letter r to stand for the length of the radius, and the letter d to stand for the length of the diameter. A diameter of a circle is twice as long as its radius.

$$d = 2 \times r$$

The quotient $C \div d$ is the same number for all circles. We use the Greek letter π (pi) to stand for this number.

$C \div d = \pi$ $C \div d \approx 3.14$

$3.14 \approx \pi$ $C \approx 3.14 \times d$

↑

"is about equal to"

Suppose a bicycle tire has a diameter of 700 mm. Let's find the circumference. Replace d in the formula with 700. We find that the circumference is 2198 mm.

$$C \approx 3.14 \times d$$
$$C \approx 3.14 \times 700$$
$$C \approx 2198 \text{ (mm)}$$

Exercises

What is the length of the diameter (d)?

1. $r = 4$	**2.** $r = 7$	**3.** $r = 15$	**4.** $r = 22$	**5.** $r = 16$
6. $r = 25$	**7.** $r = 100$	**8.** $r = 2.5$	**9.** $r = 300$	**10.** $r = 5.25$

Describe the part of the circle named.

11. $\overline{AC}$ **12.** $\overline{OC}$

13. $\overline{OB}$ **14.** Point O

What is the circumference?

15. 12 cm

16. 9 m

17. 8.5 cm

What is the circumference?

18. $d = 35$ cm   **19.** $d = 50$ cm   **20.** $d = 24$ mm   **21.** $r = 15$ cm

22. $r = 18$ cm   **23.** $r = 17$ m   **24.** $d = 3.3$ cm   **25.** $d = 1.5$ mm

26. $d = 0.6$ km   **27.** $r = 10.8$ cm   **28.** $r = 1.4$ m   **29.** $r = 6.5$ mm

More about Pi

The ancient Greeks knew that the circumference (C) of a circle divided by the length of the diameter (d) is always the same number. We call this number pi (π). Computers have calculated π to over 1,000,000 decimal places.

30. Ptolemy, a Greek mathematician, used $1131 \div 360$ to approximate π. Divide to find the value he used to the nearest thousandth.

★ **31.** Archimedes determined that π was between $22 \div 7$ and $223 \div 71$. The value of π to five decimal places is 3.14159. Was Archimedes right?

Calculator Corner

These approximations for π were used by ancient peoples. Which approximation is closest to 3.1415929. . . ?

Romans: $\pi \approx 25 \div 8$ Egyptians: $\pi \approx 256 \div 81$

Chinese: $\pi \approx 355 \div 113$

Area

Andrea is sewing squares of fabric together to make a quilt. She measures the size of the quilt by the number of squares.

The **area** of a shape is the number of square units it contains.

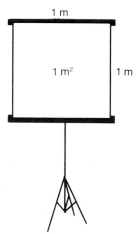

$6 \times 4 = 24$

Area $= 24$

(square units)

1 square unit

Standard units for measuring area are the **square centimeter (cm²),** the **square millimeter (mm²),** and the **square meter (m²).**

1 cm   1 cm²
1 cm

1 mm²   10 mm
10 mm

1 m

1 m²   1 m

You can find the area of a rectangle by using this formula.

Area $=$ base $\times$ height

$A = b \times h$

$A = 4 \times 2$

$= 8 \ (\text{cm}^2)$

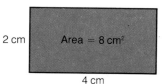

2 cm   Area $= 8 \ \text{cm}^2$

4 cm

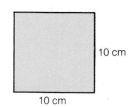

Exercises

What is the area of the rectangle?

1.

3 cm

5 cm

2.

8 cm

6 cm

3.

10 cm

10 cm

What is the area of the rectangle?

4. $b = 20$ cm
$h = 8$ cm

5. $b = 14$ m
$h = 10$ m

6. $b = 12$ mm
$h = 3$ mm

7. $b = 7$ km
$h = 23$ km

8. $b = 32$ mm
$h = 28$ mm

9. $b = 7.5$ m
$h = 8.3$ m

10. $b = 16.41$ cm
$h = 7.8$ cm

11. $b = 13.3$ km
$h = 7.1$ km

What is the area of the square?

12. $s = 9$ cm

13. $s = 12$ mm

14. $s = 20$ m

15. $s = 5$ km

16. $s = 6.3$ mm

17. $s = 7.1$ km

18. $s = 13.4$ cm

19. $s = 0.52$ m

Choose the best estimate for the area. Write *a*, *b*, or *c*.

20. an envelope   **a.** 200 cm^2 **b.** 200 mm^2 **c.** 200 m^2

21. a postage stamp   **a.** 600 cm^2 **b.** 600 mm^2 **c.** 600 m^2

22. a football field   **a.** 5000 cm^2 **b.** 5000 mm^2 **c.** 5000 m^2

23. a sheet of paper   **a.** 650 cm^2 **b.** 650 mm^2 **c.** 650 m^2

Relating Square Units of Measure

The diagram shows that 1 cm^2 contains 100 mm^2.

1 cm $= 10$ mm

1 cm$^2 = 10$ mm $\times 10$ mm
$ = 100$ mm^2

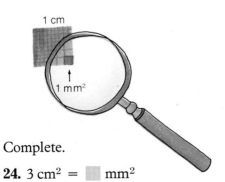

1 cm

1 mm^2

Complete.

24. 3 cm$^2 = \blacksquare$ mm^2

25. 8 cm$^2 = \blacksquare$ mm^2

26. 12 cm$^2 = \blacksquare$ mm^2

27. $\blacksquare$ cm$^2 = 500$ mm^2

28. $\blacksquare$ cm$^2 = 900$ mm^2

29. $\blacksquare$ cm$^2 = 3100$ mm^2

30. $\blacksquare$ cm$^2 = 7500$ mm^2

31. $\blacksquare$ cm$^2 = 9800$ mm^2

32. 65 cm$^2 = \blacksquare$ mm^2

33. 83 cm$^2 = \blacksquare$ mm^2

★ **34.** 1 m$^2 = \blacksquare$ cm^2

★ **35.** 1 km$^2 = \blacksquare$ m^2

Area of Parallelograms and Triangles

The **height** of a parallelogram is the length of a line segment that joins two opposite sides and is perpendicular to them.

The area of a parallelogram is the same as the area of a rectangle with the same base and height.

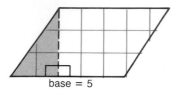

Area = base × height

$A = b \times h$

$A = 5 \times 3$

$= 15$ (square units)

A diagonal of a parallelogram divides the parallelogram into two triangles with equal areas. The area of one triangle is equal to the area of the parallelogram divided by 2.

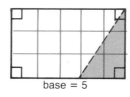

Area of Triangle = Area of Parallelogram ÷ 2

Area of Triangle = base × height ÷ 2

$A = b \times h \div 2$

$A = 4 \times 3 \div 2$

$= 6$ (square units)

Exercises

What is the area?

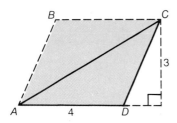

1. 12 cm, 20 cm; 12 cm, 20 cm

2. 18 mm, 9 mm; 9 mm, 18 mm

3. 15 m, 24 m; 15 m, 24 m

4. 12 cm, 32 cm; 12 cm, 32 cm

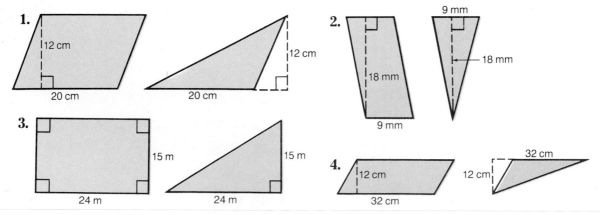

118

What is the area of the parallelogram?

5. $b = 30$ cm
$h = 4$ cm

6. $b = 12$ m
$h = 6$ m

7. $b = 60$ mm
$h = 12$ mm

8. $b = 33$ cm
$h = 10$ cm

9. $b = 300$ cm
$h = 25$ cm

10. $b = 12.3$ cm
$h = 12.3$ cm

11. $b = 60.5$ mm
$h = 75$ mm

12. $b = 16.45$ m
$h = 14.3$ m

What is the area of the triangle?

13. $b = 13$ cm
$h = 6$ cm

14. $b = 20$ mm
$h = 25$ mm

15. $b = 6$ m
$h = 6$ m

16. $b = 28$ cm
$h = 4$ cm

17. $b = 12.3$ m
$h = 25$ m

18. $b = 24$ mm
$h = 28.5$ mm

19. $b = 5.5$ m
$h = 4.8$ m

20. $b = 126$ mm
$h = 520$ mm

Area of a Trapezoid

A trapezoid has two bases, one longer than the other. The area of a trapezoid is equal to the average of the bases times the height.

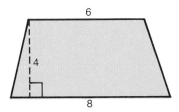

Average of the bases
$(6 + 8) \div 2 = 14 \div 2$
$= 7$ (units)

Area = Average of bases × height
Area = 7×4
$= 28$ (square units)

What is the area of the trapezoid?

21.

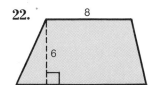

22.

23.

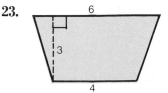

119

Area of a Circle

The area of a circle is equal to π times the length of the radius squared.

$$A = \pi \times r^2$$

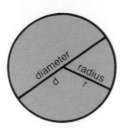

To determine the approximate area of a circle, we often use 3.14 for π.

$$A \approx 3.14 \times r^2$$
$$A \approx 3.14 \times 4^2$$
$$\approx 3.14 \times 16$$
$$\approx 50.24 \ (cm^2)$$

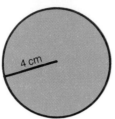

Area $\approx 50.24 \ cm^2$

Exercises

Complete.

1.

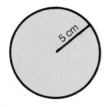

$A \approx 3.14 \times \ \boxed{}^{\ 2}$

2.

$A \approx \boxed{} \times 6^2$

3.

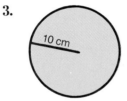

$A \approx 3.14 \times 10^2 \approx \boxed{}$

4.

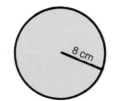

$A \approx 3.14 \times \boxed{}^{\ 2} \approx \boxed{}$

5.

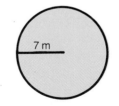

$A \approx 3.14 \times \boxed{}^{\ 2} \approx \boxed{}$

6.

$A \approx 3.14 \times \boxed{}^{\ 2} \approx \boxed{}$

What is the area of the circle?

7. $r = 6$ m

8. $r = 18$ cm

9. $r = 20$ mm

10. $r = 2.5$ m

11. $d = 40$ cm

12. $d = 160$ mm

13. $d = 8.2$ m

14. $d = 75$ cm

What is the area of the circular shape?

15. Cushion, radius 20 cm

16. Table top, radius 40 cm

17. Lamp base, diameter 16 cm

18. Clock, radius 12 cm

19. Tablecloth, radius 60 cm

20. Rug, diameter 80 cm

In Ski Circles

A ski lodge has a circular fireplace with a radius of 1 m. The owners want to put fireproof flooring with a radius of 3.5 m around the fireplace. They must cut a hole in the flooring for the fireplace.

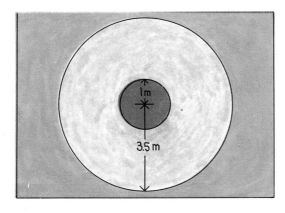

Solve.

21. What is the area covered by the fireplace?

22. What is the area of the flooring before the hole is cut for the fireplace?

★ **23.** What is the area of the flooring after the hole is cut for the fireplace?

What is the perimeter of the rectangle? (*pages 112–113*)

1. $b = 6$ cm $\quad h = 18$ cm	**2.** $b = 79$ m $\quad h = 0.4$ m

What is the circumference of the circle? (*pages 114–115*)

3. $d = 22$ cm	**4.** $r = 10$ m
5. $d = 5.7$ mm	**6.** $r = 3.2$ cm

What is the area of the rectangle? (*pages 116–117*)

7. $b = 15$ m $\quad h = 7$ m	**8.** $b = 12$ cm $\quad h = 5$ cm
9. $b = 17$ cm $\quad h = 17$ cm	**10.** $b = 0.4$ m $\quad h = 0.4$ m

What is the area of the parallelogram? (*pages 118–119*)

11. $b = 17$ cm $\quad h = 8$ cm	**12.** $b = 4.9$ mm $\quad h = 4.9$ mm

What is the area of the triangle?

13. $b = 24$ cm $\quad h = 5$ cm	**14.** $b = 5.8$ cm $\quad h = 10$ cm

What is the area of the circle? (*pages 120–121*)

15. $r = 55$ cm	**16.** $r = 7.3$ m
17. $d = 14.2$ cm	**18.** $d = 28$ mm

Problem Solving · USING FORMULAS

Formulas are often helpful in problem solving. A formula uses symbols instead of words to state a rule.

The AA Sports Club decides to put a fence around its outdoor swimming pool. It is to be 12 m by 30 m. How much fencing must the club buy?

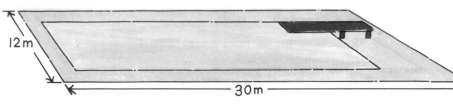

12 m

30 m

To solve a problem using a formula, first choose the correct formula.

Perimeter of a Rectangle: $p = (2 \times b) + (2 \times h)$

Next, replace the letters in the formula with the numbers they stand for. Do the arithmetic.

$p = (2 \times 12) + (2 \times 30) = 24 + 60 = 84$

The AA Sports Club needs 84 m of fencing to go around the pool.

Write the formula.

1. area of a tennis court (rectangle)

2. area of a sail (triangle)

3. distance around a circular skating rink (circle)

4. distance around the bases on a baseball diamond (square)

5. area of a handball court (rectangle)

6. area of a trampoline (rectangle)

Use a formula to solve the problem.

7. What is the perimeter of a rectangular swimming pool that is 11 m long and 7 m wide?

8. What is the area of a circular swimming pool whose radius measures 6 m?

9. What is the perimeter of a rectangular field that is 277 m long and 152 m wide?

10. What is the area of a triangular sail 8 m high and 6 m wide at its widest point?

Solve.

The children's swimming pool at the club is circular. The measure of its diameter is 8 m.

11. What is the distance around the pool?

12. How long is the radius?

13. What is the area?

A square field has sides of 245 m. A rectangular field is 200 m long by 300 m wide.

14. Which field has the greater perimeter?

15. Which field has the greater area?

The AA Sports Club decides to pave and fence 4 tennis courts. Use the diagram to solve the problem.

16. How long and how wide is each court?

17. What is the area of each court?

18. What is the total area to be paved?

19. How many meters of fencing will they need to go around the courts and between them as shown?

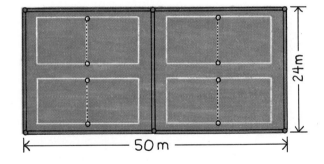

Solve.

20. A triangular sail has an area of 72 m². If the measure of the base is 8 m, how high is it?

21. What is the diameter of a circle with a circumference of 157 m?

22. What is the perimeter of a rectangle with an area of 60 m² and a length of 20 m?

★ **23.** What is the area of the largest circle that will fit entirely inside a square with a side of 4 m?

Use the figure at the right.

1. Name a pair of parallel lines.

2. Name two pairs of intersecting lines.

3. Name two pairs of vertical angles.

4. Name two rays.

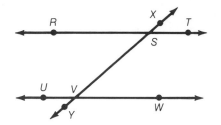

Use a protractor to draw an angle with the measure given.

5. $\angle ABC = 22°$ 6. $\angle PQR = 170°$

Use the figure at the right.

7. Name an obtuse angle.

8. Name all the acute angles.

9. Name two right angles.

10. Name an angle that is complementary to $\angle BOC$.

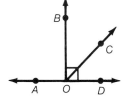

True or False? Write *T* or *F.*

11. A rhombus is a parallelogram.

12. All rectangles are squares.

13. A polygon with eight sides is called a hexagon.

14. A regular triangle has an angle with a measure of 90°.

Doreen and Jake made a diagram of the garden they want to plant in the spring. What is the perimeter or circumference of the section? What is the area?

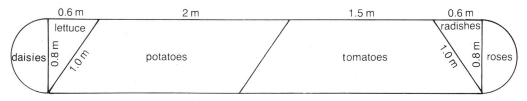

15. not used for flowers

16. daisies

17. potatoes

18. radishes

19. lettuce

20. roses

★ 21. tomatoes

Name the figure using the letters shown. (*pages 100–101*)

1.

2.
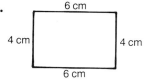

3.
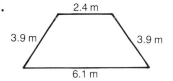

4.

Use the figure at the right. (*pages 102–105*)

5. Use a protractor to measure $\angle MQR$.

6. Name two acute angles.

7. Name an obtuse angle.

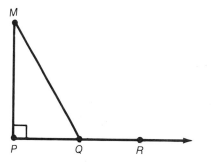

Name the figure. (*pages 106–111*)

8. a polygon with 5 sides

9. a parallelogram with right angles

What is the perimeter? (*pages 112–113*)

10.

11.

12.

What is the circumference? (*pages 114–115*)

13.
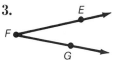

14.

15.

What is the area of the figure? (*pages 116–121*)

16. rectangle:
$b = 25$ cm
$h = 35$ cm

17. square:
$s = 5.9$ m

18. parallelogram:
$b = 12.5$ cm
$h = 6.8$ cm

19. triangle:
$b = 15.4$ m
$h = 7.5$ m

Solve. (*pages 122–123*)

20. A marble top is being cut for a circular table. If the radius is
1.5 m, what is the area of the marble top?

Clock Arithmetic

You probably are very familiar with a 12-hour clock. Did you know that often you do a special kind of arithmetic when you use it?

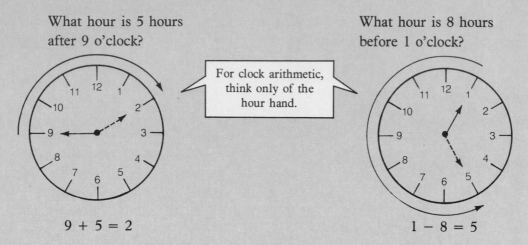

What hour is 5 hours
after 9 o'clock?

For clock arithmetic,
think only of the
hour hand.

What hour is 8 hours
before 1 o'clock?

$9 + 5 = 2$

The hour is 2 o'clock.

$1 - 8 = 5$

The hour is 5 o'clock.

To add, think of the hour hand moving in a *clockwise* direction. To subtract, think of the hour hand moving in a *counterclockwise* direction.

Add or subtract. Use the 12-hour clock.

1. 5 + 4	**2.** 5 + 6	**3.** 5 + 8	**4.** 5 + 12
5. 7 + 5	**6.** 7 + 9	**7.** 10 + 3	**8.** 10 + 10
9. 6 + 10	**10.** 8 + 7	**11.** 1 + 9	**12.** 4 + 12
13. 8 − 2	**14.** 8 − 5	**15.** 8 − 9	**16.** 8 − 12
17. 5 − 5	**18.** 5 − 9	**19.** 2 − 7	**20.** 2 − 10
21. 10 − 11	**22.** 9 − 4	**23.** 4 − 9	**24.** 3 − 12

Use the 12-hour clock. True or false?
Write *T* or *F*.

25. 4 + 8 = 8 + 4   **26.** 3 − 12 = 3   **27.** 2 − 7 = 2 + 3

It is possible to have clocks with different numbers of hours. Clock arithmetic is always done the same way.

8-Hour Clock

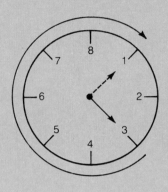

$3 + 6 = 1$

5-Hour Clock

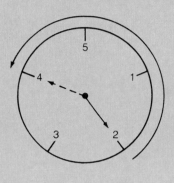

$2 - 3 = 4$

Add or subtract. Use the 8-hour clock.

28. $4 + 5$ **29.** $6 + 7$ **30.** $2 - 3$ **31.** $1 - 6$

32. $3 + 8$ **33.** $5 - 8$ **34.** $2 + 4$ **35.** $4 - 1$

Add or subtract. Use the 5-hour clock.

36. $3 + 4$ **37.** $4 + 2$ **38.** $2 - 4$ **39.** $1 - 3$

40. $2 + 5$ **41.** $2 - 5$ **42.** $2 + 2$ **43.** $5 - 1$

Use the 6-hour clock at the right.
True or False? Write *T* or *F*.

44. Clock addition is commutative.

45. Clock subtraction is commutative.

46. Clock addition is associative.

47. Clock subtraction is associative.

48. The sum of any number and 6 is the number itself.

49. Any number minus 6 is the number itself.

Write the letter for the correct answer.

Compare the numbers. Select the correct sign.

1. 1.08 ▨ 1.107
 a. <
 b. >
 c. =
 d. None of these

2. 34.6 ▨ 33.9
 a. <
 b. >
 c. =
 d. None of these

3. 3.114 ▨ 3.124
 a. <
 b. >
 c. =
 d. None of these

4. 6.666 ▨ 6.6666
 a. <
 b. >
 c. =
 d. None of these

5. 0.2080 ▨ 0.208
 a. <
 b. >
 c. =
 d. None of these

6. 3.1416 ▨ 3.14159
 a. <
 b. >
 c. =
 d. None of these

Select the equal measure.

7. 6400 cm
 a. 6.4 m
 b. 64 m
 c. 640 m
 d. None of these

8. 241 m
 a. 24.1 km
 b. 2.41 km
 c. 0.241 km
 d. None of these

9. 3.6 L
 a. 360 mL
 b. 3600 mL
 c. 36,000 mL
 d. None of these

10. 0.3 kg
 a. 30 g
 b. 300 g
 c. 3000 g
 d. None of these

11. 27 mg
 a. 0.027 g
 b. 0.27 g
 c. 2.7 g
 d. None of these

12. 75 mm
 a. 0.075 cm
 b. 0.75 cm
 c. 7.5 cm
 d. None of these

13. 450 g
 a. 0.45 kg
 b. 4.5 kg
 c. 45 kg
 d. None of these

14. 825 mL
 a. 82.5 L
 b. 8.25 L
 c. 0.825 L
 d. None of these

Identify the property.

15. $20 \times (5 \times 89) = (20 \times 5) \times 89$
 a. Commutative Property
 b. Associative Property
 c. Distributive Property
 d. None of these

16. $72{,}046 \times 1 = 72{,}046$
 a. Zero Property
 b. Associative Property
 c. Identity Property
 d. None of these

Choose the correct answer.

17. 62.701 rounded to the nearest whole number is
  a. 62
  b. 63
  c. 60
  d. None of these

18. 3.555 rounded to the nearest tenth is
  a. 3.56
  b. 3.5
  c. 3.6
  d. None of these

19. 1.0047 rounded to the nearest hundredth is
  a. 1.00
  b. 1.01
  c. 1.005
  d. None of these

20. 0.985168 rounded to the nearest thousandth is
  a. 0.99
  b. 0.986
  c. 0.985
  d. 0.984

21. 0.475 rounded to the nearest whole number is
  a. 0.0
  b. 1.0
  c. 0.5
  d. 0.4

22. 0.9902 rounded to the nearest tenth is
  a. 1.0
  b. 0.9
  c. 0.99
  d. 1.09

Estimate to determine the correct product or quotient.

23. 7×38
  a. 266
  b. 146
  c. 116
  d. 276

24. 47×89
  a. 1293
  b. 2633
  c. 4183
  d. 3183

25. 72×8163
  a. 58,736
  b. 587,736
  c. 5,877,366
  d. 58,773,666

26. 0.65×0.74
  a. 0.00481
  b. 0.0481
  c. 0.481
  d. 4.81

27. $506 \div 15$
  a. 19 R11
  b. 20 R11
  c. 33 R11

28. $66,854 \div 158$
  a. 4233 R20
  b. 423 R20
  c. 42 R3

29. $1.8424 \div 0.7$
  a. 0.2632
  b. 2.632
  c. 26.32

30. $0.008 \div 0.02$
  a. 4
  b. 0.4
  c. 0.04

Select the most appropriate unit for the measurement.

31. The distance between Chicago and Boston
  a. kilometer
  b. kilogram
  c. meter
  d. None of these

32. The weight of a box of cereal
  a. milligrams
  b. grams
  c. liters
  d. None of these

Radio and Television

Use the four-step plan to solve these problems about the beginnings of radio and television. Use the chart to answer.

How long was it between these radio and television events? Use the chart.

1. the sending of the first radio signal and the development of the transistor radio

2. the first regular television broadcasting and color television broadcasting

3. the first radio broadcast and the first useful television system

4. the first useful television system and color broadcasting

Year	Radio and Television "Firsts"
1895	Radio communication signal sent through the air
1910	Experimental radio broadcast
1929	Useful television system developed
1936	Regular television broadcasting
1947	Transistor radios developed
1953	Color television broadcasting

Suppose you are a salesperson who sells commercial air time to advertisers. What you charge your customers depends on whether you're at a radio or television station and when the commercial will be on the air. Costs are highest during prime time when most people listen or watch.

Use the chart to answer.

5. When is prime time for television? for radio?

6. A local car dealer wants to air a 30-second radio commercial at 7:00 and 9:00 in the morning and in the evening. What is the charge for this for one day?

7. On each day of its 3-day sale, an appliance store wants to air four 30-second TV commercials between 6:00 P.M. and 7:00 P.M. How much will the store pay altogether?

COSTS OF 30 SECONDS OF COMMERCIAL AIR TIME		
Time Period	**Radio**	**Television**
7:00 A.M.– 9:00 A.M.	$320	$400
9:00 A.M.–10:30 A.M.	$320	$200
10:30 A.M.–11:30 A.M.	$160	$375
12:30 P.M.– 4:00 P.M.	$160	$1300
6:00 P.M.– 7:00 P.M.	$144	$2200
8:00 P.M.–11:00 P.M.	$56	$4000
11:00 P.M.–11:30 P.M.	$56	$3600

8. Just before soap operas begin on television at 12:30 P.M., a 30-second commercial costs $600. By how much does the cost go up during the 12:30–4:00 time period?

9. What is the difference in cost between a radio commercial and a television commercial during prime time? during the slowest time?

Solve.

10. Bob Land, a radio news editor, must have all copy ready for the 6:00 p.m. news. A special news item comes in at 4:27 P.M. that will take fully 1 hour and 30 minutes to edit. Will he finish in time for the program?

11. The yearly salary of a television meteorologist is about $26,520. How much is this per month? per week?

Applying Your Skills

Department Store Sale

A buyer in a department store sometimes goes on a trip to purchase special items for a sale. After returning, the buyer fills out an expense report something like this.

City and Reason for Trip	Line Number	Date	Transportation	Hotel	Meals	Total
				A	B	C	
London	1	2/8	Whisper Airlines $599.00			?
To buy special			Round trip to			
items for the			London night flights			
October Sale	2	2/9	Bus to hotel $15.00			?
	3	2/9	Taxi and bus fares $23.75	$62.00	$31.50	?
	4	2/10	Taxi and bus fares $14.35	$62.00	$35.45	?
	5	2/11	Taxi and bus fares $21.30	$62.00	$37.35	?
	6	2/11	Bus to airport $15.00			?
	7	2/12	Airport limo.			
			to downtown Chicago $16.00			?
TOTAL EXPENSE			?	?	?	?

Complete the expense report step by step. First total each line across.

1. Line 1   2. Line 2   3. Line 3   4. Line 4

5. Line 5   6. Line 6   7. Line 7   8. Sum of Lines 1–7

What is the total for each column?

9. Column A   10. Column B   11. Column C   12. Sum of Col. A, B, and C

13. Are your answers to Questions 8 and 12 the same? If they are, the expense report balances. If the answers are not the same, check your work for mistakes.

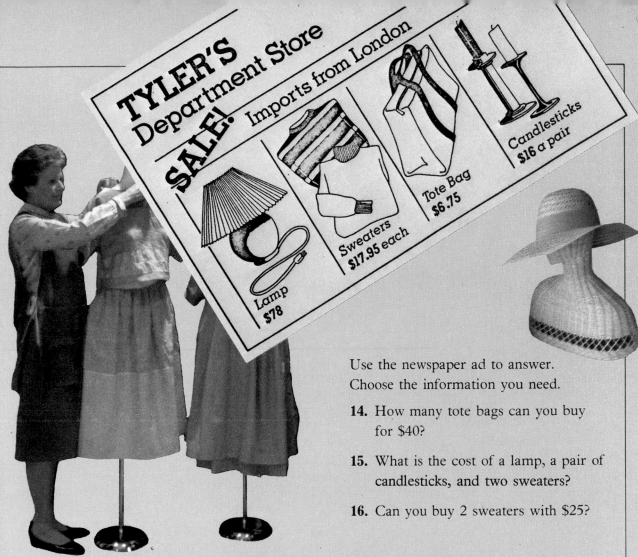

TYLER'S Department Store

SALE! Imports from London

Lamp $78

Sweaters $17.95 each

Tote Bag $6.75

Candlesticks $16 a pair

Use the newspaper ad to answer. Choose the information you need.

14. How many tote bags can you buy for $40?

15. What is the cost of a lamp, a pair of candlesticks, and two sweaters?

16. Can you buy 2 sweaters with $25?

Solve.

17. An advertising executive bought a full-page ad in the city newspaper on Monday through Saturday, for a total of $60,000. The same ad was put in the Sunday paper for $12,000. How much did all the ads cost?

18. The average income of a full-time salesperson is about $8580. About how much is this per week?

19. A newspaper ad costs $250 for 6 days. At this rate how much would the ad cost for 9 days?

20. A store buys shirts in boxes of 80 and saves $200 per box. How much is the saving per shirt?

Fixing Up Homes

These are some formulas that people in the building trades who fix up homes sometimes use:

$$P = (2 \times b) + (2 \times h) \qquad A = b \times h$$
$$P = 4 \times s \qquad\qquad\quad A = b \times h \div 2$$
$$C = \pi \times D \qquad\qquad\quad A = \pi \times r^2$$

Solve these problems that floor layers might have. Use the formulas listed above whenever possible.

Use the diagram for exercises 1–3.

12 ft.

9 ft.

1. A customer wants the whole floor area tiled. What is the area to be tiled?

2. How many square-foot tiles will cover the floor?

3. In addition to the tiles, the customer wants molding around the edge of the floor. How much molding should be ordered?

4. A different customer wants square-foot tiles that cost $1.85 per tile. How much will it cost the customer for enough tiles to cover a floor that is 216 square feet?

Use the diagram at the right for Exercises 5 and 6. Round all answers to the nearest hundredth.

5. A rug cutter cut a round rug from a square piece of carpeting. What is the area of the round rug?

6. How many feet of binding will be needed to edge the rug?

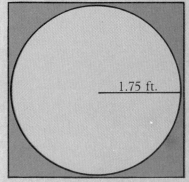

1.75 ft.

3.50 ft.

People in the painting business use a lot of math. Solve these painting problems.

7. For a room 9 ft by 18 ft, a painter charged $16.79 for a gallon of wall paint and $4.45 for 2 qt of trim paint. The labor charge was $75. How much was the total bill?

8. A painting contractor agreed to paint the walls of this square basement room including one door but no windows. What is the total surface area to be painted?

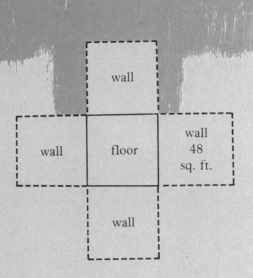

Solve.

9. The complete pattern in a particular roll of vinyl floor covering repeats every three feet. A cutter removes an 18-foot piece with complete patterns from the roll. How many times does the pattern repeat in that piece?

10. You can probably save about $172 in labor costs for 16 hours of work if you wallpaper your own 12 ft by 14 ft bedroom. About how much would you save per hour by doing it yourself?

11. Wallboard comes in sheets that are 32 feet square. How many sheets does a carpenter need to cover a room with 384 square feet of wall space?

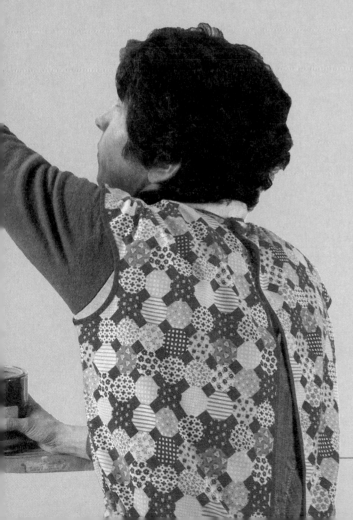

Enrichment

An Energy-Cost Formula

A **watt** is a unit of power needed to make something run. A **kilowatt**
equals 1000 watts. The rate charged for electricity is in cents per
kilowatt-hour.

$$\frac{\text{watts} \times \text{hours used}}{1000} = \text{kilowatt-hours}$$

To find the cost (C) of using an appliance, you need to know how
many watts it takes to run it (W), how many hours you use it (h), and
your electric rate.

Then you can use this formula to find the cost. $\quad C = \dfrac{W \times h \times r}{1000}$

Use the energy formula to solve. Assume that the electric rate is $.107
per kilowatt-hour. Round costs in answers to the nearest cent.

1. Suppose you have a 600-watt hair dryer that you use 50 hours per
   year. How much does it cost you to use it per year?

2. Alex Connors studied for 3 hours one evening. It began to get dark
   an hour after he started so he turned on a desk lamp with a
   100-watt bulb. How much did it cost to use the lamp while
   studying?

3. It takes one hour to bake chicken in a 3200-watt electric range
   oven. It takes only 30 minutes to bake the same chicken in a
   1500-watt microwave oven. What's the difference in cost between
   the two ways to bake chicken?

4. Tom Lopez has a 500-watt washer that takes $\frac{1}{2}$ hour per load. He
   has a 5000-watt dryer that takes $1\frac{1}{2}$ hours per load. How
   much does it cost Tom to wash and dry one load?

Steel is made from iron. If carbon makes up $\frac{1}{25}$ of the iron and $\frac{17}{1000}$ of the finished steel, is carbon added or subtracted during the steel-making process?

Number Theory and Developing Fractions

Multiples and Least Common Multiples

The Flower Cart sells roses in bunches of 4 and daisies in bunches of 6.

What is the least number of each that you can buy in order to have an equal number of roses and daisies?

When we multiply a number by 1, 2, 3, 4, and so on, we get **multiples** of that number.

Roses are sold in multiples of 4.
4, 8, 12, 16, 20, 24, 28, 32, 36, . . .

Daisies are sold in multiples of 6.
6, 12, 18, 24, 30, 36, . . .

> The three dots mean *and so on*.

Two numbers may have some multiples that are the same. We call these **common multiples** of the numbers.

Common multiples of 4 and 6: 12, 24, 36, . . .

The least of the common multiples of two numbers is called their **least common multiple (LCM).**

LCM of 4 and 6: 12   You can buy 12 of each kind of flower.

Exercises

List the next three multiples.

1. 3, 6, 9, ▨, ▨, ▨

2. 8, 16, 24, ▨, ▨, ▨

3. 20, 40, 60, ▨, ▨, ▨

4. 30, 60, 90, ▨, ▨, ▨

5. 12, 24, 36, ▨, ▨, ▨

6. 15, 30, 45, ▨, ▨, ▨

7. 14, 28, 42, ▨, ▨, ▨

8. 19, 38, 57, ▨, ▨, ▨

9. 100, 200, 300, ▨, ▨, ▨

10. 125, 250, 375, ▨, ▨, ▨

List the first five multiples of each number.

11. 2   **12.** 5   **13.** 7   **14.** 9   **15.** 10   **16.** 1

17. 11   **18.** 13   **19.** 16   **20.** 17   **21.** 40   **22.** 50

23. 25   **24.** 35   **25.** 200   **26.** 300   **27.** 150   **28.** 250

Write the LCM of the numbers.

29. 2 and 5   **30.** 4 and 5   **31.** 5 and 7   **32.** 2 and 7

33. 3 and 6   **34.** 3 and 9   **35.** 4 and 12   **36.** 5 and 10

37. 6 and 8   **38.** 6 and 9   **39.** 8 and 12   **40.** 10 and 25

41. 4 and 7   **42.** 6 and 18   **43.** 7 and 9   **44.** 12 and 18

What is the LCM of the three numbers?

45. 3, 6, and 9   **46.** 2, 4, and 8   **47.** 2, 3, and 5   **48.** 2, 5, and 7

49. 2, 4, and 5   **50.** 3, 5, and 6   **51.** 4, 6, and 9   **52.** 6, 8, and 12

53. 5, 6, and 10   **54.** 5, 8, and 20   **55.** 3, 10, and 15   **56.** 6, 7, and 12

Green Thumb

Solve.

57. Petunias are sold in flats of 6 plants. Pansies are sold in flats of 8 plants. You want to buy an equal number of petunias and pansies. What is the least number of each that you should buy?

58. A coleus plant needs water every 4 days. A jade plant needs water every 6 days. How often will they need water on the same day if you first water them on the same day?

59. During winter, a flowering cactus needs plant food every 12 days. A geranium needs it every 15 days. How often will they need food on the same day if you first feed them on the same day?

Divisibility

Can 75 stamps be shared equally by 2 friends? 3 friends? 5 friends? 9 friends? 10 friends? To find out, divide 75 by each of these numbers.

The remainder is zero when the divisor is 3 or 5. We say that 75 is **divisible** by 3 and 5.

The stamps may be shared by 3 or 5 friends.

To see if a number is divisible by 2, 5, or 10, test by checking the ones' digit.

Divisibility Test		Examples	
		75	60
By 2:	Is the ones' digit 0, 2, 4, 6, or 8?	no	yes
By 5:	Is the ones' digit 0 or 5?	yes	yes
By 10:	Is the ones' digit 0?	no	yes

Numbers that are divisible by 2 are called **even numbers.**
Numbers that are not divisible by 2 are called **odd numbers.**

60 is even.   75 is odd.

To see if a number is divisible by 3 or 9, test by adding the digits.

Divisibility Test		Examples	
		75	126
By 3:	Is the sum of the digits divisible by 3?	yes	yes
By 9:	Is the sum of the digits divisible by 9?	no	yes

$$7 + 5 = 12 \qquad 1 + 2 + 6 = 9$$

Exercises

Is the number even or odd? Write *Even* or *Odd*.

1. 27	**2.** 74	**3.** 73	**4.** 821	**5.** 730
6. 888	**7.** 415	**8.** 793	**9.** 5683	**10.** 1348

Is the first number divisible by the second? Write *Yes* or *No*.

11. 457 by 2

12. 376 by 2

13. 6582 by 2

14. 5000 by 2

15. 685 by 5

16. 500 by 5

17. 4552 by 5

18. 1790 by 5

19. 218 by 10

20. 605 by 10

21. 1090 by 10

22. 2005 by 10

23. 963 by 3

24. 705 by 3

25. 6103 by 3

26. 4122 by 3

27. 603 by 9

28. 312 by 9

29. 4650 by 9

30. 1071 by 9

True or False? Write *T* or *F*.

31. Some even numbers are divisible by 5.

32. Some numbers are not divisible by 1.

33. If a number is divisible by 10, it is also divisible by 2.

34. If a number is divisible by 6, it is divisible by 2 and 3.

A Timely Test

A year whose number is divisible by 4 is a **leap year.**

A number is divisible by 4 if the number formed by its last two digits is divisible by 4.

Number	Last two digits	Divisible by 4?
1988 ⟶	88 ⟶	Yes
2002 ⟶	02 ⟶	No

The only exception is that a century year is a leap year only when its number is divisible by 400.

Is the year a leap year? Write *Yes* or *No*.

35. 1812

36. 1776

37. 1882

38. 1986

39. 1992

40. 2001

41. 1900

42. 2000

43. 2100

If you live to be eighty years old, how many leap years will you see?

Take a Break

141

Factors and Greatest Common Factors

The number 12 is divisible by 1, 2, 3, 4, 6, and 12.

$$12 \div 1 = 12 \qquad 12 \div 4 = 3$$
$$12 \div 2 = 6 \qquad 12 \div 6 = 2$$
$$12 \div 3 = 4 \qquad 12 \div 12 = 1$$

The number 18 is divisible by 1, 2, 3, 6, 9, and 18.

$$18 \div 1 = 18 \qquad 18 \div 6 = 3$$
$$18 \div 2 = 9 \qquad 18 \div 9 = 2$$
$$18 \div 3 = 6 \qquad 18 \div 18 = 1$$

When one number is divisible by a second, the second number is called a **factor** of the first.

Factors of 12: 1, 2, 3, 4, 6, 12   Factors of 18: 1, 2, 3, 6, 9, 18

Two numbers may have some factors that are the same. We call these the **common factors** of the numbers.

Common factors of 12 and 18: 1, 2, 3, 6

The greatest of the common factors of two numbers is called their **greatest common factor (GCF).**

GCF of 12 and 18: 6

Exercises

Is the first number a factor of the second? Write *Yes* or *No*.

1. 2; 8   **2.** 4; 15   **3.** 8; 24   **4.** 9; 36

5. 7; 54   **6.** 3; 25   **7.** 16; 64   **8.** 25; 100

9. 9; 108   **10.** 10; 75   **11.** 12; 108   **12.** 100; 200

Complete.

13. factors of 4: 1, 2, ▨
factors of 8: 1, 2, 4, ▨
common factors of 4 and 8:
▨, ▨, ▨
GCF of 4 and 8: ▨

14. factors of 16: 1, 2, 4, ▨, ▨
factors of 20: 1, 2, 4, ▨, ▨, ▨
common factors of 16 and 20:
▨, ▨, ▨
GCF of 16 and 20: ▨

Write the GCF of the numbers.

15. 5 and 15   **16.** 9 and 36   **17.** 12 and 24   **18.** 10 and 25

19. 4 and 6   **20.** 9 and 12   **21.** 18 and 21   **22.** 10 and 35

23. 7 and 15   **24.** 14 and 21   **25.** 12 and 44   **26.** 16 and 18

27. 15 and 18   **28.** 14 and 28   **29.** 15 and 40   **30.** 21 and 24

31. 13 and 21   **32.** 24 and 42   **33.** 16 and 24   **34.** 28 and 32

35. 24 and 28   **36.** 25 and 30   **37.** 28 and 36   **38.** 48 and 56

Team Spirit

39. There are 36 players in the Westlake League. They have to separate into teams of equal size for a practice session. How many players can be on each team? (There is more than one answer.)

40. A group of 72 players from Roundball Camp and a group of 56 players from Central League meet to play basketball. Each group must separate into teams of equal size. All teams must have the same number of players. What is the greatest number of players that can be on each team?

41. There are 12 teachers and 42 students playing in the Student-Faculty Meet. What is the greatest number of players per team if teachers' relay teams and students' relay teams must have the same number of players?

42. You have a set of 36 chairs and a set of 42 chairs to arrange for the rally. What is the greatest number of chairs you can place in each row if you want to arrange them in rows of the same number?

Calculator Corner

The number 496 has nine factors besides 496. The sum of these nine factors is 496. What are the nine factors?

Prime Factors

Prime numbers are numbers that have exactly 2 factors.

Composite numbers are numbers that have more than two factors.

The number 7 is prime. Its factors are 7 and 1.

The number 6 is a composite number. Its factors are 1, 2, 3, and 6.

The numbers 0 and 1 are neither prime nor composite.

Every composite number can be written as a product of prime factors.

Drawing a factor tree may help you find the prime factors of a number. Factor the numbers until the end of each branch is a prime number.

We call $2 \times 3 \times 3 \times 5$ the **prime factorization** of 90.

The order of the factors may vary.

Exercises

Write the factors.

1. 9	**2.** 8	**3.** 5	**4.** 3
5. 10	**6.** 15	**7.** 16	**8.** 27
9. 28	**10.** 63	**11.** 38	**12.** 51

Is the number prime or composite? Write *Prime* or *Composite.*

13. 11	**14.** 17	**15.** 14	**16.** 22
17. 17	**18.** 35	**19.** 42	**20.** 43
21. 18	**22.** 31	**23.** 27	**24.** 37

Complete the factor tree. Write the prime factorization.

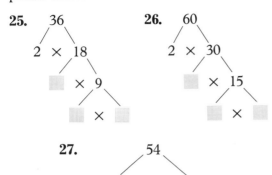

25. 36
2 × 18
▢ × 9
▢ × ▢

26. 60
2 × 30
▢ × 15
▢ × ▢

27. 54
6 × 9
▢ × ▢ × ▢ × ▢

Write the prime factorization.

28. 16	**29.** 72	**30.** 80
31. 55	**32.** 48	**33.** 44
34. 70	**35.** 54	**36.** 78
37. 95	**38.** 150	**39.** 200

Twin Primes

Twin primes are pairs of prime numbers that differ by 2, such as 11 and 13.

40. Name the twin prime of 7.

41. Name the twin prime of 19.

42. Name the pairs of twin primes between 20 and 50.

★ **43.** Three prime numbers that differ by 2 form a **prime triplet.** Name a prime triplet less than 50.

Write the LCM of the numbers.
(*pages 138–139*)

1. 6 and 9   **2.** 3 and 7

3. 5 and 15   **4.** 10 and 15

5. 4 and 9   **6.** 8 and 10

Is the first number divisible by the second? Write *Yes* or *No*.
(*pages 140–141*)

7. 694 by 2   **8.** 350 by 3

9. 1766 by 9   **10.** 1355 by 10

11. 3785 by 5   **12.** 6411 by 3

Write the GCF of the numbers.
(*pages 142–143*)

13. 7 and 28   **14.** 9 and 12

15. 15 and 25   **16.** 8 and 24

17. 16 and 36   **18.** 36 and 56

Write the prime factorization.
(*pages 144–145*)

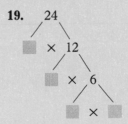

19. 24
▢ × 12
▢ × 6
▢ × ▢

20. 27   **21.** 20

22. 45   **23.** 64

24. 100   **25.** 125

Fractions

Each wheel of cheese is cut into 8 equal pieces at The Cheese Shop.

Each piece is one eighth of a whole wheel.

 $\dfrac{1}{8}$ ←— piece of a wheel
←— total number of pieces

Last week 4 wheels of cheddar cheese were in the shop, but only 3 were sold.

That is, three fourths of the wheels were sold.

$\dfrac{3}{4}$ ←— number of wheels sold
←— total number of wheels

The three wheels were shared equally by 8 people.
The amount for each person is $3 \div 8$, or $\frac{3}{8}$.
Each person has three eighths of a wheel.

$\dfrac{3}{8}$ ←— number of wheels
←— number of people sharing the wheels

The numbers $\frac{1}{8}$, $\frac{3}{4}$, and $\frac{3}{8}$ are called **fractions.**

In a fraction, we call the top number the **numerator** and the bottom number the **denominator.**

$\dfrac{1}{8}$ ←— numerator
←— denominator

Exercises

Complete.

1.

___ ←— number of pieces shaded
___ ←— total number of pieces

2.

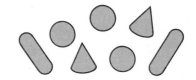

___ ←— number of ◯ cheeses
___ ←— total number of cheeses

146

What fraction of all the cheeses in the gift package have the shape shown?

3. 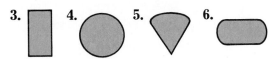 4. 5. 6.

Use the information from the inventory form. Write the fraction of the total for each type of cheese in the shop.

7. Blue

8. Cheddar

9. Edam

10. Gouda

11. Munster

12. Parmesan

13. Romano

14. Swiss

15. Romano and Parmesan

16. Edam and Gouda

INVENTORY	Date: 12-5
Cheese	No. of Wheels
Swiss	3
Edam	8
Cheddar	11
Romano	9
Parmesan	7
Munster	2
Blue	1
Gouda	6
TOTAL	47

A Fraction of Time

The Cheese Shop is open 8 hours a day for 6 days of the week. Marcia works at the shop 4 hours each day that the shop is open. Use this information to answer these questions.

17. What fraction of the hours in a day is the shop open?

18. What fraction of the hours in a week is the shop open?

19. What fraction of the hours in a week does Marcia work?

20. What fraction of the days in a week is the shop open?

21. What fraction of the hours in a day does Marcia work?

22. What fraction of the hours that the shop is open does Marcia work?

Show how you can cut this cheese into eighths with exactly three cuts.

Take a Break

147

Equivalent Fractions

The costume committee needs to replace missing buttons on old costumes. New buttons must be the same size as others on the costume.

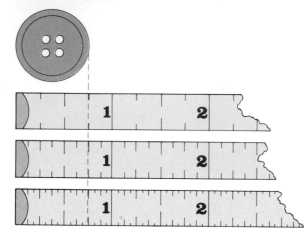

Bob measured the diameter of this button as $\frac{3}{4}$ inch.

Paula measured it as $\frac{6}{8}$ inch.

Carlos measured it as $\frac{12}{16}$ inch.

The fractions $\frac{3}{4}$, $\frac{6}{8}$, and $\frac{12}{16}$ name the same number. We call them **equivalent fractions.**

To write equivalent fractions, we multiply or divide both the numerator and the denominator by the same number.

$$\frac{3}{4} = \frac{3 \times 2}{4 \times 2} = \frac{6}{8} \qquad \frac{12}{16} = \frac{12 \div 4}{16 \div 4} = \frac{3}{4}$$

Exercises

Complete.

1. $\frac{3}{4} = \frac{3 \times 3}{4 \times 3} = \frac{\blacksquare}{\blacksquare}$

2. $\frac{7}{9} = \frac{7 \times 2}{9 \times 2} = \frac{\blacksquare}{\blacksquare}$

3. $\frac{1}{12} = \frac{1 \times 3}{12 \times 3} = \frac{\blacksquare}{\blacksquare}$

4. $\frac{4}{6} = \frac{4 \div 2}{6 \div 2} = \frac{\blacksquare}{\blacksquare}$

5. $\frac{3}{9} = \frac{3 \div 3}{9 \div 3} = \frac{\blacksquare}{\blacksquare}$

6. $\frac{10}{15} = \frac{10 \div 5}{15 \div 5} = \frac{\blacksquare}{\blacksquare}$

7. $\frac{3}{8} = \frac{3 \times 5}{8 \times \blacksquare} = \frac{15}{40}$

8. $\frac{3}{4} = \frac{3 \times \blacksquare}{4 \times 6} = \frac{18}{24}$

9. $\frac{1}{9} = \frac{1 \times \blacksquare}{9 \times \blacksquare} = \frac{4}{36}$

10. $\frac{5}{10} = \frac{5 \div 5}{10 \div \blacksquare} = \frac{1}{2}$

11. $\frac{20}{24} = \frac{20 \div \blacksquare}{24 \div 4} = \frac{5}{6}$

12. $\frac{25}{30} = \frac{25 \div \blacksquare}{30 \div \blacksquare} = \frac{5}{6}$

Complete.

13. $\dfrac{2}{9} = \dfrac{8}{\blacksquare}$

14. $\dfrac{3}{7} = \dfrac{15}{\blacksquare}$

15. $\dfrac{6}{7} = \dfrac{\blacksquare}{21}$

16. $\dfrac{2}{5} = \dfrac{\blacksquare}{15}$

17. $\dfrac{6}{9} = \dfrac{2}{\blacksquare}$

18. $\dfrac{25}{35} = \dfrac{5}{\blacksquare}$

19. $\dfrac{8}{72} = \dfrac{\blacksquare}{9}$

20. $\dfrac{35}{42} = \dfrac{\blacksquare}{6}$

21. $\dfrac{1}{2} = \dfrac{\blacksquare}{14}$

22. $\dfrac{12}{15} = \dfrac{4}{\blacksquare}$

23. $\dfrac{7}{12} = \dfrac{14}{\blacksquare}$

24. $\dfrac{28}{36} = \dfrac{\blacksquare}{9}$

25. $\dfrac{21}{45} = \dfrac{\blacksquare}{15}$

26. $\dfrac{1}{5} = \dfrac{9}{\blacksquare}$

27. $\dfrac{13}{15} = \dfrac{\blacksquare}{45}$

28. $\dfrac{18}{27} = \dfrac{2}{\blacksquare}$

Name the two equivalent fractions.

29. $\dfrac{6}{10}, \dfrac{6}{8}, \dfrac{3}{5}, \dfrac{4}{10}$

30. $\dfrac{2}{9}, \dfrac{1}{6}, \dfrac{6}{54}, \dfrac{4}{18}$

31. $\dfrac{3}{12}, \dfrac{1}{12}, \dfrac{1}{3}, \dfrac{1}{4}$

32. $\dfrac{3}{5}, \dfrac{7}{10}, \dfrac{21}{30}, \dfrac{21}{40}$

33. $\dfrac{1}{2}, \dfrac{3}{8}, \dfrac{5}{12}, \dfrac{18}{48}$

34. $\dfrac{5}{20}, \dfrac{5}{10}, \dfrac{1}{5}, \dfrac{1}{4}$

35. $\dfrac{6}{10}, \dfrac{11}{20}, \dfrac{22}{40}, \dfrac{26}{40}$

36. $\dfrac{5}{7}, \dfrac{11}{15}, \dfrac{30}{35}, \dfrac{33}{45}$

37. $\dfrac{7}{8}, \dfrac{14}{17}, \dfrac{28}{32}, \dfrac{36}{40}$

38. $\dfrac{5}{6}, \dfrac{10}{12}, \dfrac{20}{22}, \dfrac{42}{48}$

39. $\dfrac{13}{26}, \dfrac{13}{39}, \dfrac{1}{13}, \dfrac{1}{2}$

40. $\dfrac{13}{14}, \dfrac{16}{28}, \dfrac{6}{7}, \dfrac{26}{28}$

Cross Products

We can use **cross products** to check if two fractions are equivalent.

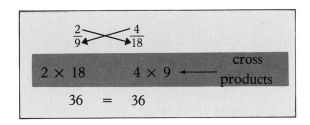

When the cross products are equal, the fractions are equivalent.
Therefore, $\dfrac{2}{9} = \dfrac{4}{18}$.

Check the cross products. Are the fractions equivalent?
Write *Yes* or *No*.

41. $\dfrac{3}{4}, \dfrac{9}{12}$

42. $\dfrac{2}{5}, \dfrac{21}{30}$

43. $\dfrac{1}{6}, \dfrac{2}{18}$

44. $\dfrac{5}{9}, \dfrac{20}{36}$

45. $\dfrac{7}{9}, \dfrac{35}{40}$

46. $\dfrac{8}{15}, \dfrac{24}{45}$

Lowest Terms

On Monday, $\frac{5}{18}$ of the vessels entering the harbor were cruise vessels and $\frac{12}{18}$ were fishing vessels.

We say that a fraction is in **lowest terms** if the GCF of the numerator and denominator is 1.

GCF of 5 and 18: 1 $\longrightarrow$ $\frac{5}{18}$ is in lowest terms.

GCF of 12 and 18: 6 $\longrightarrow$ $\frac{12}{18}$ is not in lowest terms.

A quick way to write $\frac{12}{18}$ in lowest terms is to divide both the numerator and denominator by the GCF.

$$\frac{12}{18} = \frac{12 \div 6}{18 \div 6} = \frac{2}{3}$$

Some people use slashes, like this.

Another way to write $\frac{12}{18}$ in lowest terms is to divide first by 2, then by 3.

$$\frac{12}{18} = \frac{12 \div 2}{18 \div 2} = \frac{6}{9} \longrightarrow \frac{6}{9} = \frac{6 \div 3}{9 \div 3} = \frac{2}{3} \longrightarrow \frac{12}{18} = \frac{2}{3}$$

Exercises

Write the GCF of the numerator and the denominator.

1. $\frac{4}{12}$ **2.** $\frac{6}{24}$ **3.** $\frac{10}{12}$ **4.** $\frac{15}{21}$ **5.** $\frac{12}{60}$ **6.** $\frac{24}{28}$

Is the fraction in lowest terms? Write *Yes* or *No.*

7. $\frac{5}{15}$ **8.** $\frac{2}{21}$ **9.** $\frac{6}{18}$ **10.** $\frac{2}{5}$ **11.** $\frac{2}{10}$ **12.** $\frac{27}{45}$

Complete.

13. $\frac{12}{15} = \frac{4}{\blacksquare}$ **14.** $\frac{8}{24} = \frac{1}{\blacksquare}$ **15.** $\frac{9}{18} = \frac{\blacksquare}{2}$ **16.** $\frac{48}{60} = \frac{4}{\blacksquare}$

Write in lowest terms.

17. $\frac{3}{9}$ 18. $\frac{5}{20}$ 19. $\frac{6}{10}$ 20. $\frac{15}{20}$ 21. $\frac{12}{16}$ 22. $\frac{30}{36}$

23. $\frac{3}{12}$ 24. $\frac{4}{10}$ 25. $\frac{9}{21}$ 26. $\frac{28}{32}$ 27. $\frac{24}{30}$ 28. $\frac{10}{35}$

29. $\frac{49}{56}$ 30. $\frac{28}{48}$ 31. $\frac{45}{81}$ 32. $\frac{22}{88}$ 33. $\frac{12}{26}$ 34. $\frac{18}{48}$

What do you pick up to move and put down to stay?

To learn the answer, first write each fraction in lowest terms. Then replace the fraction with the letter from the code that matches the equivalent fraction in lowest terms.

35. $\frac{14}{42}$ 36. $\frac{18}{36}$ 37. $\frac{24}{36}$ 38. $\frac{24}{42}$ 39. $\frac{24}{32}$ 40. $\frac{18}{45}$

Answer $\underline{}$ $\underline{}$ $\underline{}$ $\underline{}$ $\underline{}$ $\underline{}$
         (35) (36) (37) (38) (39) (40)

Code	A	C	E	H	I	L	M	N	O	P	R	S	T	U	W	Y
	$\frac{1}{3}$	$\frac{2}{3}$	$\frac{3}{5}$	$\frac{4}{7}$	$\frac{5}{6}$	$\frac{1}{7}$	$\frac{5}{7}$	$\frac{1}{2}$	$\frac{3}{4}$	$\frac{4}{5}$	$\frac{2}{5}$	$\frac{6}{7}$	$\frac{1}{4}$	$\frac{3}{7}$	$\frac{1}{5}$	$\frac{2}{7}$

On the Waterfront

These are facts that a reporter learned while doing research for a news story. Write the fraction in lowest terms.

41. The ice in the harbor floats because it is almost $\frac{900}{1000}$ as heavy as water.

42. On one fishing boat, $\frac{570}{690}$ of the day's catch of fish was tuna.

43. On one cruise ship, $\frac{126}{2394}$ of the passengers were visitors from foreign countries.

Comparing Fractions

A carpenter must often measure and compare fractions of an inch.

To compare fractions with like denominators, we compare their numerators.

$$\frac{3}{8} \; ? \; \frac{5}{8} \quad \Rightarrow \quad 3 < 5 \quad \Rightarrow \quad \frac{3}{8} < \frac{5}{8}$$

To compare fractions with unlike denominators, we first rewrite the fractions as equivalent fractions with a common denominator. A **common denominator** is a common multiple of the denominators. The **least common denominator (LCD)** is the LCM of the denominators.

$$\frac{3}{5} \; ? \; \frac{1}{2}$$

LCM of 5 and 2: 10

$$\frac{6}{10} \; ? \; \frac{5}{10} \quad \Rightarrow \quad 6 > 5 \quad \Rightarrow \quad \frac{3}{5} > \frac{1}{2}$$

Exercises

What is the LCM of the denominators?

1. $\frac{1}{6}, \frac{1}{3}$ **2.** $\frac{3}{4}, \frac{7}{8}$ **3.** $\frac{3}{4}, \frac{2}{3}$ **4.** $\frac{1}{2}, \frac{4}{5}$ **5.** $\frac{1}{8}, \frac{1}{6}$

6. $\frac{3}{4}, \frac{9}{10}$ **7.** $\frac{2}{5}, \frac{3}{8}$ **8.** $\frac{1}{2}, \frac{4}{9}$ **9.** $\frac{3}{8}, \frac{5}{12}$ **10.** $\frac{3}{10}, \frac{7}{30}$

Rewrite the fractions. Use the LCD for each pair.

11. $\frac{5}{6}, \frac{11}{12}$ **12.** $\frac{1}{4}, \frac{3}{8}$ **13.** $\frac{1}{3}, \frac{2}{5}$ **14.** $\frac{1}{2}, \frac{4}{7}$ **15.** $\frac{1}{4}, \frac{3}{10}$

16. $\frac{1}{6}, \frac{2}{9}$ **17.** $\frac{1}{10}, \frac{4}{15}$ **18.** $\frac{3}{5}, \frac{4}{9}$ **19.** $\frac{1}{3}, \frac{2}{9}$ **20.** $\frac{3}{8}, \frac{5}{9}$

Complete. Write < or >.

21. $\frac{7}{8}$ ▨ $\frac{5}{8}$ **22.** $\frac{2}{7}$ ▨ $\frac{6}{7}$ **23.** $\frac{5}{24}$ ▨ $\frac{8}{24}$ **24.** $\frac{11}{36}$ ▨ $\frac{6}{36}$

25. $\frac{2}{3}$ ▨ $\frac{5}{9}$ **26.** $\frac{3}{4}$ ▨ $\frac{11}{12}$ **27.** $\frac{13}{18}$ ▨ $\frac{5}{9}$ **28.** $\frac{17}{24}$ ▨ $\frac{3}{4}$

29. $\frac{1}{3}$ ▨ $\frac{5}{6}$ **30.** $\frac{2}{7}$ ▨ $\frac{1}{3}$ **31.** $\frac{2}{3}$ ▨ $\frac{3}{5}$ **32.** $\frac{3}{7}$ ▨ $\frac{1}{5}$

33. $\frac{5}{6}$ ▨ $\frac{7}{9}$ **34.** $\frac{3}{4}$ ▨ $\frac{7}{10}$ **35.** $\frac{3}{10}$ ▨ $\frac{1}{8}$ **36.** $\frac{5}{9}$ ▨ $\frac{7}{12}$

Like Numerators

To compare two fractions with like numerators, we look at the denominators.

$$\frac{1}{4} \quad ? \quad \frac{1}{3} \longrightarrow 4 \quad ? \quad 3$$

4 pieces   3 pieces

$\frac{1}{4}$ $\frac{1}{3}$

When the number of pieces is greater, the size of each piece is smaller. Therefore, $4 > 3$, but $\frac{1}{4} < \frac{1}{3}$.

Complete. Write < or >.

37. $\frac{1}{6}$ ▨ $\frac{1}{7}$ **38.** $\frac{1}{10}$ ▨ $\frac{1}{8}$ **39.** $\frac{1}{15}$ ▨ $\frac{1}{12}$ **40.** $\frac{1}{25}$ ▨ $\frac{1}{100}$

41. $\frac{5}{7}$ ▨ $\frac{5}{9}$ **42.** $\frac{3}{8}$ ▨ $\frac{3}{7}$ **43.** $\frac{9}{10}$ ▨ $\frac{9}{12}$ **44.** $\frac{12}{100}$ ▨ $\frac{12}{25}$

★ **45.** Someone mixed up these boxes of tacks on the shelves at the hardware store. Rearrange the tacks in order from the shortest to the longest.

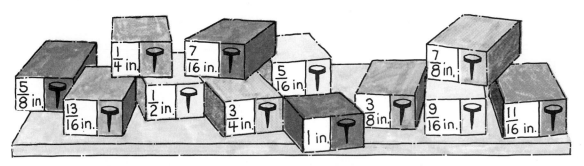

153

Mixed Numbers

A baseball has a diameter of about $2\frac{3}{4}$ inches.

A number such as $2\frac{3}{4}$ is called a **mixed number.** It means $2 + \frac{3}{4}$. A mixed number has two parts: a whole number and a fraction.

The whole number can be written as a fraction.

$$2 = \frac{?}{4} \longrightarrow 2 = 8 \div 4 \longrightarrow 2 = \frac{8}{4}$$

A mixed number can also be written as a fraction.

$$2\frac{3}{4} = 2 + \frac{3}{4} = \frac{8}{4} + \frac{3}{4} = \frac{11}{4} \rightarrow 2\frac{3}{4} = \frac{11}{4}$$

If a fraction is greater than 1, we can write it as a mixed number.

$$\frac{7}{4} = 7 \div 4 = 1 \text{ R3} \longrightarrow \frac{7}{4} = 1\frac{3}{4}$$

Any whole number may be written as a fraction with a denominator of 1.

$$2 = \frac{2}{1} \qquad 13 = \frac{13}{1}$$

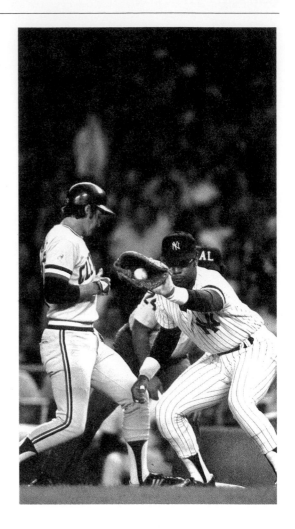

Exercises

Complete.

1. $2 = \dfrac{\blacksquare}{4}$

2. $4 = \dfrac{\blacksquare}{7}$

3. $1 = \dfrac{\blacksquare}{5}$

4. $7 = \dfrac{\blacksquare}{1}$

5. $\dfrac{9}{3} = \blacksquare$

6. $\dfrac{15}{3} = \blacksquare$

7. $\dfrac{10}{10} = \blacksquare$

8. $\dfrac{8}{1} = \blacksquare$

Complete.

9. $1\frac{1}{8} = \frac{\blacksquare}{8}$　　　　**10.** $2\frac{1}{5} = \frac{\blacksquare}{5}$　　　　**11.** $4\frac{3}{7} = \frac{\blacksquare}{7}$　　　　**12.** $3\frac{2}{5} = \frac{\blacksquare}{5}$

13. $\frac{6}{5} = 1\frac{\blacksquare}{5}$　　　　**14.** $\frac{17}{7} = 2\frac{\blacksquare}{7}$　　　　**15.** $\frac{7}{2} = 3\frac{\blacksquare}{2}$　　　　**16.** $\frac{14}{3} = 4\frac{\blacksquare}{3}$

Write as a fraction.

17. $1\frac{7}{9}$　　　**18.** $1\frac{9}{10}$　　　**19.** $2\frac{5}{6}$　　　**20.** $3\frac{4}{7}$　　　**21.** $4\frac{1}{5}$　　　**22.** $5\frac{2}{3}$

23. $6\frac{3}{8}$　　　**24.** $7\frac{1}{9}$　　　**25.** $8\frac{4}{5}$　　　**26.** $9\frac{3}{5}$　　　**27.** $5\frac{3}{4}$　　　**28.** $3\frac{2}{9}$

Write as a whole number or a mixed number.

29. $\frac{8}{5}$　　　**30.** $\frac{10}{7}$　　　**31.** $\frac{18}{9}$　　　**32.** $\frac{12}{3}$　　　**33.** $\frac{26}{7}$　　　**34.** $\frac{15}{2}$

35. $\frac{26}{9}$　　　**36.** $\frac{21}{7}$　　　**37.** $\frac{17}{4}$　　　**38.** $\frac{32}{7}$　　　**39.** $\frac{28}{4}$　　　**40.** $\frac{19}{3}$

Batter Up!

To prepare for a new baseball season, the D Street Dodgers are checking their equipment. All items must meet the new league rules.

Write the letter of the item that does *not* meet the rule given.

41. Baseballs must have a diameter less than $2\frac{3}{4}$ in.

   a. $2\frac{1}{2}$ in.　　　　**b.** $2\frac{5}{8}$ in.　　　　**c.** $2\frac{7}{8}$ in.　　　　**d.** $2\frac{7}{16}$ in.

42. Baseballs must weigh more than $5\frac{1}{8}$ oz.

   a. $5\frac{1}{4}$ oz　　　　**b.** $5\frac{3}{8}$ oz　　　　**c.** $5\frac{1}{16}$ oz　　　　**d.** $5\frac{3}{16}$ oz

43. Bats must be longer than $3\frac{1}{4}$ ft. and shorter than $3\frac{1}{2}$ ft.

   a. $3\frac{3}{8}$ ft　　　　**b.** $3\frac{5}{8}$ ft　　　　**c.** $3\frac{5}{16}$ ft　　　　**d.** $3\frac{7}{16}$ ft

Fractions to Decimals

Here is the way to write a fraction as a decimal.

The fraction $\frac{5}{8}$ means $5 \div 8$.

We can write zeros after the decimal point in the dividend. This division gives a remainder of zero.

$$8 \overline{)5} \quad \Rightarrow \quad \begin{array}{r} 0.625 \\ 8 \overline{)5.000} \\ \underline{-4\,8} \\ 20 \\ \underline{-16} \\ 40 \\ \underline{-40} \\ 0 \end{array}$$

The answer 0.625 is called a **terminating decimal.**

The fraction $\frac{1}{6}$ means $1 \div 6$.

This division never gives a remainder of zero. Instead, the digits in the quotient begin to repeat.

$$6 \overline{)1} \quad \Rightarrow \quad \begin{array}{r} 0.166\ldots = 0.1\overline{6} \\ 6 \overline{)1.000} \\ \underline{-6} \\ 40 \\ \underline{-36} \\ 40 \\ \underline{-36} \\ 4 \end{array}$$

The answer $0.1\overline{6}$ is called a **repeating decimal.** We show a repeating decimal by drawing a bar over the digit or digits that repeat.

When an answer is a repeating decimal, we often round it.

$$0.1\overline{6} = 0.166\ldots \quad \Rightarrow \quad 0.17$$

Exercises

Complete.

1. $\frac{1}{2}$ ⟶ $2\overline{)1.0}$ (0.▇)

2. $\frac{1}{5}$ ⟶ $5\overline{)1.0}$ (0.▇)

3. $\frac{1}{4}$ ⟶ $4\overline{)1.00}$ (0.▇▇)

4. $\frac{3}{20}$ ⟶ $20\overline{)3.00}$ (0.▇▇)

5. $\frac{8}{50}$ ⟶ $50\overline{)8.00}$ (0.▇▇)

6. $\frac{1}{8}$ ⟶ $8\overline{)1.000}$ (0.▇▇▇)

7. $\frac{7}{40}$ ⟶ $40\overline{)7.000}$ (0.▇▇▇)

8. $\frac{7}{16}$ ⟶ $16\overline{)7.0000}$ (0.▇▇▇▇)

9. $\frac{9}{80}$ ⟶ $80\overline{)9.0000}$ (0.▇▇▇▇)

10. $\frac{1}{20}$ ⟶ $20\overline{)1.00}$ (0.▇▇)

11. $\frac{3}{40}$ ⟶ $40\overline{)3.000}$ (0.▇▇▇)

12. $\frac{1}{16}$ ⟶ $16\overline{)1.0000}$ (0.▇▇▇▇)

Write as a decimal. Divide until the remainder is zero.

13. $\frac{2}{5}$　　　**14.** $\frac{3}{5}$　　　**15.** $\frac{3}{4}$　　　**16.** $\frac{7}{20}$　　　**17.** $\frac{3}{8}$　　　**18.** $\frac{7}{8}$

19. $\frac{9}{50}$　　　**20.** $\frac{9}{20}$　　　**21.** $\frac{9}{40}$　　　**22.** $\frac{5}{16}$　　　**23.** $\frac{16}{25}$　　　**24.** $\frac{11}{80}$

25. $\frac{1}{50}$　　　**26.** $\frac{1}{25}$　　　**27.** $\frac{1}{40}$　　　**28.** $\frac{3}{16}$　　　**29.** $\frac{7}{80}$　　　**30.** $\frac{3}{50}$

Write as a decimal. Use a bar to show repeating digits.

31. $\frac{1}{3}$　　　**32.** $\frac{2}{3}$　　　**33.** $\frac{5}{9}$　　　**34.** $\frac{7}{9}$　　　**35.** $\frac{5}{6}$　　　**36.** $\frac{7}{15}$

37. $\frac{5}{11}$　　　**38.** $\frac{9}{11}$　　　**39.** $\frac{7}{12}$　　　**40.** $\frac{13}{30}$　　　**41.** $\frac{7}{22}$　　　**42.** $\frac{5}{33}$

43. $\frac{37}{45}$　　　**44.** $\frac{28}{45}$　　　**45.** $\frac{1}{15}$　　　**46.** $\frac{1}{22}$　　　**47.** $\frac{1}{11}$　　　**48.** $\frac{1}{33}$

Winning Records

Solve.

49. Below are the records for a few teams in the first month of a recent season. Write the fraction as a decimal rounded to the nearest thousandth.

Team	$\frac{\text{Games Won}}{\text{Games Played}}$
Supersonics	$\frac{7}{8}$
Hawks	$\frac{4}{8}$
Knicks	$\frac{4}{9}$
76ers	$\frac{5}{6}$
Pistons	$\frac{2}{9}$

★ **50.** Below are the records for the same teams in the last month of the season. Write the record as a fraction $\left(\frac{\text{games won}}{\text{games played}}\right)$. Then write the fraction as a decimal.

Team	Games Won	Games Lost
Supersonics	3	2
Hawks	4	0
Knicks	0	3
76ers	3	1
Pistons	1	4

Decimals to Fractions

We can write a decimal as a fraction with a denominator of 10, 100, 1000, and so on.

$$0.3 = 3 \text{ tenths} = \frac{3}{10}$$

$$0.47 = 47 \text{ hundredths} = \frac{47}{100}$$

Rewrite the fraction in lowest terms.

$$0.018 = 18 \text{ thousandths} = \frac{18}{1000} = \frac{9}{500}$$

Some relationships between decimals and fractions are used frequently. These should be learned.

Decimal	Fraction	Decimal	Fraction
0.5	$\frac{1}{2}$	0.125	$\frac{1}{8}$
$0.\overline{3}$	$\frac{1}{3}$	$0.\overline{6}$	$\frac{2}{3}$
0.25	$\frac{1}{4}$	0.75	$\frac{3}{4}$

Exercises

Complete.

1. $0.3 = \dfrac{\blacksquare}{10}$ **2.** $0.7 = \dfrac{\blacksquare}{10}$ **3.** $0.9 = \dfrac{9}{\blacksquare}$ **4.** $0.1 = \dfrac{1}{\blacksquare}$

5. $0.19 = \dfrac{\blacksquare}{100}$ **6.** $0.03 = \dfrac{\blacksquare}{100}$ **7.** $0.67 = \dfrac{67}{\blacksquare}$ **8.** $0.09 = \dfrac{9}{\blacksquare}$

9. $0.373 = \dfrac{\blacksquare}{1000}$ **10.** $0.007 = \dfrac{\blacksquare}{1000}$ **11.** $0.951 = \dfrac{951}{\blacksquare}$ **12.** $0.009 = \dfrac{9}{\blacksquare}$

13. $0.07 = \dfrac{7}{\blacksquare}$ **14.** $0.8 = \dfrac{8}{\blacksquare}$ **15.** $0.003 = \dfrac{3}{\blacksquare}$ **16.** $0.017 = \dfrac{17}{\blacksquare}$

17. $8.3 = 8\dfrac{\blacksquare}{10}$ **18.** $4.71 = 4\dfrac{\blacksquare}{100}$ **19.** $1.007 = 1\dfrac{7}{\blacksquare}$ **20.** $4.01 = 4\dfrac{1}{\blacksquare}$

Write as a fraction or a mixed number.

21. 0.7 **22.** 0.23 **23.** 0.623

24. 0.01 **25.** 0.007 **26.** 0.039

27. 5.8 **28.** 3.9 **29.** 1.19

30. 1.03 **31.** 4.179 **32.** 6.003

Write as a fraction in lowest terms.

33. 0.4 **34.** 0.8 **35.** 0.25

36. 0.75 **37.** 0.005 **38.** 0.002

39. 0.04 **40.** 0.6 **41.** 0.015

42. 0.025 **43.** 0.125 **44.** 0.175

Complete.

45. $0.1 = \dfrac{1}{\blacksquare} = \dfrac{1}{10^1}$

46. $0.01 = \dfrac{1}{\blacksquare} = \dfrac{1}{10^{\blacksquare}}$

47. $0.001 = \dfrac{1}{\blacksquare} = \dfrac{1}{10^{\blacksquare}}$

Computer Printout

Solve.

48. The numbers on a computer printout are often decimals.

Write each decimal as a fraction in lowest terms. List the fractions in order from the least to the greatest.

```
O  0.004   0.020
O  0.105   0.036
O  0.750   0.800
O  0.500   0.250
O  0.850
```

What fraction of all the shapes have the shape shown? (*pages 146–147*)

▽△▽△▽○○○○○□□

1. △ **2.** ○ **3.** □

Complete. (*pages 148–149*)

4. $\dfrac{5}{6} = \dfrac{30}{\blacksquare}$ **5.** $\dfrac{9}{12} = \dfrac{3}{\blacksquare}$

Write in lowest terms. (*pages 150–151*)

6. $\dfrac{10}{15}$ **7.** $\dfrac{24}{30}$ **8.** $\dfrac{36}{72}$

Complete. Write < or >. (*pages 152–153*)

9. $\dfrac{7}{10} \ \blacksquare \ \dfrac{3}{10}$ **10.** $\dfrac{4}{9} \ \blacksquare \ \dfrac{11}{18}$

11. $\dfrac{2}{3} \ \blacksquare \ \dfrac{6}{7}$ **12.** $\dfrac{3}{4} \ \blacksquare \ \dfrac{5}{6}$

Write as a whole number or a mixed number. (*pages 154–155*)

13. $\dfrac{11}{7}$ **14.** $\dfrac{18}{6}$ **15.** $\dfrac{21}{9}$

Write as a decimal. (*pages 156–157*)

16. $\dfrac{3}{4}$ **17.** $\dfrac{5}{8}$ **18.** $\dfrac{8}{9}$

Write as a fraction in lowest terms. (*pages 158–159*)

19. 0.8 **20.** 0.33 **21.** 0.125

Extra practice on page 428 **159**

Problem Solving · MULTI-STEP PROBLEMS

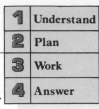

1	Understand
2	Plan
3	Work
4	Answer

The Nagels harvested 50 lb of tomatoes. The plants cost $10.75 and fertilizer cost $3.25. Tomatoes sell for 49¢ per pound. How much did they save per pound?

To answer the question, you need to solve three simpler problems.

What was the Nagels' total cost?

$$\begin{array}{r} \$10.75 \\ + 3.25 \\ \hline \$14.00 \end{array}$$

What was the Nagels' cost per pound?

$$\begin{array}{r} \$\ 0.28 \\ 50\overline{)\$14.00} \end{array}$$

What is the difference between the costs per pound?

$$\begin{array}{r} \$0.49 \\ -0.28 \\ \hline \$0.21 \end{array}$$

The Nagels save 21¢ per pound of tomatoes.

Use the set of facts to answer the questions below.

FACTS: You spent $8 for tomato plants, $2.40 for stakes, and $5.80 for fertilizer and spray. You harvested 45 lb of tomatoes.

   1. What was your total cost?

   2. What was your cost per pound of tomatoes?

FACTS: From the Garden Catalogue you can buy squash seeds in packets of 20 for 30¢, packets of 40 for 55¢, or packets of 60 for 75¢.

   3. What is the total cost of three packets of 20 seeds?

   4. What is the total cost of a packet of 20 seeds and a packet of 40 seeds?

   5. What is the least expensive way to buy exactly 60 seeds?

FACTS: You estimate that rabbits do $120 damage to your garden each year. You decide to put up a fence to keep them out. Your garden is rectangular, 20 m long and 15 m wide. Fencing costs $3.50 per meter and labor will cost $45.

6. What is the cost of the fencing for your garden?

7. What is the total cost of the fencing and the labor?

8. What is the cost per year if you spread out this total cost over a 5-year period?

9. What will be your savings per year over a 5-year period?

Solve.

10. At the Garden Shoppe, you can buy dahlia bulbs in packages of three for $4.98 or five for $8.95. Which is the greater price per bulb? How much greater?

11. Marlene spent $7.50 and Joe spent $6 growing corn in their gardens. Marlene sold 240 ears of corn at 12 for $1.75. Joe sold 180 ears of corn at 6 for $1. Who made the greater profit? How much greater?

★ **12.** Because you are a new customer, you may take $5 off the total cost of this order from the Garden Catalogue. What should be the amount of the check that you send with the order?

Catalog Number	Description	Number Wanted	Cost Per Item	Total Cost
3005H	Garden Hose	1	$5.98	
1296 H	Shovel	1	$8.98	
7448 H	Tomato Fertilizer	3	$4.98	

Credit Card Customers: See instructions on reverse side.				
			TOTAL	
	Add $2.50 shipping and handling			
	Amount to remit			

Write the LCM and the GCF of the numbers.

1. 4 and 6   **2.** 3 and 9   **3.** 5 and 7   **4.** 9 and 12

Is the first number divisible by the second? Write *Yes* or *No*.

5. 384 by 3   **6.** 705 by 10   **7.** 9710 by 2   **8.** 393 by 9

Write the prime factorization.

9. 75   **10.** 81   **11.** 56   **12.** 64

Pearl Li is buying this package of drawing pencils in shades of red, green, blue, and yellow. What fraction of all the pencils are the pencils of each color?

13. red   **14.** green   **15.** blue   **16.** yellow

Use the fractions in the picture below to answer these questions.

17. Which two fractions are equivalent?   **18.** Which fractions are in lowest terms?

19. Which fraction is less than $\frac{1}{2}$?   **20.** Which fraction is less than $\frac{2}{3}$?

 $\frac{16}{24}$ $\frac{11}{16}$ $\frac{12}{25}$ $\frac{10}{15}$

Write the mixed numbers as fractions and the fractions as mixed numbers.

21. $6\frac{1}{9}$ **22.** $10\frac{2}{3}$ **23.** $\frac{10}{9}$ **24.** $\frac{15}{7}$

Write the fractions as decimals and the decimals as fractions in lowest terms.

25. $\frac{3}{8}$ **26.** $\frac{2}{3}$ **27.** 0.27   **28.** 0.125

Solve.

29. The package of drawing pencils cost $5.98. Pearl Li is also buying three drawing pads at $2.59 each. How much change should she receive from a twenty-dollar bill?

Answer the question. (*pages 138–145*)

1. What is the LCM of 6 and 16?   **2.** Is 7136 divisible by 3?

3. What is the GCF of 28 and 32?   **4.** What is the prime factorization of 56?

What fraction of all the shapes have the shape shown? (*pages 146–147*)

5. ☆   **6.** ◯   **7.** ▭   **8.** △

Complete. (*pages 148–149*)

9. $\frac{2}{5} = \frac{4}{\blacksquare}$ **10.** $\frac{4}{7} = \frac{\blacksquare}{21}$ **11.** $\frac{4}{12} = \frac{1}{\blacksquare}$ **12.** $\frac{15}{35} = \frac{\blacksquare}{7}$

Write in lowest terms. (*pages 150–151*)

13. $\frac{6}{9}$ **14.** $\frac{5}{15}$ **15.** $\frac{15}{45}$ **16.** $\frac{54}{63}$

Complete. Write > or <. (*pages 152–153*)

17. $\frac{5}{12}$ ▨ $\frac{11}{12}$ **18.** $\frac{5}{24}$ ▨ $\frac{1}{6}$ **19.** $\frac{5}{6}$ ▨ $\frac{7}{9}$ **20.** $\frac{2}{5}$ ▨ $\frac{2}{3}$

Write as a fraction or as a mixed number. (*pages 154–155*)

21. $7\frac{1}{5}$ **22.** $2\frac{5}{8}$ **23.** $\frac{8}{5}$ **24.** $\frac{33}{7}$

Write as a decimal. Use a bar to show repeating digits. (*pages 156–157*)

25. $\frac{3}{4}$ **26.** $\frac{7}{8}$ **27.** $\frac{1}{3}$ **28.** $\frac{2}{11}$

Write as a fraction in lowest terms. (*pages 158–159*)

29. 0.39   **30.** 0.5   **31.** 0.75   **32.** 0.008

Solve. (*pages 160–161*)

33. It takes 2 hours of labor at $4.65 per hour and $12.80 in materials
to make a puppet. What should you charge to make a $5.00 profit?

Extra practice on page 429

Using Prime Factors to Find the GCF and the LCM

It is often easier to calculate the greatest common factor by using prime factors, especially if the numbers are large.

For example, this is how you would use prime factors to calculate the GCF of 90 and 108.

$$90 = 2 \times 3 \times 3 \times 5$$
$$108 = 2 \times 2 \times 3 \times 3 \times 3$$
$$GCF = 2 \times 3 \times 3 = 18$$

Multiply the common prime factors. Use each factor the least number of times that it appears.

The GCF of 90 and 108 is 18.

If the numbers have no prime factors in common, the GCF is 1.

$$20 = 2 \times 2 \times 5$$
$$27 = 3 \times 3 \times 3$$
$$GCF = 1$$

If the GCF is 1, the numbers are called **relatively prime**. The numbers 20 and 27 are relatively prime.

Write the GCF of the numbers.

1. $2 \times 3 \times 3 \times 5$
   $2 \times 2 \times 3 \times 5 \times 7$

2. $2 \times 5 \times 5 \times 7$
   $3 \times 5 \times 7 \times 7$

3. $2 \times 3 \times 5 \times 5$
   $2 \times 3 \times 3 \times 5 \times 7$

4. $2 \times 2 \times 3 \times 5$
   $2 \times 3 \times 5 \times 5$
   $3 \times 5 \times 5 \times 7$

5. $3 \times 5 \times 5 \times 7$
   $2 \times 3 \times 5 \times 11$
   $2 \times 2 \times 3 \times 5 \times 11$

6. $2 \times 3 \times 3 \times 3 \times 5 \times 7$
   $2 \times 3 \times 5 \times 5 \times 5$
   $2 \times 2 \times 2 \times 5 \times 7$

7. 48 and 168

8. 84 and 112

9. 98 and 147

10. 56, 84, and 140

11. 42, 63, and 105

12. 72, 90, and 162

Are the numbers relatively prime? Write *Yes* or *No*.

13. 14 and 15

14. 27 and 39

15. 56 and 135

16. 15, 21, and 28

17. 28, 49, and 84

18. 43, 65, and 70

You can also use prime factors to calculate the least common multiple. You again may find this method especially helpful if the numbers are large.

Here is an example of using prime factors to find the LCM of 24 and 90.

$$24 = 2 \times 2 \times 2 \times 3$$
$$90 = 2 \times 3 \times 3 \times 5$$
$$\text{LCM} = 2 \times 2 \times 2 \times 3 \times 3 \times 5 = 360$$

> Use each factor the greatest number of times that it appears.

The LCM of 24 and 90 is 360.

Write the LCM of the numbers.

19. $2 \times 3 \times 3$
$2 \times 2 \times 3 \times 7$

20. $2 \times 3 \times 3 \times 5$
$2 \times 2 \times 3 \times 5$

21. $3 \times 3 \times 5 \times 7$
$2 \times 3 \times 5 \times 7$

22. $2 \times 2 \times 2$
$2 \times 2 \times 3$
$2 \times 3 \times 5$

23. $2 \times 2 \times 2 \times 3$
$2 \times 2 \times 3 \times 3$
$2 \times 2 \times 3 \times 5$

24. $2 \times 3 \times 3 \times 5$
$2 \times 2 \times 5 \times 5$
$2 \times 3 \times 5 \times 7$

25. 54 and 84

26. 48 and 80

27. 25 and 36

28. 12, 30, and 27

29. 20, 35, and 45

30. 12, 18, and 33

Complete.

31. $24 \times 54 = $ ▨
GCF of 24 and 54 = ▨
LCM of 24 and 54 = ▨
GCF $\times$ LCM = ▨

32. $18 \times 48 = $ ▨
GCF of 18 and 48 = ▨
LCM of 18 and 48 = ▨
GCF $\times$ LCM = ▨

33. $28 \times 36 = $ ▨
GCF of 28 and 36 = ▨
LCM of 28 and 36 = ▨
GCF $\times$ LCM = ▨

True or False? Write *T* or *F*.

34. The product of any two numbers is equal to the product of the GCF and the LCM of the numbers.

35. The LCM of any two relatively prime numbers is equal to the product of the numbers.

What is the perimeter?

1.
24 in.
30 in.

2.
25.5 in.
18 in.
36 in.

3.
19.5 in.
19.5 in.
19.5 in.
9 in.

Each side is the same length. What is the perimeter?

4.
30 in.
30 in.

5.
36 in.

6.
12.5 in.
12.5 in.

What is the circumference?

7.
4 cm

8.
12 mm

9.
13 m

10.
36 in.

What is the circumference of the circle?

11. $d = 8$ mm

12. $d = 21$ cm

13. $r = 7.3$ m

14. $r = 12.8$ cm

Subtract.

15.
256
− 43

16.
875
−269

17.
733
−198

18.
300
−184

Add or subtract.

19.
63.85
+12.39

20.
71.24
+ 5.09

21.
37.89
2.4
+0.601

22.
4.756
0.08
+0.322

23.
67.59
− 3.2

24.
17.32
− 2.618

25.
6.25
−3.7146

26.
9.038
−9.019

Addition and Subtraction of Fractions

This windmill can generate $\frac{1}{12}$ the electric power needed for a nearby home. What fraction of the power would 2 windmills generate? How many windmills would be needed to generate $\frac{1}{2}$ the home's power?

Adding and Subtracting Fractions

Dan is trimming a strip of leather to make a belt. He first trimmed $\frac{7}{8}$ inch along the edge, but the strip was still too wide. He then trimmed another $\frac{5}{8}$ inch.

Add to find how much he trimmed in all.

$$\begin{array}{r} \frac{7}{8} \\ + \frac{5}{8} \\ \hline \end{array}$$

7 + 5 = 12

$$\frac{12}{8} = 1\frac{4}{8} = 1\frac{1}{2}$$

Dan trimmed $1\frac{1}{2}$ inches in all.

Subtract to find how much more he trimmed the first time.

$$\begin{array}{r} \frac{7}{8} \\ - \frac{5}{8} \\ \hline \end{array}$$

7 − 5 = 2

$$\frac{2}{8} = \frac{1}{4}$$

He trimmed $\frac{1}{4}$ inch more the first time.

To add or subtract fractions with like denominators, write the sum or difference of the numerators over the common denominator. Then write this answer in lowest terms.

Exercises

Complete.

1.
$$\frac{3}{5} \qquad \frac{3}{5}$$
$$\frac{+\frac{1}{5}}{\frac{\blacksquare}{5}} \qquad \frac{-\frac{1}{5}}{\frac{\blacksquare}{5}}$$

2.
$$\frac{5}{7} \qquad \frac{5}{7}$$
$$\frac{+\frac{1}{7}}{\frac{6}{\blacksquare}} \qquad \frac{-\frac{1}{7}}{\frac{4}{\blacksquare}}$$

3.
$$\frac{8}{11} \qquad \frac{8}{11}$$
$$\frac{+\frac{2}{11}}{\frac{\blacksquare}{11}} \qquad \frac{-\frac{2}{11}}{\frac{6}{\blacksquare}}$$

4.
$$\frac{5}{9}$$
$$\frac{+\frac{1}{9}}{\frac{\blacksquare}{9} = \frac{\blacksquare}{3}}$$

5.
$$\frac{1}{12}$$
$$\frac{+\frac{5}{12}}{\frac{\blacksquare}{12} = \frac{\blacksquare}{2}}$$

6.
$$\frac{9}{10}$$
$$\frac{-\frac{1}{10}}{\frac{\blacksquare}{10} = \frac{\blacksquare}{5}}$$

7.
$$\frac{9}{20}$$
$$\frac{-\frac{3}{20}}{\frac{\blacksquare}{20} = \frac{\blacksquare}{10}}$$

8.
$$\frac{6}{7}$$
$$\frac{+\frac{3}{7}}{\frac{\blacksquare}{7} = 1\frac{\blacksquare}{7}}$$

9.
$$\frac{4}{5}$$
$$+\ \frac{4}{5}$$
$$\frac{\blacksquare}{5} = 1\frac{\blacksquare}{5}$$

10.
$$\frac{7}{9}$$
$$+\ \frac{5}{9}$$
$$\frac{\blacksquare}{9} = 1\frac{\blacksquare}{9} = 1\frac{\blacksquare}{3}$$

11.
$$\frac{5}{6}$$
$$+\ \frac{5}{6}$$
$$\frac{\blacksquare}{6} = 1\frac{\blacksquare}{6} = 1\frac{\blacksquare}{3}$$

Add or subtract. Write the answer in lowest terms.

12.
$$\frac{4}{7}$$
$$+\ \frac{2}{7}$$

13.
$$\frac{4}{11}$$
$$+\ \frac{5}{11}$$

14.
$$\frac{8}{9}$$
$$-\ \frac{1}{9}$$

15.
$$\frac{6}{7}$$
$$-\ \frac{2}{7}$$

16.
$$\frac{3}{8}$$
$$+\ \frac{1}{8}$$

17.
$$\frac{3}{10}$$
$$+\ \frac{1}{10}$$

18.
$$\frac{5}{6}$$
$$-\ \frac{1}{6}$$

19.
$$\frac{7}{12}$$
$$-\ \frac{1}{12}$$

20.
$$\frac{5}{16}$$
$$+\ \frac{1}{16}$$

21.
$$\frac{8}{11}$$
$$-\ \frac{3}{11}$$

22.
$$\frac{8}{9}$$
$$+\ \frac{2}{9}$$

23.
$$\frac{13}{15}$$
$$+\ \frac{4}{15}$$

24.
$$\frac{7}{10}$$
$$+\ \frac{9}{10}$$

25.
$$\frac{9}{16}$$
$$+\ \frac{11}{16}$$

26.
$$\frac{7}{12}$$
$$+\ \frac{5}{12}$$

27. $\frac{4}{9} + \frac{2}{9}$

28. $\frac{9}{16} - \frac{5}{16}$

29. $\frac{9}{10} + \frac{3}{10}$

30. $\frac{3}{16} + \frac{1}{16} + \frac{5}{16}$

31. $\frac{7}{20} + \frac{9}{20} + \frac{1}{20}$

32. $\frac{1}{9} + \frac{3}{9} + \frac{5}{9}$

33. $\frac{3}{5} + \frac{3}{5} + \frac{1}{5}$

34. $\frac{7}{9} + \frac{1}{9} + \frac{7}{9}$

35. $\frac{11}{15} + \frac{2}{15} + \frac{8}{15}$

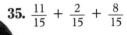

Leather Craft

Solve.

36. The leather is $\frac{3}{16}$ inch thick. Dan shaved $\frac{1}{16}$ inch along the edge. How thick is the shaved edge?

37. Dan made a crease $\frac{7}{8}$ inch from the edge. He made a second crease $\frac{3}{8}$ inch from the first one. How far from the edge is the second crease?

Adding Fractions: Unlike Denominators

A park service rents canoes and also gives canoeing lessons. Of all the visitors to the park, $\frac{2}{9}$ rent canoes and take the lessons, and $\frac{1}{3}$ only rent the canoes.

To find the fraction of visitors who rent the canoes, add $\frac{2}{9}$ and $\frac{1}{3}$.

To add fractions with unlike denominators, rewrite each fraction as an equivalent fraction with the least common denominator.

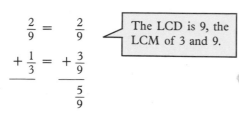

$$\begin{array}{r} \frac{2}{9} = \frac{2}{9} \\ + \frac{1}{3} = + \frac{3}{9} \\ \hline \frac{5}{9} \end{array}$$

The LCD is 9, the LCM of 3 and 9.

Canoes are rented by $\frac{5}{9}$ of the visitors to the park.

Your work will probably be simpler if you use the LCD, but any common multiple of the denominators can be used as a common denominator.

Exercises

Write the LCD for the pair of fractions.

1. $\frac{1}{4}, \frac{1}{2}$ **2.** $\frac{1}{10}, \frac{1}{5}$ **3.** $\frac{1}{21}, \frac{1}{7}$ **4.** $\frac{1}{18}, \frac{1}{6}$ **5.** $\frac{1}{14}, \frac{2}{7}$

6. $\frac{1}{15}, \frac{2}{3}$ **7.** $\frac{3}{10}, \frac{7}{20}$ **8.** $\frac{3}{10}, \frac{3}{5}$ **9.** $\frac{4}{21}, \frac{2}{3}$ **10.** $\frac{3}{35}, \frac{6}{7}$

Complete.

11. $\quad \frac{1}{2} = \frac{\blacksquare}{4}$

$\quad + \frac{1}{4} = + \frac{\blacksquare}{4}$

$\qquad\qquad \frac{\blacksquare}{4}$

12. $\quad \frac{1}{3} = \frac{\blacksquare}{9}$

$\quad + \frac{1}{9} = + \frac{\blacksquare}{9}$

$\qquad\qquad \frac{\blacksquare}{9}$

13. $\quad \frac{2}{15} = \frac{\blacksquare}{15}$

$\quad + \frac{3}{5} = + \frac{\blacksquare}{15}$

$\qquad\qquad \frac{\blacksquare}{15}$

Add. Write the answer in lowest terms.

14. $\dfrac{2}{3}$
$+\dfrac{1}{6}$

15. $\dfrac{1}{4}$
$+\dfrac{3}{8}$

16. $\dfrac{1}{2}$
$+\dfrac{5}{12}$

17. $\dfrac{2}{3}$
$+\dfrac{2}{9}$

18. $\dfrac{5}{16}$
$+\dfrac{3}{8}$

19. $\dfrac{2}{5}$
$+\dfrac{4}{15}$

20. $\dfrac{1}{6}$
$+\dfrac{5}{24}$

21. $\dfrac{5}{18}$
$+\dfrac{1}{6}$

22. $\dfrac{1}{12}$
$+\dfrac{1}{4}$

23. $\dfrac{2}{7}$
$+\dfrac{2}{21}$

24. $\dfrac{5}{16}$
$+\dfrac{3}{8}$

25. $\dfrac{2}{5}$
$+\dfrac{3}{10}$

26. $\dfrac{1}{3}$
$+\dfrac{7}{24}$

27. $\dfrac{3}{4}$
$+\dfrac{1}{8}$

28. $\dfrac{1}{15}$
$+\dfrac{3}{5}$

29. $\dfrac{3}{10} + \dfrac{1}{5} + \dfrac{2}{5}$

30. $\dfrac{1}{9} + \dfrac{4}{9} + \dfrac{1}{3}$

31. $\dfrac{1}{12} + \dfrac{1}{3} + \dfrac{5}{12}$

32. $\dfrac{1}{2} + \dfrac{1}{16} + \dfrac{5}{16}$

33. $\dfrac{1}{8} + \dfrac{1}{4} + \dfrac{1}{2}$

34. $\dfrac{1}{2} + \dfrac{1}{5} + \dfrac{1}{10}$

Rock Creek

The chart shows last year's admission records for Rock Creek State Park. Use the information in the chart to answer the following questions.

35. What fraction of the total were the Child and Senior Citizen admissions together?

36. What fraction of the total were the General and Senior Citizen admissions together?

★ **37.** What fraction of the total were *not* Senior Citizen or Complimentary admissions?

★ **38.** What fraction of the total were *not* Complimentary admissions?

ROCK CREEK STATE PARK ADMISSIONS	
Type of Admission	**Fraction of Total Visitors**
General	$\dfrac{1}{4}$
Child	$\dfrac{1}{2}$
Senior Citizen	$\dfrac{1}{8}$
Complimentary	$\dfrac{1}{8}$

Adding Fractions: Unlike Denominators

Jan Thompson is planning to construct two houses next to each other. She wants to build one house on $\frac{3}{4}$ acre of land and the other on $\frac{5}{6}$ acre. Add $\frac{3}{4}$ and $\frac{5}{6}$ to find how much land she is using for both houses.

Remember to rewrite the fractions as equivalent fractions with a common denominator.

$$\frac{3}{4} = \frac{9}{12}$$

The LCD is 12, the LCM of 4 and 6.

$$+\frac{5}{6} = +\frac{10}{12}$$
$$\overline{\qquad} \qquad \frac{19}{12} \longrightarrow \frac{19}{12} = 1\frac{7}{12}$$

Jan is using $1\frac{7}{12}$ acres of land.

Some people just multiply the denominators of the fractions to find a common denominator. Always be sure that your final answer is in lowest terms.

Exercises

Write the least common denominator for the pair of fractions.

1. $\frac{1}{3}, \frac{1}{2}$ **2.** $\frac{1}{8}, \frac{1}{6}$ **3.** $\frac{1}{12}, \frac{1}{9}$ **4.** $\frac{2}{5}, \frac{1}{6}$ **5.** $\frac{2}{9}, \frac{5}{6}$

6. $\frac{1}{4} = \frac{\blacksquare}{20}$

$+\frac{3}{5} = +\frac{\blacksquare}{20}$

$\overline{\qquad} \quad \frac{\blacksquare}{20}$

7. $\frac{5}{6} = \frac{\blacksquare}{24}$

$+\frac{5}{8} = +\frac{\blacksquare}{24}$

$\overline{\qquad} \quad \frac{\blacksquare}{24} = 1\frac{\blacksquare}{24}$

8. $\frac{5}{12} = \frac{\blacksquare}{36}$

$+\frac{7}{9} = +\frac{\blacksquare}{36}$

$\overline{\qquad} \quad \frac{\blacksquare}{36} = 1\frac{\blacksquare}{36}$

Add. Write the answer in lowest terms.

9. $\frac{1}{2}$
$+\frac{1}{5}$

10. $\frac{1}{4}$
$+\frac{1}{7}$

11. $\frac{1}{10}$
$+\frac{1}{4}$

12. $\frac{1}{6}$
$+\frac{1}{4}$

13. $\frac{1}{10}$
$+\frac{1}{6}$

14. $\frac{1}{6}$
$+\frac{1}{14}$

15. $\frac{3}{7}$
$+\frac{1}{2}$

16. $\frac{3}{4}$
$+\frac{1}{5}$

17. $\frac{1}{6}$
$+\frac{3}{4}$

18. $\frac{5}{6}$
$+\frac{1}{8}$

19. $\frac{2}{3}$
$+\frac{2}{7}$

20. $\frac{2}{9}$
$+\frac{5}{12}$

21. $\frac{3}{5}$
$+\frac{2}{3}$

22. $\frac{2}{3}$
$+\frac{3}{4}$

23. $\frac{1}{4}$
$+\frac{5}{6}$

24. $\frac{2}{5}$
$+\frac{3}{4}$

25. $\frac{7}{8}$
$+\frac{5}{6}$

26. $\frac{5}{6}$
$+\frac{3}{10}$

27. $\frac{1}{2} + \frac{1}{4} + \frac{1}{6}$

28. $\frac{1}{3} + \frac{1}{6} + \frac{1}{9}$

29. $\frac{1}{2} + \frac{1}{3} + \frac{1}{5}$

30. $\frac{1}{2} + \frac{1}{6} + \frac{2}{9}$

31. $\frac{1}{2} + \frac{2}{3} + \frac{1}{4}$

32. $\frac{1}{2} + \frac{2}{3} + \frac{3}{5}$

Piney Acres Homes

Solve.

33. One of Jan's lots has trees on $\frac{1}{6}$ acre. The other lot has trees on $\frac{2}{5}$ acre. How much of the two lots has trees?

34. The inside walls of each house will have two coats of plaster. The first will be $\frac{3}{8}$ inch thick. The second will be $\frac{1}{4}$ inch thick. What will be the total thickness of the plaster?

In each step you must move two adjacent coins, keeping them together. Make the top row match the bottom row in three steps.

Take a Break

Adding Mixed Numbers

Here's how you can add mixed numbers.

First rewrite all the fractions as equivalent fractions with a common denominator.

$$4\frac{1}{2} = 4\frac{5}{10}$$
$$+2\frac{3}{5} = +2\frac{6}{10}$$

Then add the fractions. Add the whole numbers. Regroup the answer.

$$4\frac{5}{10}$$
$$+2\frac{6}{10}$$

Write $\frac{11}{10}$ as a mixed number.

$$6\frac{11}{10} = 6 + 1\frac{1}{10} = 7\frac{1}{10}$$

Exercises

Complete.

1. $2\frac{1}{2} = 2\frac{\blacksquare}{4}$

2. $1\frac{5}{8} = 1\frac{\blacksquare}{16}$

3. $3\frac{2}{5} = 3\frac{\blacksquare}{20}$

4. $6\frac{2}{5} = 6\frac{\blacksquare}{15}$

5. $2\frac{5}{8} = 2\frac{\blacksquare}{24}$

6. $5\frac{6}{7} = 5\frac{\blacksquare}{28}$

7. $2\frac{3}{4} = 2\frac{\blacksquare}{36}$

8. $7\frac{1}{5} = 7\frac{\blacksquare}{40}$

9. $4\frac{9}{8} = 5\frac{\blacksquare}{8}$

10. $3\frac{7}{6} = 4\frac{\blacksquare}{6}$

11. $7\frac{9}{5} = 8\frac{\blacksquare}{5}$

12. $2\frac{11}{9} = 3\frac{\blacksquare}{9}$

13. $12\frac{16}{10} = 13\frac{\blacksquare}{10} = 13\frac{\blacksquare}{5}$

14. $9\frac{12}{8} = 10\frac{\blacksquare}{8} = 10\frac{\blacksquare}{2}$

15. $9\frac{16}{12} = 10\frac{\blacksquare}{12} = 10\frac{\blacksquare}{3}$

16. $6\frac{18}{10} = 7\frac{\blacksquare}{10} = 7\frac{\blacksquare}{5}$

Add.

17. $\quad 6\frac{2}{7}$
$\quad +1\frac{3}{7}$

18. $\quad 2\frac{1}{9}$
$\quad +3\frac{7}{9}$

19. $\quad 8\frac{1}{5}$
$\quad +4\frac{2}{5}$

20. $\quad 6\frac{3}{4}$
$\quad +5$

21. $\quad 8\frac{3}{5}$
$\quad +\ \frac{1}{5}$

22. $\quad 1\frac{6}{7}$
$\quad +3\frac{3}{7}$

23. $\quad 4\frac{8}{9}$
$\quad +2\frac{5}{9}$

24. $\quad 6\frac{2}{3}$
$\quad +7\frac{2}{3}$

25. $\quad 10\frac{3}{5}$
$\quad +\ \ \frac{4}{5}$

26. $\quad 12\frac{4}{7}$
$\quad +\ \ \frac{5}{7}$

Add. Write the answer in lowest terms.

27. $3\frac{7}{8}$
       $+9\frac{3}{8}$

28. $5\frac{2}{3}$
       $+4\frac{1}{4}$

29. $6\frac{7}{8}$
       $+4\frac{1}{4}$

30. $8\frac{1}{2}$
       $+7\frac{3}{5}$

31. $3\frac{9}{10}$
       $+4\frac{7}{10}$

32. $7\frac{8}{9}$
       $+7\frac{2}{3}$

33. $12\frac{4}{9} + 3\frac{5}{9}$

34. $7\frac{1}{4} + 1\frac{1}{2}$

35. $1\frac{5}{9} + \frac{7}{9} + \frac{4}{9}$

36. $4\frac{1}{2} + 3\frac{3}{4} + 1\frac{5}{8}$

From Start to Finish

37. Copy and complete the grid. Start at 0. Add $2\frac{1}{4}$ for each move up. Add $1\frac{3}{8}$ for each move right. You should finish at $14\frac{1}{2}$.

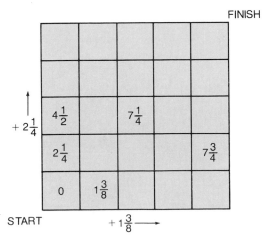

FINISH

$+2\frac{1}{4}$

$4\frac{1}{2}$		$7\frac{1}{4}$		
$2\frac{1}{4}$				$7\frac{3}{4}$
0	$1\frac{3}{8}$			

START $+1\frac{3}{8} \longrightarrow$

Add or subtract. Write the answer in lowest terms. (*pages 168–169*)

1. $\frac{1}{7}$
      $+\frac{4}{7}$

2. $\frac{5}{9}$
      $-\frac{1}{9}$

3. $\frac{7}{8}$
      $+\frac{3}{8}$

4. $\frac{7}{10}$
      $-\frac{3}{10}$

Add. Write the answer in lowest terms. (*pages 170–171*)

5. $\frac{1}{4}$
      $+\frac{3}{8}$

6. $\frac{7}{12}$
      $+\frac{3}{4}$

Add. Write the answer in lowest terms. (*pages 172–173*)

7. $\frac{3}{5}$
      $+\frac{1}{3}$

8. $\frac{1}{4}$
      $+\frac{5}{6}$

Add. Write the answer in lowest terms. (*pages 174–175*)

9. $6\frac{1}{5}$
      $+4\frac{2}{5}$

10. $7\frac{5}{6}$
       $+9\frac{1}{8}$

11. $1\frac{6}{7}$
       $+3\frac{4}{7}$

12. $2\frac{5}{6}$
       $+4\frac{1}{2}$

Extra practice on page 430

Subtracting Fractions: Unlike Denominators

There is $\frac{3}{4}$ cup milk in the carton. Ana's recipe for bread requires $\frac{1}{3}$ cup milk. To find how much milk she will have left, Ana subtracts $\frac{1}{3}$ from $\frac{3}{4}$.

To subtract fractions with unlike denominators, rewrite the fractions as equivalent fractions with a common denominator.

$$\frac{3}{4} = \frac{9}{12}$$
$$-\frac{1}{3} = -\frac{4}{12}$$
$$\frac{5}{12}$$

The LCD is 12, the LCM of 4 and 3.

Ana will have $\frac{5}{12}$ cup milk left.

Exercises

Complete.

1.
$\frac{3}{8} = \frac{\blacksquare}{8}$
$-\frac{1}{4} = -\frac{\blacksquare}{8}$
$\frac{\blacksquare}{8}$

2.
$\frac{4}{5} = \frac{\blacksquare}{10}$
$-\frac{1}{10} = -\frac{\blacksquare}{10}$
$\frac{\blacksquare}{10}$

3.
$\frac{7}{9} = \frac{\blacksquare}{18}$
$-\frac{1}{2} = -\frac{\blacksquare}{18}$
$\frac{\blacksquare}{18}$

4.
$\frac{3}{4} = \frac{\blacksquare}{12}$
$-\frac{1}{6} = -\frac{\blacksquare}{12}$
$\frac{\blacksquare}{12}$

5.
$\frac{5}{6} = \frac{\blacksquare}{18}$
$-\frac{2}{9} = -\frac{\blacksquare}{18}$
$\frac{\blacksquare}{18}$

6.
$\frac{2}{3} = \frac{\blacksquare}{12}$
$-\frac{1}{4} = -\frac{\blacksquare}{12}$
$\frac{\blacksquare}{12}$

7.
$\frac{5}{6} = \frac{\blacksquare}{12}$
$-\frac{1}{2} = -\frac{\blacksquare}{12}$
$\frac{\blacksquare}{12} = \frac{\blacksquare}{3}$

8.
$\frac{2}{3} = \frac{\blacksquare}{6}$
$-\frac{1}{6} = -\frac{\blacksquare}{6}$
$\frac{\blacksquare}{6} = \frac{\blacksquare}{2}$

9.
$\frac{7}{10} = \frac{\blacksquare}{30}$
$-\frac{1}{6} = -\frac{\blacksquare}{30}$
$\frac{\blacksquare}{30} = \frac{\blacksquare}{15}$

Subtract. Write the answer in lowest terms.

10. $\dfrac{7}{9}$ $-\dfrac{1}{3}$

11. $\dfrac{3}{4}$ $-\dfrac{5}{8}$

12. $\dfrac{17}{20}$ $-\dfrac{1}{4}$

13. $\dfrac{5}{9}$ $-\dfrac{7}{18}$

14. $\dfrac{11}{12}$ $-\dfrac{1}{4}$

15. $\dfrac{2}{3}$ $-\dfrac{3}{5}$

16. $\dfrac{4}{5}$ $-\dfrac{1}{4}$

17. $\dfrac{3}{8}$ $-\dfrac{1}{5}$

18. $\dfrac{5}{7}$ $-\dfrac{2}{3}$

19. $\dfrac{3}{4}$ $-\dfrac{5}{9}$

20. $\dfrac{8}{9}$ $-\dfrac{1}{6}$

21. $\dfrac{7}{12}$ $-\dfrac{2}{9}$

22. $\dfrac{5}{8}$ $-\dfrac{1}{6}$

23. $\dfrac{5}{6}$ $-\dfrac{7}{10}$

24. $\dfrac{4}{15}$ $-\dfrac{1}{6}$

25. $\dfrac{1}{3} - \dfrac{1}{6}$

26. $\dfrac{7}{10} - \dfrac{1}{5}$

27. $\dfrac{2}{3} - \dfrac{5}{8}$

28. $\dfrac{3}{4} - \dfrac{3}{10}$

Mince, Chop, and Grate

Ana is planning to make stuffed acorn squash. Use the measures shown on her recipe to answer the question.

29. Ana has $\dfrac{1}{3}$ cup brown rice. How much more does she need?

30. She has $\dfrac{1}{2}$ cup minced onion. How much will she have left after she makes the recipe?

31. Each squash weighs $\dfrac{7}{8}$ pound. How many pounds of squash does Ana have?

★ 32. She has $\dfrac{2}{3}$ cup chopped walnuts. Is this more or less than she needs? How much?

★ 33. She has $\dfrac{2}{5}$ cup grated cheese. Is this more or less than she needs? How much?

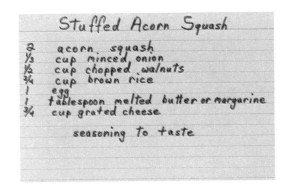

Stuffed Acorn Squash
2 acorn squash
⅓ cup minced onion
½ cup chopped walnuts
¾ cup brown rice
1 egg
1 tablespoon melted butter or margarine
¾ cup grated cheese

seasoning to taste

Subtracting Mixed Numbers

One of the largest living species of birds is the wandering albatross. It has an average wingspan of $10\frac{1}{3}$ feet. There is a record of one albatross that had a wingspan of $11\frac{5}{6}$ feet. We subtract to find how much wider than the average this was.

Write equivalent fractions with a common denominator.

$$11\frac{5}{6} = 11\frac{5}{6}$$
$$-10\frac{1}{3} = -10\frac{2}{6}$$

Subtract the fractions.

$$11\frac{5}{6}$$
$$-10\frac{2}{6}$$
$$\overline{\frac{3}{6}}$$

Subtract the whole numbers.

$$11\frac{5}{6}$$
$$-10\frac{2}{6}$$
$$\overline{1\frac{3}{6} = 1\frac{1}{2}}$$

The record wingspan was $1\frac{1}{2}$ feet wider than the average.

Exercises

Subtract.

1. $3\frac{7}{9}$
$-2\frac{2}{9}$

2. $5\frac{6}{7}$
$-1\frac{1}{7}$

3. $8\frac{2}{3}$
$-5\frac{1}{3}$

4. $2\frac{3}{5}$
$-1\frac{2}{5}$

5. $7\frac{4}{7}$
$-3\frac{2}{7}$

6. $7\frac{4}{5}$
$-\frac{1}{5}$

7. $10\frac{5}{7}$
$-\frac{2}{7}$

8. $1\frac{8}{9}$
$-\frac{1}{9}$

9. $12\frac{4}{5}$
$-\frac{2}{5}$

10. $8\frac{6}{7}$
$-\frac{2}{7}$

11. $5\frac{3}{4}$
-2

12. $8\frac{1}{5}$
-6

13. $11\frac{2}{3}$
-7

14. $5\frac{1}{4}$
-1

15. $13\frac{7}{8}$
-4

Subtract. Write the answer in lowest terms.

16. $6\frac{7}{8}$ **17.** $8\frac{3}{4}$ **18.** $17\frac{9}{10}$ **19.** $12\frac{3}{4}$ **20.** $18\frac{7}{10}$

$\quad\ -4\frac{1}{4}$ $\quad\ -2\frac{1}{2}$ $\quad\ -\ 9\frac{2}{5}$ $\quad\ -\ 4\frac{7}{20}$ $\quad\ -\ 9\frac{1}{2}$

21. $7\frac{3}{4}$ **22.** $9\frac{4}{5}$ **23.** $11\frac{2}{3}$ **24.** $10\frac{5}{9}$ **25.** $11\frac{3}{7}$

$\quad\ -2\frac{2}{3}$ $\quad\ -3\frac{1}{2}$ $\quad\ -\ 7\frac{3}{5}$ $\quad\ -\ 6\frac{1}{2}$ $\quad\ -\ 2\frac{2}{5}$

26. $8\frac{5}{12}$ **27.** $6\frac{3}{4}$ **28.** $7\frac{3}{8}$ **29.** $5\frac{9}{10}$ **30.** $20\frac{5}{6}$

$\quad\ -4\frac{3}{8}$ $\quad\ -4\frac{3}{10}$ $\quad\ -5\frac{1}{6}$ $\quad\ -4\frac{1}{6}$ $\quad\ -10\frac{3}{4}$

31. $7\frac{11}{12}$ **32.** $12\frac{3}{8}$ **33.** $13\frac{3}{4}$ **34.** $10\frac{5}{6}$ **35.** $14\frac{2}{3}$

$\quad\ -4\frac{1}{6}$ $\quad\ -11\frac{1}{5}$ $\quad\ -\ 6\frac{1}{20}$ $\quad\ -\ 3\frac{7}{9}$ $\quad\ -\ 7\frac{1}{9}$

36. $10\frac{7}{9}-2$ **37.** $2\frac{3}{4}-\frac{1}{4}$ **38.** $11\frac{2}{3}-4\frac{5}{9}$ **39.** $7\frac{1}{2}-1\frac{1}{5}$

World Records

The longest preserved beard was presented to the Smithsonian Institute in Washington, D.C. It measured $17\frac{1}{2}$ feet. The longest mustache on record measured $8\frac{1}{2}$ feet.

Use these facts to answer the question.

40. Which was longer, the longest beard or the longest mustache? How much?

41. Suppose that the man who grew the longest beard was $6\frac{1}{3}$ feet tall. How much shorter was he than his beard?

★ **42.** Suppose that the man who grew the longest mustache was $2\frac{1}{4}$ feet shorter than his mustache. Who was taller, the man with the longest beard or the man with the longest mustache?

179

Subtracting Mixed Numbers

Nick Vouros bought a 25-yard bolt of
fabric and sold $21\frac{3}{4}$ yards at the regular
price. He will sell the rest as a remnant
at a reduced price. He subtracts to find
how much fabric will be in the remnant.

Rewrite the whole number
as a mixed number.

$$25 = 24\frac{4}{4}$$
$$-21\frac{3}{4} = -21\frac{3}{4}$$

$25 = 24 + 1 = 24\frac{4}{4}$

Subtract the
fractions.

$$24\frac{4}{4}$$
$$-21\frac{3}{4}$$
$$\overline{\quad \frac{1}{4}}$$

Subtract the
whole numbers.

$$24\frac{4}{4}$$
$$-21\frac{3}{4}$$
$$\overline{3\frac{1}{4}}$$

There will be $3\frac{1}{4}$ yards of fabric in the remnant.

Exercises

Complete.

1. $4 = 3\frac{\blacksquare}{6}$

2. $9 = 8\frac{\blacksquare}{4}$

3. $6 = 5\frac{\blacksquare}{10}$

4. $13 = 12\frac{\blacksquare}{8}$

5. $10 = \blacksquare\frac{12}{12}$

6. $15 = \blacksquare\frac{9}{9}$

7. $20 = \blacksquare\frac{6}{6}$

8. $2 = \blacksquare\frac{18}{18}$

9. $\blacksquare = 3\frac{15}{15}$

10. $\blacksquare = 5\frac{8}{8}$

11. $\blacksquare = 6\frac{20}{20}$

12. $\blacksquare = 8\frac{10}{10}$

13.
$$4 = 3\frac{\blacksquare}{5}$$
$$-2\frac{3}{5} = -2\frac{3}{5}$$
$$\overline{\quad 1\frac{\blacksquare}{5}}$$

14.
$$12 = 11\frac{\blacksquare}{9}$$
$$-7\frac{4}{9} = -7\frac{4}{9}$$
$$\overline{\quad 4\frac{\blacksquare}{9}}$$

15.
$$20 = 19\frac{\blacksquare}{7}$$
$$-13\frac{6}{7} = -13\frac{6}{7}$$
$$\overline{\quad 6\frac{\blacksquare}{7}}$$

16.
$$15 = \blacksquare\frac{8}{8}$$
$$-12\frac{3}{8} = -12\frac{3}{8}$$
$$\overline{\quad \blacksquare\frac{5}{8}}$$

17.
$$9 = \blacksquare\frac{10}{10}$$
$$-1\frac{3}{10} = -1\frac{3}{10}$$
$$\overline{\quad \blacksquare\frac{7}{10}}$$

18.
$$45 = \blacksquare\frac{9}{9}$$
$$-37\frac{2}{9} = -37\frac{2}{9}$$
$$\overline{\quad \blacksquare\frac{7}{9}}$$

Subtract.

19. 9
$-2\frac{4}{5}$

20. 4
$-1\frac{5}{7}$

21. 12
$-5\frac{3}{4}$

22. 14
$-6\frac{9}{10}$

23. 10
$-7\frac{1}{5}$

24. 19
$-15\frac{1}{2}$

25. 15
$-9\frac{11}{16}$

26. 23
$-14\frac{5}{6}$

27. 19
$-\frac{2}{7}$

28. 25
$-\frac{3}{7}$

29. 17
$-2\frac{5}{8}$

30. 20
$-\frac{7}{10}$

31. 14
$-9\frac{3}{16}$

32. 1
$-\frac{5}{9}$

33. 1
$-\frac{7}{12}$

34. $10 - 6\frac{2}{5}$

35. $8 - 3\frac{1}{3}$

36. $14 - 10\frac{1}{7}$

37. $15 - 9\frac{1}{6}$

38. $10 - \frac{5}{16}$

39. $8 - \frac{9}{16}$

40. $7 - \frac{2}{3}$

41. $1 - \frac{7}{8}$

Remnant Table

Solve.

42. Nick Vouros also bought an 18-yard bolt of fabric. He sold all but $2\frac{1}{8}$ yards of it at the regular price. How much was sold at the regular price?

43. One customer bought a 3-yard remnant of fabric. She needs $2\frac{2}{3}$ yards to make a skirt. How much fabric will be left to trim a jacket?

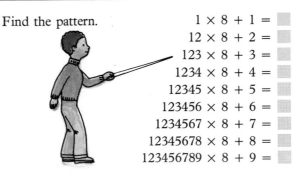

Calculator Corner

Find the pattern.

$1 \times 8 + 1 = $ ▨
$12 \times 8 + 2 = $ ▨
$123 \times 8 + 3 = $ ▨
$1234 \times 8 + 4 = $ ▨
$12345 \times 8 + 5 = $ ▨
$123456 \times 8 + 6 = $ ▨
$1234567 \times 8 + 7 = $ ▨
$12345678 \times 8 + 8 = $ ▨
$123456789 \times 8 + 9 = $ ▨

Subtracting Mixed Numbers

Sometimes before subtracting mixed numbers you may need to regroup.

In this example you cannot subtract $\frac{4}{6}$ from $\frac{3}{6}$.

$$9\frac{1}{2} = \quad 9\frac{3}{6}$$
$$-1\frac{2}{3} = -1\frac{4}{6}$$

You must first use the fact that 9 equals $8\frac{6}{6}$ to regroup.

	Regroup.		Subtract the fractions.	Subtract the whole numbers.

$$9\frac{3}{6} = 8\frac{6}{6} + \frac{3}{6} = 8\frac{9}{6}$$

Regroup.
$$9\frac{3}{6} = \quad 8\frac{9}{6}$$
$$-1\frac{4}{6} = -1\frac{4}{6}$$

Subtract the fractions.
$$8\frac{9}{6}$$
$$-1\frac{4}{6}$$
$$\frac{5}{6}$$

Subtract the whole numbers.
$$8\frac{9}{6}$$
$$-1\frac{4}{6}$$
$$7\frac{5}{6}$$

Exercises

Complete.

1. $4\frac{1}{6} = 3\frac{\square}{6}$

2. $6\frac{1}{9} = 5\frac{\square}{9}$

3. $2\frac{3}{8} = 1\frac{\square}{8}$

4. $3\frac{5}{7} = 2\frac{\square}{7}$

5. $5\frac{8}{12} = 4\frac{\square}{12}$

6. $9\frac{15}{20} = 8\frac{\square}{20}$

7. $4\frac{10}{15} = 3\frac{\square}{15}$

8. $7\frac{6}{18} = 6\frac{\square}{18}$

9.
$$9\frac{1}{5} = \quad 8\frac{\square}{5}$$
$$-1\frac{3}{5} = -1\frac{3}{5}$$
$$7\frac{\square}{5}$$

10.
$$6\frac{2}{9} = \quad 5\frac{\square}{9}$$
$$-2\frac{7}{9} = -2\frac{7}{9}$$
$$3\frac{\square}{9}$$

11.
$$7\frac{1}{3} = \quad 6\frac{\square}{3}$$
$$-5\frac{2}{3} = -5\frac{2}{3}$$
$$1\frac{\square}{3}$$

12.
$$4\frac{1}{6} = \quad 3\frac{\square}{6}$$
$$-1\frac{5}{6} = -1\frac{5}{6}$$
$$2\frac{\square}{6} = 2\frac{\square}{3}$$

13.
$$7\frac{3}{8} = \quad 6\frac{\square}{8}$$
$$-5\frac{7}{8} = -5\frac{7}{8}$$
$$1\frac{\square}{8} = 1\frac{\square}{2}$$

14.
$$7\frac{3}{10} = \quad 6\frac{\square}{10}$$
$$-2\frac{7}{10} = -2\frac{7}{10}$$
$$4\frac{\square}{10} = 4\frac{\square}{5}$$

Subtract. Write the answer in lowest terms.

15. $8\frac{1}{7}$ **16.** $6\frac{2}{9}$ **17.** $9\frac{2}{5}$

$-1\frac{3}{7}$ $-1\frac{5}{9}$ $-3\frac{9}{10}$

18. $7\frac{1}{4}$ **19.** $3\frac{1}{4}$ **20.** $7\frac{2}{7}$

$-2\frac{1}{3}$ $-2\frac{9}{10}$ $-6\frac{2}{3}$

21. $10\frac{1}{8}-2\frac{3}{8}$ **22.** $7\frac{1}{10}-4\frac{3}{5}$

23. $5\frac{2}{5}-4\frac{1}{2}$ **24.** $11\frac{3}{4}-5\frac{9}{10}$

On Wall Street

The price of a share of stock in a company often is listed as a mixed number. The increase in value of a stock is the difference between the last sale today and the last sale yesterday.

What is the increase in value for each stock?

	Company	Last Sale Yesterday	Last Sale Today
25.	Atlantis	$75\frac{3}{4}$	$77\frac{1}{2}$
26.	Daytron	$38\frac{7}{8}$	$41\frac{1}{4}$
27.	Eksonn	$89\frac{5}{8}$	$90\frac{1}{2}$
28.	NY Tesco	$100\frac{3}{4}$	$101\frac{5}{8}$
29.	Thorpe	$53\frac{7}{8}$	$54\frac{1}{2}$

Checkpoint B

Subtract. Write the answer in lowest terms. (*pages 176–177*)

1. $\frac{5}{9}$ **2.** $\frac{5}{6}$

$-\frac{1}{3}$ $-\frac{3}{8}$

Subtract. Write the answer in lowest terms. (*pages 178–179*)

3. $9\frac{4}{5}$ **4.** $11\frac{3}{8}$

$-2\frac{1}{5}$ $-6\frac{1}{8}$

5. $14\frac{3}{5}$ **6.** $19\frac{7}{8}$

$-8\frac{1}{2}$ $-8\frac{5}{12}$

Subtract. (*pages 180–181*)

7. 8 **8.** 15

$-3\frac{1}{5}$ $-9\frac{7}{8}$

9. 6 **10.** 1

$-\frac{9}{10}$ $-\frac{5}{9}$

Subtract. Write the answer in lowest terms. (*pages 182–183*)

11. $10\frac{1}{7}$ **12.** $7\frac{3}{5}$

$-1\frac{5}{7}$ $-4\frac{9}{10}$

13. $4\frac{1}{3}$ **14.** $9\frac{1}{6}$

$-3\frac{7}{8}$ $-8\frac{9}{10}$

Extra practice on page 430

183

Problem Solving · SUPPLYING INFORMATION

1	Understand
2	Plan
3	Work
4	Answer

Sometimes it may seem that some of the facts needed to solve a problem are missing. You may be able to supply information that you already know, such as a formula or a measurement fact.

For example, you are making a 15-inch square pillow in sewing class and you decide to trim the edges with fringe. Fringe is sold by the yard. How much fringe do you need?

First, find the perimeter of the pillow.

You know this formula:

$p = 4s$

$p = 4 \times 15$

$p = 60 \,(\text{in.})$

Then change inches to yards.

You know this measurement fact:

1 yd = 36 in.

$60 \div 36 = 1\frac{24}{36} = 1\frac{2}{3} \,(\text{yd})$

You need $1\frac{2}{3}$ yards of fringe.

Write the formula needed to solve the problem.

1. How much trim do you need for the edges of a rectangular placemat?

2. How much fringe do you need for the edge of a circular tablecloth?

3. How much wood do you need for a triangular corner shelf?

4. How much metal do you need for the circular base of a candle holder?

Write the measurement fact needed to solve the problem. You may want to refer to the Table of Measures on page 419.

5. Fabric is sold by the yard and the measurements on your pattern are given in feet.

6. Class length for metal shop is given in minutes and you want to know hours.

7. Cheese is sold by the pound and your recipe requires ounces.

8. Wood is sold by the foot and your directions are given in inches.

Rob is making a large circular pillow in sewing class. The diagram at the right shows his plan to lay out his pattern on the fabric.

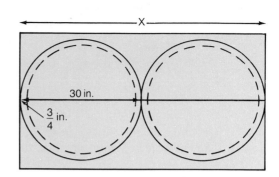

9. Rob is using x to indicate the number of yards of fabric that he must buy. What is the value of x?

10. The finished pillow will have a cord trim around the edge. Will a 2-foot piece of cord be long enough?

Nat is making a rectangular baking sheet in metal shop. She is using the sketch at the right to plan how to cut the metal.

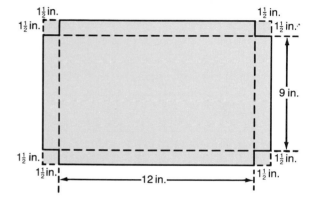

11. What are the dimensions in feet of the sheet of metal that she needs?

12. What is the baking area of the finished sheet?

Ellie's woodworking project is to make a tool rack. She sketched this top view of the rack. It shows the size and spacing of the holes.

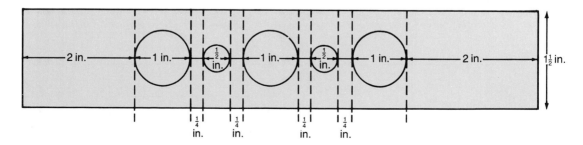

13. How many feet long will the rack be?

14. Ellie plans to put a molding around the edge of the rack. How many yards of molding must she buy?

Match.

1. $\frac{3}{5} + \frac{1}{5}$ **2.** $\frac{7}{8} + \frac{5}{8}$ **3.** $\frac{15}{16} - \frac{3}{16}$ **4.** $\frac{7}{10} - \frac{3}{10}$

A. $\frac{2}{5}$ **B.** $\frac{3}{4}$ **C.** $\frac{4}{5}$ **D.** $1\frac{1}{2}$

Add or subtract. Write your answer in lowest terms.

5. $\begin{array}{r} \frac{3}{4} \\ + \frac{5}{6} \\ \hline \end{array}$ **6.** $\begin{array}{r} 7 \\ - \frac{1}{3} \\ \hline \end{array}$ **7.** $\begin{array}{r} 6\frac{1}{2} \\ + 4\frac{5}{8} \\ \hline \end{array}$ **8.** $\begin{array}{r} 9\frac{1}{4} \\ - 5\frac{2}{5} \\ \hline \end{array}$ **9.** $\begin{array}{r} 16\frac{3}{8} \\ + 7 \\ \hline \end{array}$

10. $\begin{array}{r} \frac{7}{8} \\ - \frac{1}{4} \\ \hline \end{array}$ **11.** $\begin{array}{r} 1\frac{4}{9} \\ - \frac{7}{9} \\ \hline \end{array}$ **12.** $\begin{array}{r} 3\frac{9}{10} \\ + 5\frac{1}{2} \\ \hline \end{array}$ **13.** $\begin{array}{r} 4\frac{1}{4} \\ - \frac{7}{8} \\ \hline \end{array}$ **14.** $\begin{array}{r} 23\frac{8}{15} \\ + 7\frac{2}{3} \\ \hline \end{array}$

15. $\begin{array}{r} \frac{2}{3} \\ + \frac{1}{6} \\ \hline \end{array}$ **16.** $\begin{array}{r} \frac{4}{5} \\ - \frac{4}{15} \\ \hline \end{array}$ **17.** $\begin{array}{r} \frac{17}{18} \\ - \frac{1}{2} \\ \hline \end{array}$ **18.** $\begin{array}{r} \frac{2}{3} \\ + \frac{7}{9} \\ \hline \end{array}$ **19.** $\begin{array}{r} \frac{1}{7} \\ + \frac{5}{14} \\ \hline \end{array}$

You bought these materials at a remnant table to make a quilted wall hanging. Do you have too much or not enough of each material? How much?

	Material	Yards Needed	Yards Bought
20.	blue cotton cloth	$2\frac{3}{4}$	$3\frac{5}{8}$
21.	cotton batting	$1\frac{1}{4}$	$1\frac{1}{2}$
22.	seam tape	$5\frac{1}{2}$	8
23.	red felt	$\frac{3}{4}$	$\frac{7}{8}$
24.	white felt	$\frac{7}{8}$	$1\frac{1}{8}$
25.	black felt	$1\frac{1}{4}$	$1\frac{5}{8}$

Solve.

26. Decorative beads cost 25¢ per dozen. You need 72 white beads and 36 red beads for the wall hanging. How much will the beads cost?

Add or subtract. Write the answer in lowest terms. (*pages 168–169*)

1. $\dfrac{4}{11}$
$+\dfrac{5}{11}$

2. $\dfrac{8}{9}$
$-\dfrac{1}{9}$

3. $\dfrac{11}{12}$
$-\dfrac{7}{12}$

4. $\dfrac{3}{8}$
$+\dfrac{7}{8}$

Add. Write the answer in lowest terms. (*pages 170–175*)

5. $\dfrac{5}{8}$
$+\dfrac{1}{4}$

6. $\dfrac{2}{3}$
$+\dfrac{1}{12}$

7. $\dfrac{2}{3}$
$+\dfrac{1}{5}$

8. $\dfrac{1}{6}$
$+\dfrac{9}{10}$

9. $6\dfrac{2}{9}$
$+2\dfrac{5}{9}$

10. $5\dfrac{1}{4}$
$+1\dfrac{2}{3}$

11. $8\dfrac{3}{5}$
$+3\dfrac{4}{5}$

12. $6\dfrac{1}{2}$
$+8\dfrac{5}{6}$

Subtract. Write the answer in lowest terms. (*pages 176–183*)

13. $\dfrac{7}{15}$
$-\dfrac{1}{3}$

14. $\dfrac{1}{2}$
$-\dfrac{3}{10}$

15. $\dfrac{8}{9}$
$-\dfrac{5}{6}$

16. $\dfrac{5}{6}$
$-\dfrac{3}{10}$

17. $13\dfrac{5}{7}$
$-7\dfrac{2}{7}$

18. $4\dfrac{11}{12}$
$-1\dfrac{1}{12}$

19. $12\dfrac{9}{10}$
$-5\dfrac{1}{2}$

20. $8\dfrac{3}{4}$
$-1\dfrac{2}{5}$

21. 15
$-9\dfrac{7}{8}$

22. 6
$-1\dfrac{3}{10}$

23. $7\dfrac{2}{9}$
$-5\dfrac{1}{3}$

24. $11\dfrac{1}{6}$
$-4\dfrac{3}{4}$

Solve. (*pages 184–185*)

25. Wood for a picture frame costs 39¢ per foot. What will be the cost of the wood for a rectangular picture frame that measures 22 in. by 38 in.?

What a Computer Can Do

We hear so much about computers that sometimes it seems as if they can do anything. Some people seem to think that if they have a problem, no matter what it is, a computer will solve it. This is not true. Here are some things a computer cannot do.

- Decide which shirt you should wear.
- Enjoy a beautiful sunset.
- Tell you whether something you're thinking of doing is good or bad.
- Have its feelings hurt.
- Lose its temper.
- Fall in love.
- Anything that it hasn't been programmed to do.

Computers have no feelings or emotions. They are not able to make judgments of right and wrong or good and bad. Only people can do these things.

Computers are excellent at tasks that require difficult arithmetic calculations. They work amazingly fast. In fact, some "supercomputers" can do 100 million arithmetic operations per second. Computers have huge memories, and they remember everything they are told to remember. A computer doesn't mind doing a job that a person would find dull and boring.

Most of all, computers are very good at following directions. To solve any problem, someone must give the computer a set of directions called a **program.** Then the computer will follow the directions in the program. If the program was prepared well, the computer will then tell you the answer to your problem.

Suppose you need to buy 40 cassette tapes. The tapes cost $1.59 each. The sales tax rate is 5%. How much is your bill?

A computer program to solve the problem would look like this.

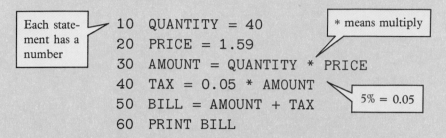

Each statement has a number

```
10   QUANTITY = 40
20   PRICE = 1.59
30   AMOUNT = QUANTITY * PRICE
40   TAX = 0.05 * AMOUNT
50   BILL = AMOUNT + TAX
60   PRINT BILL
```

* means multiply

5% = 0.05

Lines 10 and 20 show the number of tapes and the price. Line 30 tells how to figure the cost for all the tapes. Line 40 shows how to find the tax. Line 50 adds the tax to the cost of the tapes. Line 60 prints the answer, which is the total bill including the tax.

True or false? Write *T* or *F*.

1. Computers are very fast.

2. Computers forget things easily.

3. A computer can solve a problem without being told how to solve it.

4. If you make a mistake, your computer will not get mad at you.

Use the program for the cassette tape problem above to answer the following questions.

5. You want to buy 50 tapes. Rewrite line 10.

6. The tapes go on sale for $1.19 each. Rewrite line 20.

7. The sales tax rate is 6%. Rewrite line 40.

8. What will the computer print for the total bill, if the changes in Exercises 5–7 are made?

9. You decide you want the computer to print the sales tax, as well as the total bill. Write a line 70 to do this.

What is the area?

1.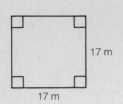
17 m
17 m

2.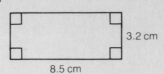
3.2 cm
8.5 cm

3.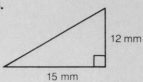
12 mm
15 mm

4.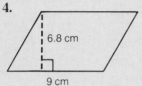
6.8 cm
9 cm

5.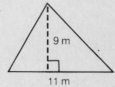
9 m
11 m

6.
12 mm

7. square:
   side, 2.4 cm

8. rectangle:
   base, 15 cm
   height, 5 cm

9. parallelogram:
   base, 46 m
   height, 39 m

10. triangle:
    base, 24.5 cm
    height, 14 cm

11. triangle:
    base, 18 mm
    height, 5.2 mm

12. circle:
    $d = 18$ mm

Multiply across the rows and down the columns to complete the grid.

13.

→ × →		
6	11	66
5	4	?
30	?	1320

14.

→ × →		
15	7	?
3	2.4	7.2
?	?	?

15.

→ × →		
3.6	4	?
2	1.7	?
?	?	?

Divide.

16. $4\overline{)340}$

17. $13\overline{)726}$

18. $49\overline{)1035}$

19. $362\overline{)8688}$

20. $5\overline{)13.5}$

21. $7\overline{)4.2}$

22. $9\overline{)0.288}$

23. $27\overline{)1.62}$

24. $0.6\overline{)5.4}$

25. $2.4\overline{)4.512}$

26. $0.38\overline{)17.1}$

27. $0.042\overline{)1.218}$

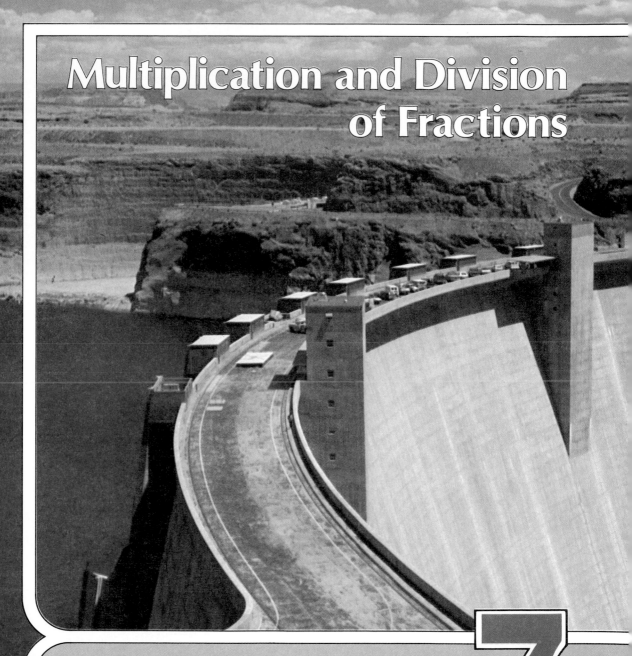

Multiplication and Division of Fractions

This dam can generate about $1\frac{1}{2}$ times as much power in July at peak water levels as in March, when levels are lowest. If the maximum March output is 730 megawatts, what is the maximum July output?

7

Multiplying Fractions and Whole Numbers

Last year Steve won 8 bowling trophies.
This year he won $\frac{3}{4}$ as many.
How many did he win?

$$\frac{1}{4} \text{ of 8 is } 8 \div 4, \text{ or } 2$$

$$\frac{3}{4} \text{ of 8 is } 3 \times 2, \text{ or } 6$$

Here's how we usually show the work.

$$\frac{3}{4} \times 8 = \frac{3 \times 8}{4}$$

$$= \frac{24}{4}$$

$$= 6$$

Steve won 6 trophies this year.

Exercises

Complete.

1. $\frac{1}{5} \times 3 = \frac{1 \times \blacksquare}{5} = \frac{\blacksquare}{5}$

   $3 \times \frac{1}{5} = \frac{3 \times \blacksquare}{5} = \frac{\blacksquare}{5}$

2. $\frac{1}{5} \times 10 = \frac{\blacksquare \times 10}{5} = \frac{\blacksquare}{5} = \blacksquare$

   $10 \times \frac{1}{5} = \frac{\blacksquare \times 1}{5} = \frac{\blacksquare}{5} = \blacksquare$

3. $\frac{1}{4} \times 2 = \frac{1 \times \blacksquare}{4} = \frac{\blacksquare}{4} = \frac{\blacksquare}{\blacksquare}$

   $2 \times \frac{1}{4} = \frac{2 \times \blacksquare}{4} = \frac{\blacksquare}{4} = \frac{\blacksquare}{\blacksquare}$

4. $\frac{1}{4} \times 5 = \frac{\blacksquare \times 5}{4} = \frac{\blacksquare}{4} = 1\frac{\blacksquare}{4}$

   $5 \times \frac{1}{4} = \frac{\blacksquare \times 1}{4} = \frac{\blacksquare}{4} = 1\frac{\blacksquare}{4}$

5. $\frac{3}{8} \times 5 = \frac{\blacksquare}{8} = 1\frac{\blacksquare}{8}$

   $5 \times \frac{3}{8} = \frac{\blacksquare}{8} = 1\frac{\blacksquare}{8}$

6. $\frac{5}{6} \times 4 = \frac{\blacksquare}{6} = \blacksquare\frac{1}{3}$

   $4 \times \frac{5}{6} = \frac{\blacksquare}{6} = \blacksquare\frac{1}{3}$

Multiply. Write the product in lowest terms.

7. $\frac{1}{7} \times 21$ **8.** $\frac{1}{8} \times 40$ **9.** $8 \times \frac{1}{2}$ **10.** $24 \times \frac{1}{8}$ **11.** $12 \times \frac{1}{3}$

12. $4 \times \frac{3}{14}$ **13.** $3 \times \frac{1}{7}$ **14.** $5 \times \frac{3}{16}$ **15.** $5 \times \frac{1}{9}$ **16.** $7 \times \frac{2}{15}$

17. $16 \times \frac{3}{4}$ **18.** $42 \times \frac{6}{7}$ **19.** $36 \times \frac{5}{9}$ **20.** $48 \times \frac{5}{6}$ **21.** $\frac{3}{4} \times 12$

22. $\frac{2}{9} \times 5$ **23.** $\frac{4}{5} \times 3$ **24.** $\frac{3}{8} \times 7$ **25.** $\frac{5}{9} \times 4$ **26.** $\frac{3}{7} \times 8$

Multiply by 24. Write the products in lowest terms.

27. $\frac{1}{8}$; $\frac{3}{8}$; $\frac{5}{8}$ **28.** $\frac{1}{12}$; $\frac{5}{12}$; $\frac{7}{12}$ **29.** $\frac{1}{6}$; $\frac{1}{2}$; $\frac{5}{6}$

Multiply by 30. Write the products in lowest terms.

30. $\frac{1}{10}$; $\frac{3}{10}$; $\frac{7}{10}$ **31.** $\frac{1}{4}$; $\frac{1}{2}$; $\frac{3}{4}$ **32.** $\frac{1}{12}$; $\frac{1}{6}$; $\frac{1}{4}$

Getting There

The gas tank of Steve's car holds 12 gal of gas. The gas gauge shows that the tank is now $\frac{1}{8}$ full. Steve knows that it takes $3\frac{1}{2}$ gal of gas to go to and from the bowling tournament.

33. How many gallons of gas are in Steve's car now?

34. Does Steve have enough gas to go to and from the tournament?

35. What is the least amount of gas that Steve must buy to go to the tournament and return?

36. How many gallons of gas must Steve buy to fill the tank?

★ **37.** This year Steve traveled a total distance of 180 mi to go to the bowling tournament. Last year he traveled $\frac{5}{6}$ of that distance, and two years ago he traveled $\frac{3}{4}$ of last year's distance to go bowling. How many miles did Steve travel in all during the last 3 years for bowling?

Multiplying Fractions

An orange juice company is looking for volunteers to test two new brands of orange juice. In the seventh grade, $\frac{3}{4}$ of the students volunteer.

Of the volunteers, $\frac{1}{2}$ will try Brand X, and $\frac{1}{2}$ will try Brand Y. What fraction of the seventh grade will try Brand X? We need to find $\frac{1}{2}$ of $\frac{3}{4}$ of the class. To do this, we multiply.

$$\frac{1}{2} \times \frac{3}{4} = \frac{1 \times 3}{2 \times 4}$$

Multiply the numerators.

Multiply the denominators.

$$= \frac{3}{8}$$

In the seventh grade, $\frac{3}{8}$ of the students will try Brand X.

BRAND X   BRAND Y

Exercises

Complete.

1. $\frac{5}{6} \times \frac{1}{4} = \frac{\blacksquare \times 1}{6 \times 4} = \frac{\blacksquare}{24}$

2. $\frac{1}{4} \times \frac{3}{8} = \frac{\blacksquare \times 3}{\blacksquare \times 8} = \frac{\blacksquare}{\blacksquare}$

3. $\frac{2}{5} \times \frac{1}{7} = \frac{2 \times \blacksquare}{5 \times \blacksquare} = \frac{\blacksquare}{\blacksquare}$

4. $\frac{2}{3} \times \frac{1}{7} = \frac{\blacksquare \times \blacksquare}{\blacksquare \times \blacksquare} = \frac{\blacksquare}{\blacksquare}$

5. $\frac{2}{7} \times \frac{1}{9} = \frac{\blacksquare \times \blacksquare}{\blacksquare \times \blacksquare} = \frac{\blacksquare}{\blacksquare}$

6. $\frac{1}{2} \times \frac{5}{9} = \frac{\blacksquare \times \blacksquare}{\blacksquare \times \blacksquare} = \frac{\blacksquare}{\blacksquare}$

7. $\frac{3}{8} \times \frac{1}{3} = \frac{\blacksquare}{24} = \frac{\blacksquare}{8}$

8. $\frac{1}{8} \times \frac{2}{5} = \frac{\blacksquare}{40} = \frac{\blacksquare}{20}$

9. $\frac{1}{4} \times \frac{6}{8} = \frac{\blacksquare}{32} = \frac{\blacksquare}{16}$ **10.** $\frac{3}{4} \times \frac{1}{6} = \frac{\blacksquare}{24} = \frac{\blacksquare}{8}$

11. $\frac{1}{5} \times \frac{5}{6} = \frac{\blacksquare}{30} = \frac{\blacksquare}{6}$ **12.** $\frac{3}{8} \times \frac{1}{6} = \frac{\blacksquare}{48} = \frac{\blacksquare}{16}$

Multiply. Write the product in lowest terms.

13. $\frac{3}{8} \times \frac{1}{7}$ **14.** $\frac{2}{3} \times \frac{7}{9}$ **15.** $\frac{3}{4} \times \frac{3}{8}$ **16.** $\frac{4}{5} \times \frac{2}{9}$ **17.** $\frac{3}{5} \times \frac{1}{8}$

18. $\frac{7}{12} \times \frac{5}{8}$ **19.** $\frac{7}{10} \times \frac{3}{5}$ **20.** $\frac{3}{4} \times \frac{5}{7}$ **21.** $\frac{5}{6} \times \frac{5}{7}$ **22.** $\frac{3}{4} \times \frac{5}{12}$

23. $\frac{7}{10} \times \frac{5}{9}$ **24.** $\frac{1}{10} \times \frac{15}{16}$ **25.** $\frac{9}{20} \times \frac{10}{16}$ **26.** $\frac{3}{4} \times \frac{4}{5}$ **27.** $\frac{5}{6} \times \frac{3}{5}$

28. $\frac{7}{8} \times \frac{4}{9}$ **29.** $\frac{5}{7} \times \frac{3}{10}$ **30.** $\frac{2}{5} \times \frac{5}{12}$ **31.** $\frac{4}{7} \times \frac{5}{12}$ **32.** $\frac{2}{15} \times \frac{3}{8}$

33. $\frac{5}{9} \times \frac{2}{7} \times \frac{3}{10}$ **34.** $\frac{5}{8} \times \frac{3}{7} \times \frac{4}{15}$ **35.** $\frac{4}{5} \times \frac{2}{9} \times \frac{6}{16}$

Hot Potatoes

The seventh-grade class made this recipe in cooking class.

POTATOES FLORENTINE

1 10-oz pkg frozen spinach $\frac{1}{4}$ c butter
3 c dried potato flakes   2 eggs
3 c hot water $\frac{1}{3}$ c grated cheese

Thaw spinach enough to separate leaves. Drain. Mix potato flakes and hot water in large bowl. Let stand until potatoes soak up water. Add butter, eggs, and cheese. Mix well. Fold in spinach. Pour into greased baking pan. Bake at 350° for 40 min. Makes 8 servings.

Solve.

36. The cooking class doubled this recipe. How much of each ingredient did they use?

37. Jamie wants to make half of this recipe to serve her family. How much of each ingredient should she use?

38. If Joe bakes the potatoes at 4:40 P.M., will they be cooked by 5:10 P.M.?

Multiplying Fractions

A fractional answer is usually expressed in lowest terms.
To do this, it is often necessary to divide
the numerator and the denominator of a
product by a common factor.

$$\frac{1}{4} \times \frac{2}{3} = \frac{1 \times 2}{4 \times 3}$$

$$= \frac{2}{12}$$

Divide a numerator
and a denominator by 2.

$$= \frac{1}{6}$$

Some people prefer to divide one of the
numerators and one of the denominators
by a common factor before multiplying.

$$\frac{1}{4} \times \frac{2}{3} = \frac{1}{\overset{}{\cancel{4}}} \times \frac{\overset{1}{\cancel{2}}}{3}$$

$$= \frac{1 \times 1}{2 \times 3}$$

Divide a numerator and
a denominator by 2.

$$= \frac{1}{6}$$

Exercises

Complete.

1. $\dfrac{1}{4} \times \dfrac{4}{5} = \dfrac{1 \times \overset{1}{\cancel{4}}}{\underset{1}{\cancel{4}} \times 5} = \dfrac{}{}$

2. $\dfrac{5}{6} \times \dfrac{1}{5} = \dfrac{\overset{1}{\cancel{5}} \times 1}{6 \times \underset{1}{\cancel{5}}} = \dfrac{}{}$

3. $\dfrac{3}{5} \times \dfrac{4}{9} = \dfrac{\overset{1}{\cancel{3}} \times 4}{5 \times \underset{3}{\cancel{9}}} = \dfrac{}{}$

4. $\dfrac{5}{6} \times \dfrac{2}{15} = \dfrac{\overset{1}{\cancel{5}} \times \overset{1}{\cancel{2}}}{\underset{3}{\cancel{6}} \times \underset{3}{\cancel{15}}} = \dfrac{}{}$

5. $\dfrac{9}{16} \times \dfrac{6}{15} = \dfrac{\overset{3}{\cancel{9}} \times \overset{3}{\cancel{6}}}{\underset{8}{\cancel{16}} \times \underset{5}{\cancel{15}}} = \dfrac{}{}$

6. $\dfrac{5}{6} \times \dfrac{2}{15} = \dfrac{\overset{}{\cancel{5}} \times \overset{1}{\cancel{2}}}{\underset{3}{\cancel{6}} \times \underset{}{\cancel{15}}} = \dfrac{}{}$

7. $\dfrac{9}{16} \times \dfrac{2}{15} = \dfrac{\overset{3}{\cancel{9}} \times \overset{}{\cancel{2}}}{\underset{}{\cancel{16}} \times \underset{5}{\cancel{15}}} = \dfrac{}{}$

8. $\dfrac{10}{21} \times \dfrac{7}{8} = \dfrac{\overset{5}{\cancel{10}} \times \overset{}{\cancel{7}}}{\underset{}{\cancel{21}} \times \underset{4}{\cancel{8}}} = \dfrac{}{}$

Multiply. Write the product in simplest form.

9. $\frac{3}{8} \times \frac{7}{9}$ **10.** $\frac{4}{7} \times \frac{5}{16}$ **11.** $\frac{2}{5} \times \frac{3}{12}$ **12.** $\frac{5}{6} \times \frac{7}{10}$

13. $\frac{3}{4} \times \frac{8}{16}$ **14.** $\frac{5}{8} \times \frac{4}{20}$ **15.** $\frac{3}{7} \times \frac{7}{9}$ **16.** $\frac{4}{5} \times \frac{10}{12}$

17. $\frac{9}{16} \times \frac{4}{6}$ **18.** $\frac{8}{12} \times \frac{3}{4}$ **19.** $\frac{8}{15} \times \frac{5}{15}$ **20.** $\frac{3}{4} \times \frac{6}{7}$

21. $\frac{2}{9} \times \frac{3}{5}$ **22.** $\frac{7}{12} \times \frac{6}{7}$ **23.** $\frac{4}{5} \times \frac{1}{2}$ **24.** $\frac{7}{8} \times \frac{3}{14}$

25. $\frac{5}{6} \times \frac{2}{5}$ **26.** $\frac{3}{4} \times \frac{1}{12}$ **27.** $\frac{9}{12} \times \frac{6}{15}$ **28.** $\frac{3}{5} \times \frac{15}{24}$

For the Birds

Solve.

29. About $\frac{2}{3}$ of the birds that use a feeder like small seeds. Of these birds, $\frac{5}{8}$ will also eat large seeds. What part of the birds that use the feeder will eat both large seeds and small seeds?

30. About $\frac{1}{6}$ of the birds in the area stay all winter. Of these, $\frac{3}{4}$ eat from the feeder. What part of the birds in the area eat from the feeder in the winter?

31. For a science report, $\frac{5}{6}$ of the students in the class wrote about birds. Of these students, $\frac{3}{10}$ wrote about bluebirds. What part of the students in the class wrote about bluebirds?

Multiplying Mixed Numbers

The New Age Dance Troupe needs costumes for its production of *The Nutcracker*. They need $2\frac{1}{8}$ yd of blue cloth for each toy soldier costume. If there are 12 toy soldiers, how much blue cloth is needed for the toy soldier costumes?

To multiply mixed numbers, first write the mixed number as a fraction. It sometimes helps to write a whole number with a denominator of 1.

$$2\frac{1}{8} \times 12 = \frac{17}{\cancel{8}_2} \times \frac{\cancel{12}^3}{1}$$

$$= \frac{51}{2} = 25\frac{1}{2}$$

For the toy soldier costumes, $25\frac{1}{2}$ yd of blue cloth is needed.

To multiply two mixed numbers, you first write both mixed numbers as fractions.

$$2\frac{1}{3} \times 1\frac{2}{5} = \frac{7}{3} \times \frac{7}{5}$$

$$= \frac{49}{15} = 3\frac{4}{15}$$

Exercises

Complete.

1. $\frac{3}{5} \times 2\frac{1}{7} = \frac{3}{5} \times \frac{\blacksquare}{7}$

2. $2\frac{2}{7} \times 4\frac{1}{4} = \frac{\blacksquare}{7} \times \frac{\blacksquare}{4}$

3. $2\frac{1}{5} \times 3\frac{1}{2} = \frac{\blacksquare}{5} \times \frac{\blacksquare}{2}$

4. $1\frac{1}{3} \times 3\frac{1}{2} = \frac{\blacksquare}{3} \times \frac{\blacksquare}{2}$

Multiply. Write the product in lowest terms.

5. $1\frac{4}{5} \times 2\frac{2}{9}$

6. $6\frac{2}{9} \times 1\frac{5}{8}$

7. $4\frac{2}{5} \times 1\frac{7}{8}$

8. $8\frac{1}{3} \times 2\frac{1}{10}$

9. $4\frac{2}{3} \times 3\frac{3}{8}$

10. $5\frac{1}{4} \times 2\frac{1}{8}$

11. $3\frac{1}{9} \times 1\frac{1}{4}$

12. $2\frac{1}{3} \times 1\frac{1}{5}$

13. $9\frac{1}{3} \times 2\frac{1}{4}$ **14.** $1\frac{3}{4} \times 1\frac{7}{8}$

15. $3\frac{1}{9} \times 1\frac{1}{14}$ **16.** $3\frac{3}{4} \times 1\frac{1}{9}$

Multiply by $3\frac{1}{2}$.

17. 2   **18.** $\frac{1}{8}$ **19.** $1\frac{1}{2}$ **20.** $\frac{2}{5}$

Multiply by $2\frac{3}{4}$.

21. $\frac{2}{11}$ **22.** $3\frac{1}{3}$ **23.** 8   **24.** $2\frac{1}{2}$

Multiply by $1\frac{7}{8}$.

25. $\frac{4}{5}$ **26.** $1\frac{1}{3}$ **27.** $4\frac{1}{5}$ **28.** $3\frac{2}{7}$

Backstage

There are 10 snowflakes in the cast of *The Nutcracker*. What is the total number of yards needed to make the 10 costumes?

29. white cloth: $2\frac{3}{4}$ yd each

30. white lace: $3\frac{1}{4}$ yd each

31. silver ribbon: $2\frac{1}{8}$ yd each

32. white thread: $5\frac{1}{2}$ yd each

★ **33.** Each costume for the 12 toy soldiers needs $1\frac{1}{8}$ yd of gold trim. Gold trim costs $4.50 per yard. What is the cost of the gold trim?

Checkpoint A

Multiply. Write the product in lowest terms. (*pages 192–193*)

1. $\frac{5}{6} \times 48$ **2.** $\frac{3}{8} \times 40$

3. $\frac{2}{7} \times 12$ **4.** $\frac{8}{9} \times 10$

Multiply. (*pages 194–195*)

5. $\frac{1}{8} \times \frac{3}{5}$ **6.** $\frac{4}{11} \times \frac{2}{9}$

7. $\frac{3}{4} \times \frac{5}{7}$ **8.** $\frac{6}{13} \times \frac{2}{11}$

Multiply. Write the product in lowest terms. (*pages 196–197*)

9. $\frac{3}{4} \times \frac{5}{6}$ **10.** $\frac{8}{13} \times \frac{7}{24}$

11. $\frac{9}{16} \times \frac{2}{3}$ **12.** $\frac{11}{15} \times \frac{10}{33}$

Multiply. Write the product in lowest terms. (*pages 198–199*)

13. $3\frac{1}{5} \times 2\frac{1}{2}$ **14.** $6\frac{2}{3} \times 5\frac{1}{4}$

15. $12\frac{1}{2} \times 5\frac{2}{5}$

Reciprocals

Reciprocals are a pair of numbers whose product is 1.

$$3 \times \frac{1}{3} = 1 \qquad\qquad \frac{5}{6} \times \frac{6}{5} = 1 \qquad\qquad \frac{7}{8} \times \frac{8}{7} = 1$$

These numbers are reciprocals of each other:

$$3 \text{ and } \frac{1}{3} \qquad\qquad \frac{5}{6} \text{ and } \frac{6}{5} \qquad\qquad \frac{7}{8} \text{ and } \frac{8}{7}$$

The product of 0 and any number is always 0, never 1.
Therefore, the number 0 has no reciprocal.

$$0 \times 0 = 0 \qquad\qquad 0 \times 1 = 0 \qquad\qquad 0 \times a = 0$$

Exercises

Complete.

1. $\frac{1}{9} \times \underline{} = 1$
     2. $\frac{3}{20} \times \underline{} = 1$
     3. $7 \times \underline{} = 1$

4. $21 \times \underline{} = 1$
     5. $\frac{7}{9} \times \underline{} = 1$
     6. $\underline{} \times 11 = 1$

Write the reciprocal.

7. $\frac{1}{5}$ **8.** $\frac{7}{9}$ **9.** $\frac{4}{5}$ **10.** $\frac{5}{9}$ **11.** $\frac{8}{11}$ **12.** $\frac{5}{7}$

13. $\frac{3}{4}$ **14.** $\frac{12}{13}$ **15.** $\frac{11}{14}$ **16.** $\frac{12}{21}$ **17.** $\frac{19}{20}$ **18.** $\frac{13}{14}$

19. $\frac{3}{5}$ **20.** $\frac{4}{7}$ **21.** 8   **22.** 16   **23.** 25   **24.** 141

Multiply. Are the two numbers reciprocals?

25. $3\frac{1}{8} \times \frac{8}{25}$ **26.** $8\frac{4}{5} \times \frac{5}{39}$ **27.** $4\frac{1}{6} \times \frac{6}{25}$ **28.** $9\frac{2}{5} \times \frac{5}{47}$

29. $7\frac{4}{5} \times \frac{5}{44}$ **30.** $8\frac{1}{5} \times \frac{5}{41}$ **31.** $12\frac{3}{4} \times \frac{4}{51}$ **32.** $6\frac{3}{8} \times \frac{8}{51}$

Write the mixed number as a fraction. Then write the reciprocal.

33. $3\frac{1}{9}$ **34.** $1\frac{1}{5}$ **35.** $8\frac{7}{9}$ **36.** $4\frac{1}{5}$ **37.** $10\frac{1}{7}$ **38.** $14\frac{7}{8}$

39. $17\frac{1}{2}$ **40.** $25\frac{1}{6}$ **41.** $20\frac{3}{8}$ **42.** $15\frac{5}{9}$ **43.** $2\frac{18}{23}$ **44.** $12\frac{5}{8}$

Are the numbers reciprocals? Write *Yes* or *No*.

45. $\frac{8}{9}$ and $\frac{9}{8}$ **46.** $5\frac{1}{4}$ and $2\frac{1}{4}$ **47.** $3\frac{1}{6}$ and $\frac{6}{19}$ **48.** $\frac{1}{5}$ and 5   **49.** 7 and $\frac{1}{7}$

50. 8 and $\frac{8}{1}$ **51.** $2\frac{1}{2}$ and $\frac{5}{2}$ **52.** $\frac{9}{12}$ and $\frac{4}{3}$ **53.** $\frac{12}{16}$ and $\frac{3}{4}$ **54.** $\frac{2}{3}$ and $\frac{12}{8}$

Solve.

55. $\frac{2}{3} \times a = 1$ **56.** $d \times \frac{3}{7} = 1$ **57.** $\frac{3}{8} \times g = 1$ **58.** $4 \times c = 1$

59. $\frac{5}{9} \times f = 1$ **60.** $h \times \frac{1}{6} = 1$ **61.** $b \times 8 = 1$ **62.** $e \times \frac{2}{7} = 1$

Number Facts

True or False? Write *T* or *F*.

63. The reciprocal of 1 is 0.

★ **64.** A fraction less than 1 has a reciprocal less than 1.

★ **65.** A fraction with a numerator of 1 and whose denominator is a whole number has a whole number reciprocal.

★ **66.** The reciprocal of a mixed number is a fraction less than one.

★ **67.** The numbers $\frac{3}{5}$, $\frac{1}{3}$, and 5 are reciprocals because their product is 1.

Calculator Corner

Are these numbers reciprocals?

8 and 0.125   0.25 and 2.5   16 and 0.0625

2.5 and 0.4   1.25 and 0.08   3.2 and 0.3125

Dividing Fractions and Whole Numbers

Each of four boards is cut in half to make two shelves.

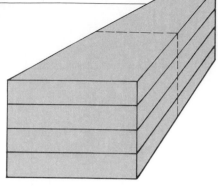

How many shelves will there be? $4 \times 2 = 8$

How many halves are there in 4? $4 \div \frac{1}{2} = 8$

There will be 8 shelves. There are 8 halves in 4.

To divide by a fraction, multiply by the reciprocal of the divisor.

Here is another example.

Shelves take up $\frac{3}{4}$ of the wall space. If there are 3 sections of shelves, how much of the wall does each section take? Each section uses $\frac{1}{4}$ of the wall space.

$$\frac{3}{4} \div 3 = \frac{3}{4} \times \frac{1}{3}$$

$$= \frac{\overset{1}{\cancel{3}}}{4} \times \frac{1}{\underset{1}{\cancel{3}}} = \frac{1}{4}$$

Exercises

Complete.

1.

How many fourths are in 3?

$$3 \div \frac{1}{4} = 3 \times \frac{\rule{1cm}{0.4pt}}{1} = \blacksquare$$

2.

How many eighths are in 4?

$$4 \div \frac{1}{8} = 4 \times \frac{8}{\rule{1cm}{0.4pt}} = \blacksquare$$

3.

How many thirds are in 2?

$$2 \div \frac{1}{3} = 2 \times \frac{\rule{1cm}{0.4pt}}{\rule{1cm}{0.4pt}} = \blacksquare$$

4.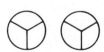

How many halves are in 5?

$$5 \div \frac{1}{2} = 5 \times \frac{\rule{1cm}{0.4pt}}{\rule{1cm}{0.4pt}} = \blacksquare$$

Complete.

5. $9 \div \frac{3}{4} = 9 \times \frac{\blacksquare}{3} = \blacksquare$

6. $8 \div \frac{4}{7} = 8 \times \frac{7}{\blacksquare} = \blacksquare$

7. $\frac{8}{9} \div 12 = \frac{8}{9} \times \frac{\blacksquare}{\blacksquare} = \frac{\blacksquare}{\blacksquare}$

8. $6 \div \frac{9}{10} = 6 \times \frac{\blacksquare}{\blacksquare} = \frac{\blacksquare}{\blacksquare} = 6\frac{\blacksquare}{\blacksquare}$

Divide. Write the quotient in lowest terms.

9. $8 \div \frac{2}{3}$

10. $\frac{3}{4} \div 9$

11. $\frac{8}{9} \div 4$

12. $6 \div \frac{2}{3}$

13. $\frac{6}{7} \div 12$

14. $9 \div \frac{9}{10}$

15. $\frac{5}{6} \div 10$

16. $12 \div \frac{7}{8}$

17. $\frac{3}{14} \div 7$

18. $15 \div \frac{9}{10}$

19. $16 \div \frac{5}{8}$

20. $\frac{3}{5} \div 15$

21. $18 \div \frac{3}{5}$

22. $\frac{7}{8} \div 14$

23. $30 \div \frac{2}{3}$

24. $20 \div \frac{15}{16}$

25. $\frac{8}{15} \div 32$

26. $\frac{14}{15} \div 21$

27. $36 \div \frac{3}{4}$

28. $72 \div \frac{8}{9}$

Interior Designs

Solve.

29. Steve is making frames. He uses $\frac{1}{3}$ of a piece of molding to make each frame. How many frames can he make out of 13 pieces of molding?

30. Jacki is using boards and cement blocks to make shelves for her apartment. Each shelf uses $\frac{1}{2}$ of a board and 2 cement blocks. Jacki has 7 boards and 16 cement blocks. How many shelves can she make?

If a chicken and a half lays an egg and a half in 1 day, how many eggs will 5 chickens lay in 6 days?

Division of Fractions

Paul needs $\frac{3}{8}$ yd of leather cord for each sandal he makes. How many sandals can Paul make if he has $\frac{3}{4}$ yd?

To find how many $\frac{3}{8}$ yd pieces there are in $\frac{3}{4}$ yd, we divide.

To divide by a fraction, multiply by the reciprocal of the divisor.

To divide by $\frac{3}{8}$, we multiply by its reciprocal, $\frac{8}{3}$.

$$\frac{3}{4} \div \frac{3}{8} = \frac{3}{4} \times \frac{8}{3}$$

$$= \frac{\overset{1}{\cancel{3}}}{\underset{1}{\cancel{4}}} \times \frac{\overset{2}{\cancel{8}}}{\underset{1}{\cancel{3}}}$$

$$= \frac{1 \times 2}{1 \times 1} = 2$$

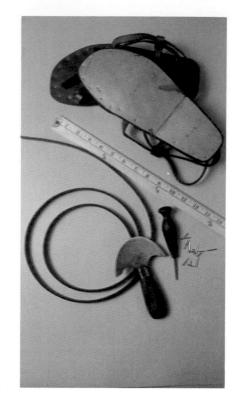

Paul can make 2 sandals from $\frac{3}{4}$ yd of leather cord.

Exercises

Complete.

1. $\frac{1}{7} \div \frac{2}{3} = \frac{1}{7} \times \frac{\blacksquare}{\blacksquare} = \frac{\blacksquare}{\blacksquare}$

2. $\frac{2}{3} \div \frac{3}{4} = \frac{2}{3} \times \frac{\blacksquare}{\blacksquare} = \frac{\blacksquare}{\blacksquare}$

3. $\frac{4}{7} \div \frac{3}{5} = \frac{4}{7} \times \frac{\blacksquare}{\blacksquare} = \frac{\blacksquare}{\blacksquare}$

4. $\frac{5}{8} \div \frac{2}{3} = \frac{5}{8} \times \frac{\blacksquare}{\blacksquare} = \frac{\blacksquare}{\blacksquare}$

5. $\frac{2}{9} \div \frac{3}{4} = \frac{2}{9} \times \frac{\blacksquare}{\blacksquare} = \frac{\blacksquare}{\blacksquare}$

6. $\frac{1}{2} \div \frac{4}{5} = \frac{1}{2} \times \frac{\blacksquare}{\blacksquare} = \frac{\blacksquare}{\blacksquare}$

7. $\frac{3}{10} \div \frac{5}{7} = \frac{3}{10} \times \frac{\blacksquare}{\blacksquare} = \frac{\blacksquare}{\blacksquare}$

8. $\frac{1}{4} \div \frac{6}{7} = \frac{1}{4} \times \frac{\blacksquare}{\blacksquare} = \frac{\blacksquare}{\blacksquare}$

Divide. Write the answer in lowest terms.

9. $\frac{3}{4} \div \frac{7}{8}$

10. $\frac{1}{5} \div \frac{9}{10}$

11. $\frac{2}{3} \div \frac{7}{9}$

12. $\frac{5}{8} \div \frac{7}{12}$

13. $\frac{4}{5} \div \frac{2}{3}$

14. $\frac{5}{12} \div \frac{5}{7}$

15. $\frac{7}{10} \div \frac{11}{15}$

16. $\frac{3}{8} \div \frac{9}{10}$

17. $\frac{5}{9} \div \frac{5}{6}$

18. $\frac{9}{14} \div \frac{6}{7}$

19. $\frac{5}{8} \div \frac{2}{3}$

20. $\frac{7}{8} \div \frac{21}{22}$

21. $\frac{3}{5} \div \frac{3}{10}$

22. $\frac{3}{8} \div \frac{6}{10}$

23. $\frac{8}{9} \div \frac{2}{3}$

24. $\frac{9}{16} \div \frac{2}{4}$

25. $\frac{3}{8} \div \frac{7}{12}$

26. $\frac{9}{10} \div \frac{3}{4}$

27. $\frac{4}{5} \div \frac{14}{15}$

28. $\frac{8}{15} \div \frac{16}{25}$

29. $\frac{12}{15} \div \frac{3}{10}$

30. $\frac{9}{16} \div \frac{3}{20}$

31. $\frac{10}{21} \div \frac{5}{14}$

32. $\frac{7}{10} \div \frac{14}{15}$

On the Calculator

You can use a calculator to multiply or divide fractions. Of course, the answer on the calculator will be in decimal form. Study these examples.

$$\frac{4}{5} \times \frac{3}{8} \longrightarrow \boxed{4} \div \boxed{5} \boxed{\times} \boxed{3} \div \boxed{8} \boxed{=} \mathit{0.3}$$

$$\frac{3}{8} \div \frac{2}{3} = \frac{3}{8} \times \frac{3}{2} \longrightarrow \boxed{3} \div \boxed{8} \boxed{\times} \boxed{3} \div \boxed{2} \boxed{=} \mathit{0.5625}$$

Complete to show the sequence of steps necessary to do the arithmetic on the calculator. If you have a calculator, use it to do the multiplication or division.

33. $\frac{3}{4} \times \frac{2}{5} \longrightarrow \boxed{3} \div \boxed{} \boxed{\times} \boxed{2} \div \boxed{}$

34. $\frac{4}{5} \div \frac{2}{3} \longrightarrow \boxed{4} \div \boxed{} \boxed{\times} \boxed{3} \div \boxed{}$

35. $\frac{5}{8} \times \frac{3}{10} \longrightarrow \boxed{5} \div \boxed{} \boxed{\times} \boxed{} \div \boxed{}$

36. $\frac{3}{5} \div \frac{5}{6} \longrightarrow \boxed{3} \div \boxed{} \boxed{\times} \boxed{} \div \boxed{}$

Write the sequence of buttons that you would push to do the arithmetic on a calculator. If you have a calculator, use it to do the multiplication or division.

37. $\frac{7}{8} \times \frac{3}{5}$

38. $\frac{3}{8} \div \frac{1}{5}$

39. $\frac{5}{16} \times \frac{3}{10}$

40. $\frac{2}{5} \div \frac{2}{3}$

Dividing Mixed Numbers

At the Jolly Roller Amusement Park the snack bar music plays constantly. Each tape takes about $1\frac{1}{4}$ hours. How many tapes does it take to keep the music going for 10 hours? To answer the question you divide 10 by $1\frac{1}{4}$.

$$10 \div 1\frac{1}{4} = 10 \div \frac{5}{4}$$

Write the mixed number as a fraction.

$$= 10 \times \frac{4}{5}$$

$$= \frac{\overset{2}{\cancel{10}}}{1} \times \frac{4}{\cancel{5}} = 8$$

It takes 8 tapes to play for 10 hours.

Exercises

Complete.

1. $\frac{2}{3} \div 1\frac{1}{6} = \frac{\blacksquare}{3} \div \frac{\blacksquare}{6}$

$= \frac{\blacksquare}{3} \times \frac{\blacksquare}{\blacksquare}$

2. $2\frac{3}{8} \div 1\frac{1}{2} = \frac{\blacksquare}{8} \div \frac{\blacksquare}{2}$

$= \frac{\blacksquare}{\blacksquare} \times \frac{\blacksquare}{\blacksquare}$

Divide. Write the quotient in lowest terms.

3. $4\frac{1}{2} \div 3$

4. $7\frac{4}{5} \div 13$

5. $13\frac{3}{4} \div 11$

6. $5\frac{2}{3} \div 17$

7. $2\frac{5}{8} \div 7$

8. $1\frac{3}{7} \div 5$

9. $2\frac{3}{5} \div 13$

10. $12\frac{2}{9} \div 10$

11. $7\frac{1}{5} \div \frac{9}{12}$

12. $2\frac{1}{2} \div \frac{3}{4}$

13. $5\frac{3}{5} \div \frac{7}{10}$

14. $4\frac{1}{2} \div \frac{1}{4}$

15. $8\frac{1}{8} \div \frac{5}{16}$

16. $13\frac{1}{3} \div \frac{3}{4}$

17. $9\frac{1}{5} \div \frac{2}{10}$

18. $3\frac{5}{9} \div \frac{8}{12}$

Divide. Write the quotient in lowest terms.

19. $2\frac{4}{5} \div 1\frac{1}{3}$ **20.** $1\frac{1}{8} \div 1\frac{1}{16}$

21. $2\frac{5}{6} \div 2\frac{1}{2}$ **22.** $3\frac{2}{3} \div 1\frac{2}{9}$

23. $8\frac{4}{5} \div 2\frac{3}{4}$ **24.** $10\frac{2}{3} \div 2\frac{1}{6}$

25. $9\frac{2}{7} \div 1\frac{1}{4}$ **26.** $12\frac{1}{2} \div 2\frac{1}{2}$

Using Estimates

You can estimate to decide if your answer is reasonable.

EXAMPLE Does $5\frac{1}{4} \div 4\frac{2}{3}$ equal $1\frac{1}{8}$?

To round a mixed number, compare the fraction with $\frac{1}{2}$. If the fraction is greater than or equal to $\frac{1}{2}$, round up. If the fraction is less than $\frac{1}{2}$, round down.

$$5\frac{1}{4} \approx 5 \qquad 4\frac{2}{3} \approx 5$$

So, $5\frac{1}{4} \div 4\frac{2}{3}$ is about equal to $5 \div 5$, or 1. The answer, $1\frac{1}{8}$, is reasonable.

Estimate to see if the answer is reasonable. If it is not, divide to obtain an exact answer.

27. $7\frac{1}{2} \div 5 = 90$ **28.** $9 \div 4\frac{1}{2} = 2$

29. $8\frac{3}{4} \div 2\frac{3}{4} = 3\frac{2}{11}$

30. $1\frac{4}{5} \div 2\frac{7}{10} = 1\frac{1}{2}$

Checkpoint B

Write the reciprocal. (*pages 200–201*)

1. $\frac{2}{7}$ **2.** $\frac{8}{9}$

3. $10\frac{3}{4}$ **4.** $7\frac{4}{15}$

Divide. Write the quotient in lowest terms. (*pages 202–203*)

5. $15 \div \frac{3}{8}$ **6.** $12 \div \frac{2}{13}$

7. $25 \div \frac{10}{11}$ **8.** $18 \div \frac{4}{7}$

Divide. Write the quotient in lowest terms. (*pages 204–205*)

9. $\frac{3}{5} \div \frac{6}{7}$ **10.** $\frac{5}{9} \div \frac{10}{21}$

11. $\frac{7}{8} \div \frac{11}{12}$ **12.** $\frac{9}{16} \div \frac{27}{28}$

Divide. Write the quotient in lowest terms. (*pages 206–207*)

13. $6\frac{7}{8} \div 2\frac{1}{2}$ **14.** $8\frac{1}{4} \div 3\frac{6}{7}$

15. $10\frac{3}{4} \div 5\frac{1}{8}$ **16.** $12\frac{3}{8} \div 6\frac{3}{5}$

Problem Solving · USING ESTIMATES

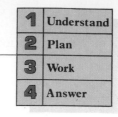

1	Understand
2	Plan
3	Work
4	Answer

Estimates are often useful in problem solving. Sometimes an estimate can help you decide whether the answer you have is reasonable.

EXAMPLE Suppose the regular plane fare to Atlanta is $120.85. A special weekday rate reduces the fare by $\frac{1}{3}$. Is the reduced fare $108.95?

Round the price.   Estimate $\frac{1}{3}$ of the price.   Subtract.

$120.85 \approx \$120$ $\frac{1}{3} \times 120 = 40$ $120 - 40 = 80$

The reduced fare is about $80, so $108.95 is not reasonable.

Often, an estimated answer rather than an exact answer is all you need to solve a problem.

EXAMPLE Regular bus fare to Little Rock is $18.75. Is $80 enough to buy 3 full-fare tickets and 1 half-fare ticket?

Round the numbers, then multiply. $3\frac{1}{2} \times 18.75 \approx 4 \times 20$, or 80

Yes, $80 is enough. Both numbers were rounded up, so the total cost is less than $80.

Use an estimate to check whether the given answer is reasonable. If it is not reasonable, write your estimated answer and the correct exact answer.

1. How far does a bus go in $3\frac{1}{2}$ hours at 54 miles an hour?   Answer: 503 mi

2. What is the cost of 46 bus tickets at $47.75 each?   Answer: $224.42

3. If a bus charter for 36 passengers costs $14,166, what should each passenger pay?   Answer: $39.35

4. If you bike $8\frac{3}{4}$ miles before lunch and $11\frac{1}{8}$ miles after lunch, about how far did you go?   Answer: $11\frac{7}{8}$ mi

Estimate. Then do the arithmetic to see how close your estimate is to the exact answer.

5. The bus fare to San Francisco is a third of the plane fare. If the plane fare is $97.65, about how much is the bus fare?

6. What is the value of a two-year-old bus if it has lost a third of its original value of $65,788?

7. Suppose you have $18.90 and spend half of it on souvenirs. You then spend a third of the remainder on a snack. Do you have enough to pay $4 to go to a movie?

8. You save a quarter of the cost of a trip by paying for the bus and motel 3 months in advance. How much did you save if the full price of the trip was $978?

9. Which goes farther, a bus traveling for $3\frac{1}{2}$ h at 58 miles per hour or a bus traveling for $4\frac{1}{2}$ h at 39 miles per hour?

10. Which costs more, paying half of a $421-train fare or a third of a $689.70-plane fare?

11. The hike to the top of Mount Nova is $5\frac{3}{8}$ miles along one trail and $8\frac{3}{4}$ miles along another trail. You decide to go up one trail and come back on the other. After you have hiked 6 miles, have you gone more than half the distance?

What's wrong here?

12. You are flying over mountains whose average height is 5420 ft. Your pilot rounds 5420 to 5400 and plans to fly at 5400 ft.

13. An engineer is designing a bridge. The winds can go as high as 73 miles per hour. The engineer rounds 73 to 70 and designs the bridge to withstand winds of 70 miles per hour.

Write the product or quotient in simplest form.

1. $\frac{3}{4} \times \frac{5}{8}$ 2. $\frac{4}{5} \times \frac{7}{8}$ 3. $12 \times \frac{9}{16}$ 4. $\frac{7}{15} \times 10$

5. $\frac{5}{12} \times \frac{9}{10}$ 6. $\frac{7}{10} \times \frac{13}{14}$ 7. $6\frac{2}{3} \times 3\frac{1}{5}$ 8. $1\frac{5}{8} \times 2\frac{6}{13}$

9. $5 \div \frac{3}{10}$ 10. $12 \div \frac{2}{3}$ 11. $\frac{1}{5} \div \frac{7}{10}$ 12. $\frac{2}{3} \div \frac{6}{7}$

13. $13 \div 6\frac{1}{2}$ 14. $3\frac{1}{3} \div 2\frac{1}{2}$ 15. $7\frac{1}{5} \div 1\frac{1}{5}$ 16. $5\frac{5}{8} \div 1\frac{4}{5}$

Write the reciprocal.

17. $\frac{1}{2}$ 18. 3 19. $\frac{3}{4}$ 20. $\frac{5}{8}$ 21. $1\frac{3}{5}$ 22. $8\frac{1}{2}$

A Greek philosopher who lived in the sixth century B.C. is best remembered today for his work with right triangles.

His name was $\underline{(23)}$ $\underline{(24)}$ $\underline{(25)}$ $\underline{(26)}$ $\underline{(27)}$ $\underline{(28)}$ $\underline{(29)}$ $\underline{(30)}$ $\underline{(31)}$ $\underline{(32)}$.

To learn his name, complete each sentence below. Then replace each number in the blank above with the first letter of the answer.

23. The __?__ of $\frac{2}{3}$ and 18 is 12.

24. One __?__ is another name for $(73 \div \frac{1}{5})$ days.

25. In the problem $3\frac{1}{9} \div 1\frac{1}{3}$, the quotient is 2 and one __?__.

26. One __?__ of 36 is 18.

27. The __?__ property tells us that $(\frac{3}{7} \times \frac{2}{9}) \times \frac{4}{5} = \frac{3}{7} \times (\frac{2}{9} \times \frac{4}{5})$.

28. The quotient of $22 \div 7$ is __?__ than π. $(\pi \approx 3.1416)$

29. Two numbers whose product is __?__ are called reciprocals.

30. The fraction $\frac{8}{9}$ is the __?__ of the fraction $\frac{9}{8}$.

31. The symbol $\approx$ means *is* __?__ *equal to.*

32. The product of $\frac{1}{2}$ and $\frac{2}{7}$ is one __?__.

Estimate to solve.

33. A tent usually sells for $87.98. Is $60 enough to buy it on sale at $\frac{1}{3}$ off?

Multiply. Write the product in lowest terms. (*pages 192–193*)

1. $\frac{2}{3} \times 9$ 2. $8 \times \frac{5}{8}$ 3. $\frac{5}{6} \times 10$ 4. $\frac{3}{4} \times 7$

Multiply. Write the product in lowest terms. (*pages 194–197*)

5. $\frac{1}{2} \times \frac{1}{6}$ 6. $\frac{1}{9} \times \frac{5}{8}$ 7. $\frac{5}{12} \times \frac{1}{4}$ 8. $\frac{7}{9} \times \frac{4}{3}$

9. $\frac{5}{16} \times \frac{8}{10}$ 10. $\frac{3}{4} \times \frac{8}{9}$ 11. $\frac{1}{6} \times \frac{3}{4}$ 12. $\frac{7}{30} \times \frac{5}{21}$

Multiply. Write the product in lowest terms. (*pages 198–199*)

13. $8 \times 1\frac{1}{2}$ 14. $\frac{3}{4} \times 2\frac{1}{2}$ 15. $1\frac{1}{4} \times 3\frac{1}{8}$ 16. $9\frac{1}{3} \times 2\frac{5}{8}$

Write the reciprocal. (*pages 200–201*)

17. 5 18. $\frac{5}{11}$ 19. $\frac{2}{7}$ 20. $\frac{13}{15}$ 21. $2\frac{1}{9}$ 22. $1\frac{15}{16}$ 23. $7\frac{1}{3}$

Divide. Write the quotient in lowest terms. (*pages 202–205*)

24. $\frac{6}{7} \div 7$ 25. $\frac{8}{9} \div 4$ 26. $6 \div \frac{2}{3}$ 27. $5 \div \frac{10}{13}$

28. $\frac{3}{4} \div \frac{3}{4}$ 29. $\frac{3}{8} \div \frac{6}{10}$ 30. $\frac{7}{10} \div \frac{14}{15}$ 31. $\frac{9}{16} \div \frac{3}{20}$

Divide. Write the quotient in lowest terms. (*pages 206–207*)

32. $4\frac{1}{2} \div \frac{3}{5}$ 33. $2\frac{1}{6} \div \frac{2}{3}$ 34. $5 \div \frac{7}{10}$ 35. $2\frac{3}{4} \div \frac{1}{2}$

36. $2\frac{1}{2} \div 2\frac{1}{2}$ 37. $\frac{1}{3} \div 1\frac{1}{4}$ 38. $3 \div 1\frac{1}{5}$ 39. $3\frac{1}{6} \div 2$

Solve. (*pages 208–209*)

40. A set of stereo headphones usually sells for $43.95. If the sale price is about $\frac{1}{3}$ less than the regular price, about how much will it cost to buy the set on sale?

Extra practice on page 433

Enrichment

Scientific Notation

Both the *Voyager I* and *Voyager II* spacecraft flew by the planet
Saturn. Saturn is about 1.6×10^9 km from Earth.

The number 1.6×10^9 is written in a special form.

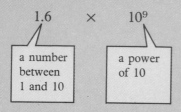

1.6   × 10^9

| a number between 1 and 10 | a power of 10 |

This form is called **scientific notation.** It is
used often in writing very large numbers.

Any number written in scientific notation
can be written in standard form.

$$1.6 \times 10^9 = 1.6 \times 1{,}000{,}000{,}000$$
$$= 1{,}600{,}000{,}000$$

A quick way to find the standard form is to think of the decimal point
moving to the right. The exponent of 10 tells you how many places.

$$1.6 \times 10^9 = 1{,}600{,}000{,}000.$$

9 places

Saturn is about 1,600,000,000 km from Earth.

Is the number written in scientific notation? Write *Yes* or *No*.

1. 24×10^7 **2.** 7×10^4 **3.** 6.9×5^2 **4.** 0.3×10^6

Write the standard form.

5. 9×10^5 **6.** 2×10^8 **7.** 8.2×10^3 **8.** 5.1×10^7

9. 7.35×10^4 **10.** 2.67×10^6 **11.** 1.8×10^1 **12.** 4.92×10^2

Voyager II was launched from Earth before *Voyager I*. It flew an indirect course of about 2,300,000,000 km to reach Saturn.

Here is how to write the number 2,300,000,000 in scientific notation.

Move the decimal point to the left to make a number between 1 and 10.

Write the number of places moved as the exponent of 10.

$$2,300,000,000. \longrightarrow 2.3 \times 10^9$$

9 places

Voyager II flew about 2.3×10^9 km to reach Saturn.

Complete.

13. $36,000,000 = 3.6 \times 10^{\blacksquare}$

14. $980,000,000,000 = 9.8 \times 10^{\blacksquare}$

15. $50,000,000,000,000 = 5 \times 10^{\blacksquare}$

16. $27,400,000,000 = 2.74 \times 10^{\blacksquare}$

Write in scientific notation.

17. 7,000,000

18. 500,000

19. 30,000,000,000

20. 3,400,000,000

21. 650,000,000

22. 92,000

23. 136,000

24. 8,040,000,000

25. 40,600,000

Write the number in scientific notation.

26. *Voyager I* took about 18,000 photographs of Saturn, its rings, and its moons.

27. The *Voyager* spacecraft discovered that Saturn has many more rings than we thought. The diameter of the largest ring is about 480,000 km.

28. The length of a year on Saturn is equal to about 29.5 Earth years.

29. Large distances are also measured in a unit called a light year. The length of a light year is about 9,460,000,000,000 km.

Maintaining Skills

Write the number using exponents.

1. 6×6 **2.** $7 \times 7 \times 7$ **3.** $1 \times 1 \times 1 \times 1 \times 1$ **4.** $9 \times 9 \times 9$

5. 11×11 **6.** 12×12 **7.** $10 \times 10 \times 10 \times 10$ **8.** 30×30

Write the number in standard form.

9. 6^2 **10.** 4^3 **11.** 10^1 **12.** 8^3 **13.** 10^6

14. 3^4 **15.** 2^5 **16.** 1^3 **17.** 7^2 **18.** 5^3

Write the number using the exponent 2.

19. 4   **20.** 16   **21.** 81   **22.** 36   **23.** 144

Write the number using the exponent 3.

24. 8   **25.** 64   **26.** 27   **27.** 125   **28.** 1

Using computers mathematicians have calculated the value of π to over 1,000,000 decimal places.

To find π to 20 places solve the equations. Write the solution in place of the variable.

$$\pi \approx 3 \cdot \underline{q}\ \underline{p}\ \underline{s}\ \underline{x}\ \underline{h}\ \underline{v}\ \underline{d}\ \underline{b}\ \underline{n}\ \underline{i}\ \underline{m}\ \underline{y}\ \underline{u}\ \underline{g}\ \underline{j}\ \underline{k}\ \underline{a}\ \underline{e}\ \underline{f}\ \underline{r} \ldots$$

29. $44 \times q = 44$ **30.** $6 + p = 10$ **31.** $s \times 6 = 6$ **32.** $9 - 4 = x$

33. $8 \times h = 72$ **34.** $v \times 18 = 36$ **35.** $3 \times 2 = d$ **36.** $12 - 7 = b$

37. $9 \times i = 45$ **38.** $5 + 3 = m$ **39.** $4 \times y = 36$ **40.** $u + 8 = 15$

41. $3 \times 3 = g$ **42.** $24 \div 8 = j$ **43.** $9 - 7 = k$ **44.** $17 + a = 20$

45. $e \times 6 = 48$ **46.** $32 \div 8 = f$ **47.** $7 + r = 13$ **48.** $2 + 1 = n$

49. A typewriter usually sells for \$315.50. If the sale price is about $\frac{1}{4}$ less than the regular price, about how much will it cost to buy the typewriter on sale?

Let p stand for the air pressure inside the wind socks. If the inside pressure is 15 pounds per square inch, write a mathematical expression involving p.

Elements of Algebra

215

Mathematical Expressions

Numbers, variables, and operation symbols are often combined to form a **mathematical expression.** Here are some examples.

Word Expression	Mathematical Expression
seven plus fifteen	$7 + 15$
eighteen subtracted from a number x	$x - 18$
seven times a number n	$7 \times n$
a number z divided by 21	$z \div 21$, or $\frac{z}{21}$

In mathematical expressions with variables, the multiplication symbol is usually omitted.

$$2n \text{ means } 2 \times n$$

Exercises

Choose the correct mathematical expression. Write a, b, or c.

1. the product of twelve and twenty-nine
   a. $12 + 29$ **b.** $29 - 12$ **c.** 12×29

2. a number q increased by 37
   a. $q + 37$ **b.** $q - 37$ **c.** $q \div 37$

3. fifteen times a number s
   a. $15 + s$ **b.** $15 - s$ **c.** $15s$

4. the quotient of a number y and 48
   a. $y + 48$ **b.** $48y$ **c.** $\frac{y}{48}$

5. seventeen less than a number d
   a. $d - 17$ **b.** $17 - d$ **c.** $\frac{d}{17}$

Write as a mathematical expression.

6. eighteen minus seven

7. forty-six times nine

8. seven more than a number p

9. fourteen less than a number q

10. a number b divided by 4

11. a number n multiplied by 12

12. a number g decreased by 3

13. a number w increased by 11

14. the sum of a number x and 13

15. the product of a number x and 5

16. the sum of a number x and a number y

17. the product of a number x and a number y

Write as a word expression.

18. $27 + 19$

19. $\frac{78}{13}$

20. $45 - 37$

21. 3×51

22. $a - 15$

23. $31v$

24. $\frac{z}{10}$

25. $18 - c$

26. $\frac{48}{h}$

27. $56 + y$

28. $35b$

29. $x + y$

30. $x - y$

31. xy

32. $\frac{x}{y}$

Making a Good Expression

Choose a variable. Then write a mathematical expression to describe the situation.

33. the number of trading cards divided by 5

34. twice the number of record albums

35. the number of patches decreased by 20

36. eighteen more than the number of posters

37. twelve times the height of the model

★ **38.** the total of the number of stamps from Australia and the number of stamps from New Zealand

Evaluating Mathematical Expressions

Each lap around the track measures 400 meters. Coach Gibby uses the expression $400n$ to represent the total distance that a student runs.

Here is how the students use this expression to find their total distance.

Number of Laps (n)	Total Distance in Meters $(400n)$
1	$400 \times 1 = 400$
2	$400 \times 2 = 800$
3	$400 \times 3 = 1200$

To **evaluate** an expression for a given number, replace the variable in the expression with the number and then do the indicated arithmetic.

Exercises

Evaluate $n + 12$ for the given value.

1. $n = 5$ **2.** $n = 49$ **3.** $n = 0$

Evaluate $\frac{36}{n}$ for the given value.

4. $n = 4$ **5.** $n = 36$ **6.** $n = 1$

Evaluate the expression. Use $n = 4$.

7. $n + 2$ **8.** $21 - n$ **9.** $n \times 5$

10. $7n$ **11.** $\frac{12}{n}$ **12.** $\frac{n}{4}$

Evaluate the expression.
Use $a = 12$ and $b = 4$.

13. $b - 3$ **14.** $3a$ **15.** $\frac{b}{4}$ **16.** $21 - a$ **17.** $38 + b$

18. $\frac{72}{a}$ **19.** $5b$ **20.** $a - b$ **21.** ab **22.** $\frac{a}{b}$

Evaluate the expression. Use $x = 6$, $y = 12$, and $z = 24$.

23. $x + 15$

24. $y - 12$

25. $3z$

26. $\frac{y}{2}$

27. $32 - z$

28. $34 + y$

29. $\frac{x}{6}$

30. $9x$

31. $y - x$

32. $z - x$

33. $\frac{z}{x}$

34. $\frac{z}{y}$

35. $x + y + z$

36. xyz

37. $3xy$

38. $2yz$

Order of Operations

In evaluating mathematical expressions, remember the order of operations. First do all the multiplications and divisions in order from left to right. Then do the additions and subtractions in order from left to right.

The example below shows how to evaluate $10 + 4c$ when $c = 3$.

Evaluate the expression.
Use $r = 2$, $s = 6$, and $t = 36$.

39. $3r - 5$

40. $4 + 2s$

41. $\frac{s}{2} + 9$

42. $10 - \frac{t}{6}$

43. $5r + s$

44. $s - \frac{t}{12}$

★ **45.** $7r - 2s$ ★ **46.** $\frac{t}{2} + 4r$ ★ **47.** $rs + \frac{s}{r}$

$10 + 4c$
$10 + 4 \times 3$ — Do the multiplication first.
$10 + \quad 12$
$\qquad 22$

Equations

You can use an equation to show that two mathematical expressions are equal. Each mathematical expression is a **side** of the equation.

$$\underbrace{6 + 2}_{} = \underbrace{15 - 7}_{}$$
$$\text{sides}$$

Often one side of an equation is a mathematical expression that contains a variable.

$$5 + x = 12 \qquad 3 = z \div 7$$

One way to solve an equation is to replace the variable with trial numbers. This is called **substitution.** The number that makes a true equation is the solution.

Solve: $86 + t = 125$
Try 40: $86 + 40 = 125$ False
Try 39: $86 + 39 = 125$ True
The solution of the equation $86 + t = 125$ is 39.

Exercises

Is 8 the solution of the equation? Write *Yes* or *No.*

1. $c + 5 = 13$ **2.** $y - 2 = 4$ **3.** $7r = 56$ **4.** $\frac{24}{m} = 3$

5. $19 + x = 37$ **6.** $25 - v = 33$ **7.** $21z = 168$ **8.** $\frac{a}{72} = 9$

Is the given number the solution of the equation? Write *Yes* or *No.*

9. $z + 25 = 94$; 79 **10.** $a - 46 = 35$; 81 **11.** $9p = 171$; 19

12. $\frac{c}{7} = 147$; 21 **13.** $\frac{76}{x} = 19$; 4 **14.** $12h = 96$; 84

220

Choose the solution of the equation. Write *a*, *b*, or *c*.

15. $m + 23 = 72$

    a. 50   **b.** 51   **c.** 49

16. $x - 14 = 27$

    a. 40   **b.** 41   **c.** 39

17. $3t = 87$

    a. 30   **b.** 31   **c.** 29

18. $\frac{r}{5} = 21$

    a. 100   **b.** 105   **c.** 95

19. $125 - d = 46$

    a. 79   **b.** 80   **c.** 81

20. $77 + q = 138$

    a. 59   **b.** 60   **c.** 61

21. $\frac{120}{y} = 8$

    a. 12   **b.** 15   **c.** 20

22. $6g = 108$

    a. 18   **b.** 19   **c.** 20

Meeting Your Match

Match the equation with its solution.

Equations	Solutions
23. $m + 49 = 68$	**A.** 17
24. $8a = 176$	**B.** 18
25. $105 - c = 88$	**C.** 19
26. $\frac{60}{t} = 3$	**D.** 20
27. $q - 6 = 17$	**E.** 21
28. $\frac{y}{3} = 6$	**F.** 22
29. $54 + x = 75$	**G.** 23

Ten classmates are having a reunion. Each person shakes hands with each other person exactly once. How many handshakes are exchanged?

Take a Break

Equations: Addition and Subtraction

Addition and subtraction of the same number are called **inverse operations.** This means that one operation "undoes" the other.

$$5 + 9 = 14 \quad \triangleright \quad 14 - 9 = 5$$

ESCALATOR

You can use inverse operations to rewrite an equation. Often this makes it easier to see the solution.

$$y + 14 = 43$$
$$y + 14 - 14 = 43 - 14$$
$$y + 0 = 29$$
$$y = 29$$
Solution: 29

$$a - 28 = 95$$
$$a - 28 + 28 = 95 + 28$$
$$a - 0 = 123$$
$$a = 123$$
Solution: 123

Use substitution to check the solution in the original equation.

$$y + 14 = 43$$
$$29 + 14 = 43 \quad \text{True}$$

$$a - 28 = 95$$
$$123 - 28 = 95 \quad \text{True}$$

When you use inverse operations to solve an equation, it is very important to do the same thing to both sides of the equation.

Exercises

What number should be subtracted from each side to solve the equation?

1. $y + 4 = 16$ **2.** $r + 46 = 95$ **3.** $x + 24 = 49$ **4.** $d + 19 = 91$

5. $m + 86 = 102$ **6.** $s + 55 = 127$ **7.** $b + 66 = 155$ **8.** $t + 15 = 108$

What number should be added to each side to solve the equation?

9. $n - 5 = 12$ **10.** $t - 36 = 57$ **11.** $a - 84 = 107$ **12.** $w - 60 = 89$

13. $b - 99 = 123$ **14.** $p - 48 = 102$ **15.** $d - 38 = 115$ **16.** $s - 87 = 142$

Complete.

17.
$$z + 15 = 22$$
$$z + 15 - 15 = 22 - \blacksquare$$
$$z = \blacksquare$$

18.
$$c - 27 = 48$$
$$c - 27 + \blacksquare = 48 + \blacksquare$$
$$c = \blacksquare$$

19.
$$b + 35 = 68$$
$$b + 35 - \blacksquare = 68 - \blacksquare$$
$$b = \blacksquare$$

Solve the equation.

20. $b + 18 = 21$ **21.** $g + 9 = 23$ **22.** $x + 15 = 42$ **23.** $m - 19 = 31$

24. $c - 28 = 49$ **25.** $a + 24 = 93$ **26.** $d - 51 = 14$ **27.** $h - 130 = 47$

28. $y + 12 = 109$ **29.** $x - 59 = 118$ **30.** $z + 52 = 191$ **31.** $v - 63 = 71$

32. $t - 36 = 48$ **33.** $c + 89 = 97$ **34.** $n + 75 = 132$ **35.** $w - 47 = 151$

Solve the first equation. Use the solution to solve
the next equation, and so on.

36. $b + 53 = 62; b = \blacksquare$
$u + b = 46; u = \blacksquare$
$s + u = 91; s = \blacksquare$

37. $c - 63 = 75; c = \blacksquare$
$a - c = 41; a = \blacksquare$
$r - a = 81; r = \blacksquare$

Find one value for each variable to make a set of true equations.

★ **38.** $g + o = 120$
$j + 27 = 63$
$o - j = 56$

★ **39.** $k - i = 14$
$e - k = 5$
$b - 18 = 83$
$i - b = 21$

★ **40.** $a + 17 = 43$
$b - a = 59$
$t + b = 91$
$o - t = 49$

Writing and Solving Equations

In two days, a diver found 137 old coins in a shipwreck. If she found 52 coins the second day, how many did she find the first day?

Writing an equation may help you to organize the given information.

Coins Found First Day		Coins Found Second Day		Total Number of Coins
n	$+$	52	$=$	137

Now, solve the equation.

$$n + 52 = 137$$
$$n + 52 - 52 = 137 - 52$$
$$n = 85$$

Then check your solution.

$$n + 52 = 137$$
$$85 + 52 = 137 \quad \text{True}$$

The diver found 85 coins the first day.

Exercises

Choose an equation to describe the situation. Write a, b, or c.

1. A number decreased by 17 is 75.
  a. $n + 17 = 75$ **b.** $n - 17 = 75$ **c.** $17 - n = 75$

2. Four more than a number is 61.
  a. $n + 4 = 61$ **b.** $4 - n = 61$ **c.** $n - 4 = 61$

3. The sum of a number and 5 is 72.
  a. $n + 72 = 5$ **b.** $n = 72 + 5$ **c.** $n + 5 = 72$

4. Thirty less than a number is 46.
  a. $30 - n = 46$ **b.** $n - 30 = 46$ **c.** $n = 46 - 30$

Use a variable to write an equation. Solve. Then answer the question.

5. What number plus 14 is 72?

6. What number minus 17 is 78?

7. What number decreased by 29 is 41?

8. What number increased by 5 is 63?

9. Twelve more than what number is 64?

10. Fifteen less than what number is 48?

11. What number added to 67 is 121?

Buried Treasure

Use a variable to write an equation.
Solve. Then answer the question.

12. A total of how many gold coins and 59 silver coins are in a collection of 124 gold and silver coins?

13. How many years after the sinking of the *Titanic* in 1913 was the sinking of the *Andrea Doria* in 1956?

★ 14. Ramond dived to a depth of 25 m, which is 18 m less than the depth of the sunken ship. What is the depth of the sunken ship?

★ 15. Karla found a coin dated 1835, which is 22 years later than the date on the coin that Phil found. What is the date on Phil's coin?

★ 16. Julie's new life line is 120 m long, which is 41 m longer than her old life line. How long was her old life line?

★ 17. Fran counted 47 kinds of fish underwater, which is 13 fewer kinds of fish than Stan counted. How many kinds of fish did Stan count?

Checkpoint A

Write as a mathematical expression. (*pages 216–217*)

1. fifty-seven minus nine

2. eight more than a number q

3. the product of a number x and 7

4. a number a divided by 15

Evaluate the expression. Use $a = 8$ and $b = 2$. (*pages 218–219*)

5. $a + 17$ 6. $a - b$

7. $5b$ 8. $\frac{a}{b}$

Is the given number a solution of the equation? (*pages 220–221*)

9. $y + 18 = 77$; 69

10. $93 - c = 53$; 39

11. $3t = 78$; 26

12. $\frac{m}{4} = 84$; 21

Solve the equation. (*pages 222–223*)

13. $s + 14 = 57$ 14. $b + 36 = 91$

15. $w - 23 = 75$ 16. $z - 38 = 23$

Write and solve an equation to answer the question. (*pages 224–225*)

17. What number minus 23 is 59?

18. The sum of what number and 55 is 121?

Equations: Multiplication and Division

Multiplication and division by the same number are inverse operations.

$$7 \times 8 = 56 \quad \Rightarrow \quad 56 \div 8 = 7$$

Use inverse operations as a shortcut to solutions. Remember to do the same thing to both sides of the equation.

$4z = 60$

$\dfrac{4z}{4} = \dfrac{60}{4}$

$1z = 15$
$z = 15$
Solution: 15

$\dfrac{n}{6} = 18$

$\dfrac{n}{6} \times 6 = \underbrace{18 \times 6}$

$n \times 1 = 108$
$n = 108$
Solution: 108

Check the solution in the original equation.

$4z = 60$ $\dfrac{n}{6} = 18$

$4 \times 15 = 60$ True $\dfrac{108}{6} = 18$ True

Exercises

What number should both sides be divided by to solve the equation?

1. $4t = 72$ **2.** $3x = 84$ **3.** $12b = 96$ **4.** $5a = 85$

5. $2k = 68$ **6.** $25m = 375$ **7.** $50z = 450$ **8.** $7r = 154$

What number should both sides be multiplied by to solve the equation?

9. $\dfrac{q}{4} = 23$ **10.** $\dfrac{s}{9} = 14$ **11.** $\dfrac{w}{15} = 7$ **12.** $\dfrac{d}{10} = 13$

13. $\dfrac{p}{12} = 9$ **14.** $\dfrac{c}{23} = 8$ **15.** $\dfrac{l}{14} = 6$ **16.** $\dfrac{n}{32} = 10$

Complete.

17. $6y = 78$

$$\frac{6y}{6} = \frac{78}{\blacksquare}$$

$$y = \blacksquare$$

18. $\frac{d}{4} = 17$

$$\frac{d}{4} \times \blacksquare = 17 \times \blacksquare$$

$$d = \blacksquare$$

19. $5n = 125$

$$\frac{5n}{\blacksquare} = \frac{125}{\blacksquare}$$

$$n = \blacksquare$$

Solve the equation.

20. $5k = 75$

21. $6x = 90$

22. $4c = 92$

23. $\frac{y}{2} = 16$

24. $\frac{n}{4} = 14$

25. $\frac{w}{3} = 32$

26. $2b = 78$

27. $\frac{a}{6} = 17$

28. $8z = 104$

29. $\frac{m}{5} = 11$

30. $\frac{s}{2} = 46$

31. $7q = 91$

32. $3g = 96$

33. $\frac{p}{7} = 15$

34. $12w = 144$

35. $\frac{a}{10} = 15$

36. $\frac{x}{14} = 14$

37. $15y = 165$

38. $11j = 121$

39. $\frac{t}{19} = 12$

A New Look

The first column shows some of the geometric formulas that you have learned. In the second column, these formulas are written with a new look. Many people consider them easier to read and use this way.

Use what you have learned about expressions to match the formulas.

40. $A = b \times h$

A. $A = \pi r^2$

41. $A = b \times h \div 2$

B. $P = 4s$

42. $A = \pi \times r^2$

C. $A = bh$

43. $C = \pi \times d$

D. $C = \pi d$

44. $P = (2 \times b) + (2 \times h)$

E. $A = \frac{bh}{2}$

45. $P = 4 \times s$

F. $P = 2b + 2h$

Use what you have learned about expressions to rewrite the formula.

★ **46.** $A = (a + b) \div (2 \times h)$

Writing and Solving Equations

Eric was always asking riddles. On his birthday he said, "Eight times my age is 360. How old am I?"

Writing an equation may help you answer his riddle. Let a equal Eric's age.

$$8 \times a = 360$$
$$8a = 360$$

Solve the equation.

$$8a = 360$$
$$\frac{8a}{8} = \frac{360}{8}$$
$$a = 45$$

Check your solution.

$$8a = 360$$
$$8 \times 45 = 360$$

True

Eric is 45 years old.

Exercises

Choose an equation to describe the situation. Write a, b, or c.

1. The product of a number and 8 is 112.

　a. $\frac{n}{8} = 112$　　　**b.** $8n = 112$　　**c.** $n = 8 \times 112$　　**d.** $112n = 8$

2. A number divided by 3 equals 42.

　a. $\frac{n}{3} = 42$　　　**b.** $\frac{3}{n} = 42$　　**c.** $3n = 42$　　　**d.** $n = \frac{42}{3}$

3. One fifth of a number is 125.

　a. $5n = 125$　　**b.** $\frac{5}{n} = 125$　　**c.** $\frac{n}{5} = 125$　　**d.** $\frac{125}{n} = 5$

4. Four times a number is 96.

　a. $4 \times 96 = n$　　**b.** $4n = 96$　　**c.** $4 = 96n$　　**d.** $\frac{n}{4} = 96$

Use a variable to write an equation. Solve. Then answer the question.

5. What number times 9 is 189?

6. Twice what number is 58?

7. What number divided by 3 is 24?

8. Triple what number is 48?

9. The product of what number and 6 is 96?

10. What number shared equally by 5 is 125?

11. One half of what number is 35?

12. One fourth of what number is 14?

The Riddler

Use a variable to write an equation. Solve. Then answer the riddle.

13. Fourteen times the number of planets in our solar system is 126. How many planets are in our solar system?

14. One fifth of the number of states in the United States is 10. How many states are in the United States?

15. Triple the number of people on a jury is 36. How many people are on a jury?

16. The product of the number of holes on a golf course and 24 is 432. How many holes are on a golf course?

17. The number of sheets of paper in a ream divided by 10 is 50. How many sheets of paper are in a ream?

18. Twice the number of items in a gross is 288. How many items are in a gross?

19. The number of original colonies times 45 is 585. How many original colonies were there?

20. One thirteenth the number of *Arabian Nights* stories is 77. How many *Arabian Nights* stories are there?

Deciding Which Operation to Use

Engineers often need to solve equations in their work.
The first step in solving an equation is to decide which operation to
use. When you see only one operation in the equation, you usually
choose the inverse of that operation. Here are some examples.

Equation	Operation in Equation	Inverse Operation (Do to Both Sides)
$t + 17 = 54$	addition of 17	subtraction of 17
$c - 42 = 37$	subtraction of 42	addition of 42
$5m = 135$	multiplication by 5	division by 5
$\frac{w}{7} = 273$	division by 7	multiplication by 7

Exercises

What should be done on both sides to solve the equation?

1. $k + 5 = 69$ **2.** $b - 12 = 42$ **3.** $4q = 76$ **4.** $\frac{m}{2} = 26$

5. $19 + a = 44$ **6.** $d + 28 = 65$ **7.** $x - 34 = 72$ **8.** $7z = 91$

9. $\frac{t}{18} = 7$ **10.** $c - 41 = 80$ **11.** $12y = 108$ **12.** $\frac{r}{3} = 17$

Solve the equation.

13. $n - 18 = 32$ **14.** $g - 37 = 91$ **15.** $\frac{w}{13} = 9$ **16.** $3v = 51$

17. $2x = 42$ **18.** $9n = 117$ **19.** $y + 58 = 64$ **20.** $\frac{a}{5} = 13$

21. $b + 45 = 71$　　　　**22.** $\frac{c}{8} = 16$　　　　**23.** $z - 12 = 34$

24. $\frac{w}{24} = 6$　　　　**25.** $6c = 132$　　　　**26.** $27x = 9$

27. $p + 35 = 174$　　　**28.** $\frac{d}{12} = 24$　　　**29.** $m + 49 = 100$

30. $\frac{r}{20} = 16$　　　　**31.** $n - 49 = 182$　　　**32.** $22t = 264$

33. $h + 124 = 212$　　**34.** $\frac{s}{25} = 15$　　　**35.** $x - 147 = 191$

36. $36a = 288$　　　　**37.** $k - 93 = 126$　　　**38.** $m + 149 = 222$

Equation Magic

Remember that a magic square is a square array of numbers in which each row, column, and diagonal has the same sum.

Solve the equation. Then replace the variable in the square with the solution of the equation. If your work is correct, the solutions will form a magic square.

a	b	c
d	e	f
g	h	j

39. $a + 28 = 44$　　　**40.** $\frac{b}{6} = 6$　　　　**41.** $13c = 104$

42. $d + 89 = 101$　　**43.** $e - 2 = 18$　　　**44.** $\frac{f}{2} = 14$

45. $g - 19 = 13$　　　**46.** $h + 58 = 62$　　　**47.** $7j = 168$

Calculator Corner

Arrange the digits 1, 3, 5, 7, and 9 in this multiplication to form the greatest product possible.

Equations with Two Variables

Some equations have two variables. When this is the case, there is usually more than one solution of the equation. Each solution is a pair of numbers.

Here are some of the solutions of the equation $x + y = 2$.

$$x + y = 2$$
$$0 + 2 = 2$$
$$1 + 1 = 2$$
$$2 + 0 = 2$$

A simpler way to show these solutions is to organize them into a chart.

$x + y = 2$

x	0	1	2
y	2	1	0

Another way to show these solutions is to write them as **ordered pairs.**

$x + y = 2$ Solutions: (0, 2) (1, 1) (2, 0)

You write the numbers in an ordered pair in the order (x, y). Since this order is usually important, (0, 2) and (2, 0) are different solutions.

Exercises

Complete the chart of solutions of the equation.

1. $x + 5 = y$

x	0	1	?	3	?	5
y	5	6	7	?	9	?

2. $x - 6 = y$

x	6	8	10	?	14	?
y	0	?	?	6	?	10

3. $4x = y$

x	0	3	?	?	12	?
y	?	?	24	36	?	60

4. $\frac{x}{7} = y$

x	0	7	?	21	?	?
y	?	?	2	?	4	5

Complete the ordered pairs of solutions of the equation.

5. $x + y = 5$ $(0, 5)$ $(1, 4)$ $(2, \;\;)$ $(3, \;\;)$ $(\;\;, 1)$ $(\;\;, 5)$

6. $x + 3 = y$ $(0, 3)$ $(1, \;\;)$ $(2, \;\;)$ $(\;\;, 6)$ $(\;\;, 7)$ $(5, \;\;)$

7. $x + 7 = y$ $(0, \;\;)$ $(2, 9)$ $(4, \;\;)$ $(\;\;, 13)$ $(8, \;\;)$ $(\;\;, 17)$

8. $x - y = 2$ $(2, 0)$ $(3, \;\;)$ $(4, \;\;)$ $(\;\;, 3)$ $(\;\;, 4)$ $(7, \;\;)$

9. $x - 4 = y$ $(4, \;\;)$ $(5, \;\;)$ $(6, 2)$ $(\;\;, 3)$ $(8, \;\;)$ $(\;\;, 5)$

Camping Out

Some problems have many possible solutions. An equation with two variables may help you to list those solutions.

Complete the equation. Then use the equation to complete the chart.

10. The temperature at home is 3°C more than it is at camp.

$c =$ temperature in °C at camp
$h =$ temperature in °C at home
$c + \;\;\; = h$

c	19	20	21	22	23	24
h	?	?	?	?	?	?

11. The weight of a camper is usually 4 lb less after camping for a week.

$b =$ weight in lb before camping
$a =$ weight in lb after camping
$b - \;\;\; = a$

b	135	138	141	144	147	150
a	?	?	?	?	?	?

12. Canteens sell for $5 each.

$c =$ number of canteens
$t =$ total cost in dollars
$\;\;\; c = t$

c	1	2	3	4	5	6
t	?	?	?	?	?	?

13. Three campers will share the cost.

$t =$ total cost in dollars
$e =$ cost in dollars for each camper
$\frac{t}{\;\;\;} = e$

t	90	96	102	108	114	120
e	?	?	?	?	?	?

Graphing Ordered Pairs

You can graph an ordered pair of numbers as a point on a number grid. The two numbers in the ordered pair are called the **coordinates** of the point on the grid.

To graph a pair of coordinates, start at 0 on the grid. The first coordinate tells you how far to move right from 0. The second coordinate tells you how far to move up.

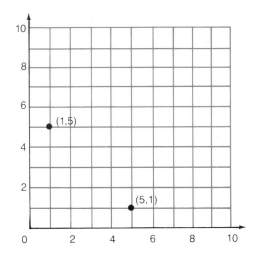

The coordinates (1, 5) name a point 1 unit to the right of 0 and 5 units up.

The coordinates (5, 1) name a point 5 units to the right of 0 and 1 unit up.

Exercises

Write the coordinates for these directions. Start at 0.

1. 4 units right and 7 units up

2. 8 units right and 3 units up

3. 2 units right and 5 units up

4. 5 units right and 2 units up

5. 1 unit right and 0 units up

6. 0 units right and 6 units up

Write the letter that names the coordinates.

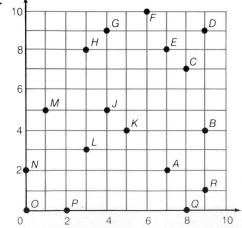

7. (7, 2)   **8.** (3, 8)

9. (6, 10)   **10.** (9, 1)

11. (4, 5)   **12.** (5, 4)

13. (3, 3)   **14.** (9, 9)

15. (8, 0)   **16.** (0, 2)

17. (2, 0)   **18.** (0, 0)

19. (9, 4)   **20.** (8, 7)

Write the coordinates for the letter.

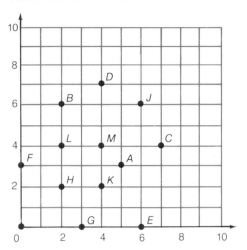

21. A	**22.** B	**23.** C
24. D	**25.** E	**26.** F
27. H	**28.** J	**29.** K
30. L	**31.** M	**32.** G

Geo-Graphing

Locate each point on a number grid.
Join the points in the given order.
Then join the last point to the first.
Name the type of quadrilateral that you
have drawn.

33. A (2, 2)   **34.** E (1, 3)
    B (5, 2)   F (8, 3)
    C (5, 8)   G (10, 7)
    D (2, 8)   H (3, 7)

35. J (3, 1)   **36.** N (8, 1)
    K (6, 4)   P (8, 6)
    L (3, 7)   Q (5, 9)
    M (0, 4)   R (0, 9)

Checkpoint B

Solve the equation. (*pages 226–227*)

1. $3a = 39$ **2.** $9z = 135$

3. $\frac{m}{2} = 41$ **4.** $\frac{t}{8} = 24$

Write and solve an equation to answer
the question. (*pages 228–229*)

5. What number divided by 3 is 21?

6. The product of what number and 7
is 154?

Solve the equation. (*pages 230–231*)

7. $q - 26 = 77$ **8.** $5r = 95$

9. $\frac{z}{14} = 3$ **10.** $b + 44 = 71$

Complete the ordered pairs of solutions
of $5x = y$. (*pages 232–233*)

11. (0, ■)   **12.** (■, 5)

13. (7, ■)   **14.** (■, 45)

Write the coordinates for the letter.
(*pages 234–235*)

15. P

16. Q

17. R

18. S

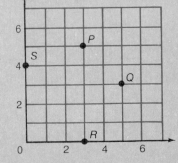

Extra practice on page 434   **235**

Problem Solving · USING EQUATIONS

1	Understand
2	Plan
3	Work
4	Answer

One equation may be used to solve problems that seem very different.

Lisa earned $8 mowing lawns. She earned $13 total mowing lawns and delivering papers. How much did she earn delivering papers?

paper earnings		lawn earnings		total earnings
x	+	8	=	13

Clark is driving 13 km to town. He knows that there are still 8 km ahead of him. How far did he already drive?

distance driven		distance to go		total distance
x	+	8	=	13

The same equation, $x + 8 = 13$, can be used to solve both problems.

$$x + 8 = 13$$
$$x + 8 - 8 = 13 - 8$$
$$x = 5$$

Check: $x + 8 = 13$
$5 + 8 = 13$ True

Lisa earned $5 delivering papers. Clark already drove 5 km.

Match the problem in the first column with an equation in the second column. Each equation will be used more than once.

1. A number a decreased by 3 is 24.

2. Three times the number a is 24.

3. One third of the number a is 24.

4. Three more than the number a is 24.

5. The product of a number a and 3 is 24.

6. The total of a number a and 3 is 24.

7. The sum of a number a and 3 is 24.

8. A number a shared equally by 3 is 24.

9. A number a minus 3 is 24.

10. Three less than a number a is 24.

A. $a + 3 = 24$

B. $a - 3 = 24$

C. $3a = 24$

D. $\frac{a}{3} = 24$

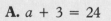

All of the problems in Exercises 11–16 can be solved using one of these equations.

$n + 4 = 20$	$4n = 20$	$n - 4 = 20$	$\frac{n}{4} = 20$

Choose and solve the correct equation for each problem. Then answer the question.

11. Nan has to buy 20 tulip bulbs for the garden. If each package contains 4 bulbs, how many packages does she have to buy?

12. The chorus is arranged in 4 rows. There are 20 students in each row. How many students are in the chorus?

13. This year there are 20 students in the Explorers' Club. This is four fewer students than last year. How many were there last year?

14. Ken has saved $4. If he and his sister put their savings together, they will have $20. What is the amount of his sister's savings?

15. Sue has agreed to pay back a loan in four equal payments. If each payment is $20, what was the amount of the loan?

16. Each of 4 friends will pay the same amount toward a magazine subscription. If the subscription costs $20, how much will each pay?

Write a problem that can be solved using the equation. Then solve the equation and answer the question.

★ **17.** $x + 5 = 12$ ★ **18.** $c - 9 = 14$ ★ **19.** $2n = 18$ ★ **20.** $\frac{t}{6} = 3$

Match.

1. a number r increased by 7

2. the product of 7 and a number r

3. twelve divided by a number r

4. twelve minus a number r

A. $7r$ **B.** $12 \div r$ **C.** $12 - r$ **D.** $r + 7$

Evaluate the expression. Use $a = 1$, $n = 4$, and $t = 20$.

5. $31 - n$ **6.** $\frac{t}{5}$ **7.** at **8.** $a + n + t$

Choose the solution of the equation. Write a, b, or c.

9. $38 + s = 54$

a. 20 **b.** 24 **c.** 16

10. $\frac{x}{12} = 3$

a. 36 **b.** 4 **c.** 15

Solve the equation.

11. $s + 11 = 34$ **12.** $42 + z = 73$ **13.** $w - 23 = 57$

14. $f - 9 = 54$ **15.** $3p = 42$ **16.** $8d = 56$

17. $\frac{a}{7} = 23$ **18.** $\frac{y}{3} = 13$ **19.** $\frac{x}{14} = 3$

Write and solve an equation to answer the question.

20. Triple what number is 51? **21.** One sixth of what number is 5?

Complete the ordered pairs of solutions to the equation. Then locate each point on a number grid and join the points in order. Name the type of figure that you have drawn.

22. $x + 2 = y$ (▮, 3) (3, ▮)

23. $\frac{x}{2} = y$ (▮, 3) (4, ▮)

24. $x - 2 = y$ (4, ▮) (▮, 0)

25. $3x = y$ (▮, 0) (1, ▮)

Choose $\frac{d}{2} = 12$ or $d - 2 = 12$ to solve the problem. Solve the equation and answer the question.

26. Two friends shared a package of trading cards equally. Each got twelve cards. How many cards were in the package?

Write as a mathematical expression. (*pages 216–217*)

1. eighty-six minus seven

2. twelve more than a number m

3. the product of a number y and 6

4. a number q divided by 3

Evaluate the expression. Use $t = 24$. (*pages 218–219*)

5. $t + 38$ **6.** $74 - t$ **7.** $9t$ **8.** $\frac{t}{8}$ **9.** $2t - 8$ **10.** $\frac{12}{t}$

Is the given number a solution of the equation? (*pages 220–221*)

11. $p + 36 = 82$; 46   **12.** $8r = 128$; 18   **13.** $\frac{m}{6} = 126$; 21

Write and solve an equation to answer the question. (*pages 222–231*)

14. What number minus 29 is 42?

15. 84 more than what number is 127?

16. What number divided by 5 is 19?

17. 6 times what number is 78?

Solve the equation.

18. $q - 29 = 13$ **19.** $b + 36 = 75$ **20.** $6m = 72$ **21.** $\frac{z}{7} = 17$

Complete the coordinates for solutions of $7x = y$. (*pages 232–233*)

22. (0, ▓)   **23.** (9, ▓)   **24.** (▓, 56)

Write the coordinates for each letter. Use the graph below. (*pages 234–235*)

25. R **26.** S **27.** M **28.** Q

Choose $3n = 54$ or $n + 3 = 54$ as the correct equation to solve the problem. Solve the equation and answer the question. (*pages 236–237*)

29. Donna needs three more trading cards to complete the set of 54. How many trading cards does Donna have?

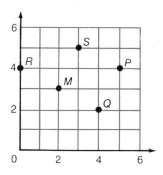

Functions

There are many times that one quantity depends on another. For example, the cost of a phone call to your friend in another state depends on the time of day that you make the call.

$$x = \text{time of day}$$
$$y = \text{cost of a 5-min phone call}$$

x	7:30 A.M.	9:30 A.M.	11:30 A.M.	1:30 P.M.	3:30 P.M.	5:30 P.M.	7:30 P.M.	9:30 P.M.	11:30 P.M.
y	$0.80	$1.94	$1.94	$1.94	$1.94	$1.28	$1.28	$1.28	$0.80

When the value of y depends on the value of x, we say that y is a **function** of x. A function can have only one value of y for each value of x.

The cost of your phone call is a function of the time that you make the call.

Does the chart show a function? Write *Yes* or *No*.

1. $x = $ cost of an item

$y = $ amount of sales tax

x	0¢ to 29¢	30¢ to 49¢	50¢ to 69¢	70¢ to 89¢
y	1¢	2¢	3¢	4¢

2. $x = $ sock size

$y = $ shoe size

x	$9\frac{1}{2}$	10	$10\frac{1}{2}$	11
y	$5 - 5\frac{1}{2}$	$6 - 6\frac{1}{2}$	$7 - 7\frac{1}{2}$	$8 - 8\frac{1}{2}$

Is y a function of x? Write *Yes* or *No*.

3. $x = $ number of minutes you talk

$y = $ cost of a long-distance phone call

4. $x = $ temperature

$y = $ cost of a long-distance phone call

5. $x = $ color of the package

$y = $ cost of mailing the package

6. $x = $ weight of the package

$y = $ cost of mailing the package

Here is another example of a function.

You know that it will take you one hour to make dinner tonight. The time that you can eat is a function of the time that you start to make dinner.

x = time that you start to make dinner
y = time that you can eat

x	5:00	5:15	5:30	5:45	6:00	6:15	6:30
y	6:00	6:15	6:30	6:45	7:00	7:15	7:30

In this function, each value of y is exactly one hour greater than the related value of x. Because each pair of values is related in exactly the same way, we say that this function has a constant rule.

x = time that you start to make dinner
y = time that you can eat
$x + 1$ (hour) $= y$

Write an equation for the rule of the function.

7.

x	2	4	6	8	10	12	14
y	4	8	12	16	20	24	28

8.

x	9	12	15	18	21	24	27
y	3	6	9	12	15	18	21

9.

x	1	2	3	4	5	6	7
y	3	5	7	9	11	13	15

10.

x	1	2	3	4	5	6	7
y	1	4	9	16	25	36	49

11. You must be at Jill's house one hour before she leaves.
x = time that Jill leaves
y = time that you must be there

12. You earn money mowing lawns at $2 an hour.
x = hours you work
y = total amount you earn

13. You need 45 min to deliver papers on your route.
x = time that you start
y = time that you finish

14. Two friends will share the profits of the car wash equally.
x = total profits
y = amount of each share

This tile pattern uses triangles, parallelograms, and trapezoids. Use the pattern to answer the questions.

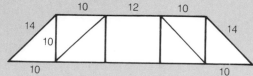

What is the perimeter of the shape?

1.   2.   3.  4.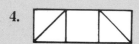

What is the area of the shape?

5.   6.   7.  8.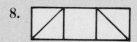

Write the letter of the equivalent fraction on the blackboard.

9. $\frac{6}{8}$ 10. $\frac{6}{18}$ 11. $\frac{12}{15}$

12. $\frac{11}{44}$ 13. $\frac{12}{28}$ 14. $\frac{3}{21}$

15. $\frac{17}{34}$ 16. $\frac{10}{15}$

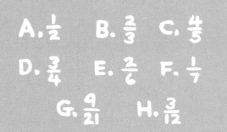

A. $\frac{1}{2}$ B. $\frac{2}{3}$ C. $\frac{4}{5}$

D. $\frac{3}{4}$ E. $\frac{2}{6}$ F. $\frac{1}{7}$

G. $\frac{9}{21}$ H. $\frac{3}{12}$

Write the fraction in lowest terms.

17. $\frac{15}{45}$ 18. $\frac{18}{66}$ 19. $\frac{9}{51}$ 20. $\frac{28}{42}$ 21. $\frac{45}{81}$ 22. $\frac{36}{63}$

What is the circumference of the circle named?

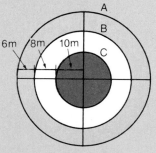

23. A   24. B   25. C

What is the area of the circle named?

26. A   27. B   28. C

29. Donna made 5 payments of $26 on a stereo. How much did she pay in all?

The ratio of the circumferences of the front and rear gears determines the difficulty of pedaling. Will the difficulty increase or decrease as the chain moves to a larger rear-wheel gear?

Ratio and Proportion

Ratio

A **ratio** is a quotient of two numbers that is used to compare one quantity to another. The seventh grade team won 7 games and lost 9 this season. You can write the ratio of wins to losses as shown below.

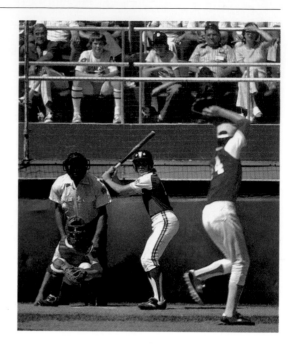

$$7 \text{ to } 9 \qquad 7:9 \qquad \frac{7}{9}$$

When a ratio is written as a fraction, you can simplify the fraction.

Last season, the seventh grade team won 10 games and lost 5.

The ratio of wins to losses is $\frac{10}{5}$, or $\frac{2}{1}$. In lowest terms, the ratio 10 to 5 is 2 to 1.

Exercises

Write the ratio as a fraction in lowest terms.

1. 3 to 7 **2.** 7 to 8 **3.** 6:5 **4.** 9 to 5 **5.** 8:7

6. 12:15 **7.** 14:7 **8.** 24 to 9 **9.** 100:10 **10.** 5 to 15

11. 18:81 **12.** 45:15 **13.** 17:51 **14.** 80:1240 **15.** 3:117

Write the ratio of responses as a fraction in lowest terms. Use the Product Survey Chart on the right.

16. excellent to good

17. poor to excellent

18. fair to good

19. excellent to total

20. good to fair

21. poor to total

22. poor to fair

PRODUCT SURVEY CHART	
Opinion	Number of Responses
Excellent	550
Good	125
Fair	40
Poor	15

A teacher is 152 cm tall and a student is 120 cm tall. Write the ratio as a fraction in lowest terms.

23. What is the ratio of the teacher's height to the student's height?

24. What is the ratio of the student's height to the teacher's height?

Central Junior High has 225 students and 9 teachers. Write the ratio as a fraction in lowest terms.

25. What is the ratio of students to teachers?

26. What is the ratio of teachers to students?

Last year the athletic department spent $275 for uniforms and equipment, $125 for swimming pool maintenance, $320 for transportation, and $30 for telephone. Write the ratio of the amount spent as a fraction in lowest terms.

27. swimming pool maintenance to telephone

28. uniforms and equipment to transportation

29. telephone to uniforms and equipment

30. transportation to telephone

31. transportation to uniforms and equipment

32. swimming pool maintenance to transportation

Estimating Ratios

We can estimate the ratio of the length of $\overline{AB}$ to the length of $\overline{CD}$. It looks as if $\overline{CD}$ is about 5 times as long as $\overline{AB}$. We guess that $\overline{AB}:\overline{CD}$ is about 1:5. Using a ruler, we find that $\overline{AB}$ is 2 cm and $\overline{CD}$ is 10.4 cm. The estimate 1:5 is close to the actual measurement of 2:10.4, or 1:5.2.

A   B

C   D

Guess the ratio of $\overline{AB}:\overline{CD}$. Check your estimate by measuring.

33.

A   B

C   D

34.

A   B

C   D

Rate

You may use a ratio to compare quantities of different kinds. Such a ratio is called a **rate.** Suppose you pay $3.50 to have 14 letters printed on a T-shirt. You are paying at a rate of $3.50 for 14 letters. You can find the cost per letter, or the **unit rate,** by dividing the amount of money by the number of letters.

money $\longrightarrow$ $\dfrac{\$3.50}{14} = \dfrac{\$.25}{1}$ $\longleftarrow$ letters

The unit rate is $.25 per letter.

Exercises

Complete.

1. $\dfrac{40}{10} = \dfrac{\blacksquare}{1}$

2. $\dfrac{300}{15} = \dfrac{\blacksquare}{1}$

3. $\dfrac{304}{16} = \dfrac{\blacksquare}{1}$

4. $\dfrac{1694}{22} = \dfrac{\blacksquare}{1}$

5. $\dfrac{962}{26} = \dfrac{\blacksquare}{1}$

6. $\dfrac{1394}{34} = \dfrac{\blacksquare}{1}$

7. $\dfrac{1083}{19} = \dfrac{\blacksquare}{1}$

8. $\dfrac{2640}{48} = \dfrac{\blacksquare}{1}$

Complete the unit rate.

9. 250 m in 10 minutes = ▨ m per min

10. 56 light bulbs in 7 cartons = ▨ light bulbs per carton

11. 432 pens in 12 boxes = ▨ pens per box

12. 75 pages in 15 minutes = ▨ pages per minute

13. $360 for 20 lessons = ▨ per lesson

14. $129.50 for 37 hours = ▨ per hour

15. $1872 for 6 months' rent = ▨ per month

16. $28.50 for 30 dozen eggs = ▨ per dozen

Find the unit rate.

17. A printing press prints 3000 pages in 60 minutes.

18. A stitcher is paid $54.90 for 366 pockets.

19. A delivery company charges $173.30 for 1733 packages.

20. An accountant completes 30 tax forms in $7\frac{1}{2}$ hours.

21. The Flower Shop charges $187.50 for 25 bouquets.

22. Leslie is paid $465.60 to deliver 582 copies of the Daily News.

23. Furniture Builders charges $259.50 to assemble 30 chairs.

24. The Urban Press paid $20.20 for 202 message units.

25. Brad receives $126.75 for selling 169 magazine subscriptions.

26. It costs $180 to make 3000 copies of a poster.

27. A typist types 1950 words in 30 minutes.

28. The Photo Shop charges $20.88 for 72 color prints.

Marty's Food Mart

The price of 224 g of jumbo shrimp is $4.59 at Marty's Food Mart.
The price of 1 g, or the unit price, is shown below.

$$\frac{\$4.59}{224} = \$.02 \text{ when rounded to the nearest cent.}$$

The unit price is $.02 per gram. This may be written as $.02/g.

Find the unit price.

29.

30.

Is the price correct? Write *Yes* or *No*.

★ **31.**

★ **32.**

Proportions

The hours worked by two store clerks are shown below.

Bryan worked 48 hours in 6 days.

$$\frac{48}{6} = \frac{8}{1}$$

Becky worked 40 hours in 5 days.

$$\frac{40}{5} = \frac{8}{1}$$

Becky and Bryan both averaged 8 hours per day. The ratios $\frac{40}{5}$ and $\frac{48}{6}$ are equal. An equation which states that two ratios are equal is called a **proportion.** Here are two ways to write a proportion.

$$\frac{40}{5} = \frac{48}{6} \qquad 40:5 = 48:6$$

We read the proportion as *40 is to 5 as 48 is to 6.*

Exercises

Are the ratios equal? Write *Yes* or *No.*

1. $\frac{2}{4}$ $\frac{1}{2}$

2. $\frac{2}{1}$ $\frac{1}{2}$

3. $\frac{2}{4}$ $\frac{2}{3}$

4. $\frac{7}{7}$ $\frac{3}{3}$

5. $\frac{12}{10}$ $\frac{6}{5}$

6. $\frac{6}{10}$ $\frac{60}{100}$

7. $\frac{4}{3}$ $\frac{8}{7}$

8. $\frac{18}{2}$ $\frac{9}{1}$

9. $\frac{15}{20}$ $\frac{30}{100}$

10. $\frac{7}{15}$ $\frac{14}{35}$

11. $\frac{42}{7}$ $\frac{54}{6}$

12. $\frac{9}{81}$ $\frac{5}{25}$

Write as ratios. Are they equal? Write *Yes* or *No.*

13. 1 out of 2 votes
5 out of 10 votes

14. 6 out of 7 days
7 out of 8 days

15. 3 absent out of 25
4 absent out of 30

16. 15 wins out of 21 games
10 wins out of 14 games

17. 85 correct out of 100
165 correct out of 200

18. 120 sold out of 125
360 sold out of 370

Write as a proportion in the two ways shown.

19. 1 is to 2 as 4 is to 8

20. 3 is to 5 as 21 is to 35

21. $5.00 is to 4 as $1.25 is to 1

22. $120 is to $7.50 as $4 is to $.25

Match with an equal ratio. Then write a proportion in two ways.

23. 21 to 36 votes

24. 1 box for a dollar

25. 30 jobs in 1 hour

26. 20¢ for 1 apple

27. 4 children per ball

28. 4 out of 5 trucks

29. 12 out of 20 people

30. 14 to 18 cups

31. 26 weeks in 6 months

32. 36 months in 3 years

33. 300 m in 45 seconds

34. 50 names in 1 column

A. $7:12$

B. $3:5$

C. $16:4$

D. $7:9$

E. $\frac{12}{12}$

F. $\frac{8}{10}$

G. $\frac{80}{4}$

H. $\frac{90}{3}$

I. $\frac{100}{2}$

J. $\frac{13}{3}$

K. $\frac{20}{3}$

L. $\frac{12}{1}$

Proportion Recreation

You can use the numbers 1, 2, 4, 8 to write the proportions shown.

$$\frac{1}{2} = \frac{4}{8} \qquad \frac{1}{4} = \frac{2}{8} \qquad \frac{2}{1} = \frac{8}{4} \qquad \frac{4}{1} = \frac{8}{2}$$

Write as many proportions as you can using all four numbers.

35. 2, 3, 10, 15

36. 6, 11, 18, 33

37. 5, 6, 10, 12

Calculator Corner

Here are test-drive results for cars.

How many kilometers per liter does each car get?

Round to the nearest tenth.

Car	Distance	Gasoline
Espirit GT	364.9 km	28.7 L
Voyager	501.3 km	34.4 L
Panther SXII	206.3 km	21.2 L

Solving a Proportion

If drill bits cost $3 for a package of two, how much will 8 drill bits cost? We can use a proportion to solve this problem.

Write n for the number you want to find. $3 is to 2 drill bits as $n is to 8 drill bits.

$$\frac{3}{2} = \frac{n}{8}$$

To solve a proportion, we complete two equal ratios. We can find a fraction equivalent to $\frac{3}{2}$ with the denominator 8.

$$\frac{3}{2} = \frac{3 \times 4}{2 \times 4} = \frac{12}{8} \quad \text{So, } n = 12.$$

Eight drill bits cost $12.

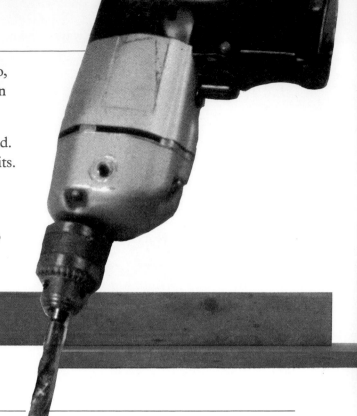

Exercises

Complete the equivalent fraction.

1. $\frac{4}{5} = \frac{\blacksquare}{10}$ **2.** $\frac{5}{6} = \frac{\blacksquare}{24}$ **3.** $\frac{8}{30} = \frac{\blacksquare}{15}$ **4.** $\frac{14}{21} = \frac{\blacksquare}{3}$

5. $\frac{3}{4} = \frac{6}{\blacksquare}$ **6.** $\frac{3}{4} = \frac{\blacksquare}{16}$ **7.** $\frac{3}{\blacksquare} = \frac{15}{20}$ **8.** $\frac{\blacksquare}{4} = \frac{18}{24}$

Solve the proportion.

9. $\frac{2}{7} = \frac{n}{21}$ **10.** $\frac{2}{7} = \frac{s}{28}$ **11.** $\frac{x}{7} = \frac{10}{35}$ **12.** $\frac{z}{7} = \frac{12}{42}$

13. $\frac{7}{9} = \frac{21}{n}$ **14.** $\frac{8}{24} = \frac{n}{6}$ **15.** $\frac{10}{26} = \frac{n}{13}$ **16.** $\frac{15}{x} = \frac{5}{9}$

17. $\frac{18}{24} = \frac{3}{n}$ **18.** $\frac{x}{8} = \frac{20}{32}$ **19.** $\frac{28}{a} = \frac{7}{9}$ **20.** $\frac{16}{30} = \frac{8}{n}$

21. $\frac{36}{42} = \frac{a}{7}$ **22.** $\frac{a}{14} = \frac{22}{28}$ **23.** $\frac{12}{20} = \frac{36}{x}$ **24.** $\frac{18}{n} = \frac{36}{42}$

25. $\frac{81}{36} = \frac{x}{4}$ **26.** $\frac{10}{n} = \frac{30}{42}$ **27.** $\frac{16}{25} = \frac{32}{x}$ **28.** $\frac{15}{28} = \frac{30}{n}$

Write the proportion using equal ratios. Then solve.

29. 1 is to 3 as 2 is to x

30. 1 is to 4 as 2 is to y

31. 1 is to 5 as p is to 10

32. 1 is to 6 as h is to 18

33. 2 is to 4 as 4 is to j

34. 2 is to k as 4 is to 9

35. 4 is to 12 as 20 is to a

36. b is to 27 as 1 is to 3

37. 10 kg is to 15 cm as 2 kg is to b cm

38. b kg is to 3 cm as 20 kg is to 30 cm

39. 5 adults is to 15 children as x adults is to 30 children

40. 3 hits is to 7 times at bat as 9 hits is to b times at bat

41. 5 wins is to 7 games as 10 wins is to x games

42. $2 for 1 hour is the same as $16 for a hours

Converting Measures

You can use a proportion to convert measures.

EXAMPLE Convert 8 m to cm.

1 m is to 100 cm as 8 m is to n cm.

$$\text{m} \longrightarrow \frac{1}{100} = \frac{8}{n} \longleftarrow \text{m}$$
$$\text{cm} \longrightarrow \qquad\qquad \longleftarrow \text{cm}$$

$$8 \text{ m} = 800 \text{ cm}$$

> Remember
> 1 m = 100 cm.

Use a proportion to convert the measure.

43. 9 m to centimeters

44. 7 L to milliliters

45. 5000 g to kilograms

46. 15 cm to millimeters

47. 31 km to meters

48. 900 g to kilograms

Solve.

49. Jim Phillips bought a 1300 g box of nails. Use a proportion to find how many kilograms he purchased.

★ **50.** A 2.7 kg box of bolts cost $54. What is the cost of 800 g?

Cross Multiplying

You can cross multiply to solve or check a proportion. Look at the proportion shown below.

$$\frac{40}{50} = \frac{8}{10}$$

The numbers 40, 50, 8 and 10 are called the **terms** of the proportion. When you cross multiply the terms of a proportion, the cross products are equal.

$$\frac{40}{50} = \frac{8}{10}$$
$$40 \times 10 = 50 \times 8$$
$$400 = 400$$

Solve this proportion.

$$\frac{12}{7} = \frac{60}{n}$$

Cross multiply.

$$12 \times n = 7 \times 60$$
$$12n = 420$$
$$\frac{12n}{12} = \frac{420}{12}$$
$$n = 35$$

You can check your answer by rewriting the proportion with 35 in place of n.

$$\frac{12}{7} = \frac{60}{35}$$
$$12 \times 35 = 7 \times 60$$
$$420 = 420 \quad \checkmark$$

Exercises

Find the cross products. Are the ratios equal? Write *Yes* or *No*.

1. $\frac{3}{2}$ $\frac{12}{8}$

2. $\frac{5}{15}$ $\frac{2}{6}$

3. $\frac{5}{6}$ $\frac{7}{8}$

4. $\frac{7}{28}$ $\frac{2}{8}$

5. $\frac{10}{4}$ $\frac{15}{6}$

6. $\frac{4}{9}$ $\frac{3}{5}$

7. $\frac{5}{2}$ $\frac{20}{8}$

8. $\frac{9}{10}$ $\frac{15}{20}$

Solve by cross multiplying.

9. $\frac{21}{x} = \frac{6}{2}$ 10. $\frac{14}{a} = \frac{7}{2}$

11. $\frac{x}{5} = \frac{10}{2}$ 12. $\frac{12}{9} = \frac{x}{6}$

13. $\frac{28}{n} = \frac{12}{3}$ 14. $\frac{25}{10} = \frac{15}{a}$

15. $\frac{4}{12} = \frac{n}{30}$ 16. $\frac{4}{n} = \frac{14}{35}$

17. $\frac{14}{12} = \frac{175}{x}$ 18. $\frac{v}{9} = \frac{143}{117}$

19. $\frac{0.7}{2.8} = \frac{n}{0.8}$ 20. $\frac{0.2}{a} = \frac{0.9}{2.7}$

21. $\frac{1.6}{0.8} = \frac{n}{0.6}$ 22. $\frac{n}{0.26} = \frac{0.1}{0.65}$

23. $\frac{0.4}{x} = \frac{0.32}{0.08}$ 24. $\frac{0.1}{0.15} = \frac{4}{a}$

Using Proportions

Solve.

25. A car travels 168 km on 14 L of gas. How far does it travel on 29 L of gas?

26. A machine produces 990 wheels in 6 hours. How many wheels are made in 13 hours?

27. Juan paid $5.76 for a 3.6 kg box of detergent. At that rate, how much will a 10.5 kg box of detergent cost?

28. A secretary typed 6 pages in 45 minutes. At that rate, how many pages can be typed in 4 hours? Hint: Change hours to minutes.

Checkpoint A

Write the ratio as a fraction in lowest terms. (*pages 244–245*)

1. 7 to 14 2. 15 to 3

3. 9:12 4. 20:30

Write the unit rate. (*pages 246–247*)

5. Motor oil: 12 cans for $20.28

6. Lunch bags: 50 for $1.25

7. Magnetic clips: 33 for $2.64

8. Paper plates: 55 for $1.10

Match with an equal ratio. Then write as a proportion in two ways. (*pages 248–249*)

9. $\frac{13}{52}$ 10. $\frac{3}{5}$ A. $\frac{57}{95}$ B. $\frac{1}{4}$

11. $\frac{13.5}{2.7}$ 12. $\frac{1.3}{15.6}$ C. $\frac{5}{1}$ D. $\frac{1}{12}$

Solve the proportion using equal ratios. (*pages 250–251*)

13. $\frac{5}{7} = \frac{n}{21}$ 14. $\frac{8}{25} = \frac{16}{n}$

15. $\frac{a}{4} = \frac{9}{12}$ 16. $\frac{56}{x} = \frac{112}{30}$

Solve the proportion by cross multiplication. (*pages 252–253*)

17. $\frac{4}{6} = \frac{6}{x}$ 18. $\frac{12}{9} = \frac{n}{6}$

19. $\frac{x}{12} = \frac{15}{9}$ 20. $\frac{1.2}{n} = \frac{8}{4}$

Scale Drawings

A **scale drawing** is a representation of a real object. The scale gives the ratio of the size in the drawing to the size of the actual object.

Here is a scale drawing of a bicycle.

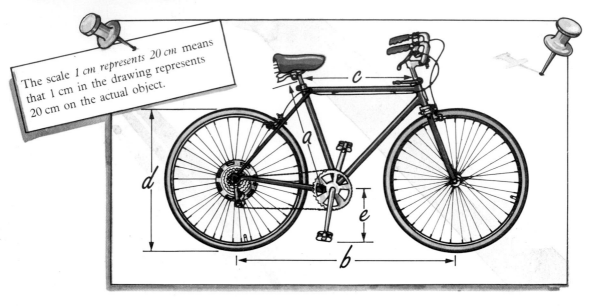

The scale *1 cm represents 20 cm* means that 1 cm in the drawing represents 20 cm on the actual object.

To find the actual size of the part marked by the letter *a*, we measure the length *a*. It is 3 cm. Then we write a proportion using the scale.

$$\frac{1}{20} = \frac{3}{n}$$ ← scale drawing
← actual object

$$1 \times n = 20 \times 3$$
$$n = 60$$

The measurement on the actual bicycle is 60 cm.

Exercises

Solve.

1. $\frac{1}{20} = \frac{5}{n}$ **2.** $\frac{1}{20} = \frac{7}{n}$ **3.** $\frac{1}{16} = \frac{5.5}{n}$ **4.** $\frac{1}{16} = \frac{7.4}{n}$

5. $\frac{1}{24} = \frac{2.5}{n}$ **6.** $\frac{1}{30} = \frac{3.8}{n}$ **7.** $\frac{1}{40} = \frac{84}{n}$ **8.** $\frac{1}{8} = \frac{76.4}{n}$

What is the measurement on the actual bicycle? Use the scale: 1 cm represents 20 cm.

9. *b*   **10.** *c*   **11.** *d*   **12.** *e*

In the drawing of the bicycle frame, 1 mm represents 16 mm. What is the measurement of each part on the actual frame?

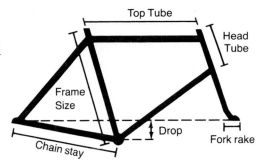

13. top tube   **14.** head tube

15. frame size   **16.** chain stay

17. fork rake   **18.** drop

Draw a line segment to represent the length of each object. Let 1 cm represent 5 cm.

19. a 5 cm bolt   **20.** a 10 cm hammer

21. a 15 cm pair of scissors   **22.** a 90 cm shovel

Let 1 cm represent 1 m.

23. a 6 m length of wire   **24.** a door 2.1 m high

25. a garage 2.7 m high   **26.** a ladder 3.9 m long

Seeing Is Believing

In order to show important details, an object may be drawn larger than its actual size.

When an object is drawn 5 times its actual size, the drawing has the scale: 5 cm represents 1 cm.

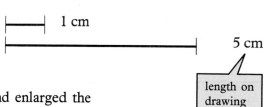

27. A scientist photographed a thumbprint and enlarged the photograph 10 times its actual size. The thumbprint is 18 cm wide in the photograph. What is the actual width of the thumbprint?

Maps

In the map below, 8 mm represents 100 km. Suppose we look at the map and estimate that the distance from Chicago to Toledo is about 400 km. You can check this estimate by copying the scale on a piece of paper and measuring the distance from Chicago to Toledo as shown below. The estimate of 400 km is a good one.

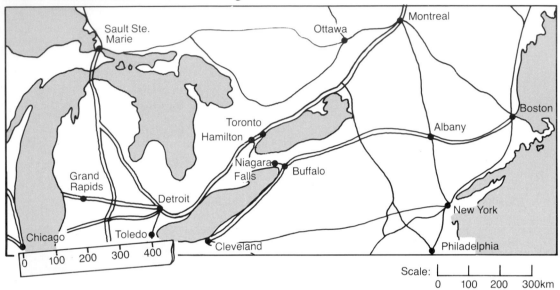

Exercises

Estimate the actual distance in kilometers. Check your estimate.

1. Chicago to Detroit

2. Chicago to Cleveland

3. Buffalo to New York

4. Boston to Philadelphia

5. Toronto to Hamilton

6. Grand Rapids to Albany

7. Montreal to Cleveland

8. Chicago to Boston

9. Toronto to New York

10. Albany to Cleveland

Find the shorter distance. Write *a* or *b*.

11. a. Grand Rapids to Toledo
b. Toledo to Chicago

12. a. New York to Philadelphia
b. Cleveland to Toledo

13. a. Montreal to Boston
b. Buffalo to Ottawa

14. a. Hamilton to Detroit
b. New York to Albany

Use the scale shown in the map to find the actual distance.

15. Los Angeles to Blythe

16. Tucson to Yuma

17. Flagstaff to Needles through Williams

18. Barstow to San Diego through Los Angeles

19. Tucson to Flagstaff through Phoenix

20. Needles to Yuma through Blythe and Phoenix

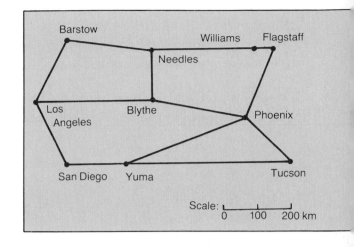

On the Map

21. A family in Tucson visits relatives in Williams. They travel through Phoenix and Flagstaff. How many kilometers do they travel to get to Williams?

22. How many kilometers will a group travel from San Diego to Blythe if they travel through Los Angeles? How many km will they travel if they go through Yuma and Phoenix?

23. A family lives in Yuma and wants to visit Phoenix and Tucson. They plan to travel to Tucson and then to Phoenix. Would the route be shorter or longer if they travel to Phoenix, then to Tucson?

★ **24.** A car uses about one liter of gasoline for a distance of 14 km on the highway. About how many liters of gasoline will the same car use on a trip from Los Angeles to Phoenix through Blythe?

From a piece of paper, cut out a rectangular region with a width-to-length ratio of 1 to 5. Cut the region into 5 pieces as shown on the right. Rearrange the 5 pieces to form a square.

Take a Break

Similar Triangles

Similar triangles have the same shape but not always the same size. In similar triangles, the **corresponding angles** are congruent and the **corresponding sides** are in proportion.

Triangles *JKL* and *PQR* are similar. The corresponding angles are marked alike. Here are the corresponding angles.

$$\angle J \text{ and } \angle P \qquad \angle K \text{ and } \angle Q \qquad \angle L \text{ and } \angle R$$

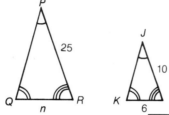

Notice that $\overline{KL}$ is opposite $\angle J$ and that $\overline{QR}$ is opposite the corresponding angle, $\angle P$. We say that $\overline{KL}$ corresponds to $\overline{QR}$.

Here are the corresponding sides of the two triangles.

$$\overline{JK} \text{ and } \overline{PQ} \qquad \overline{KL} \text{ and } \overline{QR} \qquad \overline{LJ} \text{ and } \overline{RP}$$

To find the length of $\overline{QR}$, we write a proportion using corresponding sides.

$$\frac{JL}{PR} = \frac{KL}{QR} \quad \Rightarrow \quad \frac{10}{25} = \frac{6}{n}$$

$$10 \times n = 25 \times 6$$

$$10n = 150$$

$$\frac{10n}{10} = \frac{150}{10}$$

The length of $\overline{QR}$ is 15 units.

$$n = 15$$

Exercises

Is the statement about similar triangles *JKL* and *PQR* true or false? Write *True* or *False*.

1. $\dfrac{JL}{PR} = \dfrac{KL}{QR}$ **2.** $\dfrac{JK}{PR} = \dfrac{KL}{QR}$ **3.** $\dfrac{PR}{JL} = \dfrac{LK}{RQ}$

Triangles *ABC* and *XYZ* are similar.
Name the corresponding angle.

4. $\angle A$ **5.** $\angle B$ **6.** $\angle C$

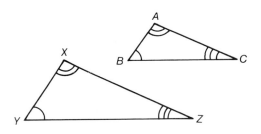

Name the corresponding side.

7. $\overline{AB}$ **8.** $\overline{BC}$ **9.** $\overline{AC}$

Complete.

10. $\dfrac{AB}{XY} = \dfrac{AC}{\blacksquare}$ **11.** $\dfrac{BC}{YZ} = \dfrac{AB}{\blacksquare}$ **12.** $\dfrac{AC}{\blacksquare} = \dfrac{BC}{YZ}$

For each pair of similar triangles, find *n*.

13.

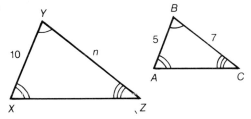

14.

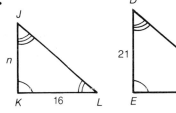

15.

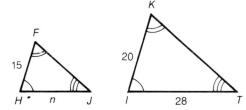

16.

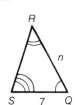

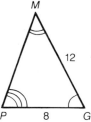

Similar Polygons

Polygons *MORT* and *NACK* are similar. The corresponding angles
are $\angle M$ and $\angle N$; $\angle O$ and $\angle A$; $\angle R$ and $\angle C$; $\angle T$ and $\angle K$.

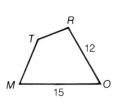

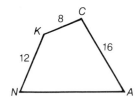

Name the corresponding side.

17. $\overline{KC}$ **18.** $\overline{MT}$ **19.** $\overline{CA}$ **20.** $\overline{MO}$

★ **21.** What is the length of $\overline{NA}$?

259

Similar Triangle Applications

You can use similar triangles to find the height of an object without actually measuring it. In the diagram shown below, the utility pole casts a shadow that is 6 m long. The lamppost is 7 m high and casts a shadow that is 2 m long.

Triangles *ABC* and *DEF* are similar, so you can write and solve a proportion to find the height of the utility pole.

$$\frac{h}{7} = \frac{6}{2}$$
$$2 \times h = 7 \times 6$$
$$2h = 42$$
$$h = 21$$

The height of the utility pole is 21 m.

Exercises

The two triangles are similar. Complete the proportion.

1. $\frac{h}{15} = \frac{\blacksquare}{6}$

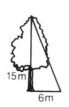

2. $\frac{h}{16} = \frac{\blacksquare}{8}$

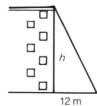
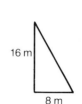

The two triangles are similar. Find *h*.

3.

4.

260

5.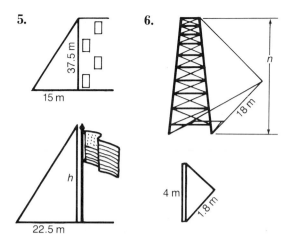

37.5 m

15 m

6.

n

18 m

4 m

1.8 m

h

22.5 m

In and Out of the Sun

Solve.

7. Jenny wanted to find the width of the river. She made the measurements as shown in the diagram. Triangles *APB* and *CDB* are similar. What is the width of the river?

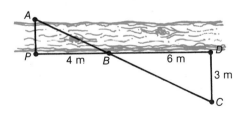

A

P   4 m   B   6 m   D

3 m

C

★ **8.** To find the height of the pole, Leo made use of the shadows as suggested by the diagram below. Leo is 1.6 m tall and his shadow is 0.8 m long. The pole's shadow is 5 m long. Triangles *DCA* and *EBA* are similar. How tall is the pole?

E   D

A   B   C

Checkpoint B

Find the measure of the actual object. (*pages 254–255*)

1. A saw is drawn 10 cm long. 1 cm represents 6 cm.

2. A house is drawn 9 cm long. 1 cm represents 3 m.

Use the scale in the map to find the distance in kilometers. (*pages 256–257*)

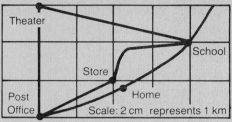

Theater

School

Store

Post Office

Home

Scale: 2 cm represents 1 km

3. theater to school

4. home to post office to theater

Triangles *ABC* and *DEF* are similar. Find the length of $\overline{DF}$. (*pages 258–259*)

5.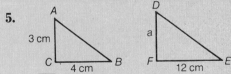

A

3 cm

C   4 cm   B

D

a

F   12 cm   E

6. If $\overline{DE}$ measures 15 cm, what is the length of $\overline{AB}$?

Solve. (*pages 260–261*)

Triangles *FDB* and *AEC* are similar.

7. What is the height of the pole?

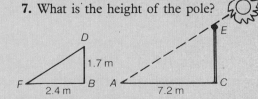

D

1.7 m

F   2.4 m   B

A   7.2 m   C

E

Problem Solving · USING PROPORTIONS

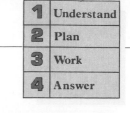

You can use proportions to solve a wide range of problems.

Carol spends 17 hours in a 2-week period practicing on the guitar for the school's talent show. How many hours does she practice in 5 weeks?

The problem asks for the number of hours practiced in 5 weeks.

The given facts include the rate of 17 h in (per) 2 weeks, and the unknown number of hours in 5 weeks.

The proportion is $\frac{17}{2} = \frac{n}{5}$.
hours
weeks

$$2n = 17 \times 5$$
$$\frac{2n}{2} = \frac{85}{2}$$
$$n = 42\frac{1}{2}$$

Therefore, in 5 weeks Carol practices $42\frac{1}{2}$ hours.

Write the proportion for solving the problem. Use n for the unknown number.

1. In a typing class, Steve typed 75 words in 2 minutes. At this rate, how many words can he type in 12 minutes?

2. The students in room 402 are making fruit punch for the end-of-term party. The fruit punch contains 5 parts of apple juice to 2 parts of cranberry juice. If 12 L of apple juice are used, how much cranberry juice should be used?

3. Jerry is sewing a new emblem on the school banner. The sewing machine makes 60 stitches on a 15 cm edge of the emblem. How many stitches will be made on a 25 cm edge?

Solve.

4. The student-teacher ratio at the Beechwood Junior High School is 53:2. There are 18 teachers. How many students are there?

5. Seven out of every 10 students at Lindsay Junior High attended the school picnic. If Lindsay Junior High has 2050 students, how many students attended the picnic?

6. At Brookfield Junior High, 13 out of every 300 students have paper routes. If there are 104 students with paper routes, how many students attend Brookfield Junior High?

7. The ratio of headphones in the language lab to the number of students who are taking a foreign language is 5:20. If there are 36 headphones in the language lab, how many students are taking a foreign language?

8. Of the 200 students who took part in a survey, 40 of them said they got their part-time jobs through the school's placement office. If there are 1750 students with part-time jobs, about how many of them got their jobs through the placement office?

9. The school office purchased 50 letter pads at $1.40 each and 24 memo pads. If the ratio of the price of one letter pad to the price of one memo pad is 1:4, what was the total cost?

10. In a typing test, Frances typed 136 words in 4 minutes. At that same rate, how long will it take her to type 3300 words?

11. In the school cafeteria, the cook uses 6.75 kg of meat to serve 60 people. How many people can be served with 24.3 kg of meat?

12. The Athletic Department bought a dozen cans of tennis balls at $2.50 each and 3 tennis rackets. If the ratio of the price of one can of balls to the price of one racket was 1:14, what was the total cost?

★ **13.** The ratio of boys to girls is 4:3 in one class. If there are 3 more boys than girls, how many boys and girls are in the class?

Write the ratio as a fraction in lowest terms.

1. number of excellent responses to number of good responses

2. number of fair responses to number of good responses

PRODUCT SURVEY	
Opinion	Number of Responses
Excellent	175
Good	35
Fair	10

Match with the correct answer.

3. A record makes 6000 revolutions in 5 minutes. What is the rate per second?   **a.** 300/s   **b.** 60/s   **c.** 20/s

4. The Photo Shop charges $10.44 for 36 color prints. What is the unit rate?   **a.** 19¢   **b.** 39¢   **c.** 29¢

Are the ratios equal? Write *Yes* or *No*.

5. $\frac{7}{15}$ $\frac{14}{30}$

6. $\frac{25}{40}$ $\frac{55}{80}$

7. $\frac{11}{12}$ $\frac{22}{24}$

8. $\frac{30}{100}$ $\frac{15}{20}$

Solve.

9. $\frac{20}{n} = \frac{60}{84}$

10. $\frac{36}{48} = \frac{6}{b}$

11. $\frac{14}{18} = \frac{56}{a}$

12. $\frac{42}{63} = \frac{k}{21}$

Find the actual length or distance. Let 5 cm represent 1 km.

13. A beam is 12 cm long in a scale drawing.

14. The distance from home to school is 2.5 cm in a map.

Find the height of the tree.

15. Triangles *MNP* and *QRS* are similar. $\overline{QR}$ = 4 m, $\overline{RS}$ = 25 m, and $\overline{NP}$ = 125 m.

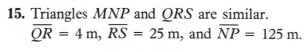

16. A bottling machine at Juice Quencher fills 125 bottles per minute. Each bottle contains 0.5 L of juice. How many liters of juice will be needed if the machine is to fill bottles for 8 hours?

Write as a fraction in lowest terms. (*pages 244–247*)

1. 8 cm : 32 cm

2. 9 red squares to 12 squares

3. 9 tablets for $2.55

4. 125 liters in 5 days

Write as a proportion in two ways. (*pages 248–249*)

5. 3 is to 4 as 75 is to 100

6. $90 for 9 tickets; $140 for 14 tickets

Solve the proportion. (*pages 250–253*)

7. $\dfrac{3}{x} = \dfrac{15}{35}$

8. $\dfrac{9}{11} = \dfrac{a}{33}$

9. $\dfrac{b}{40} = \dfrac{2}{5}$

10. $\dfrac{7}{63} = \dfrac{1}{d}$

In the map shown, 1 cm represents 50 km. Find the actual distance. (*pages 254–257*)

11. Main Junction to Sun City

12. West Enterprise to Sun City

13. Main Junction to West Enterprise

14. Main Junction to West Enterprise through Sun City

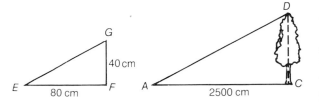

Triangles *ABC* and *DEF* are similar. Find the missing length. (*pages 258–259*)

15. Line segment *DF*
16. Line segment *BC*

Solve. (*pages 260–263*)

17. Triangles *EFG* and *ACD* are similar. How tall is the tree?

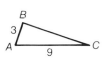

18. The student-teacher ratio at the Broody Junior High School is 106 : 4. There are 36 teachers. How many students are there?

Enrichment

Managing Information

Suppose you had to write a report for your science class. You have decided to report on "Volcanoes on Mars". How on earth would you find information on this subject?

If you're like most students, you would go to your library. There, you would look in books, encyclopedias, and magazines for information about your subject. Since "Volcanoes on Mars" is not a common subject, you might have a hard time finding enough information.

Soon, a computer may be able to help with your report. Some libraries have systems for doing computer data searching. If you give the computer the topic you're interested in, the computer will search its memory for information on this topic. The computer stores information from thousands of books, magazines, and newspapers. It will tell you where you can find facts about your topic.

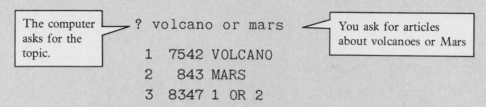

The computer asks for the topic.

? volcano or mars

You ask for articles about volcanoes or Mars

```
1   7542 VOLCANO
2    843 MARS
3   8347 1 OR 2
```

The computer tells you that there are 7542 volcano references in its memory (1). There are 843 items about Mars (2). And there are 8347 items about either volcanoes or Mars (1 or 2). Since you want to know about volcanoes on Mars, you change your input slightly.

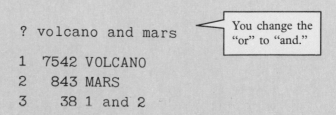

? volcano and mars

You change the "or" to "and."

```
1   7542 VOLCANO
2    843 MARS
3     38 1 and 2
```

This time the computer tells you that there are 38 references in its memory that are about both volcanoes and Mars (1 and 2). These are the articles you would be interested in.

Now you could have the computer print a brief summary of some or all of the articles about Martian volcanoes. It would also give the name and page number of the magazines and books. If you wanted to read the whole article, you could now locate the book or magazine.

Many businesses must be able to manage vast amounts of information. Often, they use computers. Otherwise, it would soon become too slow, expensive, and difficult to look up the facts and figures they need.

Many people work with computer terminals right on their desks. For example, travel agents use the computer to give them up-to-date information on which hotels have rooms available and the cost. They also use them to find which airlines fly to a certain city, when the flights are, and the cost. The computer can store information about thousands of hotels, airlines, and railroads all over the world.

Answer each question.

1. You are doing research on professional athletes. Which of the following would you type to the computer?
   a. ? baseball and football and basketball
   b. ? baseball or football or basketball

2. You want information about the relation of vitamins or protein to health. Which of the following would you type to the computer?
   a. ? health and (vitamins or protein)
   b. ? health or (vitamins and protein)

Maintaining Skills

Choose the best answer. Write *a*, *b*, *c*, or *d*.

Write as a decimal.

1. $\frac{4}{5}$
   a. 0.08
   b. 1.25
   c. 0.8
   d. None of these

2. $\frac{3}{8}$
   a. $2.6\overline{6}$
   b. 0.375
   c. 0.038
   d. None of these

3. $\frac{7}{9}$
   a. $0.7\overline{7}$
   b. 0.8
   c. 1.25714
   d. None of these

Write as a fraction in lowest terms.

4. 0.6
   a. $\frac{6}{10}$
   b. $\frac{2}{5}$
   c. $\frac{3}{5}$
   d. None of these

5. 0.57
   a. $\frac{34}{50}$
   b. $\frac{5}{7}$
   c. $\frac{57}{100}$
   d. None of these

6. 0.225
   a. $\frac{9}{40}$
   b. $\frac{225}{100}$
   c. $\frac{45}{200}$
   d. None of these

Multiply.

7. 9.56
   ×100
   a. 956
   b. 0.0956
   c. 95.6

8. 3.8
   ×10
   a. 380
   b. 0.38
   c. 38

9. 0.3
   ×100
   a. 3
   b. 0.03
   c. 30

Add.

10. 6.37
   +2.59
   a. 8.86
   b. 0.0896
   c. 8.96

11. 4.3
   +8.24
   a. 12.54
   b. 8.67
   c. 0.867

12. 6.39
   +2.7
   a. 0.909
   b. 9.09
   c. 6.66

13. 3.65 + 68
   a. 4.33
   b. 71.65
   c. 61.65
   d. None of these

14. 7.2 + 12.75 + 14
   a. 13.61
   b. 3.395
   c. 33.95
   d. None of these

15. 8.06 + 17 + 6.3
   a. 31.36
   b. 8.86
   c. 3.136
   d. None of these

What is the least common multiple (LCM)?

16. 3 and 8   **a.** 18
               b. 24
               c. 12

17. 7 and 21   **a.** 7
               b. 147
               c. 21

18. 12 and 30   **a.** 6
               b. 360
               c. 60

What is the prime factorization?

19. 30   **a.** $3 \times 5 \times 2$
      b. 6×5
      c. 10×3
      d. None of
          these

20. 56   **a.** $2 \times 2 \times 7$
      b. $7 \times 2 \times 4$
      c. $7 \times 2 \times 6$
      d. None of
          these

21. 98   **a.** 14×7
      b. $4 \times 3 \times 7$
      c. $7 \times 7 \times 2$
      d. None of
          these

What is the greatest common factor (GCF)?

22. 6 and 18   **a.** 2
               b. 18
               c. 6

23. 15 and 45   **a.** 45
               b. 9
               c. 15

24. 36 and 48   **a.** 8
               b. 12
               c. 144

Write as a whole number or mixed number.

25. $\frac{23}{9}$ **a.** $2\frac{6}{9}$

       b. $2\frac{5}{9}$

       c. $2\frac{2}{3}$

       d. None of
           these

26. $\frac{24}{3}$ **a.** 6

       b. $7\frac{4}{3}$

       c. 8

       d. None of
           these

27. $\frac{17}{8}$ **a.** $1\frac{9}{8}$

       b. $2\frac{1}{4}$

       c. $2\frac{1}{8}$

       d. None of
           these

Solve.

28. Saul ran 5.9 km on Monday, 3.75 km on Wednesday, and 8 km on
     Friday. How many kilometers did he run that week?

          a. 17.65 km

          b. 14.42 km

          c. 16.65 km

          d. None of these

Comparing Costs

A **unit price** is the cost per unit of a product.
Shoppers can save money by comparing unit prices of
different sizes of the same product.

PHOTO ALBUMS
$3.65 | $5.95
16-page | 40-page

Suppose you want to buy a photograph album. Your favorite store sells
16-page albums for $3.65 and 40-page albums for $5.95. Both albums
are the same kind and quality. Which is the better buy?

You need to solve two small problems to answer. Divide each selling
price by the number of pages in the album. Round answers to the
nearest cent.

$$\$0.228 = \$.23 \qquad \qquad \$0.148 = \$.15$$
$$16\overline{)\$3.65} \qquad \qquad \qquad 40\overline{)\$5.95}$$

The 40-page album costs less per page and is the better bargain.

Which is the better buy? Write *A* or *B*. Round unit prices to the
nearest cent. Assume the items you are comparing are the same kind
and quality.

	Item	A			B	
		Amount	**Cost**		**Amount**	**Cost**
1.	Water glasses	6	$10.99	or	4	$3.99
2.	Notebook paper	44 sheets	$1.51	or	200 sheets	$1.07
3.	Yarn	4 oz	$1.59	or	2 oz	$1.19
4.	Spiral notebook	250 pages	$3.97	or	230 pages	$2.37
5.	Pencil lead	30 pieces	$1.15	or	12 pieces	$ .60
6.	Pencils	1 dozen	$1.85	or	12 dozen	$18.00
7.	Paperclips	100	$3.90	or	500	$6.48
8.	Tape	60 yd	$1.79	or	100 yd	$1.35

Some supermarkets display unit prices. The store manager and price controller prepare price information for computer processing.

Complete these unit price tags. Round missing unit prices to the nearest thousandth. Round missing retail prices to the nearest cent.

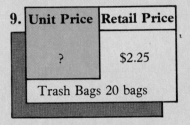

9.

Unit Price	Retail Price
?	$2.25

Trash Bags 20 bags

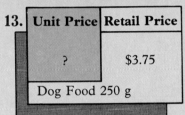

10.

Unit Price	Retail Price
.572 per portion	?

Haddock 4 fish portions

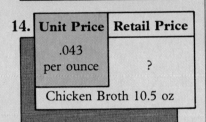

11.

Unit Price	Retail Price
?	$2.92

Laundry Powder 49 oz

12.

Unit Price	Retail Price
.071 per yard	?

Plastic Wrap 34.8 yd

13.

Unit Price	Retail Price
?	$3.75

Dog Food 250 g

14.

Unit Price	Retail Price
.043 per ounce	?

Chicken Broth 10.5 oz

Solve. Supply information that may be missing.

15. Laundry liquid can be bought at $2.46 per quart or at $6.55 per gallon. Which is the better buy? To the nearest cent, how much less does the better buy cost?

16. A drug store sells three different sizes of the same brand of toothpaste:
3 oz at $1.19   7 oz at $1.74   9 oz at $2.18
To the nearest thousandth, what is the unit price of each sized tube? Which is the best buy?

17. A quart of paint costs $4.05 and a gallon costs $10.40. A $3\frac{1}{2}$ gal can is available at $30.78. What is the least expensive way to buy $3\frac{1}{2}$ gallons of paint?

World Travel

In her job as travel agent, Margo Sawyer uses a calculator for quick computation of customers' travel expenses. She uses her computer terminal to find out plane schedules, ticket prices, and to confirm reservations. Margo also uses her terminal to keep track of details such as payments, passenger lists, and special needs of travelers. However, most of Margo's time is spent helping people travel for the least cost.

Use the cutouts from travel booklets to solve. Carefully choose the facts you need.

1. Lois Kemler will fly from Houston to New York in three weeks. There she will board a plane for Rome where she will attend business meetings for a week. Upon her return to New York, Lois will fly coach back home to Houston. What is the least amount that her air fare could be?

EAST-WEST AIR LINES

Houston-New York or New York-Houston

$550 first class, $232 coach, $228 night flight, $189 super saver (reservation 14 days in advance).

OCEAN AIRWAYS
ON-YOUR-WAY SPECIALS
Round-Trip Air Fares from New York Included

To	Spend 1 week	Spend Thurs.-Mon.
London	$410	$379
Paris	$533	$433
Rome	$642	$579

Jack Thorne is a tour director. He guides groups on foreign tours and makes sure that everything runs smoothly. Because he is thoroughly familiar with the countries on each tour, he can answer tourists' questions, such as, "How much does it cost in United States money?"

The worth of foreign money in United States money is called the **rate of exchange.** A rate of exchange can vary daily.

The chart shows some possible rates of exchange. Use the chart to find the equivalent cost in U.S. money. Round to the nearest cent.

2. dinner costing 16 English pounds

3. cuckoo clock costing 119 Swiss francs

4. guide book costing 2650 Italian lira

5. bulbs costing 230 Dutch guilders

6. stamps costing 5 French francs

Country	Rate of Exchange
England	$1.849 per English pound
France	$ .175 per French franc
Switzerland	$ .543 per Swiss franc
Italy	$.0008 per Italian lira
Netherlands	$ .395 per Dutch guilder

There are usually charges for cancelling a tour. Use the chart to solve.

7. Mr. and Mrs. Herbert had each paid $545 for a Tarlow tour of Europe. Twenty-four days before leaving, they had to cancel their trip. How much were they charged altogether for their cancellation?

TARLOW TOURS	
Number of Days Before Trip	**Cancellation Charge**
42 or more	Your $75 deposit
22–42	⅕ of tour cost
8–21	½ of tour price
1–7	⅗ of tour price

A Little at a Time

Sale! · FROST FREE ·

on Refrigerators
Pay $560.50 (full price)
or $61.39 down and
$25 for 24 months

Instead of paying the full cost of expensive items in cash, people sometimes make a down payment at the time of purchase and pay the rest in monthly installments, a little at a time. It costs more to buy on the installment plan, because stores add a finance charge for the service. These are the three steps you need to find the finance charge on the refrigerator in the newspaper ad.

Multiply the monthly installment amount by the number of months.

$$\begin{array}{r} \$\ 25 \\ \times\, 24 \\ \hline \$600 \end{array}$$

Then, add the down payment.

$$\begin{array}{r} \$600.00 \\ +\ \ 61.39 \\ \hline \$661.39 \end{array}\quad \text{Total cost}$$

Find the difference between the total cost and $560.50.

$$\begin{array}{r} \$661.39 \\ -\ 560.50 \\ \hline \$100.89 \end{array}\quad \text{Finance charge}$$

What are the total cost and the finance charge?

	Item	Price	Down Payment	Monthly Payment	Number of Months
1.	Television set	$ 375.25	$ 60.45	$ 20	18
2.	Living Room Set	$ 499.00	$ 80.00	$ 40	12
3.	Automobile	$ 7925.00	$ 400.00	$250	36
4.	Boat	$ 9257.00	$1100.00	$265	36
5.	Rug	$ 2554.00	$ 500.00	$100	24
6.	Camper	$17,205.00	$2000.00	$500	36

A credit advisor may suggest to people that their monthly payments for installment purchases should be no greater than $\frac{1}{5}$ their total monthly earnings.

Based on this information, can these people afford the monthly payments? Write *Yes* or *No*.

	Monthly Earnings	Monthly Payment
7.	$ 500	$125
8.	$ 750	$ 90
9.	$1320	$175

	Annual Earnings	Monthly Payment
10.	$ 8750	$152
11.	$15,906	$290

Which installment plan has a lower total cost?

12. 24 payments of $72 or 8 payments of $214

13. 12 payments of $45 or 3 payments of $160

Solve.

14. Suppose you bought a stereo and agreed to pay 12 monthly payments of $24 each. You have made 8 payments. How much have you paid so far?

15. Suppose you bought a camera and agreed to pay $73 in 12 monthly installments. You have made 7 payments. How much do you still owe?

Enrichment

Scale Measurement

A draftsperson is someone who draws accurate plans for engines, machinery, or buildings. A draftsperson may use a scale like the one below to measure distances and may use 1 inch to represent 1 foot or $\frac{1}{2}$ inch to represent 1 foot.

A draftsperson writes 1″ for one inch and 1′ for one foot. Using that way of writing, the scale below can be written as 1″ = 1′0″. On the scale, $2\frac{3}{10}$ have been marked off.

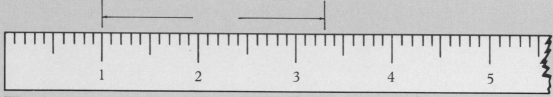

What is the actual length of each distance on the scale 1″ = 1′-0″?

1.
2.
3.
4.
5.

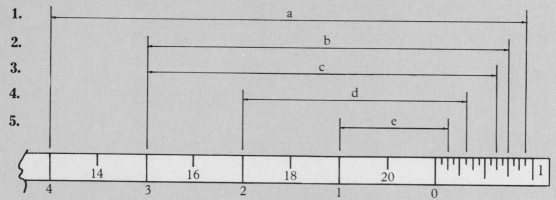

What is the actual length on the scale $\frac{1}{2}$″ = 1′-0″?

6.
7.
8.
9.

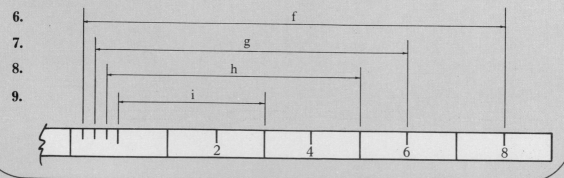

276

At almost 18 ft tall, a full-grown giraffe is the tallest of all animals. What percent of its adult height is a newborn giraffe that stands 6 ft tall?

Percents

Meaning of Percents

A **percent** compares a number to 100. The symbol % means *per hundred*. You can think of a percent as the ratio of a number to 100.

50% is the ratio of 50 to 100.

Suppose a farmer has plowed 92 hundredths of a field.

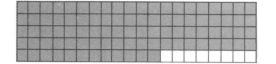

The ratio $\frac{92}{100}$ represents the part of the field that is plowed. $\frac{92}{100} = 92\%$

The ratio $\frac{100}{100}$ represents the whole field. $\frac{100}{100} = 100\%$

The part of the field that is unplowed is $100\% - 92\%$, or 8%. The ratio $\frac{8}{100}$ represents the unplowed part. $\frac{8}{100} = 8\%$

Exercises

Write as a percent.

1. $\frac{99}{100}$ **2.** $\frac{57}{100}$ **3.** $\frac{9}{100}$ **4.** $\frac{49}{100}$ **5.** $\frac{27}{100}$ **6.** $\frac{7}{100}$

7. 85 out of 100   **8.** 8 out of 100   **9.** 42 per 100   **10.** 5 out of 100

11. 16 per 100   **12.** 56 hundredths   **13.** 98 per 100   **14.** 13 hundredths

15. 3¢ tax per 100¢   **16.** $11 interest per $100   **17.** 9 rows plowed out of 100

18. 8¢ out of 100¢   **19.** $15 per $100   **20.** 5 out of 100 students

Complete the percent.

21. Tomatoes
30% ripe
▨% not ripe

22. Flowers
60% in bloom
▨% not in bloom

23. Seeds
45% planted
▨% not planted

24. Fence
▨% painted
10% not painted

Solve.

25. If 85% of the hay is mowed, what percent of the hay is not mowed?

26. If 40% of the crop has been picked, what percent of the crop is not picked?

Shady Shapes

Express the shaded area as a percent of the whole square. Express the unshaded area as a percent of the whole square. Use 3.14 for π. Hint: Remember the formulas for area.

27.

28.

29.

30.

31.

32.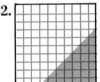

33.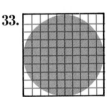

34.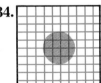

Chris can mow a lawn 100 m square in 4 hours. If she mows a lawn 50 m square at the same rate, how long will it take her?

100 m

Take a Break

Decimals and Percents

Credit card users at the Midwest Bank represent 0.65 of the customers. You can write the decimal 0.65 as a percent.

$$0.65 = \frac{65}{100} = 65\%$$

At the Midwest Bank, 65% of the customers use credit cards.

Decimals can be written as percents, and percents can be written as decimals. Study these examples.

Writing a Percent

$$0.45 = \frac{45}{100} = 45\%$$

$$0.07 = \frac{7}{100} = 7\%$$

We need a denominator of 100.

$$0.725 = \frac{725}{1000}$$

$$= \frac{725}{1000} = \frac{725 \div 10}{1000 \div 10}$$

$$= \frac{72.5}{100} = 72.5\%$$

Writing a Decimal

$$6\% = \frac{6}{100} = 0.06$$

$$78\% = \frac{78}{100} = 0.78$$

We want a whole number in the numerator.

$$5.4\% = \frac{5.4}{100}$$

$$= \frac{5.4}{100} = \frac{5.4 \times 10}{100 \times 10}$$

$$= \frac{54}{1000} = 0.054$$

Exercises

Complete to write the decimal as a percent.

1. $0.09 = \frac{\blacksquare}{100} = \blacksquare\%$

2. $0.71 = \frac{\blacksquare}{100} = \blacksquare\%$

3. $0.125 = \frac{\blacksquare}{1000} = \frac{\blacksquare}{100} = \blacksquare\%$

4. $0.60 = \frac{\blacksquare}{100} = \blacksquare\%$

5. $0.05 = \frac{\blacksquare}{100} = \blacksquare\%$

6. $0.064 = \frac{\blacksquare}{1000} = \frac{\blacksquare}{100} = \blacksquare\%$

Complete to write the percent as a decimal.

7. $84\% = \frac{\blacksquare}{100} = 0.\blacksquare$

8. $6\% = \frac{\blacksquare}{100} = 0.\blacksquare$

9. $20.5\% = \frac{\blacksquare}{100} = \frac{\blacksquare}{1000} = 0.\blacksquare$

10. $4\% = \frac{\blacksquare}{100} = 0.\blacksquare$

11. $95\% = \frac{\blacksquare}{100} = 0.\blacksquare$

12. $8.2\% = \frac{\blacksquare}{100} = \frac{\blacksquare}{1000} = 0.\blacksquare$

Write as a percent.

13. 0.37   **14.** 0.01   **15.** 0.81   **16.** 0.85   **17.** 0.40

18. 0.3   **19.** 0.7   **20.** 0.015   **21.** 0.21   **22.** 0.849

23. 0.52   **24.** 0.333   **25.** 0.74   **26.** 0.05   **27.** 0.125

28. 0.2   **29.** 0.065   **30.** 0.66   **31.** 0.913   **32.** 0.47

Write as a decimal.

33. 25%   **34.** 44%   **35.** 63%   **36.** 8%   **37.** 75%

38. 1%   **39.** 33.3%   **40.** 50%   **41.** 20%   **42.** 1.6%

43. 80%   **44.** 66.7%   **45.** 1.5%   **46.** 95%   **47.** 5%

Taking the Credit

Solve.

48. A credit card company makes charges of 1.5% per month for customers who do not pay their entire bill. Write the percent as a decimal.

49. More than 0.75 of the money deposited in the Midwest Bank is in checks. Write the decimal as a percent.

50. The Midwest Bank's lending rate is 15.75%. Write the percent as a decimal.

★ **51.** Depositors with savings accounts under $10,000 have 0.689 of all savings accounts at the Midwest Bank. What percent of the savings accounts at the Midwest Bank have balances over $10,000?

Percents and Fractions

A frostless refrigerator may use about 40% more electricity per month than a regular refrigerator. We can write 40% as a fraction in lowest terms.

$$40\% = \frac{40}{100} = \frac{2}{5}$$

A frostless refrigerator uses about $\frac{2}{5}$ more electricity per month than a regular refrigerator.

To write a percent as a fraction in lowest terms, first write the percent as the ratio of a number to 100. Then write the ratio as a fraction in lowest terms.

$$8\% = \frac{8}{100} = \frac{2}{25} \qquad\qquad 2.5\% = \frac{2.5}{100} = \frac{25}{1000} = \frac{1}{40}$$

Exercises

Complete. Write the fraction in lowest terms.

1. $10\% = \frac{10}{100} = \blacksquare$

2. $30\% = \frac{30}{100} = \blacksquare$

3. $90\% = \frac{90}{100} = \blacksquare$

4. $35\% = \frac{35}{100} = \blacksquare$

5. $5\% = \frac{5}{100} = \blacksquare$

6. $85\% = \frac{85}{100} = \blacksquare$

7. $48\% = \frac{48}{100} = \blacksquare$

8. $24\% = \frac{24}{100} = \blacksquare$

9. $36\% = \frac{36}{100} = \blacksquare$

10. $8.3\% = \frac{8.3}{100} = \frac{\blacksquare}{1000}$

11. $98.9\% = \frac{98.9}{100} = \frac{\blacksquare}{1000}$

12. $14.7\% = \frac{14.7}{100} = \frac{\blacksquare}{1000}$

13. $6.9\% = \frac{6.9}{100} = \frac{\blacksquare}{1000}$

Write as a fraction in lowest terms.

14. 25%	**15.** 1%	**16.** 60%	**17.** 50%	**18.** 45%
19. 20%	**20.** 40%	**21.** 80%	**22.** 5%	**23.** 2%
24. 8%	**25.** 12%	**26.** 70%	**27.** 65%	**28.** 6%
29. 12.1%	**30.** 66.7%	**31.** 87.5%	**32.** 37.2%	**33.** 62.8%

Complete the chart. Write the fractions in lowest terms.

	Percent	Decimal	Fraction
34.	10%	?	?
35.	12.5%	?	?
36.	20%	?	?
37.	25%	?	?
38.	37.5%	?	?
39.	40%	?	?
40.	50%	?	?
41.	60%	?	?
42.	62.5%	?	?
43.	75%	?	?
44.	80%	?	?
45.	87.5%	?	?

Fractional Percents

Sometimes a percent is a mixed number or a fraction. Here's how to write $33\frac{1}{3}\%$ as a fraction.

$$33\frac{1}{3}\% = \frac{33\frac{1}{3}}{100} = 33\frac{1}{3} \div 100$$
$$= \frac{100}{3} \times \frac{1}{100} = \frac{1}{3}$$

Complete to write the percent as a fraction in lowest terms.

46. $66\frac{2}{3}\% = 66\frac{2}{3} \div 100 = \underline{\quad}$

47. $12\frac{1}{2}\% = 12\frac{1}{2} \div 100 = \underline{\quad}$

48. $\frac{1}{4}\% = \frac{1}{4} \div \underline{\quad} = \underline{\quad}$

49. $1\frac{3}{4}\% = 1\frac{3}{4} \div \underline{\quad} = \underline{\quad}$

Write the percent as a fraction in lowest terms.

50. $6\frac{2}{3}\%$ **51.** $5\frac{1}{2}\%$ **52.** $\frac{1}{2}\%$ **53.** $20\frac{1}{4}\%$ **54.** $12\frac{2}{3}\%$ **55.** $7\frac{1}{2}\%$

Fractions and Percents

World Tours requires you to pay a deposit of $\frac{2}{5}$ of the cost of a trip at the time you make a reservation. What percent of the cost is the amount of the deposit?

To write a fraction as a percent, first write the fraction as hundredths. Then name the percent.

$$\frac{2}{5} = \frac{?}{100} \quad \Rrightarrow \quad \frac{2}{5} = \frac{2 \times 20}{5 \times 20} = \frac{40}{100} = 40\%$$

World Tours requires a deposit of 40% of the cost of the trip when you make a reservation.

You may also write a fraction as a percent by first writing it in decimal form.

$$\frac{1}{8} \quad \Rrightarrow \quad 8\overline{)1.000}^{\,0.125} \quad \Rrightarrow \quad 12.5\%$$

Sometimes, a two-place decimal and a fraction may be used to express a percent.

$$\frac{2}{3} \quad \Rrightarrow \quad 3\overline{)2.00}^{\,0.66\frac{2}{3}} \quad \Rrightarrow \quad 66\frac{2}{3}\%$$

Exercises

Complete.

1. $\frac{1}{4} = \frac{\blacksquare}{100} = \blacksquare\%$

2. $\frac{1}{5} = \frac{\blacksquare}{100} = \blacksquare\%$

3. $\frac{4}{5} = \frac{\blacksquare}{100} = \blacksquare\%$

4. $\frac{1}{20} = \frac{\blacksquare}{100} = \blacksquare\%$

5. $\frac{1}{25} = \frac{\blacksquare}{100} = \blacksquare\%$

6. $\frac{1}{10} = \frac{\blacksquare}{100} = \blacksquare\%$

7. $\frac{3}{5} \quad \Rrightarrow \quad 5\overline{)3.00}^{\,0.\blacksquare} \quad \Rrightarrow \quad \blacksquare\%$

8. $\frac{3}{8} \quad \Rrightarrow \quad 8\overline{)3.000}^{\,0.\blacksquare} \quad \Rrightarrow \quad \blacksquare\%$

9. $\frac{5}{8} \quad \Rrightarrow \quad 8\overline{)5.000}^{\,0.\blacksquare} \quad \Rrightarrow \quad \blacksquare\%$

10. $\frac{3}{50} \quad \Rrightarrow \quad 50\overline{)3.00}^{\,0.\blacksquare} \quad \Rrightarrow \quad \blacksquare\%$

11. $\frac{1}{7} \quad \Rrightarrow \quad 7\overline{)1.00}^{\,0.\blacksquare\frac{2}{7}} \quad \Rrightarrow \quad \blacksquare\%$

12. $\frac{2}{9} \quad \Rrightarrow \quad 9\overline{)2.00}^{\,0.\blacksquare\frac{2}{9}} \quad \Rrightarrow \quad \blacksquare\%$

Write as percents.

13. $\frac{1}{2}$; $\frac{2}{2}$

14. $\frac{1}{3}$; $\frac{2}{3}$; $\frac{3}{3}$

15. $\frac{1}{4}$; $\frac{2}{4}$; $\frac{3}{4}$; $\frac{4}{4}$

16. $\frac{1}{5}$; $\frac{2}{5}$; $\frac{3}{5}$; $\frac{4}{5}$; $\frac{5}{5}$

17. $\frac{1}{8}$; $\frac{3}{8}$; $\frac{5}{8}$; $\frac{7}{8}$; $\frac{8}{8}$

18. $\frac{1}{12}$; $\frac{5}{12}$; $\frac{7}{12}$; $\frac{11}{12}$; $\frac{12}{12}$

19. $\frac{1}{25}$; $\frac{2}{25}$; $\frac{3}{25}$; $\frac{4}{25}$; $\frac{9}{25}$

Rounding Percents

Sometimes you may need to round percents. For example, consider a writing $\frac{7}{9}$ as a percent.

$$\frac{7}{9} = 7 \div 9 = 0.777777\ldots.$$

To the nearest whole percent:

$$\frac{7}{9} = 77.7777\ldots\% \approx 78\%$$

To the nearest tenth of a percent:

$$\frac{7}{9} = 77.7777\ldots\% \approx 77.8\%$$

Round to the nearest whole percent.

20. 66.6666%　　**21.** 33.$\overline{3}$%　　**22.** 88.$\overline{8}$%

Write as a percent, to the nearest whole percent and the nearest tenth of a percent.

23. $\frac{3}{8}$　　　**24.** $\frac{5}{9}$　　　**25.** $\frac{1}{3}$

Checkpoint A

Write as a percent. (*pages 278–279*)

1. 4 hundredths

2. $\frac{82}{100}$

3. 56 per 100

4. 6¢ on 100¢

Write as a percent. (*pages 280–281*)

5. 0.2

6. 0.69

7. 0.33

8. 0.125

Write as a decimal. (*pages 280–281*)

9. 32%

10. 7%

11. 50%

12. 95.5%

Write as a fraction in lowest terms. (*pages 282–283*)

13. 75%

14. 8%

15. 8.2%

16. 87.5%

Write as a percent. (*pages 284–285*)

17. $\frac{5}{8}$

18. $\frac{11}{25}$

19. $\frac{7}{10}$

20. $\frac{5}{6}$

21. $\frac{2}{3}$

22. $\frac{3}{8}$

Finding a Percent of a Number

A television commercial claims that 80% of the people questioned preferred *Clean and Bright.* If 75 people were questioned, how many preferred *Clean and Bright?*

To answer this question, we can write and solve an equation. Let n be the number of people who preferred *Clean and Bright.*

$$\text{What number is 80\% of 75?}$$
$$n = 80\% \times 75$$

To solve the equation, we must first write 80% as either a decimal or a fraction.

Using a decimal

$80\% = 0.80$

$n = 80\% \times 75$

$n = 0.80 \times 75$

$n = 60$

or

Using a fraction

$80\% = \frac{80}{100} = \frac{4}{5}$

$n = 80\% \times 75$

$n = \frac{4}{5} \times 75$

$n = 60$

Out of 75 people questioned, 60 preferred *Clean and Bright.*

Exercises

Complete.

1. a is 10% of 60

$a = 0.1 \times \blacksquare$

$a = \blacksquare$

2. b is 50% of 100

$b = 0.5 \times \blacksquare$

$b = \blacksquare$

3. c is 25% of 200

$c = 0.\blacksquare \times \blacksquare$

$c = \blacksquare$

4. d is 25% of 80

$d = \frac{1}{4} \times \blacksquare$

$d = \blacksquare$

5. e is 50% of 150

$e = \frac{1}{\blacksquare} \times \blacksquare$

$e = \blacksquare$

6. f is 7% of 400

$f = \frac{\blacksquare}{\blacksquare} \times 400$

$f = \blacksquare$

Solve. Use a decimal to write the percent.

7. 25% of 80 is a

8. 40% of 100 is b

9. 15% of 70 is c

10. 2% of 90 is d

11. 10% of 40 is e

12. 30% of 75 is f

13. 63% of 70 is g

14. 50% of 84 is h

15. 25% of 96 is k

Solve. Use a fraction to write the percent.

16. 50% of 40 is m

17. 20% of 120 is n

18. 75% of 52 is p

19. 40% of 60 is q

20. 95% of 60 is r

21. 8% of 50 is u

22. 12% of 50 is v

23. $66\frac{2}{3}$% of 96 is w

24. $33\frac{1}{3}$% of 48 is x

Solve.

25. 70% of 60 is y

26. 40% of 70 is z

27. 80% of 90 is a

28. 4% of 78 is b

29. $33\frac{1}{3}$% of 100 is c

30. 7% of 63 is d

31. 95% of 70 is e

32. 2% of 45 is f

33. 9% of 25 is g

Complete.

34. 1% of 200 is ▒

$\frac{1}{2}$% of 200 is ▒

$1\frac{1}{2}$% of 200 is ▒

35. 1% of 600 is ▒

0.5% of 600 is ▒

2.5% of 600 is ▒

36. 1% of 1200 is ▒

0.25% of 1200 is ▒

9.25% of 1200 is ▒

Approximating Percents

You can approximate a percent of a number by rounding.

54% of 168 ≈ 50% of 200, or 100

Round to tens.

Round to hundreds.

Round to the highest place to approximate the answer.

37. 48% of 1156

38. 32% of 87

39. $16\frac{1}{2}$% of 430

40. $9\frac{1}{4}$% of 78

41. 31% of 2292

42. $5\frac{1}{8}$% of 20

★ **43.** Out of 1200 people questioned, $48\frac{1}{2}$% had never used *Clean and Bright*. How many of the people questioned had used *Clean and Bright?*

Finding the Percent One Number Is of Another

Suppose you have a job waiting on tables and the customers at one table leave you a tip of $6. If their total bill is about $40, what percent of the total bill is the tip?

To answer this question, write and solve an equation. Let n stand for the decimal form of the percent to be found.

$$\text{What percent of \$40 is \$6?}$$
$$n \times 40 = 6$$

Divide both sides by 40. $\quad n = \dfrac{6}{40}$

$$= 0.15$$
$$= 15\%$$

The tip is 15% of the total.

Exercises

Complete to write the equation.

1. What percent of 10 is 9?
$n \times 10 = $ ▩

2. 24 is what percent of 32?
$24 = n \times$ ▩

3. What percent of 24 is 12?
$n \times$ ▩ $= 12$

4. 45 is what percent of 135?
▩ $= n \times 135$

Solve the equation to find n as a percent.

5. $n \times 200 = 150$

6. $n \times 60 = 15$

7. $n \times 45 = 9$

8. $n \times 15 = 5$

9. $n \times 120 = 80$

10. $n \times 70 = 10$

Solve.

11. What percent of 18 is 9?

12. What percent of 28 is 21?

13. What percent of 10 is 8?

14. What percent of 10 is 5?

15. What percent of 55 is 11?

16. What percent of 48 is 12?

17. What percent of 24 is 18?

18. What percent of 32 is 16?

19. What percent of 50 is 20?

20. What percent of 60 is 24?

21. What percent of 64 is 16?

22. What percent of 80 is 24?

23. What percent of 280 is 70?

24. What percent of 375 is 75?

25. 4 is what percent of 80?

26. 16 is what percent of 25?

27. 5 is what percent of 20?

28. 13 is what percent of 65?

29. 36 is what percent of 180?

30. 260 is what percent of 650?

On the Job

What percent of the bill is the amount of the tip left by these customers?

31. Bill: $10.00; Tip: $1.50

32. Bill: $12.00; Tip: $2.40

33. Bill: $12.00; Tip: $1.50

34. Bill: $32.00; Tip: $4.00

35. Bill: $18.50; Tip: $3.70

36. Bill: $24.00; Tip: $4.20

In one week Carl earned wages of $80 and tips of $64.

37. What percent of his wages were his tips?

38. What percent of his total earnings were the tips?

★ **39.** Deductions of $12.75 were taken from Carl's wages. To the nearest whole percent, what percent of his wages were deducted?

Calculator Corner

Which station broadcasts music for the greatest percent of the time?

WADD — 19 out of 110 hours
WDIV — 95 out of 168 hours
WPRT — 45 out of 78 hours
WMUL — 84 out of 155 hours
KSUB — 58 out of 125
KSQR — 75 out of 135

Finding the Original Number

There are 70 students from Grade 7 in the band at Larson Junior High School. If 35% of the members of the band are seventh graders, how many students are there in the band?

Let n stand for the total number of students in the band.

$$35\% \text{ of what number is } 70?$$
$$35\% \times n = 70$$
$$0.35 \times n = 70$$

Divide both sides by 0.35. $\quad n = \dfrac{70}{0.35}$

$$n = 200$$

There are 200 students in the band in all.

Exercises

Complete to write the equation.

1. 50% of n is 14

$0.50 \times \boxed{} = 14$

2. 60% of what number is 20?

$0.60 \times n = \boxed{}$

3. 36 is 25% of what number?

$36 = \boxed{} \times n$

4. 50 is 5% of n

$50 = \boxed{} \times n$

Choose the correct equation. Write a, b, or c.

5. 10% of n is 25

a. $0.10 \times n = 25$

b. $0.10 = n \times 25$

c. $n = 0.10 \times 25$

6. 40% of what number is 30?

a. $0.40 = n \times 30$

b. $30 = 0.40 \times n$

c. $n = 40 \times 30$

Solve.

7. 20% of f is 6

8. 20% of g is 8

9. 50% of c is 17

10. 60% of p is 21

11. 40% of q is 10

12. 25% of d is 12

13. 80% of n is 52

14. 70% of a is 16.8

15. 50% of b is 12.5

16. 3% of m is 24.9

17. 5% of c is 4,000

18. 10% of d is 45,000

19. 65% of f is $1.95

20. 55% of h is $52.25

21. 85% of k is $5,000,000

22. 70% of what number is 140?

23. 2% of what number is 8?

24. 15% of what number is 300?

25. 40% of what number is 360?

26. 10% of what amount is $3.20?

27. 8% of what number is 518?

28. 58% of what number is 261?

29. 45% of what amount is $95.40?

On the Calculator

Percent equations all have the same form.

$$\text{Factor} \times \text{Factor} = \text{Product}$$

To solve an equation like this using a calculator, you must either multiply or divide. You multiply to find the product. You divide the product by a known factor to find the other factor.

EXAMPLE 1	**EXAMPLE 2**	**EXAMPLE 3**
$0.60 \times 20 = x$	$r \times 500 = 200$	$0.25 \times n = 140$
	$r = \frac{200}{500}$	$n = \frac{140}{0.25}$
$0.60 \boxed{\times} 20 \boxed{=} 12$	$200 \boxed{\div} 500 \boxed{=} 0.40$	$140 \boxed{\div} 0.25 \boxed{=} 560$

Write the multiplication or division necessary to solve the equation using a calculator. Solve with a calculator if you have one.

30. $r \times 60 = 540$

31. $0.60 \times 540 = p$

32. $d \times 324 = 540$

33. $0.60 \times 324 = x$

34. $r \times 540 = 60$

35. $0.60 \times b = 540$

The Three Cases of Percents

50% of the 120 members of the Bear Mountain Club went on the hike. The first example below shows that 50% of 120 is 60. Thus, 60 members of the club went on the hike. These examples show the three cases of percent problems.

EXAMPLE   Find 50% of 120.
$n = 50\% \times 120$
$\quad = 0.50 \times 120 \quad = 60$
50% of 120 is 60.

EXAMPLE   What percent of 200 is 120?
$n \times 200 = 120$
$n = \frac{120}{200}$
$\quad = 0.60 \quad = 60\%$
120 is 60% of 200.

EXAMPLE   40% of what number is 150?
$40\% \times n = 150$
$0.40 \times n = 150$
$n = \frac{150}{0.40} \quad = 375$
40% of 375 is 150.

Exercises

Match the exercise with the equation.

1. 60% of what number is 420?

2. Find 40% of 160.

3. 40% of what number is 160?

4. What percent of 420 is 140?

5. Find 60% of 420.

6. What percent of 640 is 160?

A. $n = 60\% \times 420$

B. $n \times 420 = 140$

C. $60\% \times n = 420$

D. $n = 40\% \times 160$

E. $n \times 640 = 160$

F. $40\% \times n = 160$

Solve.

7. What percent of 400 is 60?

8. What is 5% of 500?

9. 20% of what number is 70?

10. What percent of 1000 is 50?

11. 62% of what number is 341?

12. Find 80% of 425.

13. 8% of what number is 520?

14. Find 8% of 55.

15. 7% of what number is 56?

16. What percent of 300 is 96?

17. What is 75% of 80?

18. What percent of 25 is 24?

19. Find 17% of 1200.

20. What percent of 400 is 72?

21. 37% of what number is 259?

Along the Trail

22. Bear Trail is 65% as long as Chief Trail. If Chief Trail is 8.6 km long, how long is Bear Trail?

23. The chair lift travels over the Winding River for 0.2 km of its 0.6 km trip. What percent of the chair lift's trip is over the Winding River?

★ 24. After climbing 1080 m the explorer was 60% of the way to the mountain top. How far was the explorer from the mountain top?

Checkpoint B

Solve. (*pages 286–287*)

1. 50% of 74

2. 75% of 56

3. $33\frac{1}{3}$% of 54

4. 25% of 44

Solve. (*pages 288–289*)

5. What percent of 30 is 6?

6. What percent of 450 is 27?

7. 18 is what percent of 25?

8. 36 is what percent of 144?

Solve. (*pages 290–291*)

9. 30% of r is 24.6

10. 75% of n is $25.50

11. 60% of m is 18

12. 85% of p is 68.

Solve. (*pages 292–293*)

13. What is 72% of 25?

14. What percent of 60 is 3?

15. 40% of what number is 10?

16. 35% of what number is 21?

Extra practice on page 438

Problem Solving · SIMPLIFYING PROBLEMS

1	Understand
2	Plan
3	Work
4	Answer

Sometimes you can make a problem simpler by rewording it. You can use easier words, supply information you know, and omit anything that is not really necessary to solve the problem.

EXAMPLE

Station KHWX-TV shows cartoons for 3 h each Saturday morning. This is 40% of the time used for children's shows during a week. How much time does KHWX devote to shows for children during one week?

Write the problem in a simpler, more familiar form.

40% of what number is 3?

Let n be the number. Write and solve an equation.

$$40\% \times n = 3$$
$$0.40 \times n = 3$$
$$n = \frac{3}{0.40}$$
$$= 7.5$$

Station KHWX-TV devotes 7.5 h to children's shows in one week.

Complete the simpler problem and the equation. Solve.

1. In a survey of 240 viewers, 150 people said they watch *Star Ships* each week. What percent of the viewers questioned watch *Star Ships* each week?

   What percent of 240 is 150?
   $n \times 240 = $ ▢

2. KHWX broadcasts commercials for 20% of each hour of prime time. How many minutes of each hour are used for commercials during prime time?

   20% of ▢ min is what number?
   $0.20 \times $ ▢ $ = n$

3. KHWX broadcasts 18 h each day. For what percent of a day is KHWX on the air?

   What percent of ▢ h is 18 h?
   $n \times $ ▢ $ = 18$

294

Solve.

4. About 76 million households in the United States have at least one TV set. About 38 million households have more than one set. Of the households that have TVs, about what percent have more than one set?

5. The number of TV stations in California is equal to the sum of all the TV stations in New York and Ohio. If there are 54 TV stations in California, and 30 in New York, how many TV stations are there in Ohio?

6. The number of TV stations in Kentucky recently was 55% of the number of TV stations in Indiana. If there were 11 TV stations in Kentucky, how many were there in Indiana?

7. Recently, there were 40 radio stations in Wyoming. If 75% of these stations were AM or AM-FM stations, how many were FM stations only?

8. The number of FM stations in North Dakota recently was 12.5% of the number of FM stations in Tennessee. If there were 80 FM stations in Tennessee, how many were there in North Dakota?

Recently, there were 12 TV stations in Colorado, and 25% more in Louisiana than in Colorado. Use this information for Problems 9–12.

9. How many more TV stations were there in Louisiana than in Colorado?

10. How many TV stations were there in Louisiana in all?

★ **11.** What percent of the number of stations in Colorado was the number of stations in Louisiana?

★ **12.** The average number of broadcast hours per week for public TV stations in the United States in a recent year was 94.1 h. What was the average number of broadcast hours per day? What percent of each day was the average daily broadcast time for public TV stations in that year? Round the answer to the nearest tenth of a percent.

Match.

1. 0.06   **2.** 0.827   **3.** 0.5   **4.** $\frac{3}{8}$ **5.** $\frac{29}{100}$ **6.** $\frac{2}{3}$

A. 50%   **B.** 6%   **C.** 82.7%   **D.** $66\frac{2}{3}\%$ **E.** $37\frac{1}{2}\%$ **F.** 29%

Write as a decimal.

7.    **8.**    **9.**    **10.**

Write as a fraction in lowest terms.

11. 80%   **12.** 9%   **13.** 36%   **14.** $62\frac{1}{2}\%$

Solve.

15. What is 15% of 80?   **16.** What percent of 60 is 12?

17. 19 is what percent of 95?   **18.** 25% of what number is 18?

19. 70 is what percent of 80?   **20.** 32% of what number is 160?

Solve. Round to the nearest tenth.

21. What is 7% of 35?   **22.** What percent of 28 is 21?

23. 24% of what number is 192?   **24.** What is 65% of 300?

Solve.

25. The number of TV stations in Idaho in a recent year was $66\frac{2}{3}\%$ of the number of TV stations in Oklahoma. If there were 8 stations in Idaho, how many were there in Oklahoma?

Write as a percent. (*pages 278–281*)

1. 0.01 **2.** 0.84 **3.** $\frac{2}{100}$ **4.** 18 hundredths

5. 0.355 **6.** 0.569 **7.** 0.06 **8.** 0.3

Write as a decimal. (*pages 280–281*)

9. 76% **10.** 3% **11.** 60% **12.** 4.3% **13.** 16%

Write as a fraction in lowest terms. (*pages 282–283*)

14. 14% **15.** 8% **16.** 60% **17.** $37\frac{1}{2}$% **18.** $66\frac{2}{3}$%

Write as a percent. (*pages 284–285*)

19. $\frac{3}{10}$ **20.** $\frac{1}{2}$ **21.** $\frac{7}{25}$ **22.** $\frac{7}{9}$ **23.** $\frac{1}{3}$

Solve. (*pages 286–291*)

24. What is 10% of 50? **25.** 20% of 55 is how much?

26. What percent of 60 is 15? **27.** 18 is what percent of 36?

28. 15% of what number is 3? **29.** 3% of what number is $.24?

Solve. Round to the nearest tenth. (*pages 292–293*)

30. What is 10% of 56? **31.** What percent of 4 is 2.5?

32. 40% of what number is 16? **33.** What is 5% of $45.60?

Solve. (*pages 294–295*)

34. The number of FM stations in Washington, D.C. recently was 20% of the number of FM stations in Kansas. If there were 9 stations in Washington, D.C., how many were there in Kansas?

Extra practice on page 439

Percents and Proportions

25% of the 120 swimmers, which is 30 swimmers, will swim in the relay races.

Some people find it helpful to think of percent facts as proportions. For example, here is how to write *25% of 120 is 30* as a proportion.

Write 25% as the ratio of 25 to 100.

$$25\% = \frac{25}{100}$$

This is sometimes called the **rate.**

Write a ratio to compare 30 to 120.

$$\frac{30}{120}$$

The number 120 is called the **base** because it is used as the basis of comparison. The number 30 is compared to the base and is called the **percentage.**

Now write a proportion to state that these two ratios are equal.

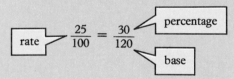

rate $\quad \dfrac{25}{100} = \dfrac{30}{120} \quad$ percentage

base

Complete the proportion. Then name the rate, the base, and the percentage.

1. 10% of 200 is 20

$$\frac{\blacksquare}{100} = \frac{\blacksquare}{200}$$

2. 50% of 160 is 80

$$\frac{50}{\blacksquare} = \frac{80}{\blacksquare}$$

3. 15% of 60 is 9

$$\frac{15}{100} = \frac{\blacksquare}{\blacksquare}$$

4. 120 is 60% of 200

$$\frac{\blacksquare}{100} = \frac{\blacksquare}{200}$$

5. 70 is 20% of 350

$$\frac{20}{\blacksquare} = \frac{70}{\blacksquare}$$

6. 18 is 25% of 72

$$\frac{25}{100} = \frac{\blacksquare}{\blacksquare}$$

Write as a proportion.

7. 50% of 10 is 5

8. 20% of 35 is 7

9. 45% of 60 is 27

10. 12 is 80% of 15

11. 84 is 70% of 120

12. 11 is 44% of 25

You can use proportions as another way to solve the three cases of percent problems.

50% of 112 is a	b% of 150 is 60	75% of c is 135
rate = 50%	rate = b%	rate = 75%
base = 112	base = 150	base = c
percentage = a	percentage = 60	percentage = 135

$$\frac{50}{100} = \frac{a}{112}$$

$$50 \times 112 = 100a$$
$$5600 = 100a$$
$$56 = a$$

$$\frac{b}{100} = \frac{60}{150}$$

$$150b = 100 \times 60$$
$$150b = 6000$$
$$b = 40$$
$$b\% = 40\%$$

$$\frac{75}{100} = \frac{135}{c}$$

$$75c = 100 \times 135$$
$$75c = 13{,}500$$
$$c = 180$$

Complete the proportion. Then solve.

13. x is 20% of 75

$$\frac{\blacksquare}{100} = \frac{\blacksquare}{75}$$

14. 35 is y% of 700

$$\frac{\blacksquare}{100} = \frac{\blacksquare}{700}$$

15. 3 is 12% of z

$$\frac{12}{100} = \frac{\blacksquare}{\blacksquare}$$

Write and solve a proportion to answer the question.

16. What is 25% of 60?

17. 90% of what number is 36?

18. What percent of 350 is 105?

19. What is 30% of 80?

20. 60% of what number is 51?

21. What percent of 300 is 45?

22. What is 45% of 160?

23. 20% of what number is 25?

24. What percent of 1500 is 375?

25. What is 12% of 475?

26. There were 400 runners entered in the marathon. Of these, 75% reached the finish line. How many reached the finish line?

27. There are 36 women entered in the road race. This is 45% of all the runners in the race. How many runners are in the race?

28. Of the 120 runners entered in the track meet, 18 are from your school. What percent of all the runners is this?

Maintaining Skills

Write each sentence as an equation.

1. A distance increased by 6 km equals 15 km.

2. Seven pages less than the total number of pages is 24.

3. A price divided by 9 equals $50.

4. Ken's age divided by 6 is 3.

5. The money in Jenney's pocket times 5 equals $1.50.

6. Bobby ran for 25 minutes today. This is 7 minutes less than yesterday.

Solve and check.

7. $a + 3 = 41$ **8.** $7 + b = 19$ **9.** $n - 4.2 = 7.8$

10. $6 = c - 1.1$ **11.** $62 + d = 141$ **12.** $15 = m + 15$

13. $6 \times e = 72$ **14.** $f \times 2 = 5.6$ **15.** $\frac{p}{3} = 6$

16. $4 = \frac{h}{9}$ **17.** $\frac{k}{2.2} = 4$ **18.** $70 = 5 \times r$

Add or subtract. Write the answer in lowest terms.

19. $\begin{array}{r} \frac{4}{7} \\ + \frac{1}{7} \\ \hline \end{array}$ **20.** $\begin{array}{r} \frac{1}{2} \\ + \frac{2}{8} \\ \hline \end{array}$ **21.** $\begin{array}{r} \frac{2}{3} \\ + \frac{1}{4} \\ \hline \end{array}$ **22.** $\begin{array}{r} \frac{7}{8} \\ - \frac{3}{8} \\ \hline \end{array}$ **23.** $\begin{array}{r} \frac{5}{6} \\ - \frac{1}{3} \\ \hline \end{array}$

24. $\begin{array}{r} 1\frac{1}{8} \\ + 2\frac{7}{8} \\ \hline \end{array}$ **25.** $\begin{array}{r} 2\frac{1}{4} \\ + 3\frac{5}{8} \\ \hline \end{array}$ **26.** $\begin{array}{r} 7\frac{1}{9} \\ - 2\frac{7}{9} \\ \hline \end{array}$ **27.** $\begin{array}{r} 9\frac{1}{3} \\ - 2\frac{1}{4} \\ \hline \end{array}$ **28.** $\begin{array}{r} 6\frac{1}{2} \\ - 1\frac{3}{4} \\ \hline \end{array}$

29. How many cups of water are there in all?

Percent Applications

A company reserves 1% of construction costs to buy art for its new buildings. How much may be spent on art for a building that costs $5,000,000?

11

Percent Applications

Suppose you are given this list of information about the brass section of an orchestra.

You could use the information to answer the three questions below.

BRASS SECTION
15 members
40% play the horn
3 members play the trombone
Brass section makes up 12% of orchestra

1. How many members play the horn?
2. What percent of the brass section play the trombone?
3. How many members are in the whole orchestra?

Rewrite the questions, write an equation for each, and then solve.

What number is 40% of 15?   What percent of 15 is 3?   12% of what number is 15?

$$n = 40\% \times 15$$

$$n = 0.40 \times 15$$

$$n = 6$$

$$n\% \text{ of } 15 = 3$$

$$n = \frac{3}{15}$$

$$n = 0.20$$

$$n = 20\%$$

$$12\% \text{ of } n = 15$$

$$0.12 \times n = 15$$

$$n = \frac{15}{0.12}$$

$$n = 125$$

You can now answer the three questions as follows:
1. Six members play the horn.
2. Twenty percent play the trombone.
3. The orchestra has 125 members.

Exercises

Write an equation to solve the problem.

1. What number is 75% of 200?

2. 10% of 325 is what number?

3. 9 is what percent of 90?

4. 4 is what percent of 50?

5. 4% of what number is 2?

6. 50% of what number is 86?

Solve.

7. What percent of 65 is 13?

8. 20% of what number is 420?

9. What number is 20% of 415?

10. What percent of 20 is 2?

11. $5\frac{1}{2}$% of 100 is what number?

12. What number is 2.5% of $430?

13. 90% of what number is 72?

14. 30 is what percent of 250?

15. $4.32 is what percent of $36?

16. 16% of 140 is what number?

17. $10\frac{1}{4}$% of what number is 2.05?

18. $33\frac{1}{3}$% of $39.93 is what amount?

19. 5.35 is what percent of 214?

20. 15% of what number is 96?

A Whole String

Solve.

21. The percussion section of an orchestra has 8 drum players. This number represents 40% of the section. How many players are in the percussion section?

22. A total of 2500 people attended the end-of-season performance of the local orchestra. Of this total, 750 people sat in the first balcony. What percent of the people sat in the first balcony?

23. In the chart shown, what percent of the musicians in the string section play each instrument? Round your answer to the nearest tenth of a percent.

24. The woodwind section has 6 clarinetists, who make up 12.5% of the section. How many players are in the woodwind section?

STRING SECTION	
Instrument	**Number**
Violin	34
Viola	11
Cello	13
Bass	9
Harp	1
Total String Section	?

Calculator Corner

The cost of constructing a new music hall is estimated at 2.5 million dollars. What percent of the money comes from each source? Round to the nearest tenth of a percent.

Gifts from companies	$755,000	Grants	$800,000
Private donations	$575,500	Loan	$314,500
Phone-a-thon	$ 55,000		

Sales Tax

When Tony Ramsey bought a tape recorder that was marked $27.25, he had to pay a 5% **sales tax.** A **sales tax rate** of 5% means that 5¢ is added to the price for every $1 of the purchase.

The sales tax on Tony's tape recorder is 5% of $27.25.

What number is 5% of $27.25?

$$n = 5\% \times \$27.25$$
$$= 0.05 \times \$27.25$$
$$= \$1.3625$$

$1.3625 rounded to the nearest cent is $1.36. We find the total cost by adding the sales tax to the marked price.

Total cost = $27.25 + $1.36 = $28.61

Tony paid $28.61 for his tape recorder.

Exercises

Solve.

1. 3% of $15   **2.** 4% of $20   **3.** 5% of $30   **4.** 6% of $45

5. 7% of $58   **6.** 8% of $62   **7.** 5.5% of $70   **8.** 4.25% of $80

Find the sales tax. Round to the nearest cent.

9. marked price: $20.25
    sales tax rate: 6%

10. marked price: $13.75
     sales tax rate: 7%

Find the total cost. Round to the nearest cent.

11. marked price: $9.25
     sales tax rate: 4%

12. marked price: $14.90
     sales tax rate: 5%

13. marked price: $18.30
sales tax rate: 6%

14. marked price: $21.50
sales tax rate: 7%

15. marked price: $24.60
sales tax rate: 8%

16. marked price: $31.20
sales tax rate: 9%

17. marked price: $150.10
sales tax rate: 3%

18. marked price: $210.50
sales tax rate: 8%

19. marked price: $16.65
sales tax rate: 3.5%

20. marked price: $20.85
sales tax rate: 5.5%

21. marked price: $19.90
sales tax rate: $6\frac{1}{4}$%

22. marked price: $27.45
sales tax rate: $7\frac{1}{2}$%

23. marked price: $36.81
sales tax rate: $2\frac{3}{4}$%

24. marked price: $250.70
sales tax rate: 6.75%

Using Sales Tax Tables

Suppose you want to find the sales tax on an item marked $.79. In the portion of the tax table shown, find the line marked *$.70–$.89*. Since $.79 falls between $.70 and $.89, the tax on $.79 is $.04.

Use the tax table to find the sales tax. There is a 5% tax on each item.

25. What is the total cost of a notebook marked $1.19?

26. What is the total cost of a pen marked $.89?

27. Julie buys an eraser marked $.45, a ruler marked $.39, and a clipboard marked $2.19. What is the total cost?

5% SALES TAX TABLE			
Amount of Sale	Tax	Amount of Sale	Tax
$.10–$.29	$.01	$7.70–$7.89	$.39
.30– .49	.02	7.90– 8.09	.40
.50– .69	.03	8.10– 8.29	.41
.70– .89	.04	8.30– 8.49	.42
.90–1.09	.05	8.50– 8.69	.43
1.10–1.29	.06	8.70– 8.89	.44
1.30–1.49	.07	8.90– 9.09	.45
1.50–1.69	.08	9.10– 9.29	.46
1.70–1.89	.09	9.30– 9.49	.47
1.90–2.09	.10	9.50– 9.69	.48
2.10–2.29	.11	9.70– 9.89	.49
2.30–2.49	.12	9.90–10.09	.50
2.50–2.69	.13	10.10–10.29	.51
2.70–2.89	.14	10.30–10.49	.52
2.90–3.09	.15	10.50–10.69	.53

Solve.

28. Jennifer paid $6.25 in sales tax when she purchased stereo speakers. The sales tax rate was 5%. What was the marked price of the speakers?

★ **29.** A guitar is priced at $45.95. With tax the price is $48.71. What is the rate of sales tax to the nearest percent?

Simple Interest

If you deposit money in the bank, the bank pays you **interest** for the use of your money. The money deposited is called the **principal.** The number of years the money is left in the bank is the **time.** The interest earned in that time is determined by the yearly **rate.**

interest = principal × rate × time
$$i = p \times r \times t$$

A principal of $225 is deposited into a savings account for one year. The interest rate per year is 6%. What is the interest?

$$i = p \times r \times t$$
$$= \$225 \times 6\% \times 1$$
$$= \$13.50$$

The interest is $13.50.

You can also use this formula to find the interest you pay when you borrow money.

Exercises

Name the principal, rate, time, and interest.

1. Brad deposited $250 in a savings account for 1 year. The bank pays an interest rate of 8%. Brad earns $20 on the money.

2. Catherine earns $285 on $1000 that she deposited for three years at an interest rate of 9.5%.

3. Shelley borrowed $650 for 1 year. The rate of interest was 20%. She paid $130 to borrow this money.

4. Steven deposited $1000 in a money market certificate for 1 year at 12%. His money earned $120.

Find the interest. Round to the nearest cent.

5. principal: $200
    rate: $5\frac{1}{2}\%$
    time: 1 year

6. principal: $200
    rate: 13%
    time: 1 year

7. principal: $1000
    rate: 18%
    time: 1 year

8. principal: $750
    rate: $6\frac{1}{4}\%$
    time: $\frac{1}{4}$ year

9. principal: $2300
    rate: $12\frac{1}{4}\%$
    time: $\frac{1}{2}$ year

10. principal: $450
    rate: 10%
    time: $\frac{1}{4}$ year

11. principal: $20,000
    rate: 16%
    time: 1 year

12. principal: $15,000
    rate: $12\frac{1}{2}\%$
    time: $\frac{1}{2}$ year

13. principal: $7500
    rate: 13.5%
    time: 2 years

Time Is Money

You can write 9 months or 26 weeks as a fraction of a year.

Number of months in a year = 12

Number of weeks in a year = 52

9 months = $\frac{9}{12}$ year = $\frac{3}{4}$ year

26 weeks = $\frac{26}{52}$ year = $\frac{1}{2}$ year

Find the interest. Round to the nearest cent.

14. principal: $592
    rate: $12\frac{1}{4}\%$
    time: 3 months

15. principal: $450.67
    rate: $9\frac{3}{4}\%$
    time: 6 months

16. Verna deposited $200 in the Thrift Club's account. The interest rate is $5\frac{3}{4}\%$. How much interest will the money earn in 3 months?

17. Carl's parents obtained an education loan of $3000. The interest rate is 7%. What will the interest be after 3 months?

★ **18.** Kim borrows $1600 at 9% for 1 year to pay for a course in refrigeration. She promises to repay the principal plus the interest at the end of the year. How much will she have to pay?

★ **19.** Alan's parents deposited $2000 in a money market fund. At the end of 1 year the interest was $240. What was the rate?

Discounts

A **discount** is a decrease in the price of an item. A **discount rate** is a percent of the original price. Suppose the original price of a tennis racket is $36.50 and you buy it at a 40% discount. The amount of discount is 40% of $36.50.

40% of $36.50 is what number?

$$40\% \text{ of } \$36.50 = 0.40 \times \$36.50$$
$$= \$14.60$$

amount of discount

You can subtract the amount of discount from the original price to find the **sale price.**

$$\$36.50 - \$14.60 = \$21.90$$

sale price

Exercises

Find the discount.

1. original price: $50
discount rate: 25%

2. original price: $59.90
discount rate: 10%

3. original price: $15.98
discount rate: 50%

4. original price: $45.60
discount rate: 15%

5. original price: $75
discount rate: 20%

6. original price: $108
discount rate: 16%

Find the sale price.

7. original price: $90
discount rate: 30%

8. original price: $150
discount rate: 35%

9. original price: $140.50
discount rate: 18%

10. original price: $205
discount rate: 15%

11. original price: $16.80
discount rate: 5%

12. original price: $29.90
discount rate: 10%

13. original price: $64
discount rate: $12\frac{1}{2}\%$

14. original price: $96
discount rate: $8\frac{1}{3}\%$

15. original price: $99
discount rate: $33\frac{1}{3}\%$

Which store has the lower sale price on the same item?

16. The Attic   original price: $50
                   discount rate: 20%
       Front Porch original price: $45
                   discount rate: 30%

17. Shoe Lane   original price: $63
                   discount rate: $33\frac{1}{3}$%
       Hat World   original price: $59
                   discount rate: 30%

18. More Shirts original price: $17
                   discount rate: 15%
       Game Room original price: $36
                   discount rate: 25%

Odds and Ends

Solve.

19. At Jane's Sports Store, sleeping bags are on sale at a 20% discount. What is the sale price of a bag originally priced at $28.95?

20. The Sports Shop is selling soccer balls at a 40% discount. What is the sale price of a ball that was originally priced at $9.95?

★ **21.** At a clearance sale, tennis shoes originally marked $22.50 are on sale for $15.75. What is the rate of discount?

★ **22.** When Alice bought a shirt for $14.40, she saved 20% of the original price. What was the original price?

Checkpoint A

Solve. (*pages 302–303*)

1. $7\frac{1}{2}$% of 100 is what number?

2. 17 is what percent of 68?

3. 20% of what number is 7?

Find the total price. Round to the nearest cent. (*pages 304–305*)

4. marked price: $17.50
    sales tax rate: $5\frac{1}{2}$%

5. marked price: $7889
    sales tax rate: $4\frac{1}{2}$%

Find the interest. Round to the nearest cent. (*pages 306–307*)

6. principal: $250
       rate: 7.75%
       time: 1 year

7. principal: $1000
       rate: $11\frac{3}{4}$%
       time: $\frac{1}{2}$ year

8. principal: $25,000
       rate: $13\frac{1}{2}$%
       time: 3 years

Find the sale price. (*pages 308–309*)

9. original price: $89.75
    discount rate: 20%

10. original price: $44.95
     discount rate: $33\frac{1}{3}$%

11. original price: $175.00
     discount rate: 15%

Extra practice on page 440

Circle Graphs

A **circle graph** shows how a total amount has been divided into parts according to percents. The total amount is 100%. To find what part of the whole each section represents, multiply the percent for that section by the total amount.

The circle graph shows that in a recent year, 7% of the population in the United States was under five years old. Notice that the total population for that year was estimated at 218 million.

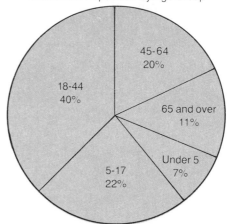

Recent U.S. Population By Age Group

Total Estimate: 218 Million

The number of children under five years old is calculated as follows:

What number is 7% of 218 million?

$$n = 7\% \text{ of } 218 \text{ million}$$
$$= 0.07 \times 218 \text{ million}$$
$$= 15.26 \text{ million}$$

The number of children under five years old is 15.26 million.

Exercises

Write the percent in each age category. Use the circle graph above.

1. 5 – 17   **2.** 18 – 44   **3.** 45 – 64   **4.** 65 and over

5. 17 and under   **6.** 18 – 64   **7.** 45 and over   **8.** 64 and under

How many people are in each age category? Use the circle graph above.

9. 5 – 17   **10.** 18 – 44   **11.** 45 – 64   **12.** 65 and over

13. 17 and under   **14.** 18 – 64   **15.** 45 and over   **16.** 64 and under

Use the circle graph on the right to answer the question.

17. How many students play violins?

18. How many students play cellos?

19. How many students play violas?

Find the percent of the orchestra that play the instrument. Round your answer to the nearest tenth of a percent.

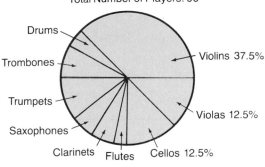

Composition of the School Orchestra
Total Number of Players: 96

20. trumpets: 10 players

21. saxophones: 6 players

22. clarinets: 5 players

23. flutes: 3 players

24. drums: 4 players

25. trombones: 8 players

Drawing Circle Graphs

We can make a circle graph to picture the information in the table on the right.

To find the part of the circle you will use for sports, find the part of the total pages that sports occupy.

$$\frac{16}{64} = \frac{1}{4}, \text{ or } 25\%$$

Then find $\frac{1}{4}$, or 25%, of the number of degrees in a circle, 360°.

$$25\% \text{ of } 360° = \frac{1}{4} \times 360° = 90°$$

You can show that sports occupy 25% of the circle by drawing an angle of 90° as shown.

CONTENTS OF SCHOOL MAGAZINE	
Kind of Material	**Number of Pages**
Fiction	32
Essays	8
Sports	16
Puzzles	8
Total	64

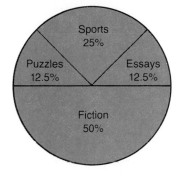

Find the number of degrees in each angle.

26. fiction   **27.** puzzles   **28.** essays

★ **29.** Sixty students took part in a survey; 45% liked swimming, 15% liked basketball, 25% liked tennis, 10% liked soccer, and 5% hiking. Draw a circle graph to picture this information.

Budget

A **budget** is a plan you make to be sure that your income will be enough to cover your expenses. When you make up a budget, you may have to estimate your income and expenses. One way to show a budget is with a circle graph. The circle graph shows the Clinton family's budget for one year. If their yearly income is $19,500, how much do they plan to spend on food this year?

From the graph, you can see that the Clintons expect to spend 21.9% of their income on food.

What number is 21.9% of $19,500?

$$n = 21.9\% \times \$19,500$$
$$= 0.219 \times \$19,500$$
$$= \$4270.50$$

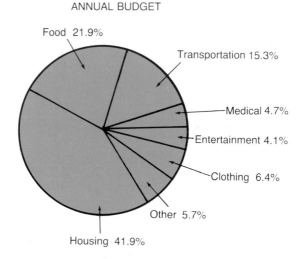

ANNUAL BUDGET

Food 21.9%

Transportation 15.3%

Medical 4.7%

Entertainment 4.1%

Clothing 6.4%

Other 5.7%

Housing 41.9%

The Clintons expect to spend $4270.50 on food.

Exercises

What percent of the annual income is planned for the expense? Use the circle graph above.

1. medical
2. transportation
3. clothing

4. entertainment
5. housing
6. other

Find the amount that is budgeted for the expense.

7. total income: $20,000
  food: 21.9%

8. total income: $30,000
  housing: 49.9%

9. total income: $27,500
  clothing: 6.4%

10. total income: $29,750
  entertainment: 4.1%

11. total income: $31,175
  transportation: 15.3%

12. total income: $39,100
  medical: 4.7%

What percent of the monthly income is budgeted for each expense?

13. housing   **14.** food   **15.** other

16. personal   **17.** transportation

18. clothing   **19.** savings and recreation

MONTHLY INCOME $4200

Food $840

Personal $273

Savings and recreation $630

Other $210

Transportation $525

Clothing $252

Housing $1470

An Expense Summary

The Davis family has a monthly income of $1500. The expense summary shows the actual amounts the family spent on some items during May.

Find the amount budgeted. Is the amount budgeted more or less than the amount spent?

20. lunch money: 5% of monthly income

21. pocket money: 4.5% of monthly income

22. telephone bill: 1.5% of monthly income

23. gasoline: 6% of monthly income

24. electric bill: 4% of monthly income

25. The amount the family spent for groceries was 10% more than they had budgeted. How much did they budget for groceries?

EXPENSE SUMMARY FOR MAY	
Expense	**Amount Spent**
Groceries	$231.00
Electric bill	48.62
Telephone bill	18.56
Gasoline	95.00
Train pass	27.00
Newspaper	13.95
Lunch money	70.15
Pocket money	67.50

A mountain is 4000 m high. One day an eagle flew halfway up the mountain. The next day the eagle flew half the distance it flew on the previous day. If the eagle continues this pattern, how many days will it take to reach the top of the mountain?

Take a Break

Percent of Increase or Decrease

When a quantity changes from one value to another, it either increases or decreases. The amount of change can be expressed as a **percent of increase** or a **percent of decrease.**

Last year 20 students at Central Village Junior High School belonged to the Mathematics Club. This year there are 26 students in the club. What is the percent of increase?

BULLETIN
MATH CLUB MEMBERSHIP
ON THE INCREASE
Check the figures!
Last year's membership | This year's membership
20 | 26
That's an increase of 30%!

First we find the amount of change.

$$26 - 20 = 6$$

The membership increased by 6.

What percent of 20 is 6?

$$n \times 20 = 6$$

$$n = \frac{6}{20}$$

$$= 0.30 = 30\%$$

The percent of increase was 30%.

If the membership this year had decreased by 6, we would say that the percent of decrease was 30%.

Sometimes, a percent of increase may be greater than 100%. Suppose the computer club increased its membership from 10 members to 25. The membership of the computer club would be increased by 150%.

$$\frac{15}{10} = 1.50 = 150\%$$

Exercises

Find the amount of change from the first number to the second number. If the change is an increase, write *I*. If the change is a decrease, write *D*.

1. 20 to 40	**2.** 30 to 75	**3.** 50 to 70	**4.** 75 to 100
5. 60 to 30	**6.** 97 to 87	**7.** 105 to 95	**8.** 136 to 99
9. 12.95 to 13	**10.** 14.5 to 13.95	**11.** 0.921 to 0.721	**12.** 0.86 to 0.715
13. 50% to 100%	**14.** 90% to 110%	**15.** 120% to 60%	**16.** 25% to 15.5%

Write as a decimal.

17. 120% **18.** 160% **19.** 240% **20.** 175% **21.** 162%

Write as a percent.

22. 1.08 **23.** 2.00 **24.** 1.80 **25.** 2.10 **26.** 1.45

Find the percent of increase or decrease.

27. 30 to 45 **28.** 46 to 92 **29.** 80 to 40 **30.** 100 to 90

31. 30 to 15 **32.** 40 to 90 **33.** 50 to 47 **34.** 27 to 24

35. 80 to 96 **36.** 32 to 17 **37.** 75 to 27 **38.** 84 to 105

39. 96 to 108 **40.** 120 to 84 **41.** 88 to 121 **42.** 212 to 53

43. 121 to 242 **44.** 350 to 175 **45.** 66 to 72.6 **46.** 90 to 72

Sales Move Up and Down

Solve.

47. Gregg is selling calendars to earn money. Last week he sold 15 calendars. This week he sold 20. What is the percent of increase?

48. Joan had 112 customers on her newspaper route. She now has 80 customers. What is the percent of decrease?

49. A paint store sold 1350 L of paint last week. This week 2700 L of paint were sold. What is the percent of increase?

50. When her car was new, Cathy made 15 round trips between work and home on one tank of gas. Now she makes only 9 round trips on one tank of gas. What is the percent of decrease?

★ **51.** After a drop of 20% in the depth of water in the Appleton Reservoir, the depth gauge read 56 m. What was the original depth?

Commission

A **commission** is the amount of money you earn for selling a product or providing a service. Many salespeople receive a percent of their total sales as commission.

For example, a salesperson who works for a commission of 20% and who sells $600 worth of goods will earn 20% of $600, or $120. In this case, the **commission rate** is 20%.

During May, Sylvia Brown sold $645.50 worth of office supplies. She received as her commission 25% of the amount of sales. What was her commission?

$$\begin{aligned}
\text{Amount of commission} &= \text{commission rate} \times \text{sales} \\
&= 0.25 \times \$645.50 \\
&= \$161.375
\end{aligned}$$

Sylvia's commission was $161.38, rounded to the nearest cent.

Exercises

Find the commission.

1. 10% of $56

2. 15% of $72

3. 20% of $878

4. $15\frac{1}{2}\%$ of $700

5. $\frac{3}{4}\%$ of $12,000

6. $18\frac{1}{2}\%$ of $400

7. 20% of $1200.75

8. 0.75% of $20,000

9. 25% of $1644.60

10. total sales: $360
    commission rate: 3.5%

11. total sales: $650
    commission rate: 5.5%

12. total sales: $420.65
    commission rate: 15%

13. total sales: $530.70
    commission rate: 20%

14. total sales: $804.75
    commission rate: 30%

15. total sales: $1014.10
    commission rate: 40%

Find the commission rate.

16. total sales: $400
    commission: $100

17. total sales: $6000
    commission: $900

Find the amount of sales.

18. commission: $350
    commission rate: 10%

19. commission: $180
    commission rate: 3%

Commission Plus Salary

Solve.

20. Dorothy Fahey's salary is $200 per week. Her commission rate is 7%. Her total pay for last week was $410. What were her total sales last week?

21. Pamela Cox receives 6.5% commission on each new insurance policy she sells. Last month she sold $3528 worth of new policies. Her total pay was $1279.32. What is her regular salary?

★ **22.** George Collins earns 18% commission on products he sells to hairstyling salons. Last week he sold $300 worth of products to one salon, $295 to another salon, and $219 to a third salon. What was his total commission?

Checkpoint B

Use the circle graph to answer the question. (*pages 310–311*)

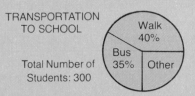

TRANSPORTATION TO SCHOOL

Total Number of Students: 300

Walk 40%
Bus 35%
Other

1. How many students walk?

2. How many students get to school by bus?

3. What percent come by other ways?

What percent is budgeted for each category? (*pages 312–313*)

4. bills

5. rent

6. food

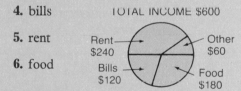

TOTAL INCOME $600

Rent $240
Other $60
Bills $120
Food $180

Solve. (*pages 314–315*)

7. percent of decrease: 35%
    original number: 160
    What is the new number?

8. new number: 108
    original number: 72
    What is the percent of increase?

Find the commission. (*pages 316–317*)

9. total sales: $725
    commission rate: 15%

10. total sales: $603.60
    commission rate: 35%

Extra practice on page 440   **317**

Problem Solving · USING CHARTS

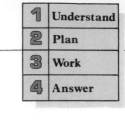

1 Understand

2 Plan

3 Work

4 Answer

Each person needs certain nutrients to remain healthy. On most food packages you can find a nutrition label that lists the number of calories and the amount of each nutrient that one serving of the product contains.

For some nutrients, the amounts are given as a percent of the U.S. Recommended Daily Allowances (U.S. RDA). The nutrition label from a can of tuna is shown.

```
        NUTRITION INFORMATION
          SERVING SIZE—6½ OZ.
      NUMBER OF SERVINGS PER CAN—1

CALORIES .......... 200    CARBOHYDRATES..... 0 g
PROTEIN............ 45 g   FAT ................ 2 g

       PERCENT OF U.S. RECOMMENDED
         DAILY ALLOWANCE (U.S.RDA)
                PER SERVING

PROTEIN........... 100    CALCIUM............. 0
VITAMIN A......... 0      IRON................ 10
VITAMIN C......... 0      VITAMIN B₆......... 40
THIAMINE (B₁)..... 2      VITAMIN B₁₂....... 100
RIBOFLAVIN (B₂)... 8      PHOSPHORUS ..... 30
NIACIN............ 120    MAGNESIUM....... 10

   INGREDIENTS: TUNA, SPRING WATER, SALT
```

What percent of the U.S. RDA of iron is contained in one serving of tuna? To find the answer, look for the heading *Percent of U.S. Recommended Daily Allowance Per Serving*. Then, under the heading you just found, look for iron. The number to the right of iron gives the percent of the U.S. RDA of iron. One serving of tuna contains 10% of the U.S. RDA of iron.

Exercises

Use the nutrition label above to answer the question.

1. What percent of the U.S. RDA of magnesium does each serving contain?

2. What percent of the U.S. RDA of phosphorus does each serving contain?

3. The tuna contains 100% of the U.S. RDA of which two nutrients?

4. The tuna contains 0% of the U.S. RDA of which three nutrients?

5. The tuna contains 120% of the U.S. RDA of which nutrient?

6. How many calories are contained in one serving of tuna?

7. How many grams of protein are contained in one serving of tuna?

Use the breakfast cereal label to answer the question.

8. If the U.S. RDA of calcium is 1200 mg, how many milligrams of calcium are contained in one serving of breakfast cereal with milk?

9. If the U.S. RDA of iron is 18 mg, how many milligrams of iron are contained in 1 serving of breakfast cereal?

10. Jerry ate 2 servings of breakfast cereal with milk. What percent of the U.S. RDA of protein was contained in the 2 servings?

BREAKFAST CEREAL

NUTRITION INFORMATION PER SERVING

| SERVING SIZE | | 1 CUP 1 OZ. (28 g) |
| SERVINGS PER CONTAINER | | 6 |

	per 1 oz. Cereal	With 1/2 Cup Vitamin D Fortified Whole Milk
CALORIES	110	190
PROTEIN	2 g	6 g
CARBOHYDRATE	25 g	31 g
FAT	0 g	4 g

% U.S. RDA PER SERVING

PROTEIN	2	10
VITAMIN A	25	25
VITAMIN C	25	25
THIAMINE	25	25
RIBOFLAVIN	25	35
NIACIN	25	25
CALCIUM	*	15
IRON	10	10

* Contains Less Than 2% of U.S. R.D.A for This Nutrient

11. If the U.S. RDA of vitamin C is 60 mg, how many milligrams of vitamin C are contained in the 2 servings of breakfast cereal with milk?

12. One medium-sized orange contains about 75 mg of vitamin C. The U.S. RDA of vitamin C is 60 mg. What percent of the U.S. RDA of vitamin C is contained in one medium-sized orange?

Use the pineapple label to answer the question.

13. If the U.S. RDA of iron is 18 mg, how many milligrams of iron does 1 serving of pineapple contain? What percent of the RDA does one serving provide?

★ 14. One large banana contains 16 mg of calcium. The U.S. RDA of calcium is about 1200 mg. Does 1 serving of pineapple contain more or less calcium than a large banana? How much more or less?

SLICED PINEAPPLE IN ITS OWN JUICE

NUTRITION INFORMATION—PER ONE CUP SERVING
SERVINGS PER CONTAINER —2

| CALORIES | 140 | CARBOHYDRATE | 25 g |
| PROTEIN | 1 g | FAT | 1 g |

% U.S. RDA PER ONE CUP SERVING

PROTEIN	2	RIBOFLAVIN (VIT. B_2)	.25
VITAMIN A	25	NIACIN	25
VITAMIN C	25	CALCIUM	4
THIAMINE (VIT. B_1)	25	IRON	4

WT. OF PINEAPPLE 10½ OZ. BEFORE ADDITION OF PINEAPPLE JUICE NECESSARY FOR PROCESSING.

What is the total price? Round to the nearest cent.

1. marked price: $132.50
   sales tax rate: 4%

2. marked price: $89.95
   sales tax rate: 6.5%

What is the interest? Round to the nearest cent.

3. principal: $900
   rate: 18%
   time: 1 year

4. principal: $1000
   rate: $7\frac{1}{4}$%
   time: 3 years

5. principal: $15,000
   rate: 10.5%
   time: 6 months

Find the sales price. Round to the nearest cent.

6. original price: $75
   discount rate: $33\frac{1}{3}$%

7. original price: $189.95
   discount rate: 15%

What percent is budgeted for each category?

8. food   **9.** savings   **10.** recreation

11. rent   **12.** bills   **13.** other

TOTAL INCOME: $1000

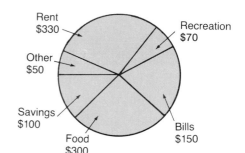

Rent $330

Recreation $70

Other $50

Savings $100

Food $300

Bills $150

Find the new number.

14. decrease: 25%
   original number: 368

15. increase: 20%
   original number: 175

Find the commission.

16. total sales: $329.50
   commission rate: 5%

17. total sales: $1815.75
   commission rate: 15%

Solve.

18. Sarah has 2 servings of breakfast cereal with milk. One serving with milk has 15% of the U.S. RDA of iron. If the U.S. RDA of iron is 18 mg, how many milligrams of iron is contained in the 2 servings that Sarah ate?

Solve. (*pages 302–303*)

1. What is 40% of 88?

2. 2 is what percent of 24?

What is the total price? Round to the nearest cent. (*pages 304–305*)

3. marked price: $8.50
   sales tax rate: 5.5%

4. marked price: $675.95
   sales tax rate: 7%

What is the interest? Round to the nearest cent. (*pages 306–307*)

5. principal, $500; rate, 12%; time, 1 year

6. principal, $18,000; rate, $7\frac{1}{2}$%; time, 6 months

Find the sale price. (*pages 308–309*)

7. original price: $150
   discount rate: 20%

8. original price: $500
   discount rate: 37.5%

What budget percent is planned for each category? (*pages 310–313*)

9. food

10. recreation

11. savings

12. other

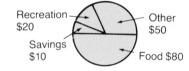

TOTAL INCOME: $160

Recreation $20

Other $50

Savings $10

Food $80

Solve. (*pages 314–315*)

13. new number: 27
   original number: 36
   What is the percent of decrease?

14. new number: 102
   original number: 85
   What is the percent of increase?

Find the commission. (*pages 316–317*)

15. total sales: $420, commission rate: 3%

Solve. (*pages 318–319*)

16. One serving of pineapple chunks contains 25% of the U.S. RDA of vitamin C. If the U.S. RDA of vitamin C is about 60 mg, about how many milligrams of vitamin C is contained in 1 serving of pineapple chunks?

Extra practice on page 441

Square Roots

You find the area of a square by multiplying the length of a side by itself.

Area of square = 4 × 4 = 4^2

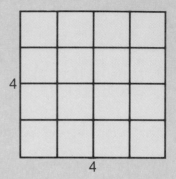

For this reason, the expression 4^2 is read as *the square of four* or *four squared.*

Because 16 = 4^2, we say that a **square root** of 16 is 4. The symbol for square root is $\sqrt{\ }$.

$$\sqrt{16} = 4$$

We read $\sqrt{16}$ as *the square root of 16.*

Many calculators have a special key that can be used to find the square root of a number.

Write the square.

1. 3^2 **2.** 5^2 **3.** 8^2 **4.** 10^2 **5.** 1^2

6. 12^2 **7.** 14^2 **8.** 15^2 **9.** 20^2 **10.** 25^2

Write the square root. Use a calculator if you wish.

11. $\sqrt{36}$ **12.** $\sqrt{49}$ **13.** $\sqrt{81}$ **14.** $\sqrt{100}$ **15.** $\sqrt{1}$

16. $\sqrt{121}$ **17.** $\sqrt{169}$ **18.** $\sqrt{256}$ **19.** $\sqrt{625}$ **20.** $\sqrt{900}$

What is the length of the side of a square with the given area?

21. Area = 64 cm²

22. Area = 144 cm²

23. Area = 324 cm²

24. Area = 1600 cm²

Often the square root of a number is not a whole number.

EXAMPLE: 18 is between   16 and   25.
             $\sqrt{18}$ is between $\sqrt{16}$ and $\sqrt{25}$.
             $\sqrt{18}$ is between   4   and   5.

A table like the one below can be used to find a value for $\sqrt{18}$. In this table, each square root is rounded to the nearest hundredth.

Number	Square Root	Number	Square Root	Number	Square Root	Number	Square Root
1	1.00	6	2.45	11	3.32	16	4.00
2	1.41	7	2.65	12	3.46	17	4.12
3	1.73	8	2.83	13	3.61	18	4.24
4	2.00	9	3.00	14	3.74	19	4.36
5	2.24	10	3.16	15	3.87	20	4.47

To use the table, find 18 in the *Number* column. Read the square root of 18 in the column to its right. The square root of 18 is *approximately* 4.24.

Use the table to find an approximate square root.

25. $\sqrt{2}$ **26.** $\sqrt{5}$ **27.** $\sqrt{9}$ **28.** $\sqrt{11}$

29. $\sqrt{15}$ **30.** $\sqrt{16}$ **31.** $\sqrt{17}$ **32.** $\sqrt{20}$

Complete. Write $<$ or $>$.

33. $\sqrt{5}$ ▨ $\sqrt{4}$ **34.** $\sqrt{5}$ ▨ $\sqrt{9}$ **35.** $\sqrt{8}$ ▨ $\sqrt{9}$

36. $\sqrt{10}$ ▨ 3   **37.** $\sqrt{17}$ ▨ 4   **38.** $\sqrt{19}$ ▨ 5

39. $\sqrt{45}$ ▨ 7   **40.** $\sqrt{84}$ ▨ 9   **41.** $\sqrt{125}$ ▨ 12

True or False? Write *T* or *F*.

42. $\sqrt{8}$ is between $\sqrt{4}$ and $\sqrt{9}$.   **43.** $\sqrt{21}$ is between $\sqrt{25}$ and $\sqrt{36}$.

44. $\sqrt{3}$ is between 1 and 2.   **45.** $\sqrt{41}$ is between 6 and 7.

46. $\sqrt{3}$ is between 1.7 and 1.8.   **47.** $\sqrt{15}$ is between 3.7 and 3.8.

48. $\sqrt{44}$ is between 6.5 and 6.6   **49.** $\sqrt{57}$ is between 7.5 and 7.6.

Maintaining Skills

Is the angle acute, obtuse, or right? Write *A*, *O*, or *R*.

1. 45°   **2.** 72°   **3.** 114°   **4.** 90°   **5.** 175°   **6.** 93°

Name the measure of the supplementary angle.

7. 71°   **8.** 39°   **9.** 115°   **10.** 6°   **11.** 135°   **12.** 90°

Estimate.

13. $1753 + 4089$ **14.** 675×89.3 **15.** $75.81 \div 3.7$ **16.** $17.57 - 3.28$

Multiply or divide. Write the answer in lowest terms.

17. $8 \times \frac{1}{7}$ **18.** $\frac{1}{2} \times \frac{1}{4}$ **19.** $\frac{3}{5} \times \frac{1}{3}$ **20.** $15 \div \frac{1}{2}$ **21.** $\frac{1}{2} \div 8$

22. $\frac{3}{4} \div \frac{6}{12}$ **23.** $1\frac{1}{2} \times 3\frac{1}{4}$ **24.** $4\frac{2}{3} \times 7\frac{1}{8}$ **25.** $5\frac{1}{4} \div 2\frac{1}{2}$ **26.** $6\frac{1}{4} \div 3$

Match with an equal ratio from the diagram. Then write a proportion.

27. $\frac{1}{2}$ **28.** $\frac{7}{8}$ **29.** $\frac{3}{5}$

30. $\frac{1}{10}$ **31.** $\frac{2}{3}$ **32.** $\frac{3}{7}$

33. $\frac{1}{4}$ **34.** $\frac{4}{9}$ **35.** $\frac{3}{8}$

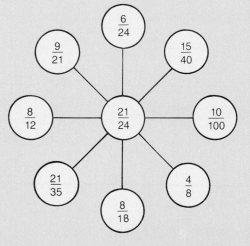

Solve the proportion.

36. $\frac{1}{4} = \frac{n}{16}$ **37.** $\frac{10}{15} = \frac{2}{b}$

38. $\frac{21}{p} = \frac{7}{8}$ **39.** $\frac{m}{13} = \frac{33}{39}$

40. $a:9$ as $42:63$

41. 4 packs is to $17.50 as 1 pack is to *r*.

42. In a class of 25 students, 10 received a grade of A on a mathematics quiz. What percent of the students did not receive an A?

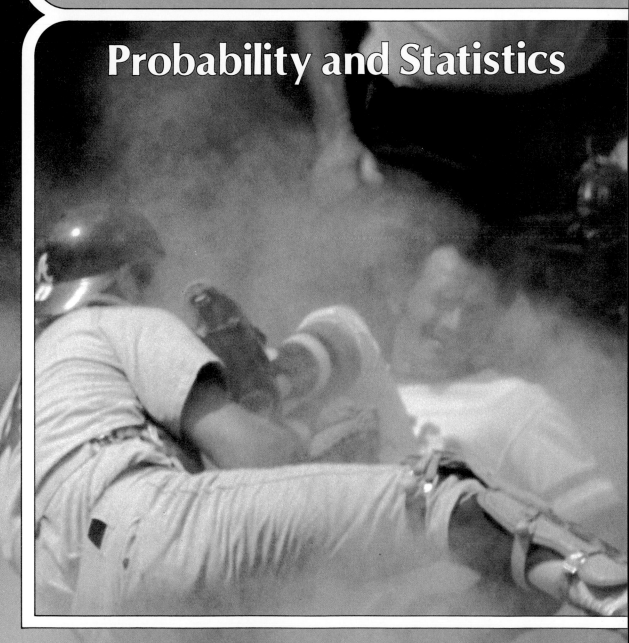

The probability of a base runner stealing home is less than the probability of stealing second base. Why do you think this is so?

Probability and Statistics

Probability

We often hear statements like these.

"There is a 10% chance of rain tonight."
"The Lancers are strong favorites for winning the soccer championship this year."

These are estimates of the chances that events will occur. The **probability** of an event is a number describing the chance that the event will happen.

If you take a coin from a bank that contains only pennies, you are *certain* to get a penny. The probability of a certain event is 1.

It would be impossible to take a dime out of that same bank. The probability of an impossible event is 0.

If an event is not impossible or certain, the probability is between 0 and 1.

EXAMPLE   "There is a 10% chance of rain tonight, and 40% tomorrow."

The events "rain tonight" and "rain tomorrow" are neither impossible nor certain. Rain tomorrow is more likely than rain tonight.

Exercises

For each event, write *0* if it is impossible, *1* if it is certain, and *between 0 and 1* otherwise.

1. July 4 will be clear and sunny.

2. A solid steel rod will float in water.

3. If you release a helium-filled balloon, it will begin to rise.

4. A cure will be found for the common cold this year.

5. There will be 30 days in February next year.

6. A penny dropped on a calendar will land on a Tuesday.

7. If an apple is dropped from a tree, it will fall towards the ground.

8. Water will freeze at 20°C.

9. There will be 30 days in November next year.

Match the probabilities and events.

10. 1   **A.** An impossible event.

11. 0.01   **B.** An event just as likely to occur as not.

12. $\frac{7}{10}$ **C.** An unlikely event.

13. 0   **D.** A certain event.

14. $\frac{1}{2}$ **E.** A nearly certain event.

15. $\frac{999}{1000}$ **F.** A somewhat likely event.

Chances Are

A weather reporter says "There is an 80% chance of rain today." The statement could mean that in the past it has rained 80 days out of every 100 days that had conditions like today's conditions.

Explain the meaning of the following statements.

16. The Cheetahs have a 50-50 chance of winning tonight.

17. All the candidates have an even chance of getting elected.

18. There is a 10% chance that an automobile built on Monday will have a defect.

19. Bernie has no chance whatsoever of setting a new marathon record.

20. It's a sure thing that next year's profits for Pat's Record Shop will be higher than this year's.

Finding Probabilities

To pick the day to clean your room, you close your eyes and mark an x on a weekly desk calendar. There are seven possible **outcomes,** the days from Monday through Sunday.

Since Thursday is one of the seven outcomes, the probability of picking Thursday is 1 out of 7, or $\frac{1}{7}$. This can be written as follows.

$$P(\text{Thursday}) = \frac{1}{7}$$

There are two weekend days, Saturday and Sunday.

$$P(\text{weekend day}) = \frac{2}{7} \qquad P(\text{weekday}) = \frac{5}{7}$$

If all the outcomes are equally likely, we use a formula to find probabilities.

$$\text{Probability} = \frac{\text{number of favorable outcomes}}{\text{total number of outcomes}}$$

Exercises

You spin the spinner shown. Complete.

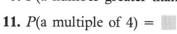

1. There are ▒ outcomes.

2. $P(3) = $ ▒

3. $P(6) = $ ▒

4. $P(2 \text{ or } 3) = $ ▒

5. $P(2, 3, \text{ or } 8) = $ ▒

6. $P(\text{even number}) = $ ▒

7. $P(\text{prime number}) = $ ▒

8. $P(\text{a number less than } 10) = $ ▒

9. $P(\text{a number greater than } 3) = $ ▒

10. $P(\text{a multiple of } 3) = $ ▒

11. $P(\text{a multiple of } 4) = $ ▒

You spin the spinner shown.

Write the given probability.

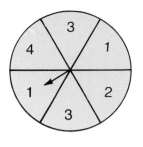

12. $P(1)$ **13.** $P(2)$

14. $P(3)$ **15.** $P(4)$

16. $P(5)$ **17.** $P(1 \text{ or } 2)$

18. $P(\text{not } 4)$ **19.** $P(\text{prime number})$

Each letter of the word *arithmetic* is written on a card. The cards are mixed, and you pick one card without looking. What is the probability?

20. $P(h)$ **21.** $P(t)$ **22.** $P(i)$ **23.** $P(t \text{ or } i)$ **24.** $P(\text{vowel})$

25. $P(\text{a letter in the word } addition)$ **26.** $P(\text{a letter in the word } metric)$

Jobability

Here are some jobs that need to be done at home. Each job is written on a piece of paper. The pieces of paper are put in a bowl, and you choose one without looking.

What is the probability?

27. You do the laundry.

28. You don't mow the lawn.

29. You get an indoor job.

30. You get an outdoor job.

★ **31.** You go first. You get "weed the garden." Then your brother chooses. What is the probability that he gets "do the laundry"?

★ **32.** Your brother goes first. He gets an indoor job. Then you choose. What is the probability that you get an outdoor job?

Counting Outcomes

Hugo and Terri are playing a board
game. They toss a coin to see who goes
first. Then they spin the spinner to see
how far to move.

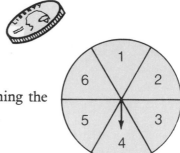

We can list all the outcomes of tossing the coin and spinning the
spinner. We use H for heads on the coin and T for tails.

$$(H, 1)\ (H, 2)\ (H, 3)\ (H, 4)\ (H, 5)\ (H, 6)$$
$$(T, 1)\ (T, 2)\ (T, 3)\ (T, 4)\ (T, 5)\ (T, 6)$$

An outcome of (T, 4), for example, means tails on the coin and 4 on
the spinner. We find that there are 12 outcomes.

Hugo goes first whenever the coin comes up heads.

$$P(\text{Hugo goes first}) = \frac{6}{12} = \frac{1}{2}.$$

$$P(\text{Hugo goes first and moves 5 spaces}) = \frac{1}{12}.$$

When we only want to know the number of outcomes, we can find out
by multiplying. There are 2 possible results for the coin. For each
result of the coin toss, there are 6 ways the spinner can come out.

$$2 \times 6 = 12 \quad \text{Outcomes for the coin and the spinner}$$

Exercises

The letters A, B, and C are written on cards. You pick a card without
looking and spin the spinner. Complete the list of outcomes.

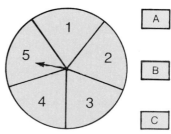

1. (A, ▦) (▦, 2) (▦, 3) (A, ▦) (A, ▦)
   (B, ▦) (B, ▦) (▦, 3) (▦, 4) (▦, 5)
   (▦, 1) (C, ▦) (C, ▦) (▦, 4) (C, ▦)

2. How many outcomes are there?

3. How many outcomes have B on the card?

4. What is the probability of getting B on the card?

5. What is the probability of getting B on the card and an odd number on the spinner?

You are going to choose a vegetable and a fruit for dinner. You have broccoli, corn, peas, and squash. You also have apples, oranges, and bananas.

6. List the outcomes. How many outcomes are there?

7. How many outcomes include peas or squash? broccoli or oranges? broccoli and oranges?

Suppose all the outcomes are equally likely. Complete.

8. P(peas or squash) = ▓

9. P(broccoli and oranges) = ▓

Short Forms

The names of government agencies sometimes read like "alphabet soup." Many abbreviations are used. There are, for example, the DOD (Department of Defense) and the SBA (Small Business Administration).

10. How many possibilities are there for each letter in an abbreviation?

11. Two-letter abbreviations are written. How many outcomes are there?

★ **12.** How many three-letter abbreviations can be written?

Calculator Corner

1. How many ways can a president, vice president, secretary, and treasurer be chosen from a class of 30 people? (*Hint:* There are 30 choices for president. Once the president is chosen there are 29 choices for vice president, and so on.)

2. How many 4-letter combinations can be made from the alphabet, if no letter can be repeated?

3. In how many different ways can 8 people be seated in a row?

Two-Step Probabilities

Four cars are displayed at City Motor Sales. They are all the same model but different colors: red, white, green, and yellow.

Carol takes a car for a drive and returns. Later, Isaac takes a car for a drive. If neither customer cared what color the car was, what is the probability that Carol drove the green car and Isaac drove the yellow car?

We can list the outcomes. The first letter shows the color of Carol's car, the second letter, the color of Isaac's car.

(r, r) (r, w) (r, g) (r, y) (w, r) (w, w) (w, g) (w, y)
(g, r) (g, w) (g, g) (g, y) (y, r) (y, w) (y, g) (y, y)

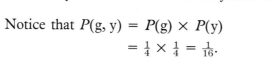

16 outcomes

$P(g, y) = \frac{1}{16}$

Probability that Carol chooses the green car: $P(g) = \frac{1}{4}$

Probability that Isaac chooses the yellow car: $P(y) = \frac{1}{4}$

Notice that $P(g, y) = P(g) \times P(y)$

$$= \frac{1}{4} \times \frac{1}{4} = \frac{1}{16}.$$

What if Isaac took a car out before Carol returned? The outcomes are now different. Isaac can't take the same car as Carol.

(r, w) (r, g) (r, y) (w, r) (w, g) (w, y)
(g, r) (g, w) (g, y) (y, r) (y, w) (y, g)

12 outcomes

$P(g, y) = \frac{1}{12}.$

Exercises

Use the information in the example above. Carol returns before Isaac takes a car.

1. How many outcomes are there?

2. In how many outcomes do they drive the same car?

3. $P(\text{they drive the same car}) = $ ▨ .

4. In how many outcomes do they drive different cars?

5. P(they drive different cars) = ▢ .

6. In how many outcomes do they both drive the red car?

7. P(both drive red car) = ▢ .

8. In how many outcomes does either person drive the red car?

9. P(either person drives red car) = ▢ .

In a game there are 3 Bonus (B) cards and 6 Forfeit (F) cards. The cards are shuffled together. The first player draws a card and replaces it before the second player draws. What is the probability?

10. P(B, B)   **11.** P(B, F)   **12.** P(F, B)   **13.** P(F, F)

The first player does not replace the card before the second player draws. What is the probability?

14. P(B, B)   **15.** P(B, F)   **16.** P(F, B)   **17.** P(F, F)

Family Matter

When a child is born, the chances are about the same that it will be a girl (G) as a boy (B).

18. P(G) = ▢   **19.** P(B) = ▢

A family has 2 children. What is the probability?

20. P(B, B)   **21.** P(B, G)   **22.** P(G, B)   **23.** P(G, G)

24. P(a boy and a girl)   **25.** P(both boys or both girls)

A family has 3 children. What is the probability?

26. P(G, G, G)   **27.** P(B, B, B)   **28.** P(neither all boys nor all girls)

★ **29.** What is the probability that a family with 6 children will have all girls?

Experimental Probability

Many times, we don't know the probability of an event. Also, all of the outcomes may not be equally likely. When this is true, we do an experiment. Then we can use the results of the experiment to estimate a probability.

Workers at Gro-Best Seeds test the corn seeds once a week. They use tally marks to record whether a seed sprouts or not.

	Week 1	Week 2
Does sprout	ͰͰͰ ͰͰͰ |||	ͰͰͰ ͰͰͰ ͰͰͰ ͰͰͰ ||
Doesn't sprout	ͰͰͰ ||	ͰͰͰ |||

Using Week 1, what is the probability that a seed will sprout?

Probability $= \dfrac{13}{20}$ — 13 seeds sprouted
— 20 seeds altogether

The probability is $\frac{13}{20}$. Of course, this is only an estimate. For a different group of seeds, the result could be different.

Exercises

Use the information in the chart above for Week 1.

1. How many seeds did not sprout? **2.** How many seeds were tested?

3. What is the probability that a seed won't sprout?

Use the information for Week 2.

4. How many seeds sprouted? **5.** How many seeds did not sprout?

6. How many seeds were tested? **7.** $P(\text{seed will sprout}) = $

8. $P(\text{seed won't sprout}) = $

The Student Council asked some students their opinion on having a school newspaper.
Here are the results of the poll.

	Grade 7	Grade 8
In favor	12	13
Not in favor	15	6
No opinion	3	1

What is the probability?

9. A 7th grader is in favor.

10. An 8th grader is not in favor.

11. An 8th grader has no opinion.

12. A student from either grade is in favor.

What Do You Expect?

The season halfway record is shown for the leading teams.

	Pumas	**Seals**	**Hawks**
w	11	15	11
l	11	10	9

13. What is the probability of each team winning its next game?

★ **14.** Which team appears most likely to be league champion?

★ **15.** Each team plays 50 games altogether. How many games would you expect each team to win?

Match the probabilities and events. (*pages 326–327*)

1. $\frac{1}{10}$ **A.** likely event

2. $\frac{97}{100}$ **B.** unlikely event

You spin the spinner. Complete. (*pages 328–329*)

3. $P(1) = $ ▦

4. $P(2 \text{ or } 3) = $ ▦

You spin the spinner, then toss a coin. (*pages 330–331*)

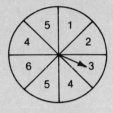

5. How many outcomes include 2 or 4?

6. How many outcomes include 2 or H?

You spin the spinner above twice. Complete. (*pages 332–333*)

7. $P(1, 1) = $ ▦   **8.** $P(2, \text{not } 3) = $ ▦

The Electrolite Co. tests light bulbs on the day they are made. The results are shown in the chart.

	Monday	**Friday**
Defect	4	2
No defect	16	18

What is the probability? (*pages 334–335*)

9. A Monday bulb is defective.

10. A Friday bulb is not defective.

Extra practice on page 442

Range and Mean

Number facts are sometimes called **data.** The data in the table are the number of floors in some buildings.

Building	City	Number of Floors
Sears Tower	Chicago	110
Empire State	New York	102
Standard Oil	Chicago	80
Chrysler	New York	77
Transamerica	San Francisco	48

We can describe the data in several ways. To find the **range,** we subtract the least number from the greatest. The range of the data in the table is 62 floors.

$$
\begin{array}{r}
110 \\
- 48 \\
\hline
62
\end{array}
$$

To find the **mean,** we divide the sum of the data by the number of items of data. The mean number of floors is 83, to the nearest whole number.

$$\frac{110 + 102 + 80 + 77 + 48}{5} = 83.4$$

Exercises

What is the range?

1. 10, 12, 13, 15, 19
   $19 - 10 = $

2. 28, 32, 47, 51, 52
   $52 - 28 = $ ▦

3. 18, 19, 23, 25, 27, 36
   $36 - $ ▦ $ = $ ▦

4. 33, 42, 47, 56, 68, 71
   ▦ $ - 33 = $ ▦

What is the mean?

5. 10, 12, 14, 18

$$\frac{10 + 12 + 14 + 18}{\blacksquare} = \frac{\blacksquare}{4} = \blacksquare$$

6. 5, 9, 11, 17, 23

$$\frac{5 + 9 + 11 + 17 + 23}{\blacksquare} = \frac{\blacksquare}{5} = \blacksquare$$

7. 15, 21, 33, 24, 16, 23

$$\frac{15 + 21 + 33 + 24 + 16 + 23}{\blacksquare} = \blacksquare$$

8. 18, 25, 16, 9, 39, 55

$$\frac{\blacksquare}{6} = \blacksquare$$

What are the range and the mean?

9. 5, 8, 11, 6, 2, 4

10. 5, 1, 3, 4, 7, 7, 9, 4

11. 17, 19, 28, 44, 37, 23

12. 41, 42, 42, 42, 50, 53

13. 54, 28, 54, 57, 54, 76

14. 88, 78, 68, 58, 48, 71

15. 203, 405, 512, 346

16. 203, 401, 378, 400, 401

17. 101, 98, 76, 113, 105

18. 56, 98, 108, 85, 123

19. 2483, 2591, 2675

20. 1800, 1738, 1894, 1522

Batting Averages

A baseball player's batting average is found by dividing the number of hits by the number of times at bat. What is the batting average for the player named?

Player	Times at Bat	Hits
Howe	404	101
Fierro	304	73
Doron	529	137
Flynn	530	120

21. Howe

22. Fierro

23. Doron

24. Flynn

★ **25.** What is the range of the batting averages?

★ **26.** What is the mean batting average?

337

Median and Mode

Seven students in the gym class counted the number of sit-ups they could do in one minute. The data are shown in the table.

Name	Number of Sit-Ups
Lisa	35
Jim	44
Lopez	48
Nancy	37
Jamie	36
Kathy	35
Ryan	48

When the data are written in order, the middle number is called the **median.**

$$35, 35, 36, 37, 44, 48, 48$$
$$\uparrow$$
median

When there are two middle numbers in a set of data that are written in order, the median is the mean of these two numbers.

Another student, Lorraine, did 39 sit-ups. We can include this in our set of data. Now there are two middle numbers.

$$35, 35, 36, 37, 39, 44, 48, 48$$

$$\begin{array}{r} 37 \\ +39 \\ \hline 76 \end{array}$$ $$\begin{array}{r} 38 \\ 2\overline{)76} \end{array}$$ 38 is the median.

A **mode** is a number which appears more often than other numbers. 35 and 48 both appear twice. They are both modes. Sometimes there is no mode.

Exercises

Arrange the data in order from least to greatest.

1. 14, 7, 8, 11, 7, 7, 6

2. 33, 19, 25, 21, 27, 33, 19

3. 56, 56, 72, 56, 68, 72, 72

4. 116, 109, 122, 109, 135, 116, 116

What is the median in the given exercise?

5. Exercise 1 **6.** Exercise 2 **7.** Exercise 3 **8.** Exercise 4

What is the mode (or modes) in the given exercise?

9. Exercise 1   **10.** Exercise 2   **11.** Exercise 3   **12.** Exercise 4

What is the median? What is the mode (or modes)?

13. 16, 15, 13, 16, 11

14. 12, 11, 9, 8, 13, 9

15. 28, 21, 23, 27, 21

16. 59, 41, 59, 52, 41, 44

17. 62, 48, 43, 53, 48, 52

18. 128, 141, 143, 128, 138

19. 135, 135, 124, 116, 142, 144

20. 130, 86, 94, 110, 88, 94

21. 210, 256, 159, 256, 234, 218

22. 536, 498, 525, 498, 252, 536

Use the chart for Exercises 23–24.

23. What are the median and the modes for the numbers of minutes practiced daily by members of the track team?

24. What is the median and the mode for the heights of members of the track team?

	TRACK TEAM									
	Lisa	Jim	Lopez	Nancy	Jamie	Kathy	Laurie	Ryan	Ellie	Ed
Minutes of Daily Practice	50	65	75	45	70	70	60	55	75	55
Height in Centimeters	146	156	159	165	168	146	156	168	146	170

Take Your Choice

Sam kept track of the colors of cars passing a checkpoint during one hour. His record is shown at the right.

25. a. What is the median?
   b. What are the modes?
   c. How can Sam's survey help the purchasing agent for a car dealership?

Colors of Cars Passing a Checkpoint	
Red	13
Blue	25
Green	22
Black	6
Brown	22
Gray	13

Using Range, Mean, Median, and Mode

Depending on the data, one or more of the numbers, range, mean, median, mode may be more helpful than another.

		MEAN MONTHLY TEMPERATURE IN °F											
City	Jan.	Feb.	Mar.	Apr.	May	Jun.	Jul.	Aug.	Sept.	Oct.	Nov.	Dec.
Nome, Alaska	6	5	7	19	35	46	50	49	42	29	16	4
Miami, Florida	67	68	71	76	78	81	82	83	82	78	72	68

	Data	Comments
Nome	Range: 50 − 4 = 46 Mean: 26	Quite a range in temperature. Mean of 26 shows a cold climate. Lowest mean monthly temperature of 4 shows it probably doesn't go extremely far below zero.
Miami	Range: 83 − 67 = 16 Mean: 76	Less range in temperature than in Nome. Mean of 76 shows a warm climate.

Exercises

1. During which months would you travel to Nome if you did not like winter weather?

2. In which city, Nome or Miami, would you be more likely to notice the change in seasons?

3. How does the growing season in Nome compare with that in Miami?

4. What is the median temperature in Nome? If you knew *only* the median temperature would it tell you whether Nome is in a warm or cold climate?

5. What is the mode of the temperatures in Nome? Is it helpful to know the mode?

6. What is the median temperature in Miami? Together with the range, does the median temperature tell you anything about the climate?

7. What is the mode of the temperatures in Miami? Is it helpful to know this?

Ups and Downs

	ELEVATIONS IN METERS				
	Highest Elevation	**Lowest Elevation**	**Elevations of Three Principal Cities**		
British Columbia	4663	0	676	375	39
Nebraska	1654	256	1219	854	356

Use these exercises to analyze the data in the table.

8. Compare the range of highest and lowest elevations of British Columbia with that of Nebraska. What does this tell you?

9. a. What is the mean elevation of the three principal cities in British Columbia?
   b. What is the mean elevation of the three principal cities in Nebraska?
   c. Using the mean elevations, could you safely predict which has the highest elevation, British Columbia or Nebraska?

Pictographs

A **pictograph** uses picture symbols to represent numbers. The pictograph below shows the number of albums sold at Sounds Swell last month. Since each represents 20 albums sold, represents 10 albums sold.

ALBUMS SOLD AT SOUNDS SWELL IN ONE MONTH	
Type	Number of Albums = 20 Albums
Classical	◉ (
Country Western	◉ ◉ ◉ ◉ ◉ ◉ ◉ ◉ ◉
Folk	(
Rock	◉ ◉ ◉ ◉ ◉ ◉ ◉ ◉ ◉ ◉ ◉ ◉
Disco	◉ ◉ ◉ ◉ ◉ ◉ ◉
Jazz	◉ ◉

Exercises

1. What type of album had the greatest sales?

2. What type of album had the smallest sales?

How many albums of each type were sold?

3. Country-Western = 20 × ▢ = ▢   **4.** Classical: 20 × ▢ = ▢

5. Jazz   **6.** Folk   **7.** Rock   **8.** Disco

MEMBERSHIP IN FAN CLUBS	
Rock Group	**Number of Fans** ★ = 1000 Fans
The Wheels	★ ★ ★ ★ ★ ★
Checkered Zebra	★ ★ ★ ★ ★ ★ ★ ★
White Limousine	★ ★ ★ ⸸
The Wild Blue	★ ★ ★ ★
Numeros	★ ★ ★ ★ ★ ★ ★ ★ ★ ⸸
Denver Boot	★ ★ ★ ★ ★ ★ ★ ★ ★

How many members are in each fan club?

9. The Wheels   **10.** Checkered Zebra   **11.** White Limousine

12. The Wild Blue   **13.** Numeros   **14.** Denver Boot

Camera Sales

The table shows the sales of cameras in the Camera Shutter chain of stores during one day.

15. Make a pictograph for the data. Use 🔲 to represent 20 cameras.

CAMERA SHUTTER CHAIN STORES	
Location of Store	**Number of Cameras Sold**
Albion	80
Boone	60
Darby	110
Chipley	95
Dove Creek	45

Show how you can copy this figure without lifting your pencil from the paper and without retracing any line.

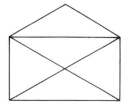

Take a Break

Bar Graphs

The bar graph below compares the highest waterfalls on some continents. The heights are given in meters. You can read the bar graph and estimate that the highest waterfall in Asia is about 350 m high.

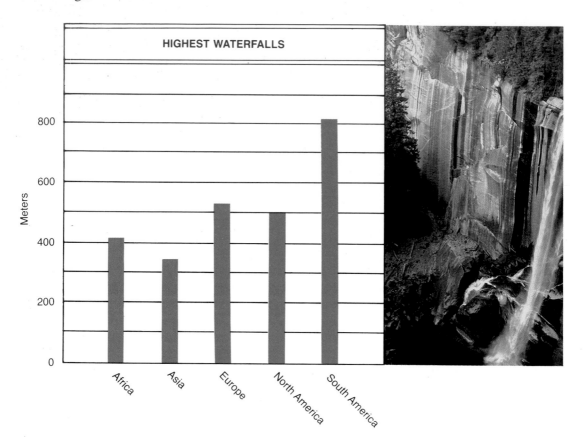

HIGHEST WATERFALLS

Meters

Exercises

Use the bar graph above to estimate the height of the highest waterfall on the given continent.

1. Africa

2. North America

3. Europe

4. South America

5. Which continent has the highest waterfall?

6. List the continents in order from shortest to highest waterfall.

The double-bar graph below compares the heights of the highest mountain and the highest active volcano on several continents. You can estimate that in Europe the highest mountain is about 5500 m high, and the highest volcano is about 3500 m high.

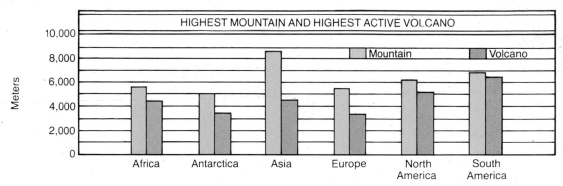

Estimate the height of the highest mountain on the continent.

7. Africa   **8.** Antarctica   **9.** Asia

10. North America   **11.** South America

Estimate the height of the highest volcano on the continent.

12. Africa   **13.** Antarctica   **14.** Asia

15. Europe   **16.** North America   **17.** South America

18. On which continent is there the greatest difference between the heights of the highest mountain and the highest volcano?

19. On which continent is there the least difference between the heights?

What's New?

Solve.

20. The table compares the numbers of newspapers in circulation in 1970 with those in circulation in 1980. Round the data to the nearest 100 and draw a double-bar graph.

NUMBERS OF NEWSPAPERS IN CIRCULATION		
Type of Newspaper	**1970**	**1980**
Semi-weekly	423	537
Weekly	8903	7159
Daily	1838	1744
Other	219	180

Line Graphs

We often use line graphs to show change over a period of time.

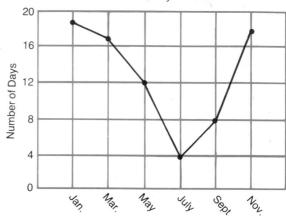

MEAN NUMBER OF DAYS WITH PRECIPITATION IN PORTLAND, OREGON

This line graph shows the change in precipitation in Portland, Oregon, during the six months.

You can see that in March the mean number of days with precipitation is 17.

Exercises

Use the graph above. What is the mean number of days with precipitation for the given month?

1. January   **2.** May   **3.** July

4. September   **5.** November

6. Which is the wettest month in Portland, Oregon?

7. Which is the dryest month in Portland, Oregon?

About what is the mean monthly temperature for the given month?

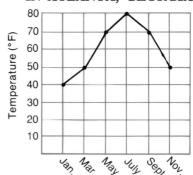

MEAN MONTHLY TEMPERATURES IN ATLANTA, GEORGIA

8. January   **9.** March   **10.** May

11. July   **12.** September   **13.** November

14. What is the difference between the highest and lowest mean temperatures?

MEAN HIGH AND LOW TEMPERATURES IN NEW ORLEANS, LA.

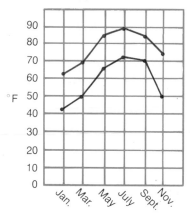

15. During which month is there the greatest difference in the mean highest and lowest temperatures?

16. During which month is there the least difference in the mean highest and lowest temperatures?

Graphing Heights

17. Make a double-line graph for the median heights for boys and girls.

18. What do you notice about your graph?

MEDIAN HEIGHT IN INCHES		
Age	**Boys**	**Girls**
8	51	50
10	54	55
12	59	60
14	64	63
16	69	64
18	70	64

What are the range, median, and mode? (*pages 336–339*)

1. 8, 6, 9, 1, 2

2. 15, 7, 7, 8, 12

Use the bar graph. (*pages 340–345*)

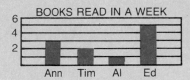

How many books were read in a week?

3. Ann   **4.** Tim   **5.** Al

Use the line graph. (*pages 346–347*)

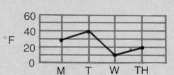

What was the temperature?

6. Mon.   **7.** Tues.

Problem Solving • MAKING PREDICTIONS

The Digitime Watch Company plans to produce digital watches in five different colors: red, blue, silver, yellow, and black. They can produce 5000 watches a month. How many should they produce of each color? To find out, they made a survey. They picked the names of 100 people by chance from the telephone book and called and asked them what colors they would choose. The results are shown in the table. Then they calculated how many watches to make of each color.

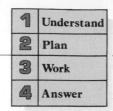

DIGITIME WATCH SURVEY	
Color	**Choices**
Red	18
Blue	12
Silver	30
Yellow	15
Black	25
Total	100

Numbers of Watches to Be Produced
Red: $\frac{18}{100} \times 5000 = 900$
Blue: $\frac{12}{100} \times 5000 = 600$
Silver: $\frac{30}{100} \times 5000 = 1500$
Yellow: $\frac{15}{100} \times 5000 = 750$
Black: $\frac{25}{100} \times 5000 = 1250$

The Production Department made a graph to display the information. The first production month was March.

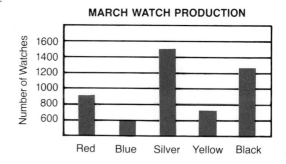

MARCH WATCH PRODUCTION

Solve.

1. The Digitime Watch Company kept track of sales during March. The results are shown in the table. They plan to base their April production figures on the March sales figures. Total production for April is again planned to be 5000 watches. Use the results in the table to calculate the number of watches of each color to be produced in April. Using your figures, make a double-bar graph comparing the March and April production figures.

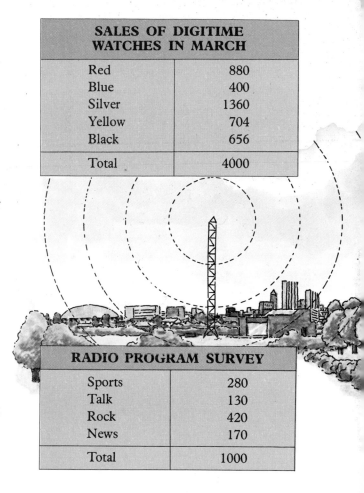

SALES OF DIGITIME WATCHES IN MARCH	
Red	880
Blue	400
Silver	1360
Yellow	704
Black	656
Total	4000

2. A radio station wants to change its afternoon format. A survey of listeners shows what the people like. The station estimates there are about 3,000,000 people in all who listen to the radio in the afternoon in their listening area. Calculate how many listeners the station might expect for each kind of program.

RADIO PROGRAM SURVEY	
Sports	280
Talk	130
Rock	420
News	170
Total	1000

3. The table shows the number of sales of some greeting cards in one year by the Hi Ya Greeting Card Company. In the next year, they plan to increase the total production of these cards to 750,000. Using these sales figures, calculate how many of each kind of card Hi Ya should produce in the next year.

YEAR'S SALES OF HI YA GREETING CARDS	
Birthday	124,000
Get Well	136,000
Valentine	152,000
Halloween	88,000
Total	500,000

You spin the spinner. Complete.

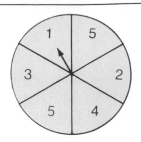

1. P(even number) = ▨   **2.** P(odd number) = ▨

3. $P(4)$ = ▨   **4.** P(not 6) = ▨

You spin the spinner twice.

5. List the outcomes.   **6.** How many outcomes are there?

7. What is $P(2, 4)$?   **8.** What is P(2, not 10)?

Use the data from the chart.

9. What is the range?

10. What is the mean?

11. What is the mode?

12. What is the median?

GLOBAL AIRWAYS NUMBER OF FLIGHTS FROM MIDVILLE TO MASON						
Mon.	Tues.	Wed.	Thurs.	Fri.	Sat.	Sun.
8	7	5	8	9	2	3

Use the graph to answer the question.

13. How many passengers were there in May?

14. About what were the profits in July?

15. What was the lowest temperature? When?

PASSENGERS

April	♀♀♀
May	♀♀♀♀
June	♀♀♀♀♀♀♀

♀ = 10,000

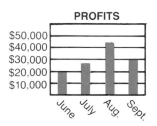

PROFITS

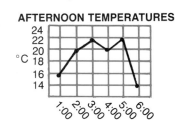

AFTERNOON TEMPERATURES

Out of one hundred people surveyed by Global Airways, seventy-five said that they preferred chicken to fish for dinner. Use this information to answer the question.

16. What is the probability that a passenger will order fish rather than chicken?

17. The chef has to prepare 8000 chicken and fish dinners. Using the results of the survey, how many of these should be chicken?

You spin the spinner, then toss a coin. (*pages 326–331*)

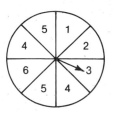

1. Is (6, 4) an impossible event?

2. How many outcomes are there?

3. How many outcomes include a 5 or 3?

You spin the spinner above twice. What is the probability? (*pages 332–333*)

4. P(1, 5)   **5.** P(3, 3)   **6.** P(2, not 5)   **7.** P(5, 5)

Quality control inspectors at the QT car tire factory test tires. The results are shown in the table. What is the probability? (*pages 334–335*)

8. A Monday tire is defective.

9. A Wednesday tire is not defective.

10. A Monday tire is not defective.

11. A tire made either day is defective.

	Monday	Wednesday
Defect	7	2
No Defect	43	48

What are the range, the mean, the median, and the mode? (*pages 336–339*)

12. 7, 9, 5, 3, 6, 6   **13.** 42, 71, 38, 25, 65, 71

Use the graph to answer the question. (*pages 342–347*)

14. How many shoppers were in the mall on Tuesday?

15. What are the sales for Kier?

16. What is the mean wind speed for July?

Day	Number of Shoppers in Mall
Tues.	👥👥👥👥 👤 = 100
Thurs.	👥👥👥👥👥👥👥👥
Sat.	👥👥👥👥👥👥👥👥👥👥👥👥

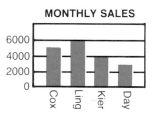

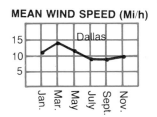

17. Hark, Inc., produces 5 different models of radios. In March, 650 Model A radios were sold out of a total sales of 8500 radios. Hark plans to produce 10,000 radios in April. How many Model A radios should they produce?

Extra practice on page 443

The Pythagorean Theorem

In a right triangle, the side opposite the right angle is called the **hypotenuse.** It is always the longest side. In the triangle shown, the side labeled c is the hypotenuse.

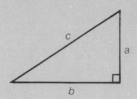

Pythagoras was a Greek mathematician who lived about 2500 years ago. He proved that all right triangles have this important property.

> If a triangle is a right triangle, the square of the length of the hypotenuse is equal to the sum of the squares of the lengths of the other two sides.

This property is usually called the **Pythagorean Theorem.** Here is how it is applied to the triangle above.

$$c^2 = a^2 + b^2$$

It is also true that if a triangle has this property, it is a right triangle.

If you know the lengths of the sides of a triangle, you can use the Pythagorean Theorem to decide if it is a right triangle.

$$c^2 = a^2 + b^2$$
$$13^2 = 5^2 + 12^2$$
$$169 = 25 + 144 \quad \text{True}$$

The triangle is a right triangle.

Is a triangle with sides of the given lengths a right triangle? Write *Yes* or *No.*

1. 3, 4, 5   **2.** 4, 5, 6   **3.** 6, 8, 10   **4.** 9, 12, 15

5. 5, 12, 14   **6.** 8, 9, 14   **7.** 8, 15, 17   **8.** 12, 16, 20

9. 25, 7, 24   **10.** 20, 11, 21   **11.** 20, 15, 25   **12.** 26, 24, 10

If you know the lengths of two sides of a right triangle, you can use the Pythagorean Theorem to calculate the length of the third side.

$$c^2 = a^2 + b^2$$
$$c^2 = 12^2 + 16^2$$
$$c^2 = 144 + 256$$
$$c^2 = 400$$
$$c = \sqrt{400} = 20$$

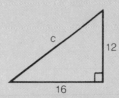

The length of the hypotenuse is 20.

What is the length of the hypotenuse? Use a calculator if you wish.

13.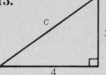

14.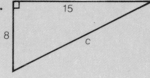

15.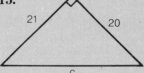

16. side $a = 7$
    side $b = 24$

17. side $a = 18$
    side $b = 24$

18. side $a = 16$
    side $b = 30$

What is the length of a diagonal of the rectangle? Use a calculator if you wish.

19.

20.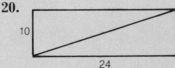

21.

Solve.

22. Your garden is in the shape of a rectangle that measures 24 m by 32 m. You want to put a diagonal walk from corner to corner across the garden. What will be the length of the walk?

23. A vacant lot is in the shape of a rectangle that measures 20 m by 21 m. You want to walk from one corner to the opposite corner. How many fewer meters do you walk if you walk diagonally across the lot rather than along two sides of the lot?

Maintaining Skills

To win at Percento, you must have 3 of 4 cards with equal value. One must be a fraction, one a decimal, and one a percent. For example, the hand at the right forms a winning hand because 0.5, $\frac{1}{2}$, and 50% are equal.

Is this a winning hand? Write *Yes* or *No*.

1.

2.

3.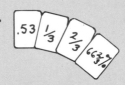

4.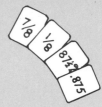

5. 5%, 0.5, $\frac{1}{2}$, $\frac{1}{20}$

6. $\frac{169}{1000}$, 16.9%, 0.169, 16%

7. 0.225, 225%, $\frac{1}{225}$, $\frac{1}{2}$

8. $\frac{1}{3}$, 0.33$\overline{3}$, 33$\frac{1}{3}$%, $\frac{2}{3}$

Name a card that will complete a winning hand.

9. $\frac{3}{10}$, $\frac{1}{3}$, 30%

10. 0.07, $\frac{7}{100}$, 70%

11. $\frac{5}{8}$, 85%, 62$\frac{1}{2}$%

12. 0.79, $\frac{79}{100}$, 77%

13. 52%, $\frac{3}{4}$, 0.52

14. 0.05, $\frac{1}{20}$, 50%

15. $\frac{9}{50}$, 18%, 60%

16. $\frac{1}{5}$, 0.2, 2%

17. $\frac{1}{4}$, 2.5, 250%

18. 44%, 0.44, $\frac{44}{50}$

19. 0.444, $\frac{9}{20}$, 45%

20. $\frac{3}{8}$, 0.48, 48%

Solve.

21. 75% of 300 people is how many?

22. 6% tax on $1.50 is how much?

23. What is 15% tip of $7.80?

24. 18 rooms are what percent of 24?

25. $30 is what percent of $80?

26. What percent of 200 homes are 125?

27. 75% of what number is 21 pets?

28. $1.65 is a 15% tip of what total?

Geometry and Measurement

Many modern buildings are made by combining simple geometric shapes and solids. What shapes and solids do you see in this hotel?

13

Congruent Figures

Figures that have the same size and shape are called **congruent figures.** If you buy a new part for your bike, you expect the new part to be congruent to the one it is replacing.

In congruent figures, measures of corresponding parts are equal. Triangles *ABC* and *DEF* shown below are congruent. The symbol for *triangle* is △. We write △ *ABC* ≅ △ *DEF*.

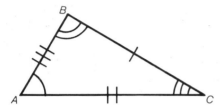
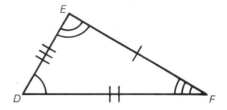

The measures of corresponding angles are equal. So, corresponding angles are congruent.

$$\angle A \cong \angle D$$
$$\angle B \cong \angle E$$
$$\angle C \cong \angle F$$

The lengths of corresponding sides are equal. So, corresponding sides are congruent.

$$\overline{AB} \cong \overline{DE}$$
$$\overline{BC} \cong \overline{EF}$$
$$\overline{AC} \cong \overline{DF}$$

When referring to two congruent polygons, it is customary to list their corresponding vertexes in the same order.

Exercises

△ *XYZ* ≅ △ *PQR*. Complete.

1. ∠*X* ≅ ▨
2. ∠*Z* ≅ ▨
3. ∠*Y* ≅ ▨
4. $\overline{XY}$ ≅ ▨
5. $\overline{YZ}$ ≅ ▨
6. $\overline{XZ}$ ≅ ▨

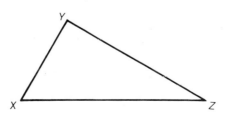
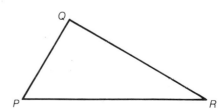

Complete the statement for each pair of congruent figures.

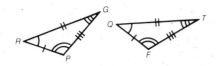
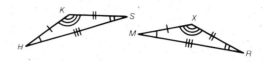

7. $\triangle RPG \cong \triangle$ ▨ **8.** $\triangle PGR \cong \triangle$ ▨ **9.** $\triangle KHS \cong \triangle$ ▨ **10.** $\triangle HSK \cong \triangle$ ▨

Quadrilateral $VRQK \cong$ Quadrilateral
$SMHG$
Write the congruent angle or side.

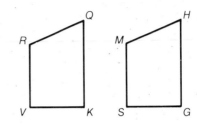

11. $\angle R$ **12.** $\angle V$ **13.** $\angle M$

14. $\overline{GH}$ **15.** $\overline{VR}$ **16.** $\overline{MH}$

Pentagon $ABCDE \cong$ Pentagon $ZVWXY$
Complete the statement.

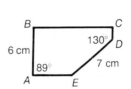
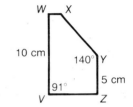

17. $VZ =$ ▨ cm **18.** $\angle E =$ ▨ °

19. $XY =$ ▨ cm **20.** $\angle B =$ ▨ °

Hidden Triangles

Diagonal $\overline{BD}$ divides parallelogram
$ABCD$ into two congruent triangles.

$\triangle ABD \cong \triangle CDB.$ Complete the
statement.

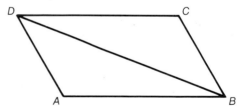

21. $\angle A \cong \angle$ ▨ **22.** $\overline{AB} \cong$ ▨

23. $\angle ADB \cong \angle$ ▨ **24.** $\angle DBA \cong \angle$ ▨

In parallelogram $LQNM,$
$\triangle LNQ \cong \triangle MQN.$ Complete the
statement.

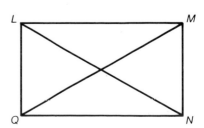

25. $\overline{LN} \cong$ ▨ **26.** $\overline{LQ} \cong$ ▨

27. $\overline{NQ} \cong$ ▨ **28.** $\angle QLN \cong \angle$ ▨

29. $\angle LNQ \cong \angle$ ▨ **30.** $\angle LQN \cong \angle$ ▨

Geometric Constructions

A **compass** and a **straightedge** are the only tools used in geometric constructions.

A compass is used to construct a circle or part of a circle, called an **arc.**

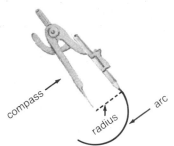

A straightedge is used to draw a line segment. You may use the edge of a ruler as a straightedge, but the markings on a ruler are not used in constructions.

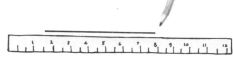

straight edge

You can use a compass to construct a circle with a radius that is congruent to a line segment such as $\overline{AB}$.

First, draw and label Point O.

$O\ \bullet$

Next, open the compass to the length of $\overline{AB}$.

Place the point of the compass on O and draw circle O.

With a compass and a straightedge you can construct a line segment that is congruent to $\overline{AB}$. First, draw a ray with endpoint Q. Next, open the compass to the length of $\overline{AB}$. Draw an arc that crosses the ray. Label the point of intersection P. $\overline{QP} \cong \overline{AB}$.

Exercises

Use a compass to construct a circle with the radius given.

1. $r = 4$ cm   **2.** $r = 6$ cm   **3.** $r = 3.5$ cm   **4.** $r = 8.6$ cm

Use a compass and straightedge to construct a line segment congruent to the given line segment.

5. _____ **6.** _____ **7.** _____

Using a compass and a straightedge, copy the design.

8.

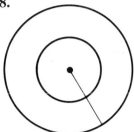

9.

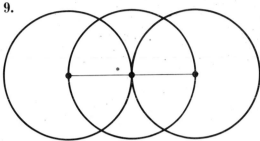

Do the construction.

A _____ B

10. Construct a line segment whose length is 2 times the length of $\overline{AB}$.

11. Construct a circle whose radius is congruent to $\overline{AB}$.

12. Construct a circle whose radius is twice as long as $\overline{AB}$.

13. Construct a circle that is congruent to Circle O.

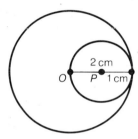

14. Construct a circle that is congruent to Circle P.

Floor Show

Geometric constructions are often used in the design of floor tiles.

15. Use a compass and straightedge to copy this design.

16. Use a compass and straightedge to design your own original pattern for floor tiles.

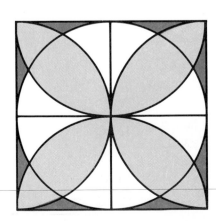

359

Constructing Congruent Angles

Drafters use geometric constructions to draw the finished plans for buildings and machinery. It may be necessary to construct an angle that is congruent to a given angle.

Follow these steps to construct an angle that is congruent to ∠A. First, draw a ray with endpoint O.

Draw an arc with center A. Then with the same radius, draw an arc with center O. Label the intersection P as shown.

Put your compass point at C and open your compass so you can draw an arc through B. Then with center P and this radius, draw an arc which intersects the other arc at Q.

Finally, draw $\overrightarrow{OQ}$. ∠QOP ≅ ∠A.

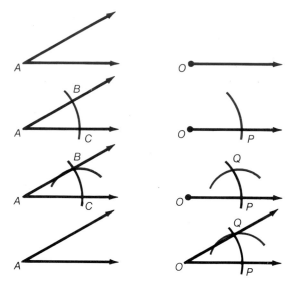

A **straight angle** is an angle with a measure of 180°. The two rays that form a straight angle together form a straight line. You can use this fact to construct the supplement of an angle.

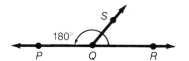

∠PQR is a straight angle.
∠PQR = 180°
∠PQS is supplementary to ∠SQR.

Exercises

Use a protractor to draw the angle. Construct an angle congruent to the given angle.

1.
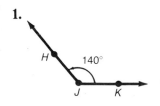

2.
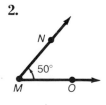

3.

4.
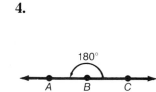

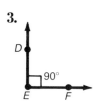

Use a protractor to draw the angle. Construct an angle that is
supplementary to the given angle.

5.

60°

6.

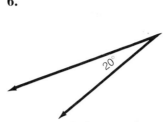

20°

7.

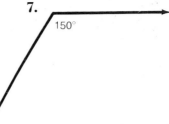

150°

Some Angle Sums

Trace △XYZ. Use your copy of
△XYZ to construct an angle with the
given measure.

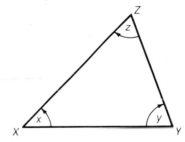

8. $x + y$　　　　**9.** $2x$

10. $180° - z$　　**11.** $2x - y$

12. $x + y + z$　　**13.** $x + 2z$

14. Draw an obtuse triangle. Use a geometric construction to show
that the sum of the measures of the angles is 180°.

15. Draw a quadrilateral. Use a geometric construction to show that
the sum of the measures of the angles is 360°.

NETWORKS

A network is a pattern made up of a number of line segments
that cross. Which of the networks below can be drawn without
lifting the pencil and without retracing a line segment?

Take a
Break

Bisectors

To **bisect** means to divide into two equal parts.

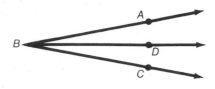

$$\angle ABD \cong \angle DBC$$
$\overrightarrow{BD}$ **bisects** $\angle ABC$.

$$\overline{XY} = \overline{YZ}$$
Point Y **bisects** $\overline{XZ}$.

$\overline{BD}$ is the **angle bisector** of $\angle ABC$.

Y is called the **midpoint** of $\overline{XZ}$.

You can construct an angle bisector using a compass and a straightedge.

1. With O as the center, draw an arc that intersects both sides of $\angle AOB$. Label the intersections X and Y.

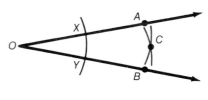

2. Open the compass to a radius that is greater than half the distance from X to Y. Using X and Y as centers, draw arcs that intersect at C.

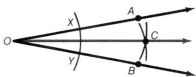

3. Draw $\overrightarrow{OC}$. $\overrightarrow{OC}$ bisects $\angle AOB$.
   $\angle AOC \cong \angle COB$.

If you bisect a straight angle, you get two right angles.

Exercises

Use the figure at the right to complete the statement.

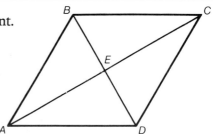

1. E is the midpoint of BD. So $\overline{BE} \cong$ ▨.

2. $\overline{AE} \cong \overline{EC}$. So, E is the midpoint of ▨.

3. $\angle ABD \cong \angle DBC$. So $\overrightarrow{BD}$ is the angle bisector of $\angle$ ▨.

Use a protractor to draw an angle with the given measure. Construct the bisector of the angle.

4.

5.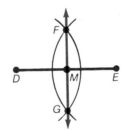

6.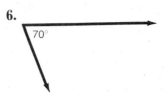

7. 60°   **8.** 140°   **9.** 42°   **10.** 168°   **11.** 90°   **12.** 180°

Draw a large figure. Construct all the angle bisectors.

13. acute triangle   **14.** obtuse triangle   **15.** scalene triangle

16. right triangle   **17.** square   **18.** rectangle

Perpendicular Bisectors

Here's how you can construct the bisector of a line segment with a compass and a straightedge.

1. Open the compass to a radius that is greater than half the distance from D to E. With D and E as centers, draw arcs that intersect at F and G.

2. Draw $\overline{FG}$. $\overline{FG}$ bisects $\overline{DE}$. M is the midpoint of $\overline{DE}$. $\overline{DM} \cong \overline{ME}$.

In this last construction, not only does $\overline{FG}$ bisect $\overline{DE}$, but $\overline{FG}$ is also perpendicular to $\overline{DE}$. We call $\overline{FG}$ the **perpendicular bisector** of $\overline{DE}$.

Construct a line segment congruent to the given line segment. Construct the perpendicular bisector of the line segment.

19. ——————————   **20.** ————————————————   **21.** —————

★ **22.** Construct an isosceles right triangle.

★ **23.** Construct a large right triangle. Construct the perpendicular bisectors of all the sides. Do you notice anything?

Symmetry

If we fold the figure shown at the right along the dotted line, one side will fit exactly on the other. We say the figure has symmetry with respect to the dotted line. We refer to the dotted line as a **line of symmetry.**

This figure has more than one line of symmetry.

Now look at this figure. Line segments have been drawn through Point *A*, and each line segment ends on the figure. Point *A* is the **midpoint** of all such line segments. We say that the figure has **point symmetry.** Point *A* is the **point of symmetry.**

If we turn a figure with point symmetry around so that it is upside down, it will match its shape in the original position.

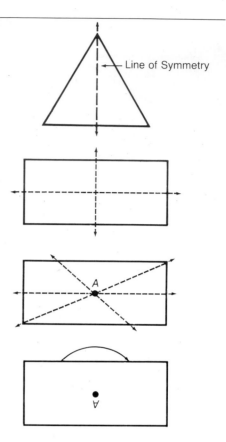

Exercises

Is the dashed line a line of symmetry? Write *Yes* or *No*.

1.
2.
3.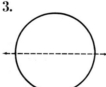
4.

Is the dot a point of symmetry? Write *Yes* or *No*.

5.
6.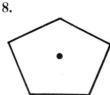
7.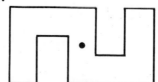
8.

Does the figure have line symmetry,
point symmetry, or both?

9. **10.**

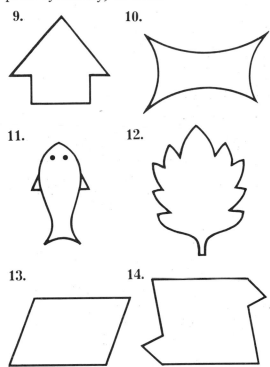

11. **12.**

13. **14.**

Figuring Symmetry

True or False? Write *T* or *F.*

15. A regular hexagon has at least six
lines of symmetry.

16. An isosceles triangle has two lines of
symmetry.

17. A diameter of a circle is a line of
symmetry of that circle.

★ **18.** Draw seven capital letters of the
alphabet that have line symmetry.

★ **19.** Which capital letters have point
symmetry?

Checkpoint A

Quadrilateral *ABCD* ≅ Quadrilateral
PQRS. Write the congruent angle or
side. (*pages 356–357*)

1. ∠*A*   **2.** ∠*S*   **3.** $\overline{BC}$ **4.** $\overline{SR}$

Do the construction. (*pages 358–359*)

5. Construct a line segment twice as
long as $\overline{PQ}$. $\overset{\bullet}{P}\rule{3cm}{0.4pt}\overset{\bullet}{Q}$

6. Construct a circle whose radius is
congruent to $\overline{PQ}$.

Use a protractor to draw the angle.
Then construct a congruent angle.
(*pages 360–361*)

7. 45°   **8.** 122°   **9.** 90°   **10.** 160°

Use a protractor to draw the angle.
Construct the angle bisector.
(*pages 362–363*)

11. 140° **12.** 80° **13.** 68° **14.** 90°

Does the figure have line symmetry,
point symmetry, or both?
(*pages 364–365*)

15. **16.**

Classifying Solids

Objects in real life have three dimensions, length, width, and height. In geometry, three-dimensional shapes are called *solids*. The flat surfaces that form many of these shapes are called **faces.** Two faces intersect at an **edge.** Three or more edges intersect at a **vertex.**

A **pyramid** has only one base. Its shape can be any polygon. The other faces of a pyramid are triangles.

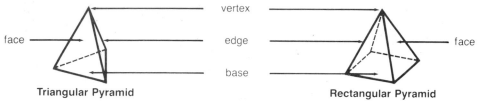

A **prism** has two congruent parallel bases whose shape is any polygon. The other faces of a prism are parallelograms.

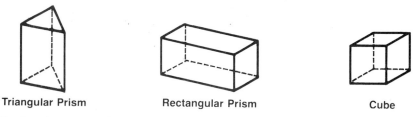

A **cylinder** has two circular bases; a **cone** has one; a **sphere** has none.

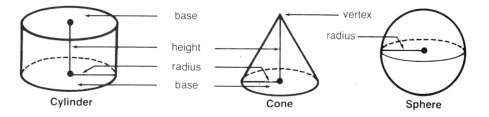

Exercises

True or False? Write *T* or *F.*

1. A rectangular prism has six faces.

2. All spheres are the same size.

3. A triangular prism has six faces.

4. A cube is a prism.

5. A sphere has no base.

6. All prisms are cubes.

7. A sphere has no edges.

8. The edges of a cube are congruent.

9. A cylinder has no vertex.

10. A cube has six congruent faces.

11. All the faces of a pyramid are triangles.

12. All the faces of a prism are rectangles.

13. The bases of a triangular prism are triangles.

14. All the faces of a triangular prism are rectangles.

15. The two bases of a cylinder may be different sizes.

16. A rectangular prism has three pairs of congruent faces.

What shape would be formed by folding and taping the pattern together?

17. **18.** **19.**

20. **21.** **22.**

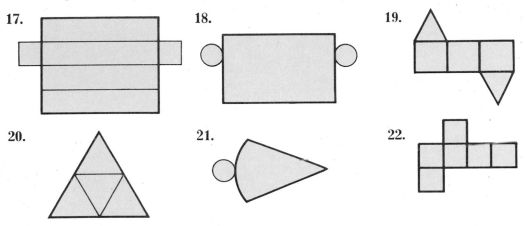

Slices of Life

Think of a plane slicing through the center of a sphere. The shape that is formed is a circle. The circle is a **cross section** of the sphere.

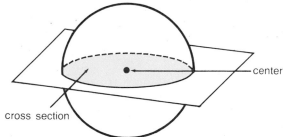

center

cross section

Name the cross section.

23. a cylinder sliced perpendicular to its bases

24. a triangular prism sliced parallel to its bases

25. a square pyramid sliced parallel to the base

26. a triangular pyramid sliced perpendicular to the base and through a vertex

Surface Area: Prisms and Pyramids

The **surface area** of a prism or pyramid is the sum of the areas of all its faces and its base.

If you cut out a figure like the one shown and fold along the dotted lines, you will have a pyramid with a square base.

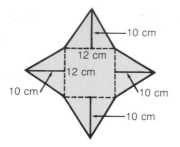

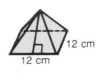

In this pyramid, the four triangular faces are congruent. So, the surface area is equal to the area of the base plus 4 times the area of one of the triangles.

Area of square $= s^2$	Area of one triangle $= b \times h \div 2$
$= 12 \times 12$	$= 12 \times 10 \div 2$
$= 144$ (cm^2)	$= 60$ (cm^2)

$$\text{Surface area} = 144 + (4 \times 60)$$
$$= 144 + 240$$
$$= 384 \ (\text{cm}^2)$$

Exercises

What is the area?

1. Top and bottom

2. Four sides

3. Surface area

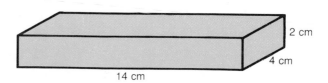

What is the surface area?

4.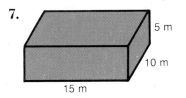

5.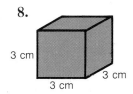

6.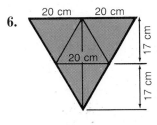

7.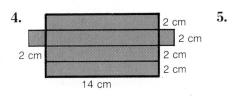

8.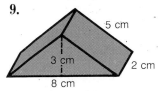

9.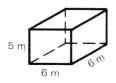

Interior Designs

A decorator wishes to make the lobby of an apartment building more attractive. The dimensions of the lobby are given at the right.

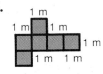

10. The floor is to be carpeted. What is the area of the floor?

11. One wall is to get mirrored tiles. What is the area of one wall?

★ **12.** The three walls that are not mirrored and the ceiling are to be painted. About 30% of the three walls is used for an entrance and for windows. What is the total surface area to be painted?

Surface Area: Cylinders

Many common objects are shaped as cylinders. The surface area of a cylinder is equal to the area of the two circular bases plus the area of the rectangle that forms the curved surface.

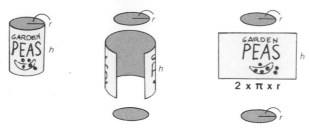

The base of the rectangle equals the circumference of one of the circles. The height of the rectangle is the height of the cylinder.

To find the surface area of the cylinder, we will use the values of the radius and height. First find the circumference.

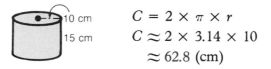

$C = 2 \times \pi \times r$
$C \approx 2 \times 3.14 \times 10$
≈ 62.8 (cm)

Find the area of the curved surface.

$A = b \times h$
$A \approx 62.8 \times 15$
≈ 942 (cm²)

Find the area of one of the bases.

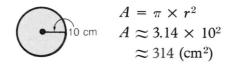

$A = \pi \times r^2$
$A \approx 3.14 \times 10^2$
≈ 314 (cm²)

Finally, add to find the total surface area.

Surface Area = Area of Curved Surface + Area of Two Bases
Surface Area $\approx$ 942   +   (2 × 314)
$\approx$ 1570 (cm²)

Exercises

Complete.

1. Area of two bases = $2 \times \pi \times$ ▨ ^{2}

2. Circumference = $2 \times \pi \times$ ▨

3. Area of curved surface = circumference × ▨

4. Surface area = ▨ + ▨

Use 3.14 for π to approximate the surface area.

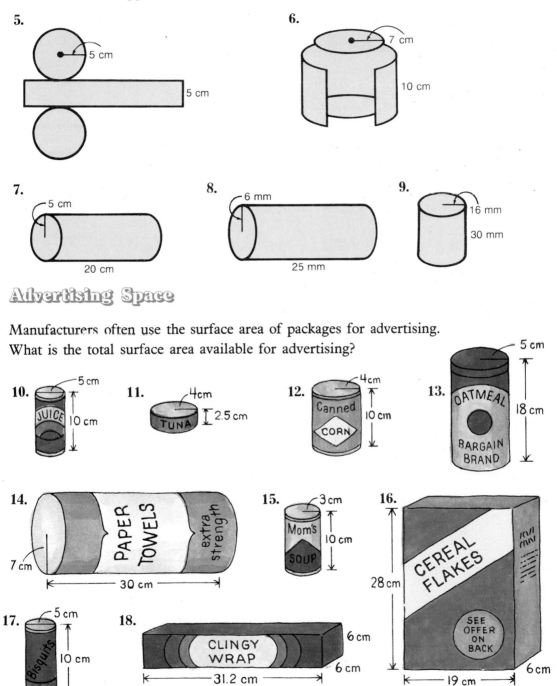

5. 5 cm, 5 cm

6. 7 cm, 10 cm

7. 5 cm, 20 cm

8. 6 mm, 25 mm

9. 16 mm, 30 mm

Advertising Space

Manufacturers often use the surface area of packages for advertising.
What is the total surface area available for advertising?

10. JUICE — 5 cm, 10 cm

11. TUNA — 4 cm, 2.5 cm

12. Canned CORN — 4 cm, 10 cm

13. OATMEAL BARGAIN BRAND — 5 cm, 18 cm

14. PAPER TOWELS extra strength — 7 cm, 30 cm

15. Mom's SOUP — 3 cm, 10 cm

16. CEREAL FLAKES SEE OFFER ON BACK — 28 cm, 19 cm, 6 cm

17. Biscuits — 5 cm, 10 cm

18. CLINGY WRAP — 6 cm, 6 cm, 31.2 cm

371

Volume: Prisms

The **volume** of a solid is the amount of space it contains. Volume is usually measured in **cubic units.**

Each layer in this prism has 4 × 2, or 8 cubic units. There are 3 layers. In all it contains 3 × 8, or 24 cubic units.

A Cubic Unit

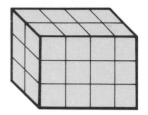

Some standard units for measuring volume are the **cubic meter (m³),** the **cubic centimeter (cm³),** and the **cubic millimeter (mm³).**

1 cm³

The volume of a prism equals the area of the base times the height.

> Volume of a prism = Area of Base × height
> $V = B \times h$

Rectangular Prism	Triangular Prism
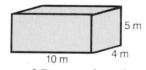	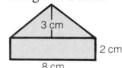

Rectangular Prism

Area of Base = $b \times h$
$\quad\quad\quad\quad\;\; = 10 \times 4$
$\quad\quad\quad\quad\;\; = 40$ (cm²)

Volume = Area of Base × height
$\quad V = 40 \times 5$
$\quad\quad\;\; = 200$ (m³)

Triangular Prism

Area of Base = $b \times h \div 2$
$\quad\quad\quad\quad\;\; = 8 \times 3 \div 2$
$\quad\quad\quad\quad\;\; = 12$ (cm²)

Volume = Area of Base × height
$\quad V = 12 \times 2$
$\quad\quad\;\; = 24$ (cm³)

Exercises

What is the volume of the prism?

1.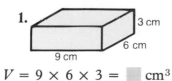

$V = 9 \times 6 \times 3 = \blacksquare$ cm³

2.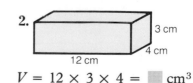

$V = 12 \times 3 \times 4 = \blacksquare$ cm³

What is the volume of the prism?

3. Area of Base: 26 cm² height: 6 cm

4. Area of Base: 3 m² height: 2 m

5. Area of Base: 20 mm² height: 15 mm

6.
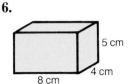
5 cm
8 cm 4 cm

7.
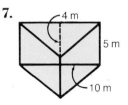
4 m
5 m
10 m

8.
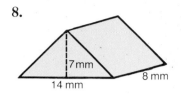
7 mm
14 mm
8 mm

More About Cubic Units

We may use what we know about the metric system to relate cubic units.

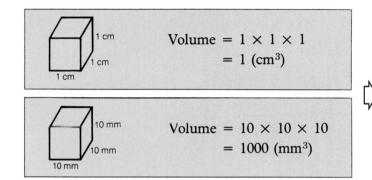

Volume = 1 × 1 × 1
= 1 (cm³)

1 cm
1 cm
1 cm

Volume = 10 × 10 × 10
= 1000 (mm³)

10 mm
10 mm
10 mm

Since 1 cm = 10 mm, the volumes of the two cubes are equal.

1 cm³ = 1000 mm³

Complete.

9. 7 cm³ = ▨ mm³

10. 6.75 cm³ = ▨ mm³

11. 545 mm³ = ▨ cm³

What is the volume of the prism in cubic millimeters?

★ **12.** Area of Base: 15 cm² height: 20 cm

★ **13.** Area of Base: 40 cm² height: 2.5 cm

Calculator Corner

Your heart pumps about 75 mL of blood every second.

1 mL = 1 cm³

About how many cubic centimeters of blood does your heart pump in a day?

Volume: Cylinders

The volume of a cylinder is found in the same way as the volume of a prism.

Volume of a cylinder = Area of Base × height
$$V = B \times h$$

The base of this planter has a radius of 20 cm. It is 35 cm high. To find how much it will hold, first find the area of the base.

$$
\begin{aligned}
A &= \pi \times r^2 \\
&\approx 3.14 \times r^2 \\
&\approx 3.14 \times 20^2 \\
&\approx 3.14 \times 400 \\
&\approx 1256 \text{ cm}^2
\end{aligned}
$$

Next, substitute 1256 for B in the formula.

$$
\begin{aligned}
V &= B \times h \\
&\approx 1256 \times 35 \\
&\approx 43{,}960 \text{ cm}^3
\end{aligned}
$$

The planter holds about 43,960 cm³.

Exercises

What is the volume?

1. $V = B \times h$
$= 50 \times \blacksquare$
$= \blacksquare$ cm³

2. $V = B \times h$
$= 13 \times \blacksquare$
$= \blacksquare$ mm³

3. $V = B \times h$
$= 18 \times \blacksquare$
$= \blacksquare$ cm³

B=50 cm²
8 cm

B=13 mm²
6 mm

B=18 cm²
5 cm

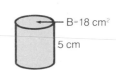

What is the volume of the cylinder?

4. Area of Base: 75 cm²
height: 10 cm

5. Area of Base: 8 m²
height: 5 m

6. Area of Base: 100 cm²
height: 24 cm

7. height: 15 cm
radius: 4 cm

8. height: 40 m
radius: 8 m

9. height: 120 mm
radius: 35 mm

10. height: 2.1 cm
radius: 1.4 cm

Applications

Solve.

11. A cylindrical silo is 25 m tall. The radius of the base is 9 m. What is the volume?

12. A cylindrical gas tank is 1.8 m long. The base has a radius of 0.6 m. What is the volume of the gas tank?

★ **13.** A container with a volume of 1000 cm³ holds 1 L. About how many liters will a cylinder hold if it has a radius of 2 m and a height of 0.5 m?

Checkpoint B

True or False? Write *T* or *F*.
(*pages 366–367*)

1. All faces of a rectangular pyramid are rectangular.

2. A cube has six faces.

3. All faces of a prism are rectangular.

What is the surface area?
(*pages 368–369*)

4.

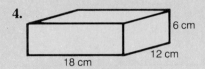
6 cm
18 cm
12 cm

What is the surface area? Use 3.14 for π. (*pages 370–371*)

5.
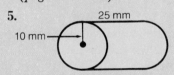
25 mm
10 mm

What is the volume of the prism?
(*pages 372–373*)

6.
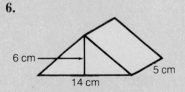
6 cm
14 cm
5 cm

7. a cube: *s* = 5 mm

What is the volume of the cylinder? Use 3.14 for π. (*pages 374–375*)

8. height: 10 mm
radius: 4 mm

9. height: 8 cm
radius: 5 cm

Extra practice on page 444

Problem Solving · DRAWING A DIAGRAM

1	Understand
2	Plan
3	Work
4	Answer

Sometimes drawing a diagram can help you to see what
you need to do to solve a problem.

EXAMPLE Suppose you want to make a frame for a picture
that is 12 cm wide by 17 cm long. To make the
frame you plan to use molding that is 5 cm wide.
What is the length of the piece of molding that
you need?

Draw a diagram of the picture and frame.

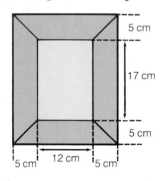

The diagram shows that the frame
adds 10 cm to both the length and
the width of the picture.

The frame must have these dimensions:

width = 12 + 10 = 22 (cm)
length = 17 + 10 = 27 (cm)

Perimeter = (2 × 22) + (2 × 27)
= 44 + 54
= 98 (cm)

You will need a piece of molding 98 cm long to make the frame.

The Jacksons are buying a rug 3 m wide
by 4 m long for a room that is 4 m by
5 m. Copy and complete the diagram to
solve.

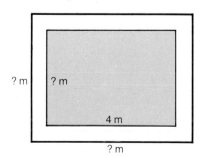

1. What is the area of the rug?

2. What is the area of the floor?

3. What is the area of the floor that
will not be covered by the rug?

376

4. The Jacksons decide to paint the walls which are 3 m high. What is the area they plan to paint?

5. Vinyl baseboards cost $2.49 per meter. What will it cost to install baseboards around the room?

6. The Jacksons decide to install a new light on the ceiling in the middle of the room. Show on your diagram how far from each side of the room the light should be installed.

Eight basketball teams played in a tournament. Here are the results of the first round of play.

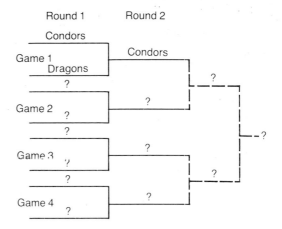

Game 1:	Condors beat the Dragons.
Game 2:	Falcons lost to the Panthers.
Game 3:	Trojans scored two points more than the Jaguars.
Game 4:	Ravens lost to the Bears.

In Round 2 the winner of Game 1 lost to the winner of Game 2. The winner of Game 3 beat the winner of Game 4. The team that beat the Condors in Round 2 won the tournament.

7. Copy and complete the diagram to show who won the tournament.

Use a diagram to solve the problem.

8. A 390 cm by 450 cm rug is on sale. Henri wants to buy it for a room that is 370 cm wide by 430 cm long. How many centimeters will Henri have to trim from the length and width of the rug to make it fit in the room?

★ **9.** The school athletic club is putting a fence around the new swimming pool. The pool is 8 m wide by 20 m long and has a concrete border 2 m wide around it. Fence posts must be 2 m apart. How many fence posts are needed?

Hexagon *FOAGLN* ≅ Hexagon *MYRTSP*.
Write the congruent side or angle.

1. ∠*F*   **2.** ∠*S*   **3.** $\overline{FN}$

Do the construction.

N ——————— *P*

4. Construct a line segment three times the length of $\overline{NP}$.

5. Use a protractor to draw an angle of 60°. Construct a congruent angle.

Use the figure to complete the statement.

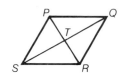

6. *T* is the midpoint of $\overline{PR}$. So $\overline{PT} \cong$ ▨.

7. ∠*PSQ* ≅ ∠*QSR*. So $\overrightarrow{SQ}$ is the angle bisector of ∠ ▨.

Does the figure have line symmetry, point symmetry, or both?

8.

9.

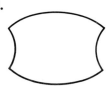

10.

Match.

11. a solid with exactly one circular base   **A.** triangular pyramid

12. a solid with exactly six rectangular faces   **B.** cone

13. a solid with only one triangular base   **C.** rectangular prism

What are the surface area and volume of the figure?

14.

40 cm   70 cm   30 cm

15.

5 cm   15 cm

16.

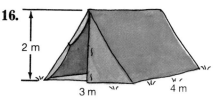

2 m   3 m   4 m

Use a diagram to solve the problem.

17. Hank is putting a rug in his hall. The hall is 10 m long and 1 m wide. The rug he has is 11 m long and 120 cm wide. How much must Hank trim off the length and width?

Hexagon $ABCDEF \cong$ Hexagon $ZYXWVU$. Write the congruent side or angle. (*pages 356–357*)

1. $\angle E$ **2.** $\angle F$ **3.** $\angle V$

4. $\overline{BC}$ **5.** $\overline{DE}$ **6.** $\overline{ZU}$

Do the construction. (*pages 358–361*) $M\underline{\hspace{2cm}}N$

7. Construct a circle whose radius is congruent to $\overline{MN}$.

8. Use a protractor to draw a 75° angle. Construct a congruent angle.

Use a protractor to draw the angle. Then construct the angle bisector. (*pages 362–363*)

9. 90°   **10.** 140°   **11.** 80°

Does the figure have line symmetry, point symmetry, or both? (*pages 364–365*)

12.   **13.**    **14.**

True or False? Write T or F. (*pages 366–367*)

15. All faces of a cube are congruent.

16. All faces of a prism are rectangular.

What is the surface area and volume? (*pages 368–375*)

17. rectangular prism:
Base: 5 cm by 7 cm
height: 9 cm

18. cylinder:
radius: 2 cm
height: 10 cm

Use a diagram to solve the problem. (*pages 376–377*)

19. Kate is tiling the floor of her kitchen. The floor is 360 cm by 420 cm, and the tiles are 20 cm by 20 cm. How many tiles will Kate need?

Extra practice on page 445   **379**

Computers in the Supermarket

Many supermarkets now use Universal Product Codes (UPC). The UPC is a code that is printed on each item. The code is made up of lines and spaces. There is a special code for each product.

There is an electronic scanner built into the check-out counter. When you check out, the cashier passes each item over the scanner. The scanner "reads" the UPC on the package.

The scanner is connected to a computer. The computer's memory contains information about each item, including the price. The computer instructs the register at the check-out counter to print the name and price of the item on the sales receipt.

The scanner is an input device. It gives information to the computer. The register is an output device. It prints information received from the computer on the receipt. The receipt also describes each item and gives the brand name as well as its price. Some computers tell whether there is tax on an item or not.

The store benefits from the UPC system because records can be kept much more efficiently and at less expense. The manager can keep track at any moment of what is selling well, how much of each product is stored in the warehouse, and what needs to be ordered.

Some supermarkets are now trying out speaking scanners. As the scanner reads the code on an item, a voice tells the name of the product and the price. This helps the shopper stay informed.

The lower portion of a supermarket receipt is shown.

1. How much was the bill before adding tax?

2. The customer had a coupon for 50¢ off on one item. How much was the total bill after deducting the coupon?

3. How much change should the customer receive from a check for $40?

4. On what day were these items bought?

5. What was the cashier's name?

```
TAX          $    .52
TOTAL        $ 31.46
COUPON TND   $    .50
CHECK TND    $ 40.00
CHANGE DUE   $
ROBERT  9
2/15/83  10.32  39657
 *   *  THANK YOU  *  *
```

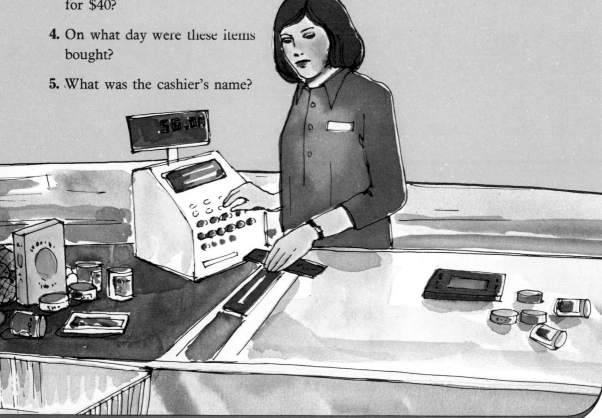

Maintaining Skills

Arrange in order from least to greatest.

1. $\frac{3}{4}$, $\frac{3}{8}$, $3\frac{1}{8}$

2. $1\frac{3}{4}$, $1\frac{11}{12}$, $3\frac{1}{4}$, $6\frac{7}{8}$

3. $13\frac{1}{3}$, $11\frac{3}{4}$, $13\frac{3}{4}$, $11\frac{7}{8}$

Answer the question.

4. What is the interest earned on $1600 at 11% for 1 year?

5. What is the amount of a 20% discount on $16.50?

6. What is the sale price of an item regularly priced at $65.80 if the discount is 20%?

7. What is the interest earned on $12,000 at 8% for 2 years?

Complete the factor tree. Write the prime factorization.

8.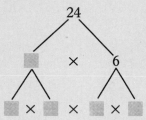

9.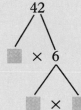

10.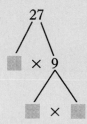

Write the LCM of the numbers.

11. 4 and 9

12. 3 and 6

13. 8 and 12

14. 4, 5, and 10

Write the GCF of the numbers.

15. 5 and 8

16. 12 and 15

17. 12 and 42

18. 9 and 36

The Morton Toy Company makes electronic games. Quality control inspectors test the games in batches of 1000 games. The data below are the number of rejects in each batch of games. Name the mean, median, mode(s) and range for each inspector.

19. Inspector 429: 4, 8, 9, 8, 5, 8

20. Inspector 211: 6, 1, 3, 7, 13, 6

21. Sara sells apples, oranges and bananas. The apples and oranges cost Sara 69¢ a pound. The bananas cost her 13¢ a pound. How much does it cost Sara to buy 40 pounds of each fruit?

Icebergs melt more quickly above water than below it. If only $\frac{1}{5}$ of an iceberg's 4000-ft thickness is above water, how many feet of the iceberg are submerged?

Integers

Integers

On a cold day, the temperature may drop below zero degrees.

Numbers less than zero are **negative numbers.** So far, you have worked mostly with numbers greater than zero. These are called **positive numbers.** Zero is neither positive nor negative.

A number line may help you picture these numbers.

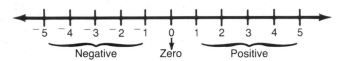

If two numbers are the same distance from zero but on opposite sides of zero, the two numbers are called **opposites.**

Number	Opposite
5	⁻5
⁻8	8
0	0

Zero is its own opposite.

The numbers 1, 2, 3, . . . and their opposites ⁻1, ⁻2, ⁻3, . . . and zero are called the **integers.**

Exercises

Is the number positive or negative? Write *Positive* or *Negative*.

1. 7   **2.** ⁻2   **3.** 12   **4.** 84   **5.** ⁻72   **6.** ⁻100

Complete.

7. The opposite of 4 is ⁻4.   **8.** The opposite of ⁻9 is 9.
    The opposite of ⁻4 is ▧.   The opposite of 9 is ▧.

9. The opposite of ⁻25 is ▧.   **10.** The opposite of 148 is ▧.
    The opposite of 25 is ▧.   The opposite of ⁻148 is ▧.

Is the number an integer? Write *Yes* or *No*.

11. 8   **12.** 0.7   **13.** $\frac{1}{4}$ **14.** ⁻14   **15.** π **16.** 0

Write the opposite of the integer.

17. ⁻1   **18.** 3   **19.** ⁻5   **20.** ⁻3   **21.** 5

22. 1   **23.** 7   **24.** 0   **25.** ⁻6   **26.** 8

27. 6   **28.** ⁻7   **29.** ⁻8   **30.** ⁻10   **31.** ⁻30

32. 45   **33.** 72   **34.** ⁻17   **35.** 100   **36.** ⁻200

37. 160   **38.** 240   **39.** 9999   **40.** ⁻1000   **41.** ⁻873

True or False? Write *T* or *F*.

42. Every integer is either positive or negative.

43. The opposite of a positive integer is a negative integer.

44. The opposite of a negative integer is a negative integer.

45. The opposite of zero is zero.

Think Positively

Write a positive or negative integer to describe the situation.

46. The temperature is 10° above zero.

47. You owe 5 dollars.

48. Your team gets a 15 yd penalty.

49. Your city is 1500 m above sea level.

50. You earn 10 dollars.

51. The temperature is 3° below zero.

52. Your team gains 6 points.

53. You dive 8 m beneath the surface.

54. You live on the 26th floor.

55. Your dad's car needs 10 gal. of gas.

56. There are 7 new students in school.

57. You lost 2 pencils last week.

Comparing Integers

You can use the number line to compare two integers. The integer to the right on the number line is the greater integer. The integer to the left is the lesser integer.

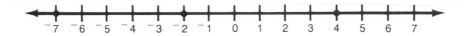

4 is to the right of 2 $\longrightarrow$ $4 > {}^-2$, or ${}^-2 < 4$

${}^-7$ is to the left of ${}^-2$ $\longrightarrow$ ${}^-7 < {}^-2$, or ${}^-2 > {}^-7$

You can write ${}^-7 < {}^-2$ and ${}^-2 < 4$ together as one statement.

$${}^-7 < {}^-2 < 4$$

This new statement can be read *${}^-2$ is between ${}^-7$ and 4.*

Exercises

Complete. Write *left* or *right* for the first blank, and $<$ or $>$ for the second blank.

1. ${}^-1$ is to the ▨ of 0; ${}^-1$ ▨ 0

2. 0 is to the ▨ of ${}^-1$; 0 ▨ ${}^-1$

3. 2 is to the ▨ of ${}^-1$; 2 ▨ ${}^-1$

4. ${}^-1$ is to the ▨ of 2; ${}^-1$ ▨ 2

5. ${}^-3$ is to the ▨ of ${}^-4$; ${}^-3$ ▨ ${}^-4$

6. ${}^-4$ is to the ▨ of 0; ${}^-4$ ▨ 0

7. 6 is to the ▨ of ${}^-7$; 6 ▨ ${}^-7$

8. ${}^-5$ is to the ▨ of ${}^-7$; ${}^-5$ ▨ ${}^-7$

9. ${}^-2$ is to the ▨ of 6; ${}^-2$ ▨ 6

10. 0 is to the ▨ of ${}^-3$; 0 ▨ ${}^-3$

Complete. Write $<$ or $>$.

11. 0 ▨ 4

12. 0 ▨ ${}^-4$

13. 4 ▨ 0

14. ${}^-4$ ▨ 0

15. 2 ▨ 4

16. 4 ▨ 2

17. ${}^-2$ ▨ 4

18. ${}^-4$ ▨ ${}^-2$

19. ${}^-2$ ▨ ${}^-4$

20. 4 ▨ ${}^-2$

21. ${}^-4$ ▨ 2

22. 0 ▨ ${}^-2$

Complete. Write < or >.

23. 3 ▨ ⁻8 **24.** ⁻9 ▨ 0 **25.** ⁻10 ▨ 4 **26.** 10 ▨ ⁻8

27. ⁻6 ▨ ⁻9 **28.** ⁻12 ▨ ⁻5 **29.** ⁻15 ▨ 11 **30.** 16 ▨ ⁻12

31. ⁻19 ▨ ⁻25 **32.** 0 ▨ ⁻34 **33.** ⁻50 ▨ 22 **34.** 99 ▨ ⁻100

Write using two < signs.

35. 2 < 4 and 4 < 6

36. ⁻3 < 0 and 0 < 3

37. ⁻7 < ⁻2 and ⁻2 < 2

38. ⁻6 < ⁻2 and ⁻2 < ⁻1

39. 4 is between 1 and 7

40. 0 is between ⁻5 and 5

41. 3 is between ⁻4 and 4

42. ⁻6 is between ⁻7 and ⁻5

List the integers in order from least to greatest.

43. 5, ⁻4, ⁻7, 0, 3, ⁻1

44. ⁻8, 6, ⁻2, 10, ⁻9, 0

45. ⁻12, 4, 0, ⁻9, ⁻10, 3

46. 0, ⁻1, 6, 2, ⁻15, 12

Above and Below

The elevation of a place is its average height above or below sea level. A positive elevation is above sea level. A negative elevation is below sea level.

List the places in the chart from least to greatest elevation.

47.

LOWEST ELEVATION OF SIX CONTINENTS	
Continent	**Lowest Elevation in Meters**
Africa	⁻156
Asia	⁻400
Australia	⁻16
Europe	⁻28
North America	⁻86
South America	⁻40

48.

ELEVATION OF SOME CALIFORNIA LOCATIONS	
Location	**Elevation in Meters**
Alameda	9
Brawley	⁻34
Calexico	2
Death Valley	⁻86
El Centro	⁻12
Salton City	⁻70

Adding Integers

You can show how to add integers by using arrows on a number line. Arrows for positive integers point to the right. Arrows for negative integers point to the left.

Mike put $4 into savings last week and $3 this week.

Li took $2 out of savings last week and $6 this week.

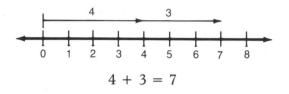

4 + 3 = 7

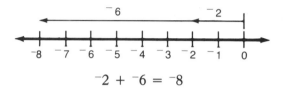

⁻2 + ⁻6 = ⁻8

Mike put a total of $7 into savings in the two weeks.

Li took a total of $8 out of savings in the two weeks.

> The sum of two positive integers is a positive integer.
> The sum of two negative integers is a negative integer.

Exercises

Add. Use the number line if you need help.

1. 1 + 5
   ⁻1 + ⁻5

2. 2 + 5
   ⁻2 + ⁻5

3. 5 + 3
   ⁻5 + ⁻3

4. 2 + 2
   ⁻2 + ⁻2

5. 7 + 1
   ⁻7 + ⁻1

6. 5 + 9
   ⁻5 + ⁻9

7. 7 + 6
   ⁻7 + ⁻6

8. 8 + 8
   ⁻8 + ⁻8

9. 6 + 9
   ⁻6 + ⁻9

10. 9 + 4
    ⁻9 + ⁻4

Add.

11. ⁻9 + ⁻9

12. ⁻7 + ⁻4

13. 8 + 2

14. 9 + 7

15. 3 + 9

16. ⁻8 + ⁻6

17. 7 + 8

18. ⁻8 + ⁻5

19. 12 + 9

20. ⁻7 + ⁻16

21. 19 + 5

22. ⁻14 + ⁻8

23. 15 + 35

24. ⁻14 + ⁻31

25. ⁻18 + ⁻45

26. 17 + 52

27. 9 + 3 + 5

28. ⁻9 + ⁻3 + ⁻5

29. ⁻4 + ⁻7 + ⁻6

30. 10 + 2 + 14

31. ⁻10 + ⁻7 + ⁻12

32. ⁻13 + ⁻11 + ⁻18

33. 27 + 18 + 35

34. ⁻27 + ⁻15 + ⁻34

35. ⁻41 + ⁻37 + ⁻13

36. 32 + 6 + 47

37. ⁻19 + ⁻9 + ⁻29

38. 16 + 52 + 7

Dollars and Sense

Write an integer to represent each number in the problem. Then add the integers and answer the question.

39. A craft business had a profit of $103 last month and a profit of $97 this month. What is the total profit for both months?

40. A woodworking business had a loss of $25 last week and a loss of $17 this week. What is the total loss for both weeks?

41. Mark took $5 out of his savings in June, $10 in July, and $8 in August. How much did he take out in all?

42. Joan saved $19 in January, $5 in February, and $12 in March. How much did she save in all?

Calculator Corner

On the first day of the month, you put 1¢ into your savings account. For each day after that, you plan to put in double the amount you put in the day before. How much will you have to put into your savings on the twentieth day?

Adding Positive and Negative Integers

You also can use arrows to show how to add a positive integer and a negative integer.

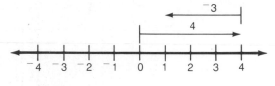

$4 + {}^-3 = 1$

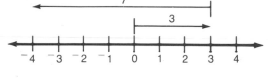

$3 + {}^-7 = {}^-4$

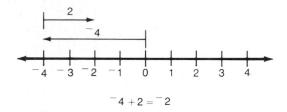

${}^-4 + 2 = {}^-2$

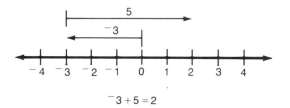

${}^-3 + 5 = 2$

The sum of an integer and its opposite is always zero.

$$4 + {}^-4 = 0 \qquad {}^-7 + 7 = 0 \qquad 0 + 0 = 0$$

> The sum of a positive integer and a negative integer may be a positive integer, a negative integer, or zero.

Exercises

Add. Use the number line if you need help.

1. $1 + {}^-1$
$1 + {}^-2$
$1 + {}^-3$

2. $3 + {}^-3$
$3 + {}^-2$
$3 + {}^-1$

3. ${}^-2 + 2$
${}^-2 + 3$
${}^-2 + 4$

4. ${}^-4 + 4$
${}^-4 + 3$
${}^-4 + 2$

Is the sum positive or negative? Write *Positive* or *Negative*.

5. $4 + {}^-1$
${}^-4 + 1$

6. $4 + {}^-5$
${}^-4 + 5$

7. ${}^-3 + 7$
$3 + {}^-7$

8. ${}^-2 + 6$
$2 + {}^-6$

Add.

9. 9 + ⁻5   **10.** 8 + ⁻3   **11.** ⁻4 + 9

12. ⁻6 + 8   **13.** 3 + ⁻8   **14.** 6 + ⁻7

15. ⁻8 + 2   **16.** ⁻7 + 1   **17.** ⁻9 + 2

18. 6 + ⁻14   **19.** 15 + ⁻7   **20.** 9 + ⁻16

21. ⁻5 + 11   **22.** ⁻10 + 10   **23.** ⁻25 + 19

24. 15 + ⁻21   **25.** 43 + ⁻21   **26.** ⁻33 + 65

Ups and Downs

Write an integer to represent each number in the problem. Then add the integers and answer the question.

27. You get on an elevator at the 11th floor and go down 7 floors. On what floor are you?

28. You get on an elevator 2 floors below ground level and go up 13 floors. On what floor are you?

★ **29.** You get on an elevator at the 9th floor and go down 10 floors. Then you go up 8 floors. On what floor are you?

★ **30.** You get on an elevator 3 floors below ground level and go up 9 floors. Then you go down 7 floors. On what floor are you?

★ **31.** You get on an elevator at the 12th floor and go down 9 floors. Then you go up 3 floors and down 8 floors. On what floor are you?

391

Subtracting Integers

The temperature was 10°C. Then there was a drop in temperature of 2°C. What was the temperature then?

There are two ways to find the temperature then.

$10 - 2 = 8°C$ $10 + {}^-2 = 8°C$

The temperature then was 8°C.

> To subtract an integer, add its opposite.

Here are some other examples.

$$6 - 10 = 6 + {}^-10 = {}^-4$$
$$4 - {}^-2 = \quad 4 + 2 = 6$$
$${}^-6 - {}^-8 = \quad {}^-6 + 8 = 2$$

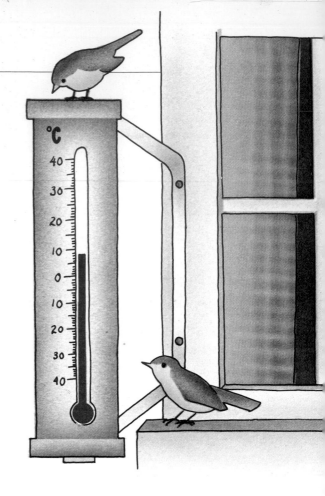

Exercises

Complete.

1. $4 - 6 = 4 + \boxed{} = {}^-2$
     2. $4 - {}^-6 = 4 + \boxed{} = 10$

3. ${}^-8 - 2 = {}^-8 + \boxed{} = {}^-10$
     4. ${}^-8 - {}^-2 = {}^-8 + \boxed{} = {}^-6$

5. ${}^-2 - 4 = {}^-2 + \boxed{} = \boxed{}$
     6. ${}^-8 - {}^-6 = {}^-8 + \boxed{} = \boxed{}$

7. $4 - {}^-4 = 4 + \boxed{} = \boxed{}$
     8. $2 - 10 = 2 + \boxed{} = \boxed{}$

Subtract.

9.	**10.**	**11.**	**12.**
$8 - 4$	$2 - 6$	${}^-4 - 10$	${}^-6 - 2$
$8 - 0$	$2 - 0$	${}^-4 - 0$	${}^-6 - 0$
$8 - {}^-4$	$2 - {}^-6$	${}^-4 - {}^-10$	${}^-6 - {}^-2$

Subtract.

13. 5 − 9

14. 3 − ⁻7

15. ⁻3 − 8

16. ⁻5 − ⁻8

17. 0 − 4

18. 0 − ⁻7

19. ⁻2 − 0

20. ⁻5 − ⁻5

21. 14 − ⁻5

22. ⁻17 − 9

23. ⁻9 − 12

24. ⁻13 − ⁻4

25. 12 − 37

26. 42 − ⁻15

Chilling Facts

Write the problem as the difference between two integers. Then subtract the integers and answer the question.

27. The greatest recorded drop in temperature is from 7°C to ⁻49°C in a single day at Browning, Montana. What is the difference between these temperatures?

28. The greatest recorded range of temperatures is from 37°C to ⁻70°C at Verkhoyansk, USSR. What is the difference between these temperatures?

29. The least recorded range of temperatures is from 31°C to 20°C on the island of Saipan. What is the difference between these temperatures?

30. A very strong wind can make a temperature of ⁻10°C feel as cold as ⁻32°C. What is the difference between these temperatures?

Multiplying Integers

You multiply positive integers just as you multiply whole numbers.

$$5 \times 2 = 10$$

To multiply a positive integer and a negative integer, a number line may help. Think of multiplication as repeated addition.

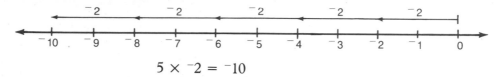

$$5 \times {}^-2 = {}^-10$$

You can use the commutative property with integers.

$$2 \times {}^-5 = {}^-10 \qquad \text{so} \qquad {}^-5 \times 2 = {}^-10$$

To see how to multiply two negative integers, look at the pattern of the products in this series of multiplications.

$$
\begin{aligned}
{}^-5 \times 2 &= {}^-10 \\
{}^-5 \times 1 &= {}^-5 \\
{}^-5 \times 0 &= 0 \\
{}^-5 \times {}^-1 &= 5 \\
{}^-5 \times {}^-2 &= 10
\end{aligned}
$$

> To continue the pattern, these products must be positive.

The product of any integer and zero is zero.

$$7 \times 0 = 0 \qquad {}^-3 \times 0 = 0 \qquad 0 \times 0 = 0$$

> The product of two positive or two negative integers is positive.
> The product of a positive integer and a negative integer is negative.

Exercises

Multiply.

1. 2 × 9
2 × ⁻9

2. 3 × 7
⁻3 × 7

3. 8 × 6
8 × ⁻6

4. 1 × 1
⁻1 × ⁻1

5. 4 × 8
⁻4 × 8

6. 9 × 3
⁻9 × ⁻3

7. 5 × 6
5 × ⁻6

8. 4 × 10
⁻4 × ⁻10

Multiply.

9. $2 \times {}^-1$	**10.** ${}^-6 \times 6$	**11.** ${}^-4 \times {}^-3$
12. ${}^-9 \times 0$	**13.** ${}^-3 \times 8$	**14.** 5×7
15. ${}^-8 \times {}^-9$	**16.** $5 \times {}^-9$	**17.** ${}^-8 \times {}^-5$
18. ${}^-1 \times 4$	**19.** 4×0	**20.** $6 \times {}^-2$
21. $10 \times {}^-2$	**22.** ${}^-7 \times {}^-11$	**23.** ${}^-13 \times 2$
24. 20×4	**25.** $2 \times {}^-30$	**26.** ${}^-10 \times {}^-6$
27. ${}^-15 \times 3$	**28.** ${}^-6 \times {}^-13$	**29.** $5 \times {}^-12$
30. ${}^-3 \times {}^-17$	**31.** $12 \times {}^-6$	**32.** ${}^-19 \times 0$

Reaching New Heights

For each km that you go above the base of Frosty Mountain, the temperature is 3°C colder than it is at the base of the mountain.

Use this information to complete the chart.

	FROSTY MOUNTAIN TEMPERATURES				
	Base of Mountain	1 km above Base	2 km above Base	3 km above Base	5 km above Base
33.	0°C	${}^-3$°C	?	?	?
34.	2°C	${}^-1$°C	?	?	?
35.	${}^-5$°C	?.	?	?	?

Dividing Integers

You divide positive integers just as you divide whole numbers.
Remember how multiplication and division are related.

$$6 \times 3 = 18 \qquad \text{so} \qquad 18 \div 3 = 6$$

Multiplication and division of integers are related in the same way.

$$6 \times {}^-3 = {}^-18 \qquad \text{so} \qquad {}^-18 \div {}^-3 = 6$$
$$^-6 \times 3 = {}^-18 \qquad \text{so} \qquad {}^-18 \div 3 = {}^-6$$
$$^-6 \times {}^-3 = 18 \qquad \text{so} \qquad 18 \div {}^-3 = {}^-6$$

> The quotient of two positive or two negative integers is positive.
> The quotient of a positive integer and a negative integer is negative.

The quotient of zero divided by any other integer is zero.

$$0 \div 8 = 0$$
$$0 \div {}^-5 = 0$$

You cannot divide an integer by zero.

$$7 \div 0 = ?$$
$$? \times 0 = 7$$

There is no solution to this equation.

Exercises

Complete.

1. $2 \times 4 = 8$
$8 \div 4 = \blacksquare$

2. $2 \times {}^-4 = {}^-8$
$^-8 \div {}^-4 = \blacksquare$

3. $^-2 \times 4 = {}^-8$
$^-8 \div 4 = \blacksquare$

4. $^-2 \times {}^-4 = 8$
$8 \div {}^-4 = \blacksquare$

5. $3 \times 3 = 9$
$9 \div 3 = \blacksquare$

6. $3 \times {}^-3 = {}^-9$
$^-9 \div {}^-3 = \blacksquare$

7. $^-3 \times 3 = {}^-9$
$^-9 \div 3 = \blacksquare$

8. $^-3 \times {}^-3 = 9$
$9 \div {}^-3 = \blacksquare$

Divide.

9. $15 \div 3$
$^-15 \div 3$

10. $18 \div 9$
$18 \div {}^-9$

11. $21 \div 7$
$^-21 \div {}^-7$

12 $24 \div 3$
$24 \div {}^-3$

13. $36 \div 9$
$^-36 \div {}^-9$

14. $48 \div 6$
$^-48 \div 6$

15. $54 \div 9$
$54 \div {}^-9$

16. $72 \div 8$
$^-72 \div {}^-8$

Divide.

17. $^-18 \div 9$ **18.** $16 \div {}^-2$ **19.** $^-30 \div {}^-5$ **20.** $56 \div {}^-7$

21. $^-24 \div {}^-4$ **22.** $^-64 \div 8$ **23.** $42 \div 6$ **24.** $6 \div {}^-3$

25. $81 \div {}^-9$ **26.** $^-7 \div 1$ **27.** $0 \div {}^-9$ **28.** $^-28 \div 7$

29. $^-26 \div 2$ **30.** $84 \div {}^-4$ **31.** $^-46 \div {}^-2$ **32.** $^-48 \div 3$

Integer Averages

Write an integer to represent each number in the problem. Then divide the integers and answer the question.

33. A diver went 12 m beneath the surface of the water in 6 minutes. What was the average change in the diver's position per minute?

34. A climber went 255 m up a mountain in 3 hours. What was the average distance climbed per hour?

35. The temperature dropped 24°C in 12 hours. What was the average change in temperature per hour?

36. A team scored a total of 396 points in 4 games. What was the average score per game?

Solve.

★ **37.** A business had a profit of $140 in May and $290 in June. What was the average profit for the two months?

★ **38.** A business had a loss of $47 in March, $105 in April, and $91 in May. What was the average loss for the three months?

★ **39.** A business had a loss of $40 in November, a profit of $400 in December, and a loss of $120 in January. What was the average profit or loss for the three months?

Solving Equations

You solve equations with integers the same way that you solve
equations with whole numbers.

You may add or subtract the same integer from both sides of an
equation.

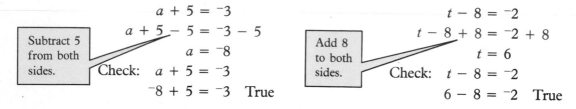

$$a + 5 = {}^-3$$
$$a + 5 - 5 = {}^-3 - 5$$

Subtract 5 from both sides.

$$a = {}^-8$$

Check: $a + 5 = {}^-3$
$${}^-8 + 5 = {}^-3 \quad \text{True}$$

$$t - 8 = {}^-2$$
$$t - 8 + 8 = {}^-2 + 8$$

Add 8 to both sides.

$$t = 6$$

Check: $t - 8 = {}^-2$
$$6 - 8 = {}^-2 \quad \text{True}$$

You may multiply or divide both sides of an equation by the same
integer.

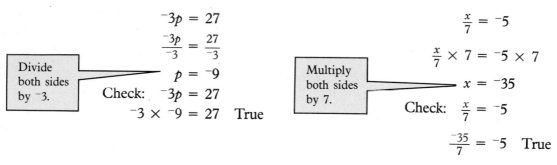

$${}^-3p = 27$$
$$\frac{{}^-3p}{{}^-3} = \frac{27}{{}^-3}$$

Divide both sides by ⁻3.

$$p = {}^-9$$

Check: ${}^-3p = 27$
$${}^-3 \times {}^-9 = 27 \quad \text{True}$$

$$\frac{x}{7} = {}^-5$$
$$\frac{x}{7} \times 7 = {}^-5 \times 7$$

Multiply both sides by 7.

$$x = {}^-35$$

Check: $\frac{x}{7} = {}^-5$

$$\frac{{}^-35}{7} = {}^-5 \quad \text{True}$$

Exercises

Complete.

1.
$$y + 8 = 3$$
$$y + 8 - \blacksquare = 3 - \blacksquare$$
$$y = \blacksquare$$

2.
$$c - 3 = {}^-9$$
$$c - 3 + \blacksquare = {}^-9 + \blacksquare$$
$$c = \blacksquare$$

3.
$$6r = {}^-42$$
$$\frac{6r}{\blacksquare} = \frac{{}^-42}{\blacksquare}$$
$$r = \blacksquare$$

4.
$$\frac{m}{{}^-5} = {}^-3$$
$$\frac{m}{{}^-5} \times \blacksquare = {}^-3 \times \blacksquare$$
$$m = \blacksquare$$

Solve the equation.

5. $n + 7 = 3$

6. $x + 9 = {}^-6$

7. $b + 20 = 5$

8. $p - 5 = {}^-4$

9. $z - 7 = {}^-9$

10. $t - 12 = {}^-10$

11. ${}^-4k = 28$

12. $6d = {}^-54$

13. ${}^-8w = {}^-56$

14. $\frac{r}{6} = {}^-3$

15. $\frac{a}{{}^-9} = 7$

16. $\frac{q}{{}^-4} = {}^-8$

17. $b + 38 = {}^-5$

18. $r - 15 = {}^-3$

19. $s + 43 = 0$

20. ${}^-12x = 48$

21. $\frac{y}{12} = {}^-5$

22. ${}^-9t = 9$

23. $\frac{a}{15} = {}^-1$

24. $n - 36 = {}^-17$

25. ${}^-1y = 45$

Name That Integer!

Choose an equation to describe the situation. Solve the equation and answer the question.

26. What integer increased by 2 is ${}^-12$?

    a. $n - 2 = {}^-12$ **b.** $n + 2 = {}^-12$ **c.** $2n = {}^-12$

27. What integer divided by 8 is ${}^-16$?

    a. $8n = {}^-16$ **b.** $\frac{n}{{}^-16} = 8$ **c.** $\frac{n}{8} = {}^-16$

28. What integer minus 45 is ${}^-15$?

    a. $n - 45 = {}^-15$ **b.** $n - {}^-15 = 45$ **c.** $\frac{n}{{}^-16} = 45$

29. The product of what integer and ${}^-12$ is 36?

    a. $\frac{n}{{}^-12} = 36$ **b.** ${}^-12n = 36$ **c.** $36n = {}^-12$

A train that is 1 km long is traveling at a speed of 1 km/min. How long will it take the train to pass through a tunnel that is 1 km long?

Graphing Ordered Pairs of Integers

In the Space Race game, you name the position of your spaceship by an ordered pair of integers on a number grid.

The grid is called the **coordinate plane.** The horizontal number line is the **x-axis.** The vertical number line is the **y-axis.** They intersect at the **origin.**

Each point in the plane is named by a pair of coordinates. They tell you how far the point is from the origin, and in what direction.

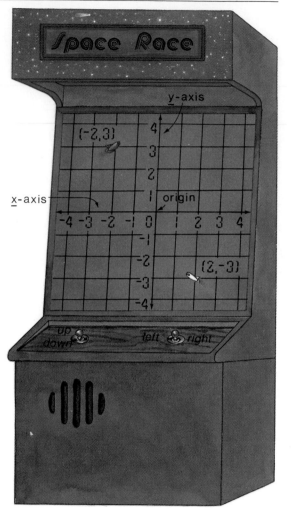

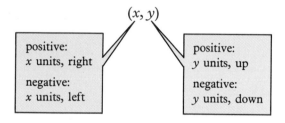

The point (2, ⁻3) is 2 units to the right of the origin and 3 units down.

The point (⁻2, 3) is 2 units to the left of the origin and 3 units up.

Exercises

Write the coordinates for these directions. Start at the origin.

1. 2 units right and 3 units up

2. 2 units left and 3 units down

3. 4 units right and 2 units down

4. 3 units left and 1 unit up

5. 1 unit right and 0 units up

6. 0 units right and 1 unit down

7. 0 units right and 1 unit up

8. 1 unit left and 0 units up

Write the letter of the point named by the coordinates.

9. (⁻3, 7)   10. (3, ⁻7)

11. (3, 7)   12. (⁻3, ⁻7)

13. (6, ⁻2)   14. (⁻8, 8)

15. (⁻5, 0)   16. (0, ⁻3)

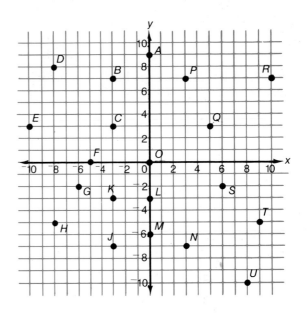

Write the coordinates of the point.

17. Q   18. T   19. A

20. U   21. C   22. M

23. E   24. O   25. G

26. R   27. H   28. K

Reflections

The points (3, 1) and (⁻3, 1) are the same distance from the y-axis, but in opposite directions. We say that the points are **reflections** of each other in the y-axis.

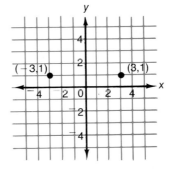

(⁻3, 1) is the reflection of (3, 1) in the y-axis.

(3, 1) is the reflection of (⁻3, 1) in the y-axis.

Locate the point on a coordinate plane. What is its reflection in the y-axis?

29. (3, 5)   30. (⁻4, 1)   31. (2, ⁻4)   32. (⁻1, ⁻5)   33. (⁻3, 0)

Locate the three points on a coordinate plane. Connect the points to form a triangle. Draw the reflection of the triangle in the y-axis.

★ 34. (3, 2), (7, 5), (2, 6)   ★ 35. (⁻4, 0), (⁻8, ⁻2), (⁻7, ⁻8)

Graphing Equations

When an equation has two variables, you can use a chart to show some of its solutions.

$$x + y = 5$$

x	0	1	2	3	4	5	6	7
y	5	4	3	2	1	0	-1	-2

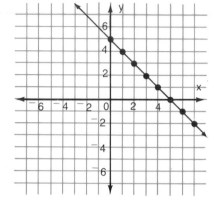

If you write these solutions as ordered pairs, you can show them as points on the coordinate plane.

(0, 5) (1, 4) (2, 3) (3, 2)
(4, 1) (5, 0) (6, ⁻1) (7, ⁻2)

Notice that the points lie on a straight line. You draw the line connecting them to show that the list of solutions is endless. This line is called the **graph** of the equation.

Exercises

Write the solutions as ordered pairs. Then draw the graph of the equation.

1. $x + y = 4$

x	0	1	2	3	4	5	6
y	4	3	2	1	0	-1	-2

2. $x - y = 3$

x	0	1	2	3	4	5	6
y	-3	-2	-1	0	1	2	3

3. $x + 2 = y$

x	0	1	2	3	4	5	6
y	2	3	4	5	6	7	8

4. $x - 5 = y$

x	0	1	2	3	4	5	6
y	-5	-4	-3	-2	-1	0	1

Copy and complete the chart. Then draw the graph of the equation.

5. $x + y = 1$

x	0	1	2	3	4	5	6
y	?	?	?	?	?	?	?

6. $x + 1 = y$

x	0	1	2	3	4	5	6
y	?	?	?	?	?	?	?

7. $x - y = 1$

x	0	1	2	3	4	5	6
y	?	?	?	?	?	?	?

8. $x - 1 = y$

x	0	1	2	3	4	5	6
y	?	?	?	?	?	?	?

On Your Own

Make a chart of solutions. Then draw the graph of the equation.

9. $x + y = 3$ **10.** $x + 4 = y$

11. $x - y = 5$ **12.** $x - 2 = y$

Checkpoint B

Multiply. (*pages 394–395*)

1. $3 \times {}^-8$ **2.** ${}^-7 \times {}^-6$

3. ${}^-1 \times 9$ **4.** 5×4

Divide. (*pages 396–397*)

5. ${}^-8 \div 2$ **6.** $25 \div {}^-5$

7. ${}^-72 \div {}^-9$ **8.** $24 \div 6$

Solve the equation. (*pages 398–399*)

9. $a + 5 = 2$ **10.** $x - 7 = 1$

11. $6q = {}^-54$ **12.** $\frac{c}{{}^-5} = 8$

Write the coordinates of the point. (*pages 400–401*)

13. A

14. B

15. C

16. D

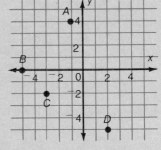

Copy and complete the chart. Then draw the graph of the equation. (*pages 402–403*)

17. $x + y = 2$

x	0	1	2	3	4	5	6
y	?	?	?	?	?	?	?

Extra practice on page 446

Problem Solving · LOGIC

1	Understand
2	Plan
3	Work
4	Answer

You can solve some problems just by using logic to organize the facts. Joe Cook, Ann Tailor, and Lee Barber are a cook, a tailor, and a barber. Their occupations do not match their last names. Joe Cook is the barber's cousin. Who is the cook?

To solve the problem, make a chart to show all the possible answers. Make an × when you have used a fact to eliminate a possibility.

No one has an occupation that matches his last name.

This fact eliminates three possibilities.

	cook	tailor	barber
Joe Cook	×		
Ann Tailor		×	
Lee Barber			×

Joe Cook is the barber's cousin.

Joe Cook cannot be the barber.

	cook	tailor	barber
Joe Cook	×		×
Ann Tailor		×	
Lee Barber			×

Make a ✓ when there is only one possibility remaining in a row or column of the chart.

Joe Cook must be the tailor.

The barber must be Ann Tailor.

	cook	tailor	barber
Joe Cook	×	✓	×
Ann Tailor		×	✓
Lee Barber			×

The cook is Lee Barber.

Each card has one of the numbers 3, 4, or 5 on the back. Match the fact to a chart.

1. The number on is prime.

2. The number on is less than

3. The number on 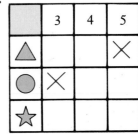 is not even.

a.

	3	4	5
△			
○		✕	
☆			

b.

	3	4	5
△			
○			
☆		✕	

c.

	3	4	5
△			✕
○	✕		
☆			

Copy the chart and organize the facts. Then answer the question.

4. Sam, Sue, and Suni each play a different instrument. The instruments are the drums, the flute, and the trumpet. Sue and the drummer are in the same algebra class. The flute player and the drummer come to Suni's house to practice. Who plays the flute?

	drums	flute	trumpet
Sam			
Sue			
Suni			

5. Anne, Arno, and Alex have lockers next to each other. Arno rides the bus with the person whose locker is at the right. Anne's locker is not next to Arno's. Who has the locker at the right?

	left	middle	right
Anne			
Arno			
Alex			

Make a chart to organize the facts. Then answer the question.

★ **6.** A train conductor is talking to three passengers named Baker, Samgrass, and Burgess. The passengers are a teacher, a musician, and a salesperson. Samgrass and the musician are neighbors. Baker and the teacher have not met before. Both the teacher and Burgess enjoy the musician's albums. Who is the salesperson?

Write the opposite of the integer.

1. 15   **2.** $^-43$ **3.** 0   **4.** 197

Complete. Write $<$ or $>$.

5. 7 ▓ $^-9$ **6.** $^-12$ ▓ 6   **7.** 0 ▓ $^-16$ **8.** $^-7$ ▓ $^-5$

Complete. Write $+$ or $-$.

9. 6 ▓ 10 $= ^-4$ **10.** $^-6$ ▓ 8 $= 2$ **11.** $^-2$ ▓ $^-6 = 4$

12. $^-9$ ▓ 3 $= ^-6$ **13.** $^-5$ ▓ $^-8 = 3$ **14.** 19 ▓ $^-15 = 4$

Solve the equations. Then locate (x, y) on a coordinate plane.

15. $x = ^-1 \times 1$
$y = ^-2 \times ^-2$

16. $x = ^-6 \div 3$
$y = ^-9 \div ^-3$

17. $x = ^-4 \times 1$
$y = 12 \div ^-4$

18. $x = ^-18 \div ^-6$
$y = 2 \div 1$

19. $x - 2 = 1$
$y + 2 = 1$

20. $^-5x = 5$
$\frac{y}{^-2} = ^-2$

Copy and complete the chart. Then draw the graph of the equation.

21. $x + y = ^-2$

x	0	1	2	3	4	5	6
y	?	?	?	?	?	?	?

22. $x - 5 = y$

x	0	1	2	3	4	5	6
y	?	?	?	?	?	?	?

Make a chart to organize the facts. Then answer the question.

23. Sara, Tara, and Lara are identical triplets who enjoy confusing people. Each wears a necklace with an initial that is not her own. No triplet tells the truth when asked her name. The triplet wearing the initial T says, "I'm Lara." Who wears each initial?

Write the opposite of the integer. (*pages 384–385*)

1. 29   **2.** ⁻11   **3.** 0   **4.** ⁻250

Complete. Write $<$ or $>$. (*pages 386–387*)

5. 5 ▨ ⁻2   **6.** ⁻3 ▨ 1   **7.** ⁻6 ▨ ⁻9   **8.** ⁻10 ▨ 0

Add, subtract, multiply, or divide. (*pages 388–397*)

9. $5 + 3$ **10.** $⁻6 + ⁻4$ **11.** $11 + ⁻5$ **12.** $⁻14 + 6$

13. $4 - 7$ **14.** $2 - ⁻9$ **15.** $⁻5 - 4$ **16.** $⁻3 - ⁻12$

17. $5 \times ⁻3$ **18.** $⁻7 \times ⁻4$ **19.** $⁻36 \div 9$ **20.** $⁻64 \div ⁻8$

Solve the equation. (*pages 398–399*)

21. $q + 4 = 1$ **22.** $r - 5 = ⁻2$ **23.** $⁻7s = 42$ **24.** $\frac{m}{4} = ⁻3$

Complete the chart. Then draw the graph of the equation.
(*pages 400–403*)

25. $x + y = 3$

x	0	1	2	3	4	5	6
y	?	?	?	?	?	?	?

26. $x - y = 5$

x	0	1	2	3	4	5	6
y	?	?	?	?	?	?	?

Copy the chart and organize the facts.
Then answer the question.
(*pages 404–405*)

27. A red, a blue, and a green card
each have one of the numbers 2, 4,
or 5 on the back. The number on
the red card is even. The number
on the blue card is not prime.
Which number is on each card?

	2	4	5
red			
blue			
green			

Rational Numbers

When you add, subtract, or multiply two integers, the answer is an integer. But the quotient of two integers is not always an integer.

$$5 + {}^-14 = {}^-9 \qquad {}^-7 - {}^-25 = 18 \qquad {}^-3 \times 17 = {}^-51 \qquad {}^-1 \div 4 = ?$$

To write the quotient ${}^-1 \div 4$, you need a different kind of number. A **rational number** is any number that can be written as the quotient of two integers. Remember that 0 can never be used as the denominator of a quotient. All of the following are rational numbers.

$$\frac{{}^-1}{4} \qquad \frac{10}{7} \qquad {}^-2\frac{1}{2}, \text{ or } \frac{{}^-5}{2} \qquad 3, \text{ or } \frac{3}{1} \qquad {}^-1.57, \text{ or } \frac{{}^-157}{100} \qquad 0.\overline{1}, \text{ or } \frac{1}{9}$$

Any repeating decimal represents a rational number. To show a repeating decimal as the quotient of two integers, you can use the facts that $0.\overline{1} = \frac{1}{9}$ and $0.\overline{01} = \frac{1}{99}$.

$$0.\overline{5} = 5 \times 0.\overline{1} = 5 \times \frac{1}{9} = \frac{5}{9}$$

$${}^-0.\overline{6} = {}^-6 \times 0.\overline{1} = {}^-6 \times \frac{1}{9} = \frac{{}^-6}{9} = \frac{{}^-2}{3}$$

$$0.\overline{45} = 45 \times 0.\overline{01} = 45 \times \frac{1}{99} = \frac{45}{99} = \frac{5}{11}$$

Numbers such as $\sqrt{2}$, $\sqrt{3}$, and π cannot be written as the quotient of two integers. These are called **irrational numbers.**

Show that the number is rational by writing it as the quotient of two integers.

1. $4\frac{1}{3}$ 2. ${}^-7\frac{3}{5}$ 3. ${}^-6\frac{1}{2}$ 4. $10\frac{2}{3}$ 5. $25\frac{1}{3}$ 6. ${}^-50\frac{3}{4}$

7. 6 8. ${}^-5$ 9. ${}^-100$ 10. 1 11. ${}^-1$ 12. 0

13. 0.3 14. ${}^-0.7$ 15. ${}^-0.27$ 16. 0.25 17. ${}^-1.9$ 18. ${}^-2.75$

19. $0.\overline{2}$ 20. ${}^-0.\overline{3}$ 21. ${}^-0.\overline{17}$ 22. $0.\overline{27}$ 23. ${}^-0.\overline{07}$ 24. $0.\overline{06}$

You can add, subtract, multiply, or divide with rational numbers. You decide if the answer is positive or negative the same way that you decide when performing the operations with integers.

Here are some examples.

$$\frac{^-7}{9} + \frac{1}{9} = \frac{^-7 + 1}{9} = \frac{^-6}{9} = \frac{^-2}{3} \qquad \frac{^-1}{7} - \frac{^-5}{7} = \frac{^-1}{7} + \frac{5}{7} = \frac{4}{7}$$

$$\frac{^-2}{5} \times \frac{^-1}{4} = \frac{2}{20} = \frac{1}{10} \qquad \frac{^-1}{5} \div \frac{3}{4} = \frac{^-1}{5} \times \frac{4}{3} = \frac{^-4}{15}$$

$$\frac{^-1}{4} + \frac{2}{3} + \frac{1}{6} = \frac{^-3}{12} + \frac{8}{12} + \frac{2}{12} = \frac{^-3 + 8 + 2}{12} = \frac{7}{12}$$

Add, subtract, multiply, or divide. Write the answer in lowest terms.

25. $\frac{1}{5} + \frac{^-4}{5}$ **26.** $\frac{3}{5} + \frac{^-1}{5}$ **27.** $\frac{^-2}{9} + \frac{5}{9}$ **28.** $\frac{^-9}{10} + \frac{1}{10}$

29. $\frac{4}{9} - \frac{^-1}{9}$ **30.** $\frac{2}{9} - \frac{7}{9}$ **31.** $\frac{^-1}{4} - \frac{3}{4}$ **32.** $\frac{^-1}{8} - \frac{^-3}{8}$

33. $\frac{2}{3} \times \frac{^-1}{3}$ **34.** $\frac{^-1}{2} \times \frac{^-3}{5}$ **35.** $\frac{^-1}{2} \times \frac{2}{7}$ **36.** $\frac{^-1}{6} \times \frac{^-3}{5}$

37. $\frac{^-1}{5} \div \frac{^-2}{3}$ **38.** $\frac{1}{2} \div \frac{^-3}{4}$ **39.** $\frac{^-1}{6} \div \frac{1}{2}$ **40.** $\frac{^-1}{10} \div \frac{^-2}{5}$

41. $\frac{^-1}{2} + \frac{^-1}{4} + \frac{^-1}{8}$ **42.** $\frac{^-1}{3} + \frac{^-1}{3} + \frac{^-1}{9}$ **43.** $\frac{^-2}{5} + \frac{^-1}{5} + \frac{4}{5}$

True or False? Write *T* or *F*.

44. Every integer is a rational number.

45. The sum of two rational numbers is always a rational number.

46. The difference of two rational numbers is always a rational number.

47. The product of two rational numbers is always a rational number.

48. The quotient of two rational numbers is *not* always a rational number.

Maintaining Skills

Choose the best answer. Write *a*, *b*, *c*, or *d*.

Evaluate the expression. Use $a = 7$ and $b = 2$.

1. $a + 19$ **a.** 12   **2.** $\frac{18}{b}$ **a.** 9   **3.** $2ab$ **a.** 272
             b. 21   **b.** 16   **b.** 28
             c. 26   **c.** 11   **c.** 11
             d. None of   **d.** None of   **d.** None of
                    these   these   these

Solve the equation.

4. $x + 5 = 7$ **a.** 12   **5.** $y - 2 = 9$ **a.** 11
                   b. 2   **b.** 7
                   c. ⁻2   **c.** ⁻7
                   d. None of these   **d.** None of these

6. $7u = 91$ **a.** 23   **7.** $\frac{v}{4} = 24$ **a.** 6
                b. 637   **b.** 3
                c. 13   **c.** 96
                d. None of these   **d.** None of these

Solve the proportion.

8. $\frac{6}{8} = \frac{f}{24}$ **a.** 18   **9.** $\frac{g}{35} = \frac{7}{49}$ **a.** 25
                   b. 24   **b.** 5
                   c. 2   **c.** 7
                   d. None of these   **d.** None of these

10. $\frac{12}{h} = \frac{2}{7}$ **a.** 14   **11.** $\frac{5}{36} = \frac{10}{k}$ **a.** 72
                   b. 42   **b.** 2
                   c. 6   **c.** 36
                   d. None of these   **d.** None of these

12. $\frac{r}{18} = \frac{3}{5}$ **a.** 9   **13.** $\frac{6}{x} = \frac{2}{17}$ **a.** 36
                   b. 16   **b.** 51
                   c. 10   **c.** 8
                   d. None of these   **d.** None of these

Solve.

14. What percent of 24 is 18?
- **a.** 7.5
- **b.** 75%
- **c.** 13.3%
- **d.** None of these

15. What is 5% of $12.60?
- **a.** $.63
- **b.** $63
- **c.** $2.52
- **d.** None of these

Find the surface area. Use 3.14 for π.

16.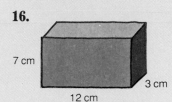
- **a.** 282 cm²
- **b.** 141 cm²
- **c.** 210 cm²
- **d.** None of these

17.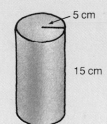
- **a.** 78.5 cm²
- **b.** 628 cm²
- **c.** 471 cm²
- **d.** None of these

Find the volume. Use 3.14 for π.

18.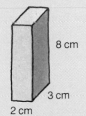
- **a.** 96 cm³
- **b.** 24 cm³
- **c.** 48 cm³
- **d.** None of these

19.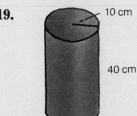
- **a.** 31.4 cm³
- **b.** 400 cm³
- **c.** 1256 cm³
- **d.** None of these

A bowl contains 15 marbles. Of these, 8 are red and 7 are blue. Jim takes out one marble. Then, without replacing the first, he removes another. What is the probability?

20. P (first blue)
- **a.** $\frac{7}{15}$
- **b.** $\frac{1}{15}$
- **c.** $\frac{7}{8}$
- **d.** None of these

21. P (both red)
- **a.** $\frac{4}{15}$
- **b.** $\frac{64}{225}$
- **c.** $\frac{1}{15}$
- **d.** None of these

Borrowing Money

Don Varland needs a new car but hasn't enough money to pay cash for it. He decides to apply for a bank auto loan. This is how Don filled out the first part of his loan application.

Don talked to a personal banking representative whose job it is to interview consumer loan applicants and grant loans. She discussed loan rates and charges with Don.

Don decided he could afford to pay back a $3000 loan in 36 monthly payments of $90.43. This is how Don found the total amount he had to repay and the finance charge.

APPLICATION FOR PERSONAL LOAN

(Fill out in full.)

1. Amount of loan *$3000*
2. Purpose of loan *car purchase*
3. Payment date each month *15th*
4. Method of payment
   ☑ Personal monthly check   ☐ Charge monthly payment to Account #_____
5. Auto Loan Information
   ☑ New   ☐ Used
   Model *2-door hardtop*
   Make *Omeratron*
   Cost *$6850*

   Personal Information (Please print)
   Name *DONALD VARLAND*
   Address *12 SPRING STREET*

Multiply the amount of payments by the number of payments.

$90.43
× 36
$3255.48 total to repay

Subtract the amount of the loan from the total amount to be repaid.

$3255.48
− 3000.00
$ 255.48 finance charge

Find the total amount to repay and the finance charge.

	Amount of Loan	Months to Repay	Monthly Payment	Total to Repay	Finance Charge
1.	$1500	12	$143.75	?	?
2.	$2000	24	$ 98.33	?	?
3.	$3500	24	$177.92	?	?
4.	$7550	36	$255.86	?	?

Solve. You'll need to use more than one step.

5. Martha Pryor wants to buy a boat for $8650. She can afford a 20% down payment but she must have a loan to pay the rest. What is the amount of the loan that Martha needs?

6. Josie Ling agrees to repay her bank loan at a rate of $155.21 per month for 24 months. What is the total repayment amount of her loan?

7. Bob Terry borrows $1000 from the Apex Loan Company to replace the roof on his house. He agrees to make monthly payments of $98.75 for 12 months. How much is the finance charge on his loan?

8. Dr. Gerald takes out a loan of $5500 toward her son's college expenses. She agrees to repay her credit union a total of $6435 in 36 months. How much does the doctor repay each month?

★ 9. Ted Downey decides to borrow $500 to pay all his bills. The finance charge for the loan is $27.40. Ted agrees to repay the loan at a rate of $43.95 per month. In how many months will the loan be repaid?

LOAN DEPARTMENT

Saving for a Rainy Day

The money put into a savings account is called a **deposit.** The money taken from an account is a **withdrawal.** A bank teller receives deposits and pays withdrawals.

Banks sometimes pay their interest four times a year, or quarterly. Interest paid on only the principal is **simple interest.**

DATE	MEMORANDUM	WITHDRAWALS	DEPOSITS/INTEREST	BALANCE
01-01-81				$300.00
01-01-81	Interest		4 13	$304.13
02-15-81	Withdrawal	304 13		$000.00
04-01-81	Deposit		200 00	$200.00
07-01-81	Interest		2 75	$202.75
10-01-81	Interest		2 79	$205.54
10-03-81	Withdrawal	105 54		$100.00
01-01-82	Interest		1 38	$101.38
01-08-82	Withdrawal	50 00		$ 51.38
01-14-82	Withdrawal	25 00		$ 26.38
02-03-82	Withdrawal	26 38		$000.00
04-01-82	Deposit		312 00	$312.00

DEPOSITOR'S RECORD. FOR DEPOSITORS USE ONLY

Mary Dowd deposits $312 in a savings account that pays interest annually at a rate of $5\frac{1}{2}\%$ per year. If she makes no other deposits or withdrawals, how much simple interest does her principal earn in one quarter?

You can use a formula to find the amount of interest.
Interest = principal × rate of interest × time
The principal earns $4.29 simple interest.

$I = p \times r \times t$
$I = \$312 \times 0.055 \times 0.25$
$I = \$4.29$

Use the formula to find the amount of simple interest. Assume that there have been no other deposits or withdrawals. Round interest to the nearest cent.

1. Deposit: $90

Rate of interest: $5\frac{1}{2}\%$

Time: $\frac{1}{4}$ year

2. Deposit: $625

Rate of interest: $5\frac{1}{4}\%$

Time: $\frac{1}{4}$ year

3. Deposit: $930

Rate of interest: $5\frac{3}{4}\%$

Time: $\frac{1}{4}$ year

Compound interest is interest paid on both the principal and on previously-earned interest. We say that interest is compounded quarterly ($\frac{1}{4}$ year), semiannually ($\frac{1}{2}$ year), monthly ($\frac{1}{12}$ year), or daily ($\frac{1}{365}$ year).

John Silks deposited $650 in a savings account. His bank pays $5\frac{1}{2}\%$ interest per year, compounded quarterly. If John made no other deposits or withdrawals, how much is in his account at the end of the second quarter?

First Quarter	Second Quarter
I = \$650 × 0.055 × 0.25	I = \$658.94 × 0.055 × 0.25
I = \$8.9375 or \$8.94	I = \$9.0604 or \$9.06
\$650 + \$8.94 = \$658.94	\$658.94 + \$9.06 = \$668

How much money is in the account at the end of the second quarter?
Round interest to the nearest cent.

4. Principal: $800

Interest: $5\frac{1}{4}\%$

compounded quarterly

5. Principal: $925

Interest: $5\frac{1}{2}\%$

compounded quarterly

6. Principal: $1175

Interest: $5\frac{1}{4}\%$

compounded quarterly

Solve. Assume that no other deposits or withdrawals are made.

7. Pam Kisby opened an account at the Apex Savings Bank with a deposit of $725. Apex pays $5\frac{1}{4}\%$ interest quarterly. How much simple interest did Pam's money earn during the first quarter?

8. In January, Dave Kinoshita deposited $1275 in the Thrift Savings Bank. Thrift pays $5\frac{1}{2}\%$ interest compounded seminannually. How much money was in Dave's account at the end of the year?

★ **9.** The principal in Gail Silver's savings account in the credit union was $2020 at the beginning of the year. Her credit union pays $5\frac{1}{2}\%$ interest compounded quarterly. How much money will be in her account at the end of the year?

★ **10.** On January 1st, Ryan McNamara had $825 in the bank. In June, he deposited $250 more. At $5\frac{3}{4}\%$ interest compounded quarterly, how much money will Ryan have in his account at the end of the year?

Applying Your Skills

Paychecks

In his job as payroll clerk at Cartland Aircraft, Gary Casarez is responsible for the accurate preparation of weekly paychecks for 1200 workers and the distribution of those checks on time. For workers who are paid at an hourly rate, Gary must know the exact number of hours they work so he can pay them the correct amount.

Workers paid hourly use a time card to keep track of their hours.

This is Debby Sharain's time card. Her regular hours are 8:00 A.M. to 4:00 P.M. with 30 minutes for lunch.

Use Debby's time card to answer. Round daily working hours down to the nearest quarter hour.

TIME CARD   **Department:**
Debby Sharain   Wing Assembly
Week of: 3-8-82   **Pay rate:** $6.50 per hr.

Day	In	Out	In	Out
Monday	7:45 AM	12:00 PM	12:30 PM	4:02 PM
Tuesday	8:00 AM	12:00 PM	12:30 PM	4:00 PM
Wednesday	7:51 AM	12:00 PM	12:30 PM	3:30 PM
Thursday	8:10 AM	12:10 PM	12:30 PM	4:00 PM
Friday	7:42 AM	12:00 PM	12:30 PM	5:30 PM

1. How many hours did Debby work on Monday? on Tuesday? on Wednesday?

2. On Thursday, Debby was late to work. How many hours did Debby work on Thursday?

3. On Friday, Debby was asked to work overtime. For this, she is paid $1\frac{1}{2}$ times her regular hourly rate for each extra hour. What is the total amount that Debby was paid for her work on Friday?

4. What was the total amount of money in Debby's paycheck at the end of the week?

416

Gross pay is the total amount of money earned by a worker. **Net pay** is the amount of earnings after all deductions, or withholdings, have been made. A payroll clerk keeps accurate records of all deductions.

Employers are required by law to deduct amounts for federal income tax and for social security tax. Tables are used to find proper deductions of income tax. The rate for social security is 13.4%. One-half of this is paid by the employer. The other half is deducted from the worker's paycheck.

Use the earnings statements to find the amount.

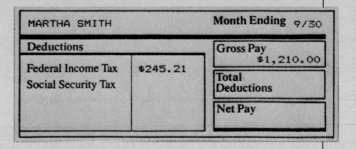

5. Martha's social security tax (6.7% of her gross pay)

6. Martha's total deductions

7. Martha's net pay

8. Alice's social security tax

9. Alice's state tax (3% of her gross pay)

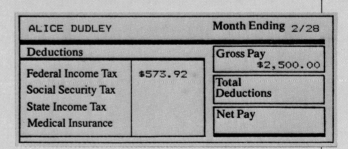

10. Alice's medical insurance (20% of $41.30, its monthly cost)

11. Alice's total deductions

12. Alice's net pay

★ 13. Richard Stuart works forty-two hours per week. He earns $9.50 per hour. His federal income tax is $312.48. What is his monthly:
    a. gross pay?
    b. social security tax?
    c. state income tax ($4\frac{1}{2}$% of his gross pay)?
    d. net pay?

Some Geometric Patterns

Line segment $\overline{XY}$ is divided into two
line segments by point A.

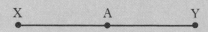

1. Make a chart like the one below. Fill in your chart to show how
many points are needed to divide $\overline{XY}$ into the given number of line
segments.

Number of Line Segments	2	3	4	5	6	10	25
Number of Points	1	?	?	?	?	?	?

What is the pattern on your chart? Write 2 formulas that show the
pattern. Use l for the number of line segments and p for the number
of points.

Rectangle ABCD is divided into two parts by line
segment $\overline{EF}$. If the line segments do not intersect inside
the rectangle, is it possible to divide ABCD into the
number of parts? *Yes* or *No*.

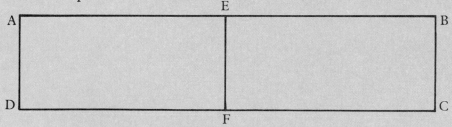

2. 3 parts by 2 line segments   **3.** 4 parts by 3 line segments

4. 5 parts by 4 line segments   **5.** 10 parts by 9 line segments

Look for a pattern in Exercises 2–5.

6. Is the relationship of parts to line segments in Exercises 2–5 the
same as the relationship of line segments to points in Exercise 1?

Table of Measures

TIME

$$60 \text{ seconds (s)} = 1 \text{ minute (min)}$$
$$60 \text{ minutes (min)} = 1 \text{ hour (h)}$$
$$24 \text{ hours} = 1 \text{ day (d)}$$
$$7 \text{ days} = 1 \text{ week}$$

$$\left. \begin{array}{l} 365 \text{ days} \\ 52 \text{ weeks} \\ 12 \text{ months} \end{array} \right\} = 1 \text{ year}$$
$$10 \text{ years} = 1 \text{ decade}$$
$$100 \text{ years} = 1 \text{ century}$$

Metric

LENGTH

$$10 \text{ millimeters (mm)} = 1 \text{ centimeter (cm)}$$
$$10 \text{ centimeters} = 1 \text{ decimeter (dm)}$$
$$\left. \begin{array}{l} 10 \text{ decimeters} \\ 100 \text{ centimeters} \end{array} \right\} = 1 \text{ meter}$$
$$10 \text{ meters} = 1 \text{ dekameter (dam)}$$
$$10 \text{ dekameters} = 1 \text{ hectameter (hm)}$$
$$\left. \begin{array}{l} 10 \text{ hectameters} \\ 1000 \text{ meters} \end{array} \right\} = 1 \text{ kilometer (km)}$$

AREA

$$100 \text{ square millimeters} = 1 \text{ square centimeter}$$
$$(\text{mm}^2) \qquad (\text{cm}^2)$$
$$10{,}000 \text{ square centimeters} = 1 \text{ square meter (m}^2)$$
$$10{,}000 \text{ square meters} = 1 \text{ hectare (ha)}$$

VOLUME

$$1000 \text{ cubic millimeters} = 1 \text{ cubic centimeter}$$
$$(\text{mm}^3) \qquad (\text{cm}^3)$$
$$1{,}000{,}000 \text{ cubic centimeters} = 1 \text{ cubic meter (m}^3)$$

MASS

$$1000 \text{ milligrams (mg)} = 1 \text{ gram (g)}$$
$$1000 \text{ grams} = 1 \text{ kilogram (kg)}$$

CAPACITY

$$1000 \text{ milliliters (mL)} = 1 \text{ liter (L)}$$

United States Customary

LENGTH

$$12 \text{ inches (in.)} = 1 \text{ foot (ft)}$$
$$\left. \begin{array}{l} 3 \text{ feet} \\ 36 \text{ inches} \end{array} \right\} = 1 \text{ yard (yd)}$$
$$\left. \begin{array}{l} 5280 \text{ feet} \\ 1760 \text{ yards} \end{array} \right\} = 1 \text{ mile (mi)}$$

AREA

$$144 \text{ square inches (in.}^2) = 1 \text{ square foot (ft}^2)$$
$$9 \text{ square feet} = 1 \text{ square yard (yd}^2)$$
$$4840 \text{ square yards} = 1 \text{ acre (A)}$$

VOLUME

$$1728 \text{ cubic inches} = 1 \text{ cubic foot (ft}^3)$$
$$27 \text{ cubic feet} = 1 \text{ cubic yard (yd}^3)$$

WEIGHT

$$16 \text{ ounces (oz)} = 1 \text{ pound (lb)}$$
$$2000 \text{ pounds} = 1 \text{ ton (t)}$$

CAPACITY

$$8 \text{ fluid ounces (fl oz)} = 1 \text{ cup (c)}$$
$$2 \text{ cups} = 1 \text{ pint (pt)}$$
$$2 \text{ pints} = 1 \text{ quart (qt)}$$
$$4 \text{ quarts} = 1 \text{ gallon (gal)}$$

UNIT 1 Extra Practice

For use after Checkpoint A

Pages 10–11

Write the standard form.

1. 3 hundred 7   **2.** 7 thousand, 5 hundred   **3.** 33 million, 286

4. 60,000 + 3000 + 200 + 9   **5.** 200,000 + 9000 + 60 + 5

Pages 12–13

Write as a decimal.

6. 9 tenths   **7.** 10 and 7 tenths   **8.** 8 and 7 hundredths

Pages 14–15

Write the decimal in standard form.

9. 291 thousandths   **10.** 23 millionths   **11.** 32 + 0.5 + 0.0008

Pages 16–17

Compare the numbers. Write < or >.

12. 39 ▦ 37   **13.** 2463 ▦ 2473   **14.** 19,408 ▦ 19,406

Pages 18–19

Arrange the numbers in order from greatest to least.

15. 2.53, 2.63, 1.53, 1.06, 1.69

For use after Checkpoint B

Pages 20–21

Round to the place underlined.

1. 3<u>9</u>2   **2.** 4<u>3</u>97   **3.** 70,<u>6</u>28   **4.** 339,<u>5</u>06

Pages 22–23

Round to the place underlined.

5. <u>5</u>.96   **6.** 0.1<u>4</u>9   **7.** 0.23<u>8</u>1   **8.** 5.09<u>4</u>9

Pages 24–25

Measure to the nearest centimeter.

9. ————————   **10.** ————————

Pages 26–31

Complete.

11. 5 m = ▦ cm   **12.** 5000 mm = ▦ m   **13.** 17 km = ▦ m

14. 6 L = ▦ mL   **15.** 19000 mL = ▦ L   **16.** 7 g = ▦ mg

Extra Practice UNIT 1

Pages 10–19

3.025 ▦ 3.026
5 < 6 so
3.025 < 3.026

Compare the numbers. Write < or >.

1. 273 ▦ 293   **2.** 30,472 ▦ 30,382

3. 214,779 ▦ 214,778   **4.** 72,605 ▦ 72,625

5. 0.23 ▦ 0.25   **6.** 1.03 ▦ 1.31   **7.** 1.029 ▦ 0.029

8. 4.6 ▦ 4.06   **9.** 0.392 ▦ 0.4   **10.** 0.621 ▦ 0.622

Pages 20–23

429.739 rounded to
the nearest hundred is
400; to the nearest
hundredth, 429.74.

Round to the place underlined.

1. 7<u>9</u>2   **2.** 8<u>2</u>51   **3.** <u>3</u>925   **4.** <u>7</u>48

5. 65,<u>2</u>31   **6.** <u>5</u>4,999   **7.** 74<u>9</u>8   **8.** 38<u>2</u>6

9. 8.<u>3</u>92   **10.** 0.4<u>8</u>3   **11.** 1.<u>1</u>9   **12.** 1.1<u>7</u>26

13. 4.3<u>8</u>6   **14.** 0.6<u>4</u>4   **15.** <u>0</u>.53   **16.** 6.1<u>3</u>8

Pages 24–25

10 mm = 1 cm

Measure to the nearest centimeter.

1. ——————————   **2.** ————————————————

Pages 26–31

1 m = 100 cm
1 L = 1000 mL
1 kg = 1000 g

Complete.

1. 4 m = ▦ cm   **2.** 9000 mm = ▦ m

3. 25 km = ▦ m   **4.** 6000 mL = ▦ L

5. 17 L = ▦ mL   **6.** 32,000 mL = ▦ L

7. 9 g = ▦ mg   **8.** 14,000 g = ▦ kg

Pages 32–33

1. Understand
2. Plan
3. Work
4. Answer

Solve.

1. During the school olympics Paul threw the ball 27.3 m,
Jane threw the ball 27.35 m, and Alice threw it 26.3 m.
Who threw the ball the farthest?

UNIT 2 Extra Practice

Pages 40–41

Solve the equation.

1. $5 + n = 13$ **2.** $17 - c = 9$ **3.** $k - 6 = 7$

Pages 42–43

Name the property illustrated.

4. $9 + 8 = 8 + 9$ **5.** $2 + (9 + 6) = (2 + 9) + 6$

Pages 44–47

Add or subtract.

6.   392
      +419

7.   4709
       2864
      +5132

8.   6.02
      +2.99

9.   0.43
        0.091
      +2.98

Pages 48–51

10.   347
       − 139

11.   460
       − 218

12.   5431
       − 2850

13.   9713
       − 2825

14.   6.25
       − 1.19

15.   8.03
       − 7.52

16.   3.4
       − 0.29

17.   7.38
       − 3.094

Pages 52–53

1.   300
       − 246

2.   700
       − 289

3.   2.001
       − 1.41

4.   5.01
       − 2.983

Pages 54–55

Find the answer.

5. $43 + 872 - 61$ **6.** $17.09 - 3.24 + 0.758$

Pages 56–57

Round to the place specified. Estimate the sum or difference.

7. nearest hundred: $6384 - 2943$ **8.** nearest tenth: $4.82 + 0.19 + 0.758$

Pages 58–59

Add or subtract.

9.   7 ft 4 in.
      +8 ft 9 in.

10.   2 c 2 oz
       − 1 c 7 oz

11.   30 min
       − 5 min 25 s

Extra Practice   UNIT 2

Pages 40–43

$3 + n = 9$

$n = 9 - 3 = 6$

Solve.

1. $9 + c = 15$ **2.** $13 - b = 4$ **3.** $a + 7 = 12$

4. $d - 8 = 7$ **5.** $16 - e = 9$ **6.** $f + 8 = 16$

Pages 44–55

$\begin{array}{r} 4.034 \\ -2.947 \\ \hline 1.087 \end{array}$

Keep the decimal point in line.

1. $\begin{array}{r} 329 \\ +658 \\ \hline \end{array}$	**2.** $\begin{array}{r} 903 \\ -274 \\ \hline \end{array}$	**3.** $\begin{array}{r} 400 \\ -283 \\ \hline \end{array}$
4. $\begin{array}{r} 7358 \\ +6877 \\ \hline \end{array}$	**5.** $\begin{array}{r} 4.32 \\ +1.94 \\ \hline \end{array}$	**6.** $\begin{array}{r} 1.672 \\ -0.925 \\ \hline \end{array}$
7. $\begin{array}{r} 0.83 \\ +0.759 \\ \hline \end{array}$	**8.** $\begin{array}{r} 3.061 \\ -1.471 \\ \hline \end{array}$	**9.** $\begin{array}{r} 2.02 \\ -1.483 \\ \hline \end{array}$

Pages 56–57

Estimate the sum.

$\begin{array}{r} 593 \\ +427 \\ \hline \end{array}$ ⇨ $\begin{array}{r} 600 \\ +400 \\ \hline 1000 \end{array}$

Round to the place specified. Estimate the sum or difference.

1. nearest whole number:
$72.43 + 6.9 + 32.6$

2. nearest hundred:
$6352 - 4913$

3. nearest tenth:
$0.83 + 0.552 + 1.09$

4. nearest hundredth:
$13.049 - 4.574$

Pages 58–59

2 ft 6 in.

+ 1 ft 7 in.

3 ft 13 in. = 4 ft 1 in.

You may need to regroup.

1. $\begin{array}{r} 3\,h\ 25\ min \\ +2\,h\ 41\ min \\ \hline \end{array}$	**2.** $\begin{array}{r} 17\,lb\ 5\ oz \\ -\ \ 8\,lb\ 3\ oz \\ \hline \end{array}$	**3.** $\begin{array}{r} 2\ pt\ 1\,c \\ +1\ pt\ 2\,c \\ \hline \end{array}$
4. $\begin{array}{r} 6\ ft\ 8\ in. \\ -2\ ft\ 9\ in. \\ \hline \end{array}$	**5.** $\begin{array}{r} 15\,h\ 35\ min \\ +16\,h\ 42\ min \\ \hline \end{array}$	**6.** $\begin{array}{r} 8\,lb\ 2\ oz \\ -3\,lb\ 9\ oz \\ \hline \end{array}$

Pages 60–61

1. Understand
2. Plan
3. Work
4. Answer

Solve.

1. There are 34 racing bicycles remaining in the store. Each costs $275 with a tax of $13.75. Seven of the bicycles are 24 in. and 8 are 21 in. How much will one bicycle cost?

UNIT 3 Extra Practice

Pages 68–71

Solve the equation.

1. $3 \times m = 15$ **2.** $g \div 6 = 7$ **3.** $1 \times 9 = n$

4. $4 \times 6 = 6 \times a$ **5.** $7 \times (3 + 4) = (7 \times 3) + (p \times 4)$

Pages 72–73

Simplify.

6. $(7 - 5) \times 6$ **7.** $20 \div 5 + 3 \times 6$ **8.** $19 - 3 \times 2 + (8 \div 2)$

Pages 74–77

9. $\begin{array}{r} 402 \\ \times 39 \\ \hline \end{array}$ **10.** $\begin{array}{r} 0.06 \\ \times 9 \\ \hline \end{array}$ **11.** $\begin{array}{r} 3.4 \\ \times 0.8 \\ \hline \end{array}$ **12.** $\begin{array}{r} 5.43 \\ \times 2.05 \\ \hline \end{array}$

Pages 78–79

Write the number in standard form.

13. 3^2 **14.** 2^5 **15.** 5^3 **16.** 10^5

Pages 80–83

Divide.

1. $55\overline{)236}$ **2.** $8\overline{)7463}$ **3.** $4\overline{)51063}$ **4.** $9\overline{)63851}$

5. $60\overline{)793}$ **6.** $21\overline{)6905}$ **7.** $48\overline{)2178}$ **8.** $73\overline{)42839}$

Pages 84–85

9. $8\overline{)2.4}$ **10.** $7\overline{)82.04}$ **11.** $25\overline{)0.72}$ **12.** $43\overline{)2.623}$

Pages 86–87

13. 3.2×10 **14.** $68.3 \div 10$ **15.** $29.52 \div 1000$

Pages 88–89

16. $0.7\overline{)9.1}$ **17.** $0.52\overline{)1.3}$ **18.** $0.24\overline{)164.4}$

Pages 90–91

Estimate the product or quotient.

19. 49×22 **20.** $74{,}840 \div 4.8$ **21.** 3.2×69.8

Extra Practice   UNIT 3

Pages 68–73

$7 \times n = 42$
$n = 42 \div 7 = 6$

Solve the equation.

1. $6 \times n = 18$ **2.** $21 \div g = 3$ **3.** $s \div 8 = 8$

4. $m \times 9 = 54$ **5.** $6 \times h = 48$ **6.** $k \div 5 = 4$

Pages 74–79

$$\begin{array}{r} 46 \\ \times 32 \\ \hline 1472 \end{array} \qquad \begin{array}{r} 4.6 \\ \times 0.32 \\ \hline 1.472 \end{array}$$

Multiply.

1. $\begin{array}{r} 39 \\ \times 12 \\ \hline \end{array}$ **2.** $\begin{array}{r} 745 \\ \times 60 \\ \hline \end{array}$ **3.** $\begin{array}{r} 208 \\ \times 35 \\ \hline \end{array}$ **4.** $\begin{array}{r} 612 \\ \times 203 \\ \hline \end{array}$

5. $\begin{array}{r} 0.09 \\ \times 8 \\ \hline \end{array}$ **6.** $\begin{array}{r} 0.73 \\ \times 0.6 \\ \hline \end{array}$ **7.** $\begin{array}{r} 5.4 \\ \times 0.72 \\ \hline \end{array}$ **8.** $\begin{array}{r} 2.04 \\ \times 0.89 \\ \hline \end{array}$

$3^3 = 3 \times 3 \times 3 = 27$

Write the number in standard form.

9. 7^2 **10.** 2^4 **11.** 3^4 **12.** 10^6

Pages 80–89

$2.5\overline{)158}$

$\begin{array}{r} 63.2 \\ 25\overline{)1580.0} \end{array}$

Divide.

1. $6\overline{)735}$ **2.** $12\overline{)6294}$ **3.** $39\overline{)24736}$

4. $7\overline{)4.34}$ **5.** $26\overline{)9.62}$ **6.** $42\overline{)270.9}$

7. $0.3\overline{)5.22}$ **8.** $6.7\overline{)2.412}$ **9.** $0.15\overline{)45.6}$

Pages 90–91

Estimate the product.
39×21
$40 \times 20 = 800$

Estimate the product or quotient.

1. $679 \div 71$ **2.** 638×43 **3.** $9868 \div 49$

4. $21,493 \div 3.4$ **5.** 7.8×23.7 **6.** 247×9.493

Pages 92–93

1. Understand
2. Plan
3. Work
4. Answer

Use the facts to write a problem. Then solve.

1. There are 35 rows of seats in the auditorium, with 10 seats per row. Tickets for the school play are $0.50. The drama club hopes to raise at least $100 for new costumes.

UNIT 4 Extra Practice

For use after Checkpoint A

**Pages
100–101**

True or False? Write *T* or *F*.

1. A ray is part of a line.

2. A line segment has one endpoint.

3. A plane is a set of points along a line.

4. The endpoint of an angle is called the vertex.

**Pages
102–105**

Use a protractor to draw the angle. Tell whether the angle is acute, right, or obtuse.

5. ∠*SEL* = 34°

6. ∠*TAN* = 172°

7. ∠*PUD* = 90°

8. ∠*COP* = 115°

**Pages
106–111**

Name the figure.

9. A polygon with 6 sides

10. A polygon with 8 sides

11. A rectangle with 4 congruent sides

12. A triangle with no congruent sides and no congruent angles

13. A parallelogram with four right angles

14. A quadrilateral with exactly one pair of parallel sides

For use after Checkpoint B

**Pages
112–113**

What is the perimeter of the figure?

1.
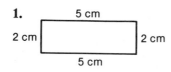
5 cm
2 cm 2 cm
5 cm

2.
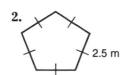
2.5 m

3.
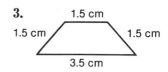
1.5 cm
1.5 cm 1.5 cm
3.5 cm

**Pages
114–115**

What is the circumference of the circle?

4. $d = 4$ cm

5. $r = 8$ mm

6. $r = 18$ m

**Pages
116–121**

What is the area of the figure?

7. rectangle:
$b = 15$ cm
$h = 20$ cm

8. parallelogram:
$b = 3.6$ m
$h = 4.5$ m

9. triangle:
$b = 8.5$ m
$h = 12$ m

10. circle:
$r = 15$ cm
$\pi \approx 3.14$

Extra Practice UNIT 4

Pages 100–105
ray line
angle plane
line segment

Name the figure using the letters shown. If the figure is an angle, tell whether it is acute, obtuse, or right.

1.
   A   B

2.
   C   D

3.
   I   H   J

4.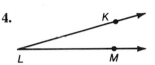
   K L M

Pages 106–111
hexagon pentagon
rhombus square
isosceles triangle
trapezoid

Name the type of polygon, triangle, or quadrilateral.

1.

2.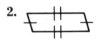

3.

Pages 112–115
Perimeter:
Distance around a polygon.
Circumference:
Distance around a circle.
$C = \pi \times d$

1. Triangle:
   $a = 6$ cm
   $b = 4$ cm
   $c = 8$ cm

2. Rectangle:
   $b = 6.5$ m
   $h = 7.4$ m

3. Circle:
   $d = 6.3$ cm
   $\pi \approx 3.14$

4. Square: $s = 9.5$ mm

Pages 116–121
Area of triangle:
$A = b \times h \div 2$

Area of circle:
$A = \pi \times r^2$

What is the area of the figure?

1. Rectangle:
   $b = 6$ m
   $h = 9$ m

2. Triangle:
   $b = 4.3$ mm
   $h = 6.1$ mm

3. Circle:
   $r = 2.5$ cm
   $\pi \approx 3.14$

Pages 122–123

1. Understand
2. Plan
3. Work
4. Answer

Use a formula to solve the problem.

1. What is the area of a rectangular piece of paper that is 17 cm wide and 23 cm long?

UNIT 5 Extra Practice

For use after Checkpoint A

Pages 138–139, 142–143

Write the LCM and GCF of the numbers.

1. 4 and 8 **2.** 3 and 5 **3.** 6 and 8 **4.** 10 and 12

Pages 140–141

Is the first number divisible by the second? Write *Yes* or *No*.

5. 378 by 2 **6.** 8621 by 3 **7.** 4392 by 9

Pages 144–145

Write the prime factorization.

8. 15 **9.** 50 **10.** 120 **11.** 175

For use after Checkpoint B

Pages 146–149

Complete.

1. $\dfrac{3}{5} = \dfrac{\blacksquare}{20}$ **2.** $\dfrac{7}{8} = \dfrac{21}{\blacksquare}$ **3.** $\dfrac{12}{18} = \dfrac{2}{\blacksquare}$ **4.** $\dfrac{30}{60} = \dfrac{\blacksquare}{2}$

Pages 150–151

Write in lowest terms.

5. $\dfrac{12}{20}$ **6.** $\dfrac{18}{40}$ **7.** $\dfrac{24}{30}$ **8.** $\dfrac{42}{63}$ **9.** $\dfrac{28}{36}$

Pages 152–153

Complete. Write $<$ or $>$.

10. $\dfrac{5}{12} \ \blacksquare \ \dfrac{7}{12}$ **11.** $\dfrac{2}{3} \ \blacksquare \ \dfrac{5}{18}$ **12.** $\dfrac{4}{5} \ \blacksquare \ \dfrac{3}{7}$ **13.** $\dfrac{1}{4} \ \blacksquare \ \dfrac{1}{6}$

Pages 154–155

Write as a whole number or a mixed number.

14. $\dfrac{20}{5}$ **15.** $\dfrac{17}{3}$ **16.** $\dfrac{25}{4}$ **17.** $\dfrac{32}{8}$ **18.** $\dfrac{29}{9}$

Pages 156–159

Write the fractions as decimals and the decimals as fractions in lowest terms.

19. $\dfrac{4}{5}$ **20.** $\dfrac{3}{8}$ **21.** $\dfrac{7}{9}$ **22.** $\dfrac{1}{3}$ **23.** $\dfrac{3}{4}$

24. 0.6 **25.** 0.225 **26.** 0.18 **27.** 0.125 **28.** 0.8

Extra Practice   UNIT 5

Pages 138–145

The LCM of 3 and 4 is 12.

The GCF of 6 and 9 is 3.

The prime factorization of 12:2 × 2 × 3

Write the LCM and GCF of the numbers.

1. 4 and 10   **2.** 5 and 20   **3.** 6 and 15

4. 8 and 12   **5.** 7 and 9   **6.** 10 and 15

7. 9 and 27   **8.** 6 and 10   **9.** 4 and 18

Write the prime factorization.

10. 16   **11.** 20   **12.** 45

13. 42   **14.** 100   **15.** 72

Pages 146–155

$\frac{2}{3}$ ▇ $\frac{3}{4}$

$\frac{2}{3} = \frac{8}{12}, \frac{3}{4} = \frac{9}{12}$

$\frac{8}{12} < \frac{9}{12}$ so $\frac{2}{3} < \frac{3}{4}$

$\frac{31}{8} = 8\overline{)31} = 3\frac{7}{8}$

Complete. Write < or >.

1. $\frac{7}{8}$ ▇ $\frac{5}{8}$ **2.** $\frac{3}{10}$ ▇ $\frac{7}{10}$ **3.** $\frac{3}{8}$ ▇ $\frac{3}{4}$

4. $\frac{5}{12}$ ▇ $\frac{1}{6}$ **5.** $\frac{4}{5}$ ▇ $\frac{7}{8}$ **6.** $\frac{2}{7}$ ▇ $\frac{1}{4}$

7. $\frac{5}{6}$ ▇ $\frac{9}{10}$ **8.** $\frac{7}{12}$ ▇ $\frac{2}{5}$ **9.** $\frac{2}{9}$ ▇ $\frac{3}{4}$

Write as a fraction or as a mixed number.

10. $\frac{35}{6}$ **11.** $\frac{21}{4}$ **12.** $2\frac{4}{5}$

Pages 156–159

$\frac{1}{4} = 4\overline{)1.00}^{\,0.25} = 0.25$

$2.75 = 2\frac{75}{100} = 2\frac{3}{4}$

Write the fractions as decimals and the decimals as fractions in lowest terms.

1. $\frac{1}{5}$ **2.** $\frac{5}{8}$ **3.** $\frac{5}{6}$

4. 0.31   **5.** 0.75   **6.** 0.15

Pages 160–161

1. Understand
2. Plan
3. Work
4. Answer

Solve.

1. Jerry spent $18.95 for a calculator. He also bought 4 packages of batteries at $0.88 per package. How much change did Jerry receive from $30?

UNIT 6 Extra Practice

Pages 168–169 Add or subtract. Write the answer in lowest terms.

1. $\dfrac{1}{5}$ $+\dfrac{3}{5}$

2. $\dfrac{5}{7}$ $-\dfrac{3}{7}$

3. $\dfrac{9}{12}$ $-\dfrac{5}{12}$

4. $\dfrac{3}{10}$ $+\dfrac{7}{10}$

5. $\dfrac{7}{9}$ $-\dfrac{1}{9}$

Pages 170–173

6. $\dfrac{2}{3}$ $+\dfrac{5}{6}$

7. $\dfrac{4}{5}$ $+\dfrac{7}{10}$

8. $\dfrac{5}{6}$ $+\dfrac{3}{4}$

9. $\dfrac{1}{3}$ $+\dfrac{1}{5}$

10. $\dfrac{3}{8}$ $+\dfrac{5}{12}$

Pages 174–175

11. $2\dfrac{2}{7}$ $+5\dfrac{1}{7}$

12. $6\dfrac{2}{5}$ $+4\dfrac{3}{10}$

13. $3\dfrac{3}{4}$ $+1\dfrac{1}{6}$

14. $4\dfrac{5}{9}$ $+2\dfrac{7}{9}$

15. $2\dfrac{7}{8}$ $+3\dfrac{1}{10}$

Pages 176–179 Subtract. Write the answer in lowest terms.

1. $\dfrac{7}{8}$ $-\dfrac{3}{8}$

2. $\dfrac{9}{10}$ $-\dfrac{1}{2}$

3. $\dfrac{11}{12}$ $-\dfrac{3}{4}$

4. $\dfrac{5}{6}$ $-\dfrac{1}{8}$

5. $\dfrac{7}{9}$ $-\dfrac{1}{6}$

6. $12\dfrac{3}{10}$ $-\ 6\dfrac{1}{10}$

7. $13\dfrac{5}{12}$ $-10\dfrac{1}{3}$

8. $9\dfrac{4}{5}$ $-2\dfrac{3}{4}$

9. $8\dfrac{3}{4}$ $-2\dfrac{1}{6}$

10. $12\dfrac{7}{12}$ $-\ 3\dfrac{1}{8}$

Pages 180–181

11. 7 $-2\dfrac{1}{3}$

12. 17 $-\ 8\dfrac{3}{4}$

13. 15 $-\ 9\dfrac{4}{5}$

14. 4 $-\ \dfrac{5}{6}$

15. 2 $-\ \dfrac{7}{9}$

Pages 182–183

16. $8\dfrac{1}{5}$ $-2\dfrac{3}{5}$

17. $6\dfrac{1}{3}$ $-3\dfrac{5}{6}$

18. $7\dfrac{1}{8}$ $-4\dfrac{2}{3}$

19. $8\dfrac{1}{6}$ $-7\dfrac{3}{4}$

20. $4\dfrac{1}{4}$ $-3\dfrac{7}{10}$

Extra Practice   UNIT 6

Pages 168–175

$$3\frac{3}{10} = 3\frac{9}{30}$$
$$+8\frac{5}{6} = 8\frac{25}{30}$$
$$\overline{11\frac{34}{30}}$$

$$= 12\frac{2}{15}$$

Add. Write the answer in lowest terms.

1. $\frac{3}{5}$
$+\frac{7}{10}$

2. $6\frac{3}{8}$
$+4\frac{7}{8}$

3. $\frac{2}{3}$
$+\frac{4}{9}$

4. $3\frac{5}{12}$
$+1\frac{1}{6}$

5. $6\frac{5}{8}$
$+3\frac{5}{6}$

6. $7\frac{2}{9}$
$+4\frac{1}{6}$

7. $9\frac{2}{3}$
$+3\frac{7}{10}$

8. $2\frac{7}{12}$
$+6\frac{3}{8}$

Pages 176–183

$$6 = 5\frac{4}{4}$$
$$-2\frac{3}{4} = 2\frac{3}{4}$$
$$\overline{3\frac{1}{4}}$$

Subtract. Write the answer in lowest terms.

1. $\frac{3}{5}$
$-\frac{1}{10}$

2. $\frac{8}{9}$
$-\frac{2}{3}$

3. $4\frac{5}{6}$
$-1\frac{1}{6}$

4. $7\frac{3}{4}$
$-2\frac{1}{8}$

5. $6\frac{2}{3}$
$-4\frac{1}{4}$

6. $7\frac{7}{8}$
$-2\frac{1}{6}$

7. $3\frac{9}{10}$
$-1\frac{5}{6}$

8. 7
$-\frac{1}{5}$

9. 3
$-\frac{6}{7}$

10. $5\frac{1}{3}$
$-2\frac{2}{3}$

11. $4\frac{1}{6}$
$-2\frac{5}{12}$

12. $3\frac{3}{8}$
$-2\frac{5}{6}$

Pages 184–185

1. Understand
2. Plan
3. Work
4. Answer

Use the information in the picture.
Solve.

1. Roger is planning to put a rug in his room. He sketched the room and marked the lengths as shown. He wants the rug to be one foot from the wall all the way around. What will be the area of the rug?

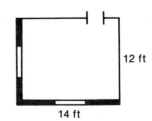

12 ft

14 ft

431

UNIT 7 Extra Practice

For use after Checkpoint A

Pages 192–195

Multiply. Write the product in lowest terms.

1. $\frac{2}{3} \times 27$
2. $14 \times \frac{5}{6}$
3. $\frac{7}{8} \times 9$
4. $\frac{3}{7} \times 15$

5. $\frac{3}{5} \times \frac{2}{5}$
6. $\frac{7}{11} \times \frac{4}{7}$
7. $\frac{2}{9} \times \frac{5}{8}$
8. $\frac{3}{7} \times \frac{4}{13}$

Pages 196–197

9. $\frac{3}{4} \times \frac{1}{6}$
10. $\frac{2}{3} \times \frac{9}{10}$
11. $\frac{6}{7} \times \frac{5}{12}$
12. $\frac{4}{5} \times \frac{3}{8}$

13. $\frac{9}{15} \times \frac{5}{9}$
14. $\frac{11}{20} \times \frac{16}{55}$
15. $\frac{8}{13} \times \frac{39}{48}$
16. $\frac{12}{15} \times \frac{9}{15}$

Pages 198–199

17. $1\frac{1}{3} \times 2\frac{1}{4}$
18. $6\frac{3}{5} \times 2\frac{5}{9}$
19. $6\frac{1}{2} \times 8\frac{1}{6}$
20. $1\frac{5}{7} \times 3\frac{3}{8}$

21. $3\frac{1}{9} \times 2\frac{5}{6}$
22. $3\frac{2}{5} \times 1\frac{2}{3}$
23. $4\frac{1}{2} \times 6\frac{1}{4}$
24. $2\frac{7}{8} \times 3\frac{4}{5}$

For use after Checkpoint B

Pages 200–201

Write the reciprocal.

1. $\frac{3}{4}$
2. $\frac{7}{8}$
3. $9\frac{4}{5}$
4. $8\frac{7}{11}$
5. $13\frac{2}{9}$

Pages 202–203

Divide. Write the quotient in lowest terms.

6. $10 \div \frac{5}{8}$
7. $\frac{3}{10} \div 18$
8. $15 \div \frac{6}{7}$
9. $\frac{9}{11} \div 24$

Pages 204–205

10. $\frac{3}{4} \div \frac{3}{5}$
11. $\frac{4}{9} \div \frac{8}{27}$
12. $\frac{7}{8} \div \frac{9}{16}$
13. $\frac{5}{12} \div \frac{15}{28}$

14. $\frac{6}{7} \div \frac{13}{14}$
15. $\frac{8}{9} \div \frac{6}{11}$
16. $\frac{4}{15} \div \frac{20}{21}$
17. $\frac{10}{11} \div \frac{5}{7}$

Pages 206–207

18. $2\frac{1}{3} \div 1\frac{1}{6}$
19. $6\frac{4}{5} \div \frac{1}{4}$
20. $7\frac{7}{8} \div 2\frac{3}{4}$
21. $8\frac{2}{5} \div \frac{3}{10}$

22. $6\frac{3}{7} \div 4\frac{1}{2}$
23. $9\frac{1}{5} \div 2\frac{5}{6}$
24. $5\frac{3}{10} \div 3$
25. $10\frac{2}{7} \div 5\frac{1}{4}$

26. $9\frac{1}{3} \div 5\frac{5}{6}$
27. $13\frac{1}{2} \div 2\frac{1}{4}$
28. $10\frac{1}{2} \div 1\frac{3}{7}$
29. $18 \div 1\frac{1}{8}$

Extra Practice   UNIT 7

Pages 192–199

$1\frac{1}{6} \times 3\frac{3}{4}$

$= \frac{7}{\cancel{6}} \times \frac{\cancel{15}^{5}}{4}$
$\quad {}_{2}$

$= \frac{35}{8} = 4\frac{3}{8}$

Multiply. Write the product in lowest terms.

1. $\frac{3}{4} \times 12$ **2.** $10 \times \frac{4}{5}$ **3.** $\frac{4}{7} \times 9$

4. $\frac{1}{3} \times \frac{4}{5}$ **5.** $\frac{1}{6} \times \frac{5}{8}$ **6.** $\frac{4}{9} \times \frac{2}{7}$

7. $\frac{3}{5} \times \frac{2}{9}$ **8.** $\frac{3}{8} \times \frac{6}{15}$ **9.** $\frac{7}{10} \times \frac{20}{21}$

10. $\frac{8}{15} \times \frac{5}{24}$ **11.** $9 \times 2\frac{1}{3}$ **12.** $1\frac{3}{4} \times 3\frac{1}{8}$

13. $5\frac{1}{5} \times 2\frac{1}{4}$ **14.** $4\frac{1}{2} \times 2\frac{5}{6}$ **15.** $3\frac{2}{7} \times 2\frac{2}{3}$

Pages 200–207

$3\frac{3}{5} \div 2\frac{1}{4}$

$= \frac{\cancel{18}^{2}}{5} \times \frac{4}{\cancel{9}}$
$\quad\quad {}_{1}$

$= \frac{8}{5} = 1\frac{3}{5}$

Divide. Write the quotient in lowest terms.

1. $8 \div \frac{4}{5}$ **2.** $\frac{3}{4} \div 9$ **3.** $15 \div \frac{6}{7}$

4. $\frac{4}{9} \div 12$ **5.** $\frac{2}{3} \div \frac{6}{7}$ **6.** $\frac{4}{5} \div \frac{4}{5}$

7. $\frac{3}{8} \div \frac{1}{4}$ **8.** $\frac{10}{12} \div \frac{5}{9}$ **9.** $\frac{7}{16} \div \frac{3}{4}$

10. $3\frac{2}{3} \div \frac{1}{6}$ **11.** $4\frac{1}{5} \div \frac{1}{2}$ **12.** $3\frac{3}{4} \div 1\frac{3}{8}$

13. $8 \div 2\frac{1}{6}$ **14.** $2\frac{1}{8} \div 1\frac{5}{6}$ **15.** $4\frac{2}{7} \div 5$

Pages 208–209

1. Understand
2. Plan
3. Work
4. Answer

Estimate to solve.

1. The cost for repairing your bicycle is $24.95. You have a coupon that reduces the cost of the repair by one fifth. About how much will you have to pay?

2. Which costs less, a two-year-old bicycle that sells for a third of the original price of $182.95 or a one-year-old bicycle that sells for half of the original price of $129.89?

UNIT 8   Extra Practice

For use after Checkpoint A

Pages 216–217

Write as a mathematical expression.

1. Six more than a number b.

2. Nine minus four.

Pages 218–219

Evaluate the expression. Use $a = 12$ and $b = 4$.

3. $a + b$

4. $\dfrac{a}{b}$

5. $6b$

6. $14 - a$

Pages 220–221

Is the given number a solution of the equation?

7. $m - 12 = 17$; 29

8. $\dfrac{n}{6} = 84$; 24

9. $4x = 96$; 24

Pages 222–225

Write and solve an equation to answer the question.

10. What number plus 6 is 15?

11. What number minus 7 is 11?

12. The sum of what number and 25 is 90?

13. What number decreased by 35 is 14?

For use after Checkpoint B

Pages 226–229

Write and solve an equation to answer the question.

1. What number divided by 4 is 5?

2. What number times 3 is 18?

Pages 230–231

Solve the equation.

3. $7p = 91$

4. $\dfrac{m}{30} = 15$

5. $t - 42 = 83$

Pages 232–233

Complete the ordered pairs of solutions of $x - 6 = y$.

6. (8, ▓)

7. (▓, 0)

8. (23, ▓)

Pages 234–235

Write the ordered pair for the letter.

9. A

10. B

11. C

12. D

13. E

14. F

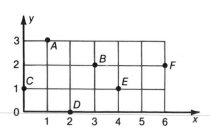

Extra Practice UNIT 8

Pages 216–219

When $a = 2$
and $c = 6$,
$ac = 2(6) = 12$

Evaluate the expression. Use $a = 2$ and $c = 6$.

1. $13 + a$ **2.** $c - a$ **3.** $\frac{c}{3}$

4. $7a$ **5.** $\frac{c}{a}$ **6.** $4ac$

Pages 220–225

$p - 9 = 7$
$p - 9 + 9 = 7 + 9$
$p + 0 = 16$
$p = 16$

Solve the equation.

1. $c + 9 = 31$ **2.** $m - 42 = 18$ **3.** $t + 15 = 83$

4. $a + 15 = 100$ **5.** $x - 60 = 8$ **6.** $y - 35 = 75$

7. $w + 69 = 87$ **8.** $z - 72 = 43$ **9.** $n - 51 = 80$

Pages 226–231

To solve an
equation, do
the same
operation
to both sides.

Solve the equation.

1. $\frac{l}{8} = 6$ **2.** $7z = 49$ **3.** $\frac{x}{15} = 3$

4. $4m = 72$ **5.** $\frac{w}{10} = 10$ **6.** $12p = 108$

7. $\frac{c}{14} = 8$ **8.** $9b = 225$ **9.** $\frac{d}{24} = 11$

Pages 232–235

$y - x = 2$
$7 - 5 = 2$
$(5, 7)$ is a
solution.

Complete the ordered pairs of solutions of $x + 2y = 13$.

1. $(1, \blacksquare)$ **2.** $(3, \blacksquare)$ **3.** $(5, \blacksquare)$

4. $(\blacksquare, 1)$ **5.** $(\blacksquare, 2)$ **6.** $(\blacksquare, 3)$

Pages 236–237

1. Understand
2. Plan
3. Work
4. Answer

Choose $m - 5 = 15$ or $\frac{m}{5} = 15$ as the correct equation to solve

the problem. Solve the equation and answer the question.

1. Alice had some nuts. She shared 5 with her friends. Now
she has 15 left. How many nuts did she start with?

**Pages
244–245**

Write the ratio as a fraction in lowest terms.

1. 3 to 12 **2.** 25 to 5 **3.** 10:15 **4.** 18:27

**Pages
246–247**

Write the unit rate.

5. Juice: 6 cans for $1.56 **6.** Cheese: 3 kg for $4.26

**Pages
248–249**

Match with an equal ratio. Then write as a proportion in two ways.

7. $\frac{2}{3}$ **8.** $\frac{17}{102}$ **9.** $\frac{7}{1}$ **A.** $\frac{29.4}{4.2}$ **B.** $\frac{42}{63}$ **C.** $\frac{1}{6}$

**Pages
250–251**

Solve the proportion using equal ratios.

10. $\frac{3}{4} = \frac{a}{36}$ **11.** $\frac{9}{13} = \frac{54}{m}$ **12.** $\frac{c}{5} = \frac{21}{35}$ **13.** $\frac{63}{n} = \frac{189}{57}$

**Pages
252–253**

Solve the proportion by cross multiplication.

14. $\frac{a}{7} = \frac{20}{28}$ **15.** $\frac{6}{9} = \frac{b}{6}$ **16.** $\frac{3}{c} = \frac{2}{4}$ **17.** $\frac{60}{12} = \frac{12.5}{n}$

For use after Checkpoint B

**Pages
254–255**

Find the measure of the actual object.

1. A table is drawn 6 cm long.
1 cm represents 4 cm.

2. A field is drawn 10 cm long.
1 cm represents 5 m.

**Pages
256–257**

On a map, 1 cm represents 2 km. What is the actual distance
represented on the map?

3. 3 cm **4.** 4.5 cm **5.** 1.2 cm **6.** 0.75 cm

**Pages
258–261**

Triangles *JFK* and *LBP* are similar.

7. What is the height of the tree?

F
2.1 m
J ↑ K
3.2 m

B
L   12.8 m   P

Pages 244–247

6 to 9 or 6:9

$\downarrow$

$\dfrac{6}{9} = \dfrac{2}{3}$

Write the ratio as a fraction in lowest terms.

1. 5 blue marbles to 20 red marbles

2. 8 oranges for $1.20

3. 7 out of 35 apples were rotten

4. 15 to 35   **5.** 6 m:27 m   **6.** 3.2:9.6

Pages 248–253

$\dfrac{2}{5} = \dfrac{6}{n}$

$2 \times n = 5 \times 6$

$n = 30 \div 2$

$n = 15$

Solve the proportion.

1. $\dfrac{2}{3} = \dfrac{a}{21}$ **2.** $\dfrac{8}{m} = \dfrac{10}{5}$ **3.** $\dfrac{n}{12} = \dfrac{27}{36}$

4. $\dfrac{5}{11} = \dfrac{15}{x}$ **5.** $\dfrac{6}{5} = \dfrac{c}{120}$ **6.** $\dfrac{8}{4} = \dfrac{6}{y}$

7. $\dfrac{w}{2.1} = \dfrac{4}{3}$ **8.** $\dfrac{6}{d} = \dfrac{4.8}{8}$ **9.** $\dfrac{1.2}{8.4} = \dfrac{e}{0.7}$

Pages 254–261

1 cm:50 km

8 cm $\diamondsuit$ 400 km

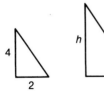

$\dfrac{2}{3} = \dfrac{4}{h}$; $h = 6$

The scale on a map is 1 cm:150 km. In kilometers, what distance does each measurement on the map represent?

1. 3 cm   **2.** 5 cm   **3.** 10 cm   **4.** 4 cm

The two triangles are similar.

5. Find h.

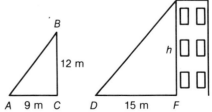

Pages 262–263

1. Understand
2. Plan
3. Work
4. Answer

1. Yesterday, 8 out of every 20 students who went to the school library checked out a book. If 90 students went to the library, how many checked out books?

UNIT 10 Extra Practice

For use after Checkpoint A

Pages 278–279

Write as a percent.

1. $18 out of $100   **2.** $\frac{45}{100}$ **3.** 16 hundredths

Pages 280–281

Write as a percent.   Write as a decimal.

4. 0.72   **5.** 0.48   **6.** 0.325   **7.** 21%   **8.** 86%   **9.** 16.2%

Pages 282–283

Write as a fraction in lowest terms.

10. 35%   **11.** 90%   **12.** 28%   **13.** 16.5%

Pages 284–285

Write as a percent.

14. $\frac{11}{20}$ **15.** $\frac{4}{5}$ **16.** $\frac{23}{40}$ **17.** $\frac{1}{6}$

For use after Checkpoint B

Pages 286–287

Solve.

1. 30% of 90 is m **2.** 12% of 150 is a **3.** 6% of 55 is n

Pages 288–289

Solve.

4. What percent of 80 is 32?   **5.** What percent of 60 is 21?

6. 18 is what percent of 75?   **7.** What percent of 124 is 93?

Pages 290–291

Solve.

8. 75% of v is $42.   **9.** 8% of c is 9.6   **10.** 63% of w is 126

Pages 292–293

Solve.

11. What is 65% of 70?   **12.** 44% of what number is 22?

13. What percent of 140 is 7?   **14.** What percent of 110 is 99?

15. 32% of what number is 24?   **16.** What number is 28% of 35?

Pages 278–285

$0.62 = \frac{62}{100} = 62\%$

$\frac{3}{4} = \frac{75}{100} = 75\%$

Write as a decimal.

1. 8% **2.** 46% **3.** 95% **4.** 6.3%

Write as a fraction in lowest terms.

5. 90% **6.** 18% **7.** 52% **8.** 17.5%

Write as a percent.

9. $\frac{19}{100}$ **10.** $\frac{19}{20}$ **11.** $\frac{3}{4}$ **12.** $\frac{5}{8}$

13. 0.09 **14.** 0.88 **15.** 0.7 **16.** 0.48

Pages 286–293

30% of what number is 24?

$0.30 \times n = 24$

$n = \frac{24}{0.30}$

$n = 80$

Solve.

1. What is 62% of 50? **2.** 90 is what percent of 150?

3. What percent of 52 is 39? **4.** 72% of what number is 61.2?

5. What is 17% of 300? **6.** What percent of 40 is 14?

7. 28% of what number is 21? **8.** 95% of what number is 76?

Pages 294–295

1. Understand
2. Plan
3. Work
4. Answer

In a recent year, there were 762 commercial television stations in the U.S. There were about $\frac{1}{3}$ as many educational stations as there were commercial stations. Solve.

1. About how many educational stations were there?

2. How many stations were there altogether?

3. The commercial stations were about what percent of all the television stations?

4. The educational stations were what percent of the commercial stations?

UNIT 11 Extra Practice

For use after Checkpoint A

Pages 302–303

Solve.

1. What percent of 45 is 18?

2. 35% of what number is 70?

Pages 304–309

Solve. Round to the nearest cent.

3. marked price: $19.95
sales tax rate: 5%
What is the total cost?

4. principal: $6000
rate: 12%
time: $\frac{1}{2}$ year
How much is the interest?

5. original price: $17.95
discount rate: 40%
How much is the sale price?

6. original price: $299
discount rate: 25%
How much is the sale price?

For use after Checkpoint B

Pages 310–311

Use the circle graph to answer the question.

1. How many 10-speed bikes are there?

2. How many 3-speed bikes are there?

3. What percent of the bikes are 5-speed?

4. How many bikes are not 1-speed?

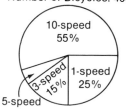

Number of Bicycles: 400

10-speed 55%

1-speed 25%

3-speed 15%

5-speed

Pages 312–313

Total income is $17,500. How much is budgeted for each expense?

5. rent: 32%

6. food: 24%

7. medical: 4.5%

Pages 314–317

Solve.

8. decrease: 28%
original number: 75
What is the new number?

9. original number: 220
new number: 407
What is the percent of increase?

10. total sales: $185
commission rate: 15%
How much is the commission?

11. total sales: $561.50
commission rate: 2%
How much is the commission?

Extra Practice UNIT 11

Pages 302–309

principal: $500
rate: 12%
time: 1 year
$i = p \times r \times t$
$i = 500 \times 0.12 \times 1$

Solve.

1. marked price: $65
   sales tax rate: 6%
   What is the total price?

2. original price: $34.50
   discount rate: 30%
   What is the sale price?

3. principal, $1750; rate, 15%; time, 6 months
   How much is the interest?

Pages 310–313

total budget: $650
rent: 34%
34% of $650
$0.34 \times 650 = 221$
rent: $221

The Ky family has a monthly
income of $2200. How much is
budgeted for each expense?

1. housing   2. food

3. transportation   4. medical

5. entertainment   6. other

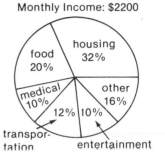

Monthly Income: $2200

food 20%
housing 32%
medical 10%
other 16%
12% 10%
transportation
entertainment

Pages 314–317

original: 60
new: 75
change: $75 - 60 = 15$
% increase:

$\frac{15}{60} = \frac{1}{4} = 25\%$

Solve.

1. original number: 150
   new number: 177
   What is the percent of
   increase?

2. original number: 45
   new number: 36
   What is the percent of
   decrease?

3. total sales, $785.50; commission rate, 8%
   How much is the commission?

Pages 318–319

1. Understand
2. Plan
3. Work
4. Answer

A serving of macaroni and cheese contains 10% of the U.S. RDA
of protein and 20% of the U.S. RDA of thiamine. Solve.

1. A serving contains 6 g of protein. How many grams of
   protein is the U.S. RDA?

2. The U.S. RDA of thiamine is 1.4 mg. How many milligrams
   of thiamine are in one serving?

UNIT 12 Extra Practice

For use after Checkpoint A

**Pages
326–327**

What is the probability?

1. a certain event

2. an impossible event

**Pages
328–329**

You spin the spinner. Complete.

3. $P(4) =$ ▓

4. $P(3) =$ ▓

5. $P(2) =$ ▓

6. $P(5) =$ ▓

**Pages
330–331**

You spin the spinner above, then toss a coin.

7. How many outcomes are there?

8. How many outcomes include a 3?

**Pages
332–333**

You spin the spinner above twice. What is the probability?

9. $P(1, 1)$

10. $P(3, 3)$

11. $P(4, 5)$

12. $P(1, 4)$

**Pages
334–335**

Find the probability.

13. spark plugs tested on Monday, 30; number defective, 6
What is the probability that a spark plug is not defective on Monday?

For use after Checkpoint B

**Pages
336–339**

Find the range, the mean, the median, and the mode.

1. 75, 71, 75, 69, 79, 81

2. 261, 250, 250, 278, 250, 301, 384

**Pages
340–341**

Is the mode, the range, or the median most accurate in describing the data?

3. 40, 42, 76, 40, 40

4. 68, 70, 95, 72, 70

**Pages
342–347**

Use the line graph to find the patient's temperature at the given time.

5. 5:00 A.M.

6. 1:00 P.M.

7. 11:00 A.M.

8. 2:00 P.M.

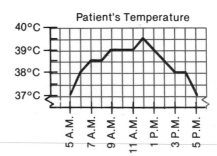

Pages 326–335

$P(3) = \dfrac{2}{8}$

$= \dfrac{1}{4}$

You spin the spinner shown. Write the probability.

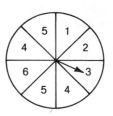

1. $P(3)$ **2.** $P(4)$ **3.** $P(5)$

You spin the spinner above and toss a coin.

4. How many outcomes are there?

5. How many outcomes include an H and a 5?

You spin the spinner above twice. What is the probability?

6. (3, 3)   **7.** (6, 1)   **8.** (2, 6)   **9.** (4, 4)

Pages 336–341

Data: 170, 170, 200,
      200, 206, 320
mean = 211
median = 200
modes = 170 and 200
range = 150

Find the range, the mean, the median, and the mode.

1. 32, 32, 45, 50, 120   **2.** 80, 85, 85, 85, 90

Does the median or the mean describe the data better?

3. 85, 84, 83, 45, 87, 82, 81

Pages 342–347

Number of
customers on
Friday: 400

Use the bar graph to find the number of customers for the day.

1. Monday   **2.** Tuesday

3. Thursday   **4.** Wednesday

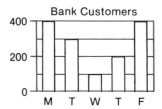

Pages 348–349

1. Understand
2. Plan
3. Work
4. Answer

1. The Lincoln Bird Harbor wants to determine the number of birds nesting in the park. They capture and tag 400 birds, which are then released. One week later they capture 25 birds and find that 5 of them are tagged. About how many birds nest in the park?

UNIT 13 Extra Practice

For use after Checkpoint A

Pages 356–357

Quadrilateral *MACK* ≅ quadrilateral *BITE*.
Write the congruent angle or side.

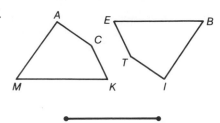

1. ∠ *K*   2. ∠ *M*   3. ∠ *I*

4. ∠ *T*   5. $\overline{MA}$ 6. $\overline{TE}$

Pages 358–359

Do the construction.

R   M

7. Construct a circle whose radius is congruent to $\overline{RM}$.

8. Construct a line segment twice as long as $\overline{RM}$.

Pages 360–363

Use a protractor to draw the angle. Then do the construction.

9. ∠ *RST*: 85°
Construct an angle congruent to ∠ *RST*.

10. ∠ *ZEN*: 120°
Construct the bisector of ∠ *ZEN*.

Pages 364–365

Does the figure have line symmetry, point symmetry or both?

11.

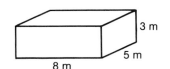

12.

For use after Checkpoint B

Pages 366–367

True or False? Write *T* or *F*.

1. A cube has 8 vertexes.

2. A cylinder has two circular bases.

Pages 368–371

What is the surface area? Use 3.14 for π.

3.

3 m

5 m

8 m

4.

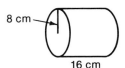

8 cm

16 cm

Pages 372–375

What is the volume? Use 3.14 for π.

5. rectangular prism
base: 21 cm by 3 cm
height: 3 cm

6. cylinder
radius: 5 mm
height: 4 mm

Pages 356–357

Congruent polygons: corresponding sides and angles are congruent.

Pentagon $LMNOP \cong$ pentagon $QRSTV$. Write the congruent side or angle.

1. $\angle L$ **2.** $\angle N$ **3.** $\angle V$

4. $\overline{LP}$ **5.** $\overline{QR}$ **6.** $\overline{ST}$

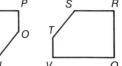

Pages 358–365

$\overrightarrow{BD}$ bisects $\angle ABC$ if $\angle ABD \cong \angle DBC$.

Draw an acute angle. Label it $\angle ABC$. Do the construction.

1. Construct an angle that is congruent to $\angle ABC$.

2. Construct the bisector of $\angle ABC$.

3. Construct an angle that is supplementary to $\angle ABC$.

Pages 366–371

Surface area = Sum of the areas of all the surfaces

What is the surface area? Use 3.14 for π.

1. rectangular prism
base: 10 cm by 12 cm
height: 13 cm

2. cylinder
radius: 5 cm
height: 25 cm

3. cylinder
radius: 5 m
height: 8 m

Pages 372–375

Volume of prism or cylinder = Area of Base × height

What is the volume? Use 3.14 for π.

1.
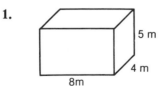

2.
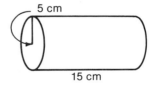

Pages 376–377

1. Understand
2. Plan
3. Work
4. Answer

Use a diagram to solve the problem.

1. Judy wants to replace the tiles on her kitchen floor. The floor is 480 cm by 600 cm, and the tiles Judy plans to use are 24 cm by 30 cm. How many tiles will she need?

445

UNIT 14 Extra Practice

For use after Checkpoint A

Pages 384–385

Write the opposite of the integer.

1. 14   **2.** 118   **3.** $^-25$ **4.** $^-30$ **5.** 9

Pages 386–387

Complete. Write < or >.

6. 5 ▨ $^-8$ **7.** 20 ▨ $^-21$ **8.** $^-14$ ▨ 8   **9.** $^-36$ ▨ 36

Pages 388–393

Add or subtract.

10. $^-9 + 13$ **11.** $^-16 + ^-17$ **12.** $19 + ^-26$ **13.** $^-20 + ^-11$

14. $7 - 30$ **15.** $8 - ^-15$ **16.** $^-6 - 14$ **17.** $^-17 - ^-27$

For use after Checkpoint B

Pages 394–397

Multiply or divide.

1. 14×9 **2.** $^-12 \times ^-3$ **3.** $^-13 \times 2$ **4.** $^-1 \times 59$

5. $^-14 \div 2$ **6.** $30 \div ^-3$ **7.** $40 \div 5$ **8.** $^-42 \div ^-6$

Pages 398–399

Solve the equation.

9. $a + 6 = 1$ **10.** $x - 9 = 3$ **11.** $5m = ^-60$ **12.** $\frac{b}{-5} = 9$

Pages 400–401

Write the coordinates of the point.

13. A **14.** B

15. C **16.** D

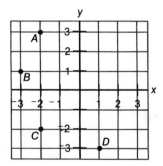

Pages 402–403

Complete the chart. Then draw the graph of the equation.

17. $x + y = 5$

x	0	1	2	3	4	5	6
y	?	?	?	?	?	?	?

Extra Practice UNIT 14

Pages 384–387

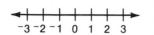

$2 > {}^-3$
$^-1 < 1$

List the integers in order from least to greatest.

1. 3, 0, $^-3$, $^-1$ **2.** $^-2$, 2, 0, $^-3$ **3.** $^-1$, $^-3$, 3, 0

4. 0, 2, 3, $^-2$ **5.** $^-3$, 0, $^-2$, 1   **6.** 4, $^-3$, 2, $^-1$

7. 3, 7, $^-2$, $^-5$ **8.** 4, $^-6$, 2, $^-3$ **9.** 0, 5, $^-1$, $^-6$

Pages 388–393

$^-8 - {}^-4 = {}^-4$
$7 + {}^-8 = {}^-1$

Add or subtract.

1. $^-9 + 7$ **2.** $14 + {}^-10$ **3.** $^-15 + {}^-12$

4. $^-21 - {}^-11$ **5.** $25 - {}^-8$ **6.** $^-7 - 18$

Pages 394–397

$^-6 \times 5 = {}^-30$
$^-48 \div {}^-8 = 6$

Multiply or divide.

7. $^-9 \times {}^-4$ **8.** $^-12 \times 7$ **9.** $20 \times {}^-8$

10. $^-24 \div {}^-8$ **11.** $36 \div 9$ **12.** $49 \div {}^-7$

Pages 398–403

$x - y = 3$

x	0	1	2	3	4	5	6
y	$^-3$	$^-2$	$^-1$	0	1	2	3

Complete the chart. Then draw the graph of the equation.

1. $x + y = 4$

x	0	1	2	3	4	5
y	?	?	?	?	?	?

2. $a - b = 2$

a	$^-2$	$^-1$	0	1	2	3
b	?	?	?	?	?	?

Pages 404–405

1. Understand
2. Plan
3. Work
4. Answer

Copy the chart and organize the facts. Then answer the question.

1. A yellow, a blue, and a green card each has one of the numbers 7, 11, or 16 on the back. The number on the yellow card is even. The number on the green card is a factor of 14. Which number is on each card?

	7	11	16
yellow	?	?	?
blue	?	?	?
green	?	?	?

Something Special

Computer Graphics

Piet Mondrian (1872–1944) was a Dutch painter who used colored lines in his paintings. You can paint similar paintings with a computer.

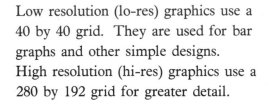

Low resolution (lo-res) graphics use a 40 by 40 grid. They are used for bar graphs and other simple designs. High resolution (hi-res) graphics use a 280 by 192 grid for greater detail.

This is a BASIC program for a lo-res graphic:

It produces this picture.

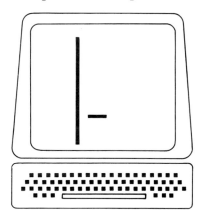

```
10   GR
20   HLIN  18, 24  AT  30
30   VLIN  4, 39  AT  15
40   END
```

JABBERWOCKY? GIBBERISH? Not at all! Let's crack the code.

GR stands for graphics. It tells the computer to get ready to draw.

H stands for horizontal and LIN stands for line. HLIN is code for horizontal line.

V stands for vertical and LIN stands for line. VLIN is code for vertical line.

HLIN 8,24 AT 10 is a horizontal line that starts at box 8 across and ends at box 24 across. It is drawn at line 10 down.

VLIN 4, 39 AT 15 is a vertical line that starts at box 4 down and ends at box 39 down. It is drawn at line 15 across.

With these statements you can create Mondrian-like compositions.

Each computer has a color code similar to the one shown. You can use the programming statements and the color code to create colored lines on the computer.

This program draws a horizontal orange line.

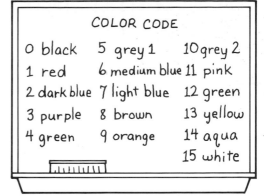

COLOR CODE

0 black   5 grey 1   10 grey 2
1 red   6 medium blue   11 pink
2 dark blue   7 light blue   12 green
3 purple   8 brown   13 yellow
4 green   9 orange   14 aqua
   15 white

```
 5   REM HORIZONTAL ORANGE LINE
10   GR
20   COLOR = 9
30   HLIN 1,39 AT 5
40   END
```

> REM statements let you write reminders into a program. The computer ignores them when the program runs.

Exercises

1. Use grid paper to decode this program. Show what the graphics would look like.

```
 10   GR
 20   COLOR = 1
 30   HLIN 1,18 AT 5
 40   HLIN 1,8 AT 12
 50   HLIN 1,18 AT 25
 60   COLOR = 6
 70   VLIN 5,39 AT 1
 80   VLIN 5,12 AT 8
 90   VLIN 5,25 AT 18
100   END
```

2. Write a program to draw a vertical purple line.

3. Write a program to draw a horizontal pink line that is 6 units long and appears in row 8 down.

4. Write a program to draw perpendicular aqua lines.

5. Write a program to draw a white square.

FOR-NEXT Statements

You can use FOR-NEXT statements to create diagonal lines. Here's how.

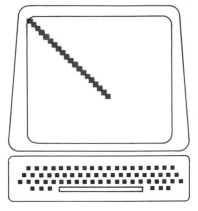

```
10  GR
20  COLOR = 1
30  FOR X = 0 to 19
40  PLOT X,X
50  NEXT X
60  END
```

FOR and NEXT are always written as a pair. They go together like socks and shoes, cup and saucer, and soap and water. FOR tells the computer how many times to do its job, whether it's counting or lighting up boxes. In the above program, the computer is being told that X is a location that will change 20 times.

PLOT is a statement that tells a computer to light up a location or box. PLOT X,X tells the computer that it should light up 0 across at 0 down, 1 across at 1 down, 2 across at 2 down, and so on. The paired address numbers are (0,0), (1,1), (2,2), (3,3), etc.

A computer grid is different from a coordinate plane. On a computer grid, 0,0 is located in the upper left corner. To reach a box, say 10,2, travel across to box 10 and down to box 2.

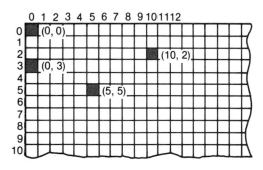

The program shown above is painting boxes with light. Since there are 20 boxes, think of 20 painters to do the job—a painter at each location. Therefore, NEXT X is like saying, "Next, please." When painter number 1 finishes, you are requesting painter number 2 to do work, and so on.

The program below gives a yellow diagonal that begins at the upper right corner and ends at the lower left corner.

```
 5   REM: YELLOW DIAGONAL
10   GR
20   COLOR = 13
30   FOR D = 39 TO 0 STEP -1
40   PLOT D, 39 - D
50   NEXT D
60   END
```

STEP −1 tells the computer to count backwards by 1's.

Exercises

1. In the program above, explain what line 30 does.

2. Explain what line 40 does.

3. Use grid paper or a computer. What will the screen show for the following program?

```
 10   GR
 20   COLOR = 4
 30   FOR X = 10 TO 30
 40   PLOT X, 10
 50   NEXT X
 60   FOR Y = 10 TO 30
 70   PLOT 30, Y
 80   NEXT Y
 90   FOR Z = 10 TO 30
100   PLOT Z, Z
110   NEXT Z
120   END
```

For Exercises 4 and 5 choose a color from the code in the previous lesson.

4. Write a program to draw a colored diagonal from the upper left corner to the lower right corner.

★ **5.** Write a program to draw a pair of intersecting diagonals. Make each diagonal a different color.

Using Frequency Tables

People who collect data must think of ways to organize the data so that it makes sense to others.

These numbers represent the ages of 20 teenagers leaving a movie theater.

17, 13, 15, 15, 14
16, 15, 13, 18, 15
19, 13, 14, 15, 16
15, 18, 17, 15, 17

Here are the same numbers arranged in order from least to greatest.

13, 13, 13, 14, 14
15, 15, 15, 15, 15,
15, 15, 16, 16, 17,
17, 17, 18, 18, 19

You can see that the number 15 appears 7 times. We say 15 has a **frequency** of 7. Study the tables below to see how to make up a **tally count** and a **frequency table** of the numbers.

TALLY COUNT

Age	Tally
13				
14			
15	⊦⊦⊦ ||
16			
17				
18			
19		

FREQUENCY TABLE

Age	Frequency
13	3
14	2
15	7
16	2
17	3
18	2
19	1
	20 = total frequency

Exercises

True or False? Write *T* or *F.*

1. The frequency of 19 is 1.

2. The frequency of 14 is 3.

3. 17 has the lowest frequency.

4. 16 has a frequency of 4.

5. 15 has the highest frequency.

6. The frequency of 13 is 2.

Write the frequency of the letter.

ALABAMA		
	Letter	Frequency
7.	A	
8.	B	
9.	L	
10.	M	

MISSISSIPPI		
	Letter	Frequency
11.	I	
12.	M	
13.	P	
14.	S	

Make up the tally count and the frequency table.

15. 9, 7, 10, 5, 7, 9, 9, 7, 6

16. 12, 14, 10, 14, 14, 12, 9, 14, 10

17. 0, 6, 12, 12, 4, 15, 12, 6, 12

18. 18, 5, 18, 6, 5, 0, 18, 18, 17

Relative Frequency

The frequency table on page 452 shows a total frequency of 20. Do you know why? The ratio of the frequency of each age to the total frequency is called the relative frequency. For example, the relative frequency of 15 is $\frac{7}{20}$.

Find the relative frequency of the number. Use the frequency table on page 452.

19. 17   **20.** 14   **21.** 19   **22.** 13   **23.** 18

24. In the word ALABAMA, find the relative frequency of *A*.

25. What is the relative frequency of *I* in MISSISSIPPI?

26. Is the relative frequency of *M* in ALABAMA greater than the relative frequency of *M* in MISSISSIPPI?

The data at right give the ages of ten   33, 33, 32, 35, 31,
employees in a certain department.   32, 33, 33, 36, 30

27. Make up a frequency table for the data.

28. Find the relative frequency of each number.

29. Which number has the highest relative frequency?

30. How many numbers have a relative frequency of $\frac{1}{10}$?

Similar Figures in the Coordinate Plane

Triangles *ABC* and *DEF* are similar.
We can use this fact to write the
following equal ratios.

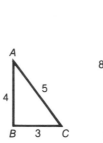

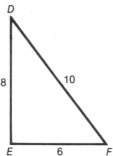

$$\frac{4}{8} = \frac{3}{6} = \frac{5}{10} \implies \frac{1}{2}$$

In the case of $\triangle ABC$ and $\triangle DEF$ the
ratio $\frac{1}{2}$ is referred to as the **scale
factor.** This means that the length of
each side in $\triangle ABC$ is $\frac{1}{2}$ the length of
the corresponding side in $\triangle DEF$.

You can use the scale factor to show
similar figures in the coordinate
plane. Study the diagram shown at
right. It is easy to see these
relationships when you count the
units in each side.

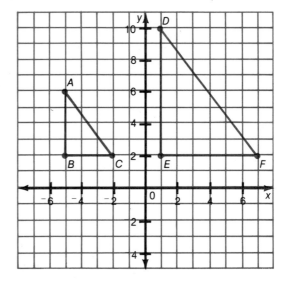

$$AB = \frac{1}{2}(DE)$$
$$BC = \frac{1}{2}(EF)$$

Can you think of a way to verify that
$AC = \frac{1}{2}(DF)$?

Exercises

Choose the correct scale factor. Write *a*, *b*, or *c*.

1. $\frac{2}{8} = \frac{6}{24} = \frac{5}{20}$ **a.** $\frac{1}{4}$ **b.** $\frac{1}{2}$ **c.** $\frac{4}{3}$

2. $\frac{12}{15} = \frac{8}{10} = \frac{16}{20}$ **a.** $\frac{4}{5}$ **b.** $\frac{2}{5}$ **c.** $\frac{5}{4}$

3. $\frac{10}{2} = \frac{20}{4} = \frac{60}{12}$ **a.** $\frac{2}{5}$ **b.** $\frac{1}{5}$ **c.** $\frac{5}{1}$

Use the diagram to find a figure similar to the one named below.

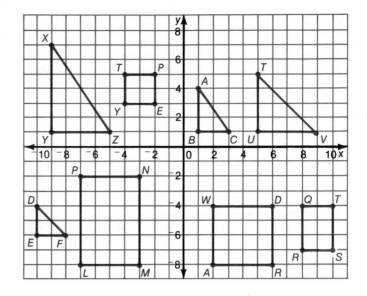

4. △ ABC   **5.** square TYPE

6. rectangle PLMN

7. △ TUV

What is the scale factor of the figures?

8. △ ABC and △ XYZ

9. △ DEF and △ TUV

10. Squares TYPE and WARD

11. Rectangles PLMN and QRST

Use the diagram shown above to find the coordinates.

12. Triangle DEF is to be enlarged to 3 times the size shown. Give the new coordinates of point D and point F. E stays in the same placc.

13. Enlarge square TYPE to 4 times the size shown. Give the new coordinates of points T, P, and E. Y stays in the same place.

14. Enlarge △ XYZ to 1½ times the size shown. Give the new coordinates for points X and Z. Y stays in the same place.

Use graph paper and a scale factor of ¾ to enlarge the figure shown at right. How many units long is the segment in the enlarged figure?

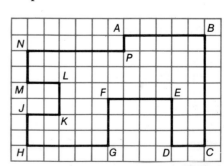

15. $\overline{BC}$ **16.** $\overline{AP}$ **17.** $\overline{LK}$ **18.** $\overline{JH}$

19. $\overline{JK}$ **20.** $\overline{MN}$ **21.** $\overline{DC}$ ★ **22.** $\overline{PE}$

455

Glossary

acute angle (p. 104) An angle measuring greater than 0° and less than 90°.

acute triangle (p. 108) A triangle in which all angles are acute.

angle (p. 100) A set of points on two rays that have the same endpoint.

angle bisector (p. 362) A ray that divides an angle into two congruent parts.

arc (p. 358) A part of a circle.

area (p. 116) The measure of the surface inside a closed figure.

Associative Property (p. 42) The way in which numbers are grouped does not affect the sum or product.

balance (p. 54) Amount of money in checking account.

bar graph (p. 344) A graph that uses bars to compare numbers.

base (p. 78) The 3 in 3^5 is the base.

base of a proportion (p. 298) The basis of comparison.

base of a rectangle (p. 112) Length of rectangle.

bisect (p. 362) To divide into two congruent parts.

budget (p. 312) A plan you make to be sure that your income will be enough to cover your expenses.

center of a circle (p. 114) The point on a plane from which all the points in a circle are the same distance.

central processing unit (p. 96) The part of a computer that actually does the assigned job.

chronological order (p. 17) Order in which events occur; the earliest event is first.

circle (p. 114) The set of all the points in a plane that are the same distance from a particular point in the plane.

circle graph (p. 310) A circle graph shows how a total amount has been divided into parts according to percents.

circumference (p. 114) The perimeter of a circle.

commission (p. 316) The amount of money you earn for selling a product or providing a service (in addition to salary).

common denominator (p. 152) Any common multiple of the denominators.

common factor (p. 142) A number which is a factor of two or more numbers.

common multiple (p. 138) A number that is a multiple of two or more numbers.

Commutative Property (p. 42) The order in which the numbers are added or multiplied does not affect the sum or product.

compass (p. 358) A tool used to construct circles or parts of circles.

complementary angles (p. 104) Two angles the sum of whose measures is 90°.

composite number (p. 144) Any number with more than two factors.

cone (p. 366) A solid with one circular base and one vertex.

congruent angles (p. 103) Angles with the same measure.

congruent figures (p. 356) Figures that have the same size and shape.

congruent line segments (p. 106) Line segments that have the same length.

coordinate plane (p. 400) A number grid on a plane with an x-axis and y-axis.

coordinates (p. 234) The two numbers in an ordered pair.

corresponding angles (p. 258) If $\triangle ABC$ is congruent to or similar to $\triangle DEF$ then $\angle A$ and $\angle D$, $\angle B$ and $\angle E$, $\angle C$ and $\angle F$ are corresponding angles.

corresponding sides (p. 258) If $\triangle ABC$ is congruent to or similar to $\triangle DEF$, then $\overline{AB}$ and $\overline{DE}$, $\overline{BC}$ and $\overline{EF}$, $\overline{AC}$ and $\overline{DF}$ are corresponding sides.

cross products (p. 149) A method used to check if two fractions are equal.

cross section (p. 367) The figure formed when a solid is sliced by a plane.

cubic centimeter (p. 28) The amount of space contained in a cube with all edges 1 cm long.

cubic units (p. 372) The units used to measure volume.

cylinder (p. 366) A solid with two parallel congruent circular bases.

data (p. 336) Number facts.

degree (p. 102) The unit of measure used to measure angles.

denominator (p. 146) The bottom number in a fraction.

deposit (p. 414) Money put into a savings account.

diagonal (p. 107) A line segment that joins two vertexes of a polygon and is not a side of the polygon.

diameter (p. 114) A line segment that joins two points on the circle and that contains the center.

discount (p. 308) A decrease in the price of an item.

discount rate (p. 308) A percent of the original price.

Distributive Property (p. 70) To multiply a sum of numbers, add first and then multiply, or multiply and then add.

divisible (p. 140) One number is divisible by another number when the division of the two numbers gives a quotient and a zero remainder.

edge (p. 366) The intersection of two faces of a solid.

equation (p. 40) A number sentence to show two numbers or quantities are equal.

equiangular (p. 111) Equal angles.

equilateral (p. 111) Equal sides.

equilateral triangle (p. 108) A triangle with three congruent sides and three congruent angles.

equivalent fractions (p. 148) Fractions that name the same number.

evaluate (p. 218) To evaluate an expression for a given number, replace the variable in the expression with the number and then do the indicated arithmetic.

even numbers (p. 140) Numbers that are divisible by 2.

expanded form (p. 10) A method of writing a number in powers of 10.

exponent (p. 78) The 4 in 10^4 is an exponent. It shows that 10 is a factor 4 times. $10^4 = 10 \times 10 \times 10 \times 10$

faces (p. 366) The flat surfaces that form a solid.

factor (p. 142) When one number is divisible by a second, the second number is called a factor of the first.

formula (p. 112) A short way of stating a rule.

fractions (p. 146) A number in the form $\frac{a}{b}$ where a and b are integers, b is not zero, and a is less than b.

function (p. 240) When the value of y depends on the value of x, we say that y is a function of x.

graph (p. 402) A line that connects the points on a coordinate plane.

greatest common factor (GCF) (p. 142) The greatest of the common factors of two numbers.

gross pay (p. 417) The total amount of money earned by a worker.

height of a rectangle (p. 112) Width of a rectangle.

hypotenuse (p. 352) The side opposite the right angle in a right triangle.

identity property (p. 70) The product of 1 and any number is that number.

input (p. 96) Information given to a computer by using a keyboard, cassette tape, etc.

integers (p. 384) The numbers 1, 2, 3, . . . , -1, -2, -3, . . . and 0.

interest (p. 306) The money that the bank pays you for use of your money.
Interest = principal × rate × time.

interest rate (p. 306) A percent used to calculate the interest, usually for a year.

intersecting lines (p. 100) Two lines that cross each other in a plane.

inverse operations (p. 222) One operation that "undoes" another.

irrational number (p. 408) Any number that cannot be written as the quotient of two integers, $\frac{a}{b}$, where b is not zero.

isosceles triangle (p. 108) A triangle with two congruent sides and two congruent angles.

leap year (p. 141) A year whose number is divisible by 4.

least common denominator (p. 152) The LCM of the denominators.

least common multiple (p. 138) The least of the common multiples of two numbers.

line (p. 100) A set of points that extends without end in two opposite directions.

line graph (p. 346) A graph used to show change over a period of time.

line of symmetry (p. 364) A line through a figure so that if the figure were folded on the line, one side would fit exactly on the other.

line segment (p. 100) A part of a line with two endpoints.

lowest terms (p. 150) A fraction is in lowest terms if the GCF of the numerator and denominator is 1.

mathematical expression (p. 216) Numbers, variables, and operation symbols are combined to form a mathematical expression.

mean (p. 336) The sum of the data items divided by the number of data items.

median (p. 338) When the data are written in order, the middle number is called the median.

memory (p. 96) The ability to store data and instructions in a computer.

midpoint (p. 362) The midpoint of a line segment divides it into two congruent parts.

mixed number (p. 154) A number that has a whole number part and a fractional part.

mode (p. 338) A number in a set of data that appears more often than other numbers.

multiples (p. 138) The product of a number and 1, 2, 3, 4, ...

negative numbers (p. 384) Numbers less than 0.

net pay (p. 417) The amount of earnings after all deductions, or withholdings, have been made.

numerator (p. 146) The top number in a fraction.

obtuse angle (p. 104) An angle that has a measure greater than 90° and less than 180°.

obtuse triangle (p. 108) A triangle with one obtuse angle.

odd numbers (p. 140) Numbers that are not divisible by 2.

opposites (p. 384) Two numbers that are the same distance from 0 on the number line.

ordered pairs (p. 232) A pair of numbers, like (3, 2), in which the order is important.

origin (p. 400) The point where the x-axis and the y-axis intersect.

outcome (p. 328) The result of a probability experiment.

output (p. 96) Information given by a computer on a TV screen, a printer, or a plotter.

parallel lines (p. 100) Two lines in a plane that do not intersect.

parallelogram (p. 110) A quadrilateral whose opposite sides are parallel.

percent (p. 278) The ratio of a number to 100. The symbol % means per hundred.

percentage (p. 298) The number compared to the base in proportions.

percent of decrease (p. 314) Amount of change of a quantity.

percent of increase (p. 314) Amount of change of a quantity.

perimeter (p. 112) The distance around a polygon.

perpendicular (p. 104) Two lines, line segments, or rays that form a right angle.

perpendicular bisector (p. 363) The bisector of a line segment that is also perpendicular to the line segment.

pictograph (p. 342) A graph that uses picture symbols to represent numbers.

plane (p. 100) A set of points on a flat surface that extends without end.

point (p. 100) An exact location.

point of symmetry (p. 364) A point A inside a figure so that all line segments passing through A with endpoints on the figure have A as their midpoint.

polygon (p. 106) A figure formed by joining three or more line segments at their endpoints.

positive numbers (p. 384) Numbers greater than 0.

prime factorization (p. 144) The product of prime numbers that name a given number, such as $2 \times 3 \times 5$ to name 30.

prime number (p. 144) A number having exactly two factors, itself and 1.

principal (p. 306) The money you deposit in the bank.

prism (p. 366) A solid with two congruent parallel bases. The bases can be any polygons.

probability (p. 326) A number that describes the chance that an event will happen.

program (p. 188) A set of directions given to a computer.

proportion (p. 248) An equation that states that two ratios are equal.

pyramid (p. 366) A solid with only one base. The base can be any polygon.

Pythagorean theorem (p. 352) If a triangle is a right triangle, the square of the length of the hypotenuse is equal to the sum of the squares of the other two sides.

radius (p. 114) The line segment that joins the center of a circle and a point on the circle.

range (p. 336) The difference between the largest number and the smallest number in a list of data.

rate (pp. 246, 298) A ratio that compares quantities of two different kinds. A rate may be expressed as a ratio, a decimal, or a percent.

rate of exchange (p. 273) The worth of foreign money in United States money.

ratio (p. 244) The quotient of two numbers when the first number is divided by the second.

rational number (p. 408) Any number that can be written as the quotient of two integers, $\frac{a}{b}$, where b is not zero.

ray (p. 100) A part of a line with one endpoint.

reciprocals (p. 200) Two numbers whose product is 1.

rectangle (p. 110) A parallelogram with four right angles.

regular polygon (p. 106) A polygon in which all sides are congruent and all angles are congruent.

relatively prime numbers (p. 164) Two numbers whose GCF is 1.

repeating decimal (p. 156) A decimal in which the division process never ends, and gives a quotient in which one or more of the digits repeat.

rhombus (p. 110) A parallelogram with four congruent sides.

right angle (p. 104) An angle measuring 90°.

right triangle (p. 108) A triangle with one right angle.

rounding (p. 20) An approximation of a quantity by dropping digits after a given place.

sale price (p. 308) The original price of an object minus the discount.

sales tax rate (p. 304) A percent amount that is added to the price of every $1 purchase.

scale (p. 254) The ratio of the size in a scale drawing to the size of the actual object.

scale drawing (p. 254) A sketch of an object with all distances in proportion to corresponding actual distances.

scalene triangle (p. 108) A triangle with no congruent sides or congruent angles.

scientific notation (p. 212) A way of naming numbers in which a given number is expressed as a product of another number between 1 and 10 and a power of 10. For example $43,000 = 4.3 \times 10^4$.

side of the equation (p. 220) Each mathematical expression on both sides of the equals sign in an equation.

sides (p. 100) The rays of an angle or the segments of a polygon.

similar triangles (p. 258) Triangles that have the same shape but not always the same size.

solution (p. 40) The number that replaces a variable to form a true equation.

sphere (p. 366) A solid, the points of which are the same distance from a point called the center.

square (p. 110) A rectangle with four congruent sides.

square root (p. 322) A number which, when multiplied by itself, equals another number. For example, $2 \times 2 = 4$. The square root of 4 is 2.

standard form (p. 10) The standard form of $700 + 60 + 3$ is 763.

straight angle (p. 360) An angle whose measure is $180°$.

straightedge (p. 358) A tool used to draw straight line segments.

substitution (p. 220) To replace the variable with trial numbers.

supplementary angles (p. 104) Two angles whose measures sum to $180°$.

surface area (p. 368) The sum of the areas of the faces of a solid.

symmetry (p. 364) A property that a figure has that makes one half of the figure identical to the other half.

terminating decimal (p. 156) A decimal in which the division process ends because a final remainder of zero is reached.

terms of a proportion (p. 252) The numbers in a proportion.

time (p. 306) The number of years that you leave your money in the bank.

trapezoid (p. 110) A quadrilateral with only one pair of parallel sides.

twin primes (p. 145) Pairs of prime numbers that differ by 2.

unit price (p. 270) The cost per unit of a product.

variable (p. 40) A letter used to stand for a number.

vertex (p. 100) The common endpoint of two rays or two segments. (p. 366) The intersection of three or more edges of a solid.

vertical angles (p. 101) Opposite angles formed by two intersecting lines.

volume (p. 372) The amount of space that a solid contains.

withdrawal (p. 414) Money taken from an account.

x-axis (p. 400) The horizontal number line on a coordinate plane.

y-axis (p. 400) The vertical number line on a coordinate plane.

Zero Property of Addition (p. 42) The sum of zero and any other number is that number.

Zero Property of Multiplication (p. 70) The product of any number and zero is zero.

Index

Credits

Cover design and art direction by Kirchoff/Wohlberg, Inc.
Photograph by Larry Voigt.

Art direction and production by Ligature Publishing Services, Inc.

Illustration

ANCO/BOSTON (Technical Art):   448-450, 452 (left), 454, 455

Leon Bishop   19, 220, 238, 327, 331, 400

Claudia Cappelle   36, 66, 116, 117, 196, 300, 360, 392, 411

Barbara Corey   68

Sharon Elzaurdia   38, 336, 337, 373, 380, 399

Larry Fredericks   32, 33, 56, 62, 115, 179, 218, 219, 224, 298, 342, 354, 391

Judith Friedman   382, 384

Arthur Grebetz   254, 295

Kaye Pomaranc   159

Francesca Rogier   149, 185

George Suyeoka   17, 18, 22, 35, 44, 75, 87, 113, 121-123, 147, 153, 160, 162, 222, 223, 226, 232, 290, 332, 349

Marjorie Waldschmidt   170, 242

Photography

Courtesy American Optical: 67

James L. Ballard and Associates, Inc.:
Applying Your Skills sections, 11, 15, 18, 20, 24, 25, 28, 42, 46, 50, 52, 54, 60, 73, 76, 82, 84, 89, 90, 94, 100, 108, 114, 138, 140, 141, 143, 144, 146, 147-149, 151, 152, 154, 155, 168, 169, 172, 173, 176, 177, 180, 181, 188, 192-194, 197, 204, 206, 216, 217, 221, 228-230, 232, 236, 237, 240, 246, 247, 250, 251, 262, 267, 281, 283, 288, 316, 326, 328, 329, 369, 374, 375, 385, 389

Lee Balterman   39, 243, 310

The Bettman Archive Inc.:   45, 71

BLACK STAR: Stephen Shanes   92-93

Jonathon Blair   178

Carolina Biological Supply Company: 43

CONTACT STOCK IMAGES:
Chuck Fishman 278;   Frank Founier 154

BRUCE COLEMAN INC.:   Keith Gunnar 395 (top);   Joy Spurr 383;   Jonathon T. Wright 395 (bottom)

Richard Estes 277

THE IMAGE BANK: 74;   T.I. Baker 23;   Ira Block 209;   Gérard Champlong 98b;   Melchoir Di Giacomo 81, 92 (left), 343;   M. Kimak 98d;   Whitney Lane 137;   Richard and Mary Magruder 150, 341;   Peter Miller 27;   Toby Molenaar 167;   Marc Romanelli 98c;   Ted Strasbinsky 99;   Alvis Upitis 26   Lou Jones 139, 198, 308, 348;

NASA: 23, 212

SPORTS ILLUSTRATED:
Walter Iooss, Jr. 325

STOCK BOSTON, INC.:   Eric Anderson 48;   Stuart Cohen 273;   Owen Franken 98e;   Bill Gillette 397;   Edith Haun 150;   Ira Kirschenbaum 92 (right);   Peter Menzel 344;   Peter Southwick 315;   Frank Wing 229;   Cary Wolinsky 244, 292

TAURUS PHOTOS: L. Rhodes 191

Transword Feature Syn.:   93

Whitney Lane 137

WOODFIN CAMP and ASSOCIATES:
Jonathon Blair 178;   John Blaustein 324;   Dick Durrance 77;   Robert French 215;   Tony Howarth 9;   William Hubbell 188;   Marvin Newman 301;   Bob Straus 32;   Leo Touchet 355;   Bill Weems 98a

Photo Research courtesy of the
Marilyn Gartman Agency

Selected Answers

UNIT 1 **Pages 10–11** **1.** 2 **3.** 1000 **5.** 1 **7.** 12 **9.** 50 **11.** 9000 **13.** 500
15. 400,000,000 **17.** 609 **19.** 5,004,000 **21.** 127,000,012,000 **23.** 348 **25.** 37,841
27. 700 + 50 + 6 **29.** 3000 + 90 + 2 **31.** 500,000 + 700 + 30 + 1
33. 700,000 + 80,000 + 8000 **35.** 2,000,000 + 300,000 + 80,000 **37.** 1,865,000,000
39. 305,610,000,000

Pages 12–13 **1.** 7 **3.** 2, 6 **5.** 4 **7.** 9 **9.** 6, 5 **11.** 0.4 **13.** 0.5 **15.** 4.2 **17.** 0.04
19. 0.50 **21.** 2.30 **23.** 5.07 **25.** 14.01 **27.** 7 tenths **29.** 3 hundredths **31.** 66 hundredths
33. 8 and 4 tenths **35.** 5 and 26 hundredths **37.** Twenty-four and $\frac{no}{100}$ **39.** Twelve and $\frac{no}{100}$
41. Answers may vary. One possible answer: To make it difficult for another person to change
the amount of the check.

Pages 14–15 **1.** 2 **3.** 217 **5.** 8 **7.** 4 **9.** 3 **11.** 0.263 **13.** 6.503 **15.** 0.019
17. 1.039 **19.** 2 + 0.9 **21.** 1 + 0.08 **23.** 6 + 0.002 + 0.0007
25. 2 + 0.4 + 0.08 + 0.007 + 0.0009 **27.** Yes **29.** No **31.** Yes **33.** 8 **35.** 4 **37.** 112
39. 1.520

Pages 16–17 **1.** >, > **3.** <, <, < **5.** > **7.** < **9.** > **11.** > **13.** > **15.** <
17. < **19.** > **21.** 82; 91; 128 **23.** 108; 41; 39 **25.** 6004; 1234; 311 **27.** 1,360,000;
1,349,724; 1,293,203; 1,267,000; 1,250,629; 870,855; 832,853

Pages 18–19 **1.** < **3.** > **5.** > **7.** > **9.** < **11.** < **13.** < **15.** > **17.** >
19. 0.328, 0.321, 0.319, 0.310, 0.309, 0.304, 0.298, 0.289, 0.275 **21.** Thursday
23. 92,060,000; 86,680,000; 87,670,000; 83,890,000; 84,690,000; 86,770,000; 104,700,000
CHECKPOINT A **1.** 809 **2.** 6750 **3.** 26,708 **4.** 73,000,080 **5.** 0.8 **6.** 0.72 **7.** 3.5 **8.** 9.04
9. 0.875 **10.** 0.000082 **11.** 3.209 **12.** 12.0806 **13.** < **14.** > **15.** > **16.** < **17.** 1.94,
1.68, 1.34, 0.93

Pages 20–21 **1.** 160 **3.** yes; up to 600 **5.** 4; no; down to 8000 **7.** 8; yes; up to 3,000,000
9. 30 **11.** 710 **13.** 4860 **15.** 1300 **17.** 27,750 **19.** 200 **21.** 1000 **23.** 3600 **25.** 12,100
27. 200,900 **29.** 4000 **31.** 8000 **33.** 21,000 **35.** 563,000 **37.** 1,578,000
39. 210,715,000,000 **41.** 162,000,000

Pages 22–23 **1.** 7 **3.** no; down to 4.7 **5.** 7; yes; up to 81.5 **7.** 3; no; down to 0.05 **9.** 4;
no; down to 0.618 **11.** 2 **13.** 8 **15.** 15 **17.** 9 **19.** 42 **21.** 0.4 **23.** 0.6 **25.** 0.3 **27.** 0.7
29. 0.1 **31.** 0.84 **33.** 0.21 **35.** 0.38 **37.** 0.43 **39.** 0.40 **41.** 0.864 **43.** 0.367 **45.** 1.268
47. 1.720 **49.** 8.011 **51.** 57,900,000; 108,100,000; 149,500,000; 227,800,000; 777,800,000;
1,426,100,000; 2,869,100,000; 4,495,600,000; 5,898,900,000

Pages 24–25 **1.** 6 cm **3.** 11 cm **5.** 52 mm **7.** 7.4 cm **9.** 3 cm **11.** 3 cm **13.** 59 mm
15. 24 mm **17.** 1 mm **19.** 6.5 cm **21.** 4.4 cm **23.** 9 **25.** 6; 5

Pages 26–27 **1.** b **3.** c **5.** 200; 500; 1200 **7.** 8; 80; 800 **9.** 80 **11.** 700 **13.** 9
15. 4000 **17.** 900 **19.** 6000 **21.** 300; 30; 3 **23.** 620; 6200; 62,000; 620,000; 6,200,000

Pages 28–29 **1.** c **3.** a **5.** 3000; 8000; 13,000 **7.** 0.003; 0.03; 0.3 **9.** 2 **11.** 17,000
13. 69 **15.** 38 **17.** 350; 3500; 35,000 **19.** 270; 2700; 27,000 **21.** 1,000,000,000 mL

Pages 30–31 **1.** b **3.** c **5.** 6000; 9000; 14,000 **7.** 0.005; 0.05; 0.5 **9.** 17 **11.** 2 **13.** 7 **15.** 3000 **17.** 8 **19.** No CHECKPOINT B **1.** 480 **2.** 7800 **3.** 15,000 **4.** 356,000 **5.** 7 **6.** 0.3 **7.** 0.65 **8.** 4.296 **9.** 4 cm **10.** 5 cm **11.** 50 mm **12.** 51 mm **13.** 300 **14.** 2000 **15.** 4 **16.** 4 **17.** 2000 **18.** 8 **19.** 6000 **20.** 3000

Pages 32–33 **1.** C; Car 14 **3.** R; 165 mph **5.** Which car has the faster lap time? Car 61 **7.** About how many thousand spectators were there? 195,000 **9.** In what order did they finish? Car 45, 1st; Car 16, 2nd; Car 13, 3rd **11.** 25,000 km **13.** Car 54

Page 34 **1.** 17,800 **3.** 5672 **5.** 0.478 **7.** 0.891 **9.** MT, NM, AZ, NV, CO, WY, UT, ID **11.** 300,000; 300,000; 200,000; 400,000; 300,000; 300,000; 200,000; 300,000 **13.** 1; 2; 2; 1; 2; 2; 2; 2 **15.** C **17.** B **19.** H **21.** F **23.** compare, land

Pages 36–37 **1.** a **3.** b **13.** Burlington **15.** Burlington, Juneau, Reno, Atlanta, Seattle, Phoenix, Honolulu **17.** 8° **19.** 7° **21.** 72° **23.** 62° **25.** 67°

Page 38 **1.** C **3.** A **5.** B **7.** 3000 C **9.** 7000 L **11.** 50,000 L **13.** 10,000 L **15.** 6000 L **17.** 90 **19.** 750 **21.** 27 **23.** > **25.** < **27.** <

UNIT 2 **Pages 40–41** **1.** T **3.** F **5.** T **7.** No **9.** Yes **11.** No **13.** Yes **15.** No **17.** No **19.** No **21.** Yes **23.** No **25.** 10 **27.** 8 **29.** 14 **31.** 20 **33.** 6 **35.** Answers may vary. One possible solution is given: $a - 2 = 4$, $10 + 6 = b$, $c + 2 = 16$, $d + 0 = 1$, $2 + 3 = e$, $15 - f = 3$, $g - 0 = 0$, $1 + h = 4$, $6 + 4 = i$

Pages 42–43 **1.** 7; 7 **3.** 14; 14 **5.** 7, 12; 9, 12 **7.** 3 **9.** 1 **11.** 9 **13.** 2 **15.** 6 **17.** 3 **19.** 0, 5 **21.** Zero **23.** Commutative **25.** Commutative **27.** Commutative **29.** human hair **31.** a, b, c **33.** No

Pages 44–45 **1.** 29; 30; 31; 32 **3.** 24; 54; 104; 114 **5.** 92 **7.** 423 **9.** 400 **11.** 1110 **13.** 866 **15.** 11,565 **17.** 11,467 **19.** 18,992 **21.** 59 **23.** 14,295 **25.** 56,938 **27.** 1,343,242 **29.** 1105 **31.** 125 **33.** 1240 **35.** 652 **37.** 2100 **39.** 260 **41.** No **43.** Sum of numbers in each row and in each column is the same; yes

Pages 46–47 **1.** 15; 1.5; 0.15 **3.** 807; 80.7; 8.07 **5.** 5.03 **7.** $9.57 **9.** 20.633 **11.** 20.04 **13.** 6.834 **15.** 11 **17.** $9.14 **19.** 24.31 **21.** $1.68 **23.** 9 **25.** 22 km **27.** $.75; $2.00; $2.80; $1.20; $6.00

Pages 48–49 **1.** 15; 16; 17 **3.** 101; 100; 99 **5.** 31 **7.** 8 **9.** 72 **11.** 430 **13.** 552 **15.** 3520 **17.** 2319 **19.** 8897 **21.** 466 **23.** 7944 **25.** 44,347 **27.** $565 **29.** $585 **31.** 9; 1 **33.** 155; 45 **35.** 15 **37.** 18 **39.** 16 **41.** 60 **43.** 87 **45.** 80 **47.** 100

Pages 50–51 **1.** 3.; 0.3; 0.03 **3.** 558.; 55.8; 5.58 **5.** 0.2 **7.** 0.10 **9.** 0.005 **11.** $1.65 **13.** 0.563 **15.** 0.014 **17.** 0.59 **19.** 17.24 **21.** 1.6 **23.** $.34 **25.** Yes; 72 min CHECKPOINT A **1.** 8 **2.** 6 **3.** 3 **4.** 10 **5.** Zero **6.** Commutative **7.** Associative **8.** 16,757 **9.** 2400 **10.** 10.43 **11.** 0.826 **12.** $40.44 **13.** 19.19 **14.** 312 **15.** 1908 **16.** 2.174 **17.** 3.789 **18.** 12.5 **19.** $1.45

Pages 52–53 **1.** 14 **3.** 208 **5.** 113 **7.** 114 **9.** 435 **11.** 39 **13.** 191 **15.** 198 **17.** 33.5 **19.** 0.5642 **21.** 77.52 **23.** 0.3434 **25.** 128 **27.** 642 **29.** 3638 **31.** $7.61 **33.** $22.32 **35.** $370.59 **37.** 4; 8, 4 **39.** 7, 8; 6 **41.** 6, 1; 8 **43.** 0; 1; 1, 5 **45.** 63 **47.** 595

Pages 54–55 **1.** 99; 83; 107 **3.** 4.6; 2.6; 7.6 **5.** 30 **7.** 2.17 **9.** $1.15 **11.** 908 **13.** 190 **15.** 154 **17.** 258 **19.** $89.37; $83.16; $108.24; $93.29; $83.31

Pages 56–57 **1.** 1 **3.** 1 **5.** 7.3 **7.** 0.4 **9.** 500 **11.** 1,300,000 **13.** 4000; 3900 **15.** $200; $157 **17.** 6; 5.4 **19.** No **21.** Yes **23.** Yes **25.** Yes **27.** No **29.** Answers may vary. Incorrect entries were made as follows. **18.** 839 for 389 **19.** 34 for 3.4 **20.** missing decimals **22.** 886 for 86 **27.** $5.89 for $35.89 **28.** + for −

Pages 58–59 **1.** 2 **3.** 1 **5.** 5 **7.** 3 c 7 oz **9.** 7 ft 1 in. **11.** 11 yd 0 ft **13.** 9 qt 0 pt **15.** 96 lb 6 oz **17.** 2 h 45 min CHECKPOINT B **1.** 341 **2.** 93 **3.** 5.31 **4.** 0.345 **5.** 86 **6.** 2.566 **7.** $22.95 **8.** 12,418 **9.** 6000 **10.** 10,700 **11.** 11.3 **12.** 1250 **13.** 1.08 **14.** 8 ft 6 in. **15.** 1 lb 8 oz

Pages 60–61 **1.** 60A5621 **3.** 50 cm **5.** Yes **7.** $47.24 **9.** $2.98 **11.** 61.9 kg **13.** $13.49, $6.51 or $15.74, $4.26

Page 62 **1.** 9 **3.** 3 **5.** Commutative **7.** 15,780 **9.** $9.72 **11.** 1206 **13.** 7.15 **15.** 6929 **17.** 3.41 **19.** 28 **21.** 9.14 **23.** $8.51 **25.** 1400 **27.** 2.1 **29.** 1 ft 6 in **31.** 8 min 15 s **33.** $5.49

Pages 64–65 **1.** 73 **3.** 1525 **5.** 121, 301 **13.** 78 **15.** 2714 **17.** 10, 422 **19.** 1,150,301 **21.** LXXXVIII **23.** MCDXCII **25.** $\overline{\overline{XX}}$CMXVI **27.** $\overline{MDXXXIV}$

Page 66 **1.** 150,064 **3.** 1274 **5.** $42.27 **7.** 18.9 **9.** 2885 **11.** 2703 **13.** $31.11 **15.** 31.83 **17.** 1.007, 2.58 **19.** 2.58; 3.9 **21.** 2.58; 2.58 **23.** 1.007; 2.58; 4 **25.** 4; 1.007; 1.007

UNIT 3 **Pages 68–69** **1.** T **3.** F **5.** T **7.** Yes **9.** Yes **11.** No **13.** 3 **15.** 8 **17.** 9 **19.** 2 **21.** 7 **23.** 12 **25.** 24 **27.** 8 **29.** 15 **31.** 3 **33.** 0 **35.** 72 **37.** fingers **39.** ENIAC **41.** 6 **43.** 7 **45.** 12

Pages 70–71 **1.** Identity **3.** Distributive **5.** Commutative **7.** 4 **9.** 4 **11.** 2 **13.** 3 **15.** 2 **17.** 4 **19.** 6 **21.** 5 R5 **23.** 6 R4 **25.** 5, 9, 4; 4, 7, 3; 3, 7

Pages 72–73 **1.** 7; 42; 40 **3.** 4; 20; 27 **5.** b **7.** b **9.** c **11.** 2 **13.** 17 **15.** 56 **17.** 1 **19.** 18 **21.** 11 **23.** 0 **25.** 18 **27.** 18 **29.** D **31.** A **33.** C **35.** B **37.** $(12 + 4) \div 2 − 3 − 2$ **39.** $(12 − 4 − 2) \times 3 + 2$

Pages 74–75 **1.** 129; 132; 135 **3.** 5600; 6160; 6720 **5.** 1548 **7.** 24,522 **9.** 1222 **11.** 10,915 **13.** 75,257 **15.** 1,514,016 **17.** 319,662 **19.** 269,262 **21.** 2,993,904 **23.** 2,015,236 **25.** 107,139 **27.** 476,861 **29.** 4476

Pages 76–77 **1.** 14.4; 1.44; 0.144 **3.** 0.32 **5.** 14.56 **7.** 0.215 **9.** 5.13 **11.** 27.72 **13.** $7.38 **15.** 1.968 **17.** 9.05535 **19.** $.84 **21.** 0.00312 **23.** 36.96 **25.** 2.431 **27.** 16.4025 **29.** $69.30 **31.** $83.66 **33.** $62.70

Pages 78–79 **1.** 2; 3; 4 **3.** 3 **5.** 3 **7.** 6^2 **9.** 4^4 **11.** 7^2 **13.** 10^4 **15.** 3^4 **17.** 16 **19.** 1 **21.** 32 **23.** 16 **25.** 100 **27.** 10,000 **29.** 1,000,000 **31.** 3^2 **33.** 10^2 **35.** 100^2 **37.** 4^2 **39.** 6^2 **41.** $(8 \times 10^3) + (3 \times 10^2) + (1 \times 10^1) + 5$ **43.** $(4 \times 10^5) + (6 \times 10^4) + (5 \times 10^3) + (2 \times 10^2) + (9 \times 10^1) + 7$ **45.** $(8 \times 10^4) + (7 \times 10^2) + (7 \times 10^1) + 5$ **47.** $(8 \times 10^7) + (6 \times 10^6)$ **49.** $(1 \times 10^8) + (4 \times 10^7) + (2 \times 10^6)$ **51.** 1×10^9

1. 35 **2.** 9 **3.** 27 **4.** 7 **5.** 3 **6.** 9 **7.** 4 **8.** 5 **9.** 21 **10.** 42 **11.** 34,704 **12.** 13,632 **13.** 39,675 **14.** 41,888 **15.** 1.9 **16.** 24.4776 **17.** 20.824 **18.** 192.9188 **19.** 16 **20.** 1000 **21.** 1 **22.** 144

Pages 80–81 **1.** 2; 21 R2; 217 **3.** 9 R8; 99 R3; 993 R6 **5.** 124 **7.** 128 **9.** 27 R2 **11.** 43 R8 **13.** 116 R5 **15.** 2982 **17.** 898 **19.** 520 R2 **21.** 608 R3 **23.** 507 R7 **25.** 7458 R1 **27.** 9050 R2 **29.** 11,534 R4 **31.** 127 **33.** 112 **35.** 123 **37.** 39 R2 **39.** 48 pompoms

Pages 82–83 **1.** 2 R11; 2 R17; 24 R26 **3.** 1 R27; 10 R270; 109 **5.** 12 R14 **7.** 12 R54 **9.** 55 R18 **11.** 326 R2 **13.** 569 R62 **15.** 1042 R25 **17.** 2 R102 **19.** 13 R277 **21.** 175 R132 **23.** 140 R434 **25.** 29 **27.** 11 R108 **29.** 5 **31.** 49 **33.** 236 **35.** 12,768 meals/week; 663,936 meals

Pages 84–85 **1.** 0.8 **3.** 0.007 **5.** 0.7 **7.** 0.013 **9.** 9; 0.9; 0.09; 0.009 **11.** 13; 1.3; 0.13; 0.013 **13.** 0.12 **15.** 0.316 **17.** 0.888 **19.** 9.06 **21.** 1.05 **23.** 0.6 **25.** 2.3 **27.** 0.021 **29.** 0.23 **31.** 0.007 **33.** 10.66 **35.** 1.97 **37.** 4.671 **39.** 13.333 **41.** 4.283 **43.** 7.804

Pages 86–87 **1.** 30.; 37.0; 3.70 **3.** 8000.; 8300.0; 8314.000 **5.** 4.; 4.58; 45.87 **7.** 74 **9.** 62 **11.** 90.6 **13.** 531 **15.** 354 **17.** 40 **19.** 721.4 **21.** 804,000 **23.** 3100 **25.** 2.84 **27.** 21.63 **29.** 0.06 **31.** 0.862 **33.** 38.4 **35.** 180 **37.** 0.128 **39.** Answers may vary.

Pages 88–89 **1.** 3; 16. **3.** 896; 28 **5.** 140; 4. **7.** 14 **9.** 1064.16 **11.** 3.5 **13.** 2.5 **15.** 1.3 **17.** 20.9 **19.** 1.4 **21.** 30 **23.** 17 **25.** 77.7 **27.** 14 km **29.** 41 call boxes

Pages 90–91 **1.** *b* **3.** *b* **5.** *b* **7.** *b* **9.** 2000 **11.** 5600 **13.** 320 **15.** 30 **17.** 5 **19.** 50 **21.** 200 **23.** 57.9 **25.** 56.115 **27.** 17.6 **1.** 75 R3 **2.** 535 R6 **3.** 604 R1 **4.** 13,468 R5 **5.** 14 R6 **6.** 92 R2 **7.** 24 R273 **8.** 6 R691 **9.** 0.89 **10.** 2.315 **11.** 0.083 **12.** 4.8 **13.** 740 **14.** 58.3 **15.** 7.2 **16.** 0.0834 **17.** 3.95 **18.** 1.58 **19.** 19.8 **20.** 2.25 **21.** 2400 **22.** 150,000 **23.** 200 **24.** 500

Pages 92–93 Answers may vary for Exercises 1, 3, 5, 7, 13, 15, and 17. One possible solution is given. **1.** What is the cost of 4 student's tickets? $12 **3.** How much more does an adult ticket cost? $1.50 **5.** How many adult tickets can be bought with $36? 8 tickets **7.** There were 2657 home fans and 1125 visitors. 1532 more home fans **9.** How much farther did Sven throw the javelin? 1.36 m **11.** How long did it take the winner to run the race? 53 min 10 s **13.** What was the difference between the fastest and slowest time? 6 min 56 s **15.** What was the total cost of admissions for the 2346 fans? $9,970.50 **17.** How much did each player get? $17,328.25

Page 94 **1.** 9 **3.** 7 **5.** 7 **7.** 17 **9.** 10 **11.** 5.6 **13.** 5 **15.** 0.28 **17.** 0.3 **19.** 4 **21.** 0.0018 **23.** 16 **25.** 1000 **27.** 20 **29.** Answers may vary. One possible solution is given. Do they have enough money to buy the bicycle? No

Pages 96–97 **1.** output **3.** input **5.** output **7.** output **9.** output **11.** output **13.** output **15.** output **17.** memory

Page 98 **1.** 43,751 **3.** 58,135 **5.** 24.742 **7.** $6.78 **9.** 8 ft 1 in **11.** 11 h 25 min **13.** 5 yd 2 ft **15.** THE **17.** ARCH

UNIT 4   Pages 100–101 Answers may vary for Exercises 1, 3, 5, and 7. One possible solution is given. **1.** ∠*CDE* **3.** $\overleftrightarrow{HK}$ **5.** $\overleftrightarrow{NR}$, $\overleftrightarrow{SY}$ **7.** $\overline{NA}$, $\overline{AR}$, $\overline{NR}$, $\overline{SB}$, $\overline{BY}$, $\overline{SY}$, $\overline{AB}$ **9.** F **11.** F **13.** F Answers may vary for Exercises 15 and 17. One possible solution is given. **15.** the corner of a window **17.** the lines between floor tiles **19.** ∠3 **21.** ∠5 **23.** There are 6 angles with *Q* as the vertex.

Pages 102–103 1. 40° **3.** 60° **5.** 140° **7.** 180° **9.** 60° **11.** 130° **21.** ∠*DOE* **23.** ∠*AOF*

Pages 104–105 1. Acute **3.** Obtuse **5.** complementary **7.** complementary **9.** supplementary **11.** complementary **13.** 60° **15.** 10° **17.** 75° **19.** 60° **21.** 176° **23.** Yes **25.** No **27.** ∠1 = 145°, ∠2 = 35°, ∠3 = 145°, ∠4 = 35°, ∠5 = 145°, ∠6 = 35°, ∠7 = 145°, ∠8 = 35° **29.** ∠1, ∠3, ∠5, ∠7 **31.** ∠1, ∠2; ∠3, ∠4; ∠5, ∠6; ∠7, ∠8

Pages 106–107 1. Quadrilateral **3.** Octagon **5.** Triangle **7.** Hexagon **9.** sides: 12; angles: 90° **11.** sides: 7; angles: 60° **13.** 3, 0 **15.** Pentagon, 2 **17.** 4 **19.** 97

Pages 108–109 1. right **3.** acute **5.** equilateral **7.** isosceles **9.** 65° **11.** 45° **13.** 23° **15.** 69° **17.** *c, e* **19.** *b, d* **27.** 540° **29.** 1080°

Pages 110–111 1. *b, c, d, e* **3.** *b, c, d, e* **5.** *c, e* **9.** N **11.** A **13.** square or rectangle **15.** square CHECKPOINT A **1.** F **2.** F **3.** T **4.** T **8.** obtuse **9.** acute **10.** right **11.** 7, 120° **12.** 15, 60° **13.** 67° **14.** 9° **15.** 45° **16.** 60° **17.** rhombus **19.** parallelogram

Pages 112–113 1. 14 cm **3.** 7.3 m **5.** 41 mm **7.** 28 cm **9.** 344.2 mm **11.** 11 m **13.** 244 cm **15.** 7.8 m **17.** 68 cm **19.** 9.52 cm **21.** P = 8 × s **23.** Yes; Because (2 × *b*) + (2 × *h*) = 2 × (*b* + *h*); Distributive

Pages 114–115 1. 8 **3.** 30 **5.** 32 **7.** 200 **9.** 600 **11.** diameter **13.** radius **15.** 37.68 cm **17.** 53.38 cm **19.** 157 cm **21.** 94.2 cm **23.** 106.76 m **25.** 4.71 mm **27.** 67.824 cm **29.** 40.82 mm **31.** 3.14 is between 223 ÷ 71 and 22 ÷ 7.

Pages 116–117 1. 15 cm² **3.** 100 cm² **5.** 140 m² **7.** 161 km² **9.** 62.25 m² **11.** 94.43 km² **13.** 144 mm² **15.** 25 km² **17.** 50.41 km² **19.** 0.2704 m² **21.** *b* **23.** *a* **25.** 800 **27.** 5 **29.** 31 **31.** 98 **33.** 8300 **35.** 1,000,000

Pages 118–119 1. 240 cm²; 120 cm² **3.** 360 m²; 180 m² **5.** 120 cm² **7.** 720 mm² **9.** 7500 cm² **11.** 4537.5 mm² **13.** 39 cm² **15.** 18 m² **17.** 153.75 m² **19.** 13.2 m² **21.** 104 square units **23.** 15 square units

Pages 120–121 1. 5 **3.** 314 **5.** 8; 200.96 **7.** 113.04 m² **9.** 1256 mm² **11.** 1256 m² **13.** 52.7834 m² **15.** 1256 cm² **17.** 200.96 cm² **19.** 11,304 cm² **21.** 3.14 m² **23.** 35.325 m² CHECKPOINT B **1.** 48 cm **2.** 158.8 m **3.** 69.08 cm **4.** 62.8 m **5.** 17.898 mm **6.** 20.096 cm **7.** 105 m² **8.** 60 cm² **9.** 289 cm² **10.** 0.16 m² **11.** 136 cm² **12.** 24.01 mm² **13.** 60 cm² **14.** 29 cm² **15.** 9498.5 cm² **16.** 167.3306 m² **17.** 158.2874 cm² **18.** 615.44 mm²

Pages 122–123 1. $A = b \times h$ **3.** $C = \pi \times d$ **5.** $A = b \times h$ **7.** 36 m **9.** 858 m **11.** 25.12 m **13.** 50.24 m² **15.** the square field **17.** 300 m² **19.** 172 m **21.** 50 m **23.** 12.56 m²

Page 124 Answers may vary for Exercises 1 and 3. One possible solution is given. **1.** $\overleftrightarrow{RT}$, $\overleftrightarrow{UW}$ **3.** $\angle RSX$, $\angle VST$; $\angle XST$, $\angle RSV$ **7.** $\angle AOC$ **9.** $\angle BOD$, $\angle BOA$ **11.** T **13.** F **15.** 11 m; 3.76 m² **17.** 6 m; 1.6 m² **19.** 2.4 m; 0.24 m² **21.** 6.2 m, 1.68 m²

Pages 126–127 **1.** 9 **3.** 1 **5.** 12 **7.** 1 **9.** 4 **11.** 10 **13.** 6 **15.** 11 **17.** 12 **19.** 7 **21.** 11 **23.** 7 **25.** T **27.** F **29.** 5 **31.** 3 **33.** 5 **35.** 3 **37.** 1 **39.** 3 **41.** 2 **43.** 4 **45.** F **47.** F **49.** T

Pages 128–129 **1.** *a* **3.** *a* **5.** *c* **7.** *b* **9.** *b* **11.** *a* **13.** *a* **15.** *b* **17.** *b* **19.** *a* **21.** *a* **23.** *a* **25.** *b* **27.** *c* **29.** *b* **31.** *a*

APPLYING YOUR SKILLS **Pages 130–131** **1.** 52 years **3.** 19 years **5.** 8:00–11:00 P.M.; 7:00–10:30 A.M. **7.** $6600 **9.** $3680; $144 **11.** $2210; $510 **Pages 132–133** **1.** $599.00 **3.** $117.25 **5.** $120.65 **7.** $16.00 **9.** $704.40 **11.** $104.30 **15.** $129.90 **17.** $72,000 **19.** $375 **Pages 134–135** **1.** 108 sq ft **3.** 42 ft **5.** 9.62 sq ft **7.** $96.24 **9.** 6 times **11.** 12 sheets **Page 136** **1.** $3.21 **3.** $.26

UNIT 5 **Pages 138–139** **1.** 12, 15, 18 **3.** 80, 100, 120 **5.** 48, 60, 72 **7.** 56, 70, 84 **9.** 400, 500, 600 **11.** 2, 4, 6, 8, 10 **13.** 7, 14, 21, 28, 35 **15.** 10, 20, 30, 40, 50 **17.** 11, 22, 33, 44, 55 **19.** 16, 32, 48, 64, 80 **21.** 40, 80, 120, 160, 200 **23.** 25, 50, 75, 100, 125 **25.** 200, 400, 600, 800, 1000 **27.** 150, 300, 450, 600, 750 **29.** 10 **31.** 35 **33.** 6 **35.** 12 **37.** 24 **39.** 24 **41.** 28 **43.** 63 **45.** 18 **47.** 30 **49.** 20 **51.** 36 **53.** 30 **55.** 30 **57.** 24 flats **59.** Every 60th day

Pages 140–141 **1.** Odd **3.** Odd **5.** Even **7.** Odd **9.** Odd **11.** No **13.** Yes **15.** Yes **17.** No **19.** No **21.** Yes **23.** Yes **25.** No **27.** Yes **29.** No **31.** T **33.** T **35.** Yes **37.** No **39.** Yes **41.** No **43.** No

Pages 142–143 **1.** Yes **3.** Yes **5.** No **7.** Yes **9.** Yes **11.** Yes **13.** 4; 8; 1, 2, 4; 4 **15.** 5 **17.** 12 **19.** 2 **21.** 3 **23.** 1 **25.** 4 **27.** 3 **29.** 5 **31.** 1 **33.** 8 **35.** 4 **37.** 4 **39.** Answers may vary. One possible solution is 6 teams with 6 players on each team. **41.** 6 players

Pages 144–145 **1.** 1, 3, 9 **3.** 1, 5 **5.** 1, 2, 5, 10 **7.** 1, 2, 4, 8, 16 **9.** 1, 2, 4, 7, 14, 28 **11.** 1, 2, 19, 38 **13.** Prime **15.** Composite **17.** Prime **19.** Composite **21.** Composite **23.** Composite **25.** 2; 3, 3; $2 \times 2 \times 3 \times 3$ **27.** 2, 3, 3, 3; $2 \times 3 \times 3 \times 3$ **29.** $2 \times 2 \times 2 \times 3 \times 3$ **31.** 5×11 **33.** $2 \times 2 \times 11$ **35.** $2 \times 3 \times 3 \times 3$ **37.** 5×19 **39.** $2 \times 2 \times 2 \times 5 \times 5$ **41.** 17 **43.** 3, 5, 7 CHECKPOINT A **1.** 18 **2.** 21 **3.** 15 **4.** 30 **5.** 36 **6.** 40 **7.** Yes **8.** No **9.** No **10.** No **11.** Yes **12.** Yes **13.** 7 **14.** 3 **15.** 5 **16.** 8 **17.** 4 **18.** 4 **19.** 2; 2; 2, 3; $2 \times 2 \times 2 \times 3$ **20.** $3 \times 3 \times 3$ **21.** $2 \times 2 \times 5$ **22.** $3 \times 3 \times 5$ **23.** $2 \times 2 \times 2 \times 2 \times 2 \times 2$ **24.** $2 \times 2 \times 5 \times 5$ **25.** $5 \times 5 \times 5$

Pages 146–147 **1.** 3; 4 **3.** $\frac{4}{11}$ **5.** $\frac{3}{11}$ **7.** $\frac{1}{47}$ **9.** $\frac{8}{47}$ **11.** $\frac{2}{47}$ **13.** $\frac{9}{47}$ **15.** $\frac{16}{47}$ **17.** $\frac{8}{24}$ **19.** $\frac{24}{168}$ **21.** $\frac{4}{24}$

Pages 148–149 **1.** 9, 12 **3.** 3, 36 **5.** 1, 3 **7.** 5 **9.** 4, 4 **11.** 4 **13.** 36 **15.** 18 **17.** 3 **19.** 1 **21.** 7 **23.** 24 **25.** 7 **27.** 39 **29.** $\frac{6}{10}$, $\frac{3}{5}$ **31.** $\frac{3}{12}$, $\frac{1}{4}$ **33.** $\frac{3}{8}$, $\frac{18}{48}$ **35.** $\frac{11}{20}$, $\frac{22}{40}$ **37.** $\frac{7}{8}$, $\frac{28}{32}$ **39.** $\frac{13}{26}$, $\frac{1}{2}$ **41.** Yes **43.** No **45.** No

Pages 150–151 **1.** 4 **3.** 2 **5.** 12 **7.** No **9.** No **11.** No **13.** 5 **15.** 1 **17.** $\frac{1}{3}$ **19.** $\frac{3}{5}$ **21.** $\frac{3}{4}$ **23.** $\frac{1}{4}$ **25.** $\frac{3}{7}$ **27.** $\frac{4}{5}$ **29.** $\frac{7}{8}$ **31.** $\frac{5}{9}$ **33.** $\frac{6}{13}$ **35.** $\frac{1}{3}$ **37.** $\frac{2}{3}$ **39.** $\frac{3}{4}$ **41.** $\frac{9}{10}$ **43.** $\frac{1}{19}$

Pages 152–153 **1.** 6 **3.** 12 **5.** 24 **7.** 40 **9.** 24 **11.** $\frac{10}{12}, \frac{11}{12}$ **13.** $\frac{5}{15}, \frac{6}{15}$ **15.** $\frac{5}{20}, \frac{6}{20}$ **17.** $\frac{3}{30}, \frac{8}{30}$ **19.** $\frac{3}{9}, \frac{2}{9}$ **21.** > **23.** < **25.** > **27.** > **29.** < **31.** > **33.** > **35.** > **37.** > **39.** < **41.** > **43.** > **45.** $\frac{1}{4}, \frac{5}{16}, \frac{3}{8}, \frac{7}{16}, \frac{1}{2}, \frac{9}{16}, \frac{5}{8}, \frac{11}{16}, \frac{3}{4}, \frac{13}{16}, \frac{7}{8}, 1$

Pages 154–155 **1.** 8 **3.** 5 **5.** 3 **7.** 1 **9.** 9 **11.** 31 **13.** 1 **15.** 1 **17.** $\frac{16}{9}$ **19.** $\frac{17}{6}$ **21.** $\frac{21}{5}$ **23.** $\frac{51}{8}$ **25.** $\frac{44}{5}$ **27.** $\frac{23}{4}$ **29.** $1\frac{3}{5}$ **31.** 2 **33.** $3\frac{5}{7}$ **35.** $2\frac{8}{9}$ **37.** $4\frac{1}{4}$ **39.** 7 **41.** c **43.** b

Pages 156–157 **1.** 5 **3.** 2, 5 **5.** 1, 6 **7.** 1, 7, 5 **9.** 1, 1, 2, 5 **11.** 0, 7, 5 **13.** 0.4 **15.** 0.75 **17.** 0.375 **19.** 0.18 **21.** 0.225 **23.** 0.64 **25.** 0.02 **27.** 0.025 **29.** 0.0875 **31.** $0.\overline{3}$ **33.** $0.\overline{5}$ **35.** $0.8\overline{3}$ **37.** $0.\overline{45}$ **39.** $0.58\overline{3}$ **41.** $0.3\overline{18}$ **43.** $0.8\overline{2}$ **45.** $0.0\overline{6}$ **47.** $0.\overline{09}$ **49.** 0.875, 0.5, 0.444, 0.833, 0.222

Pages 158–159 **1.** 3 **3.** 10 **5.** 19 **7.** 100 **9.** 373 **11.** 1000 **13.** 100 **15.** 1000 **17.** 3 **19.** 1000 **21.** $\frac{7}{10}$ **23.** $\frac{623}{1000}$ **25.** $\frac{7}{1000}$ **27.** $5\frac{8}{10}$ **29.** $1\frac{19}{100}$ **31.** $4\frac{179}{1000}$ **33.** $\frac{2}{5}$ **35.** $\frac{1}{4}$ **37.** $\frac{1}{200}$ **39.** $\frac{1}{25}$ **41.** $\frac{3}{200}$ **43.** $\frac{1}{8}$ **45.** 10 **47.** 1000; 3 CHECKPOINT B **1.** $\frac{5}{12}$ **2.** $\frac{5}{12}$ **3.** $\frac{2}{12}$ **4.** 36 **5.** 4 **6.** $\frac{2}{3}$ **7.** $\frac{4}{5}$ **8.** $\frac{1}{2}$ **9.** > **10.** < **11.** < **12.** < **13.** $1\frac{1}{7}$ **14.** 3 **15.** $2\frac{1}{3}$ **16.** 0.75 **17.** 0.625 **18.** $0.\overline{8}$ **19.** $\frac{4}{5}$ **20.** $\frac{33}{100}$ **21.** $\frac{1}{8}$

Pages 160–161 **1.** $16.20 **3.** 90¢ **5.** 1 packet of 60 **7.** $290 **9.** $62 **11.** Marlene; $3.50

Page 162 **1.** 12, 2 **3.** 35, 1 **5.** Yes **7.** Yes **9.** $3 \times 5 \times 5$ **11.** $2 \times 2 \times 2 \times 7$ **13.** $\frac{8}{25}$ **15.** $\frac{7}{25}$ **17.** $\frac{16}{24}, \frac{10}{15}$ **19.** $\frac{12}{25}$ **21.** $\frac{55}{9}$ **23.** $1\frac{1}{10}$ **25.** 0.375 **27.** $\frac{27}{100}$ **29.** $6.25

Pages 164–165 **1.** 30 **3.** 30 **5.** 15 **7.** 24 **9.** 49 **11.** 21 **13.** Yes **15.** Yes **17.** No **19.** 252 **21.** 630 **23.** 360 **25.** 756 **27.** 900 **29.** 1260 **31.** 1296; 6; 216; 1296 **33.** 1008; 4; 252; 1008 **35.** T

Page 166 **1.** 108 in. **3.** 192 in. **5.** 108 in. **7.** 25.12 cm **9.** 40.82 m **11.** 25.12 mm **13.** 45.844 m **15.** 213 **17.** 535 **19.** 76.24 **21.** 40.891 **23.** 64.39 **25.** 2.5354

UNIT 6   **Pages 168–169** **1.** 4, 2 **3.** 10, 11 **5.** 6, 1 **7.** 6, 3 **9.** 8, 3 **11.** 10, 4, 2 **13.** $\frac{9}{11}$ **15.** $\frac{4}{7}$ **17.** $\frac{2}{5}$ **19.** $\frac{1}{2}$ **21.** $\frac{5}{11}$ **23.** $1\frac{2}{15}$ **25.** $1\frac{1}{4}$ **27.** $\frac{2}{3}$ **29.** $1\frac{1}{5}$ **31.** $\frac{17}{20}$ **33.** $1\frac{2}{5}$ **35.** $1\frac{2}{5}$ **37.** $1\frac{1}{4}$ in.

Pages 170–171 **1.** 4 **3.** 21 **5.** 14 **7.** 20 **9.** 21 **11.** 2; 1; 3 **13.** 2; 9; 11 **15.** $\frac{5}{8}$ **17.** $\frac{8}{9}$ **19.** $\frac{2}{3}$ **21.** $\frac{4}{9}$ **23.** $\frac{8}{21}$ **25.** $\frac{7}{10}$ **27.** $\frac{7}{8}$ **29.** $\frac{9}{10}$ **31.** $\frac{5}{6}$ **33.** $\frac{7}{8}$ **35.** $\frac{5}{8}$ **37.** $\frac{3}{4}$

Pages 172–173 **1.** 6 **3.** 36 **5.** 18 **7.** 20; 15; 35, 11 **9.** $\frac{7}{10}$ **11.** $\frac{7}{20}$ **13.** $\frac{4}{15}$ **15.** $\frac{13}{14}$ **17.** $\frac{11}{12}$ **19.** $\frac{20}{21}$ **21.** $1\frac{4}{15}$ **23.** $1\frac{1}{12}$ **25.** $1\frac{17}{24}$ **27.** $\frac{11}{12}$ **29.** $1\frac{1}{30}$ **31.** $1\frac{5}{12}$ **33.** $\frac{17}{30}$ acre

Pages 174–175 **1.** 2 **3.** 8 **5.** 15 **7.** 27 **9.** 1 **11.** 4 **13.** 6, 3 **15.** 4, 1 **17.** $7\frac{5}{7}$ **19.** $12\frac{3}{5}$ **21.** $8\frac{4}{5}$ **23.** $7\frac{4}{9}$ **25.** $11\frac{2}{5}$ **27.** $13\frac{1}{4}$ **29.** $11\frac{1}{8}$ **31.** $8\frac{3}{5}$ **33.** 16 **35.** $2\frac{7}{9}$ **37.** Row 1 (bottom): $2\frac{3}{4}$; $4\frac{1}{8}$; $5\frac{1}{2}$; Row 2: $3\frac{5}{8}$; 5; $6\frac{3}{8}$; Row 3: $5\frac{7}{8}$; $8\frac{3}{8}$; 10; Row 4: $6\frac{3}{4}$; $8\frac{1}{8}$; $9\frac{1}{2}$; $10\frac{7}{8}$; $12\frac{1}{4}$; Row 5: 9; $10\frac{3}{8}$; $11\frac{3}{4}$; $13\frac{1}{8}$ CHECKPOINT A **1.** $\frac{5}{7}$ **2.** $\frac{4}{9}$ **3.** $1\frac{1}{4}$ **4.** $\frac{2}{5}$ **5.** $\frac{5}{8}$ **6.** $1\frac{1}{3}$ **7.** $\frac{14}{15}$ **8.** $1\frac{1}{12}$ **9.** $10\frac{3}{5}$ **10.** $16\frac{23}{24}$ **11.** $5\frac{3}{7}$ **12.** $7\frac{1}{3}$

Pages 176–177 **1.** 3; 2; 1 **3.** 14; 9; 5 **5.** 15; 4; 11 **7.** 10; 6; 4; 1 **9.** 21; 5; 16; 8 **11.** $\frac{1}{8}$ **13.** $\frac{1}{6}$ **15.** $\frac{1}{15}$ **17.** $\frac{7}{40}$ **19.** $\frac{7}{36}$ **21.** $\frac{13}{36}$ **23.** $\frac{2}{15}$ **25.** $\frac{1}{6}$ **27.** $\frac{1}{24}$ **29.** $\frac{5}{12}$ c **31.** $1\frac{3}{4}$ lb **33.** Less; $\frac{7}{20}$ c

Pages 178–179 **1.** $1\frac{5}{9}$ **3.** $3\frac{1}{3}$ **5.** $4\frac{2}{7}$ **7.** $10\frac{3}{7}$ **9.** $12\frac{2}{5}$ **11.** $3\frac{3}{4}$ **13.** $4\frac{2}{3}$ **15.** $9\frac{7}{8}$ **17.** $6\frac{1}{4}$
19. $8\frac{2}{5}$ **21.** $5\frac{1}{12}$ **23.** $4\frac{1}{15}$ **25.** $9\frac{1}{35}$ **27.** $2\frac{9}{20}$ **29.** $1\frac{11}{15}$ **31.** $3\frac{3}{4}$ **33.** $7\frac{7}{10}$ **35.** $7\frac{5}{9}$ **37.** $2\frac{1}{2}$
39. $6\frac{3}{10}$ **41.** $11\frac{1}{6}$ ft

Pages 180–181 **1.** 6 **3.** 10 **5.** 9 **7.** 19 **9.** 4 **11.** 7 **13.** 5; 2 **15.** 7; 1 **17.** 8; 7
19. $6\frac{1}{5}$ **21.** $6\frac{1}{4}$ **23.** $2\frac{4}{5}$ **25.** $5\frac{5}{16}$ **27.** $18\frac{5}{7}$ **29.** $14\frac{3}{8}$ **31.** $4\frac{13}{16}$ **33.** $\frac{5}{12}$ **35.** $4\frac{2}{3}$ **37.** $5\frac{5}{6}$
39. $7\frac{7}{16}$ **41.** $\frac{1}{8}$ **43.** $\frac{1}{3}$ yd

Pages 182–183 **1.** 7 **3.** 11 **5.** 20 **7.** 25 **9.** 6; 3 **11.** 4; 2 **13.** 11; 4, 1 **15.** $6\frac{5}{9}$ **17.** $5\frac{1}{2}$
19. $\frac{7}{20}$ **21.** $7\frac{3}{4}$ **23.** $\frac{9}{10}$ **25.** $1\frac{3}{4}$ **27.** $\frac{7}{8}$ **29.** $\frac{5}{8}$ CHECKPOINT B **1.** $\frac{2}{9}$ **2.** $\frac{11}{24}$ **3.** $7\frac{3}{5}$ **4.** $5\frac{1}{4}$
5. $6\frac{1}{10}$ **6.** $11\frac{11}{24}$ **7.** $4\frac{4}{5}$ **8.** $5\frac{1}{8}$ **9.** $5\frac{1}{10}$ **10.** $\frac{4}{9}$ **11.** $8\frac{3}{7}$ **12.** $2\frac{7}{10}$ **13.** $\frac{11}{24}$ **14.** $\frac{4}{15}$

Pages 184–185 **1.** $P = (2 \times b) + (2 \times h)$ **3.** $A = b \times h \div 2$ **5.** 1 yd = 3 ft
7. 1 lb = 16 oz **9.** $1\frac{3}{4}$ yd **11.** $1\frac{1}{4}$ ft by 1 ft **13.** $\frac{3}{4}$ ft

Page 186 **1.** C **3.** B **5.** $1\frac{7}{12}$ **7.** $11\frac{1}{8}$ **9.** $23\frac{3}{8}$ **11.** $\frac{2}{3}$ **13.** $3\frac{3}{8}$ **15.** $\frac{5}{6}$ **17.** $\frac{4}{9}$ **19.** $\frac{1}{2}$ **21.** too
much; $\frac{1}{4}$ yd **23.** too much; $\frac{1}{8}$ yd **25.** too much; $\frac{3}{8}$ yd

Pages 188–189 **1.** T **3.** F **5.** 10 QUANTITY = 50 **7.** 40 TAX = 0.06 * AMOUNT **9.** 70
PRINT TAX

Page 190 **1.** 289 m² **3.** 90 mm² **5.** 49.5 m² **7.** 5.76 cm² **9.** 1794 m² **11.** 46.8 mm²
13. 20; 44 **15.** 14.4; 3.4; 7.2, 6.8, 48.96 **17.** 55 R11 **19.** 24 **21.** 0.6 **23.** 0.06 **25.** 1.888
27. 29

UNIT 7 **Pages 192–193** **1.** 3, 3; 1, 3 **3.** 2, 2, 1; 2; 1, 2, 1; 2 **5.** 15, 7; 15, 7 **7.** 3
9. 4 **11.** 4 **13.** $\frac{3}{7}$ **15.** $\frac{5}{9}$ **17.** 12 **19.** 20 **21.** 9 **23.** $2\frac{2}{5}$ **25.** $2\frac{2}{9}$ **27.** 3; 9; 15 **29.** 4; 12;
20 **31.** $7\frac{1}{2}$; 15; $22\frac{1}{2}$ **33.** $1\frac{1}{2}$ gal **35.** 2 gal **37.** $442\frac{1}{2}$

Pages 194–195 **1.** 5, 5 **3.** 1, 2; 7, 35 **5.** 2, 1, 2; 7, 9, 63 **7.** 3, 1 **9.** 6, 3 **11.** 5, 1
13. $\frac{3}{56}$ **15.** $\frac{9}{32}$ **17.** $\frac{3}{40}$ **19.** $\frac{21}{50}$ **21.** $\frac{25}{42}$ **23.** $\frac{7}{18}$ **25.** $\frac{9}{32}$ **27.** $\frac{1}{2}$ **29.** $\frac{3}{14}$ **31.** $\frac{5}{21}$ **33.** $\frac{1}{21}$ **35.** $\frac{1}{15}$
37. 5 oz spinach; $1\frac{1}{2}$ c potato; $1\frac{1}{2}$ c water; $\frac{1}{8}$ c butter; 1 egg; $\frac{1}{6}$ c cheese

Pages 196–197 **1.** 1; 5 **3.** 4; 15 **5.** 9; 40 **7.** 3; 40 **9.** $\frac{7}{24}$ **11.** $\frac{1}{10}$ **13.** $\frac{3}{8}$ **15.** $\frac{1}{3}$ **17.** $\frac{3}{8}$
19. $\frac{8}{45}$ **21.** $\frac{2}{15}$ **23.** $\frac{2}{5}$ **25.** $\frac{1}{3}$ **27.** $\frac{3}{10}$ **29.** $\frac{5}{12}$ **31.** $\frac{1}{4}$

Pages 198–199 **1.** 15 **3.** 11, 7 **5.** 4 **7.** $8\frac{1}{4}$ **9.** $15\frac{3}{4}$ **11.** $3\frac{8}{8}$ **13.** 21 **15.** $3\frac{1}{3}$ **17.** 7
19. $5\frac{1}{4}$ **21.** $\frac{1}{2}$ **23.** 22 **25.** $1\frac{1}{2}$ **27.** $7\frac{7}{8}$ **29.** $27\frac{1}{2}$ yd **31.** $21\frac{1}{4}$ yd **33.** $60.75 CHECKPOINT A
1. 40 **2.** 15 **3.** $3\frac{3}{7}$ **4.** $8\frac{8}{9}$ **5.** $\frac{3}{40}$ **6.** $\frac{8}{99}$ **7.** $\frac{15}{28}$ **8.** $\frac{12}{143}$ **9.** $\frac{5}{8}$ **10.** $\frac{7}{39}$ **11.** $\frac{3}{8}$ **12.** $\frac{2}{9}$ **13.** 8
14. 35 **15.** $67\frac{1}{2}$

Pages 200–201 **1.** 9; 1 **3.** 1; 7 **5.** 9; 7 **7.** $\frac{5}{1}$ **9.** $\frac{5}{4}$ **11.** $\frac{11}{8}$ **13.** $\frac{4}{3}$ **15.** $\frac{14}{11}$ **17.** $\frac{20}{19}$ **19.** $\frac{5}{3}$
21. $\frac{1}{8}$ **23.** $\frac{1}{25}$ **25.** Yes **27.** Yes **29.** No **31.** Yes **33.** $\frac{28}{9}$, $\frac{9}{28}$ **35.** $\frac{79}{9}$, $\frac{9}{79}$ **37.** $\frac{71}{7}$, $\frac{7}{71}$ **39.** $\frac{35}{2}$,
$\frac{2}{35}$ **41.** $\frac{163}{8}$, $\frac{8}{163}$ **43.** $\frac{64}{23}$, $\frac{23}{64}$ **45.** Yes **47.** Yes **49.** Yes **51.** No **53.** No **55.** $\frac{3}{2}$ **57.** $\frac{8}{3}$
59. $\frac{9}{5}$ **61.** $\frac{1}{8}$ **63.** F **65.** T **67.** F

Pages 202–203 **1.** 4, 12 **3.** 3, 6 **5.** 4, 12 **7.** 1, 2; 12, 27 **9.** 12 **11.** $\frac{2}{9}$ **13.** $\frac{1}{14}$ **15.** $\frac{1}{12}$
17. $\frac{3}{98}$ **19.** $25\frac{3}{5}$ **21.** 30 **23.** 45 **25.** $\frac{1}{60}$ **27.** 48 **29.** 39 frames

Pages 204–205 **1.** 3, 3; 2, 14 **3.** 5, 20; 3, 21 **5.** 4, 8; 3, 27 **7.** 7, 21; 5, 50 **9.** $\frac{6}{7}$ **11.** $\frac{6}{7}$
13. $1\frac{1}{5}$ **15.** $\frac{21}{22}$ **17.** $\frac{2}{3}$ **19.** $\frac{15}{16}$ **21.** 2 **23.** $1\frac{1}{3}$ **25.** $\frac{9}{14}$ **27.** $\frac{6}{7}$ **29.** $2\frac{2}{3}$ **31.** $1\frac{1}{3}$ **33.** 4, 5; 0.3
35. 8, 3, 10; 0.1875 **37.** $7 \div 8 \times 3 \div 5$; 0.525 **39.** $5 \div 16 \times 3 \div 10$; 0.09375

Pages 206–207 **1.** 2, 7; 2, 6; 7 **3.** $1\frac{1}{2}$ **5.** $1\frac{1}{4}$ **7.** $\frac{3}{8}$ **9.** $\frac{1}{5}$ **11.** $9\frac{3}{5}$ **13.** 8 **15.** 26 **17.** 46 **19.** $2\frac{1}{10}$ **21.** $1\frac{2}{15}$ **23.** $3\frac{1}{5}$ **25.** $7\frac{3}{7}$ **27.** No; $1\frac{1}{2}$ **29.** Yes CHECKPOINT B **1.** $\frac{7}{2}$ **2.** $\frac{9}{8}$ **3.** $\frac{4}{43}$ **4.** $\frac{15}{109}$ **5.** 40 **6.** 78 **7.** $27\frac{1}{2}$ **8.** $31\frac{1}{2}$ **9.** $\frac{7}{10}$ **10.** $1\frac{1}{6}$ **11.** $\frac{21}{22}$ **12.** $\frac{7}{12}$ **13.** $2\frac{3}{4}$ **14.** $2\frac{5}{36}$ **15.** $2\frac{4}{41}$ **16.** $1\frac{7}{8}$

Pages 208–209 Estimates may vary for Exercises 1 and 3. One possible estimate is given. **1.** No; 200; 189 mi **3.** No; $350; $393.50 **5.** $32.55 **7.** Yes **9.** bus at 58 mph **11.** No **13.** Round 73 to 80.

Page 210 **1.** $\frac{15}{32}$ **3.** $6\frac{3}{4}$ **5.** $\frac{3}{8}$ **7.** $21\frac{1}{3}$ **9.** $16\frac{2}{3}$ **11.** $\frac{2}{7}$ **13.** 2 **15.** 6 **17.** $\frac{2}{1}$ **19.** $\frac{4}{3}$ **21.** $\frac{5}{8}$ **23.** product **25.** third **27.** associative **29.** one **31.** about **33.** Yes

Pages 212–213 **1.** No **3.** No **5.** 900,000 **7.** 8200 **9.** 73,500 **11.** 18 **13.** 7 **15.** 13 **17.** 7×10^6 **19.** 3×10^{10} **21.** 6.5×10^8 **23.** 1.36×10^5 **25.** 4.06×10^7 **27.** 4.8×10^5 **29.** 9.46×10^{12}

Page 214 **1.** 6^2 **3.** 1^5 **5.** 11^2 **7.** 10^4 **9.** 36 **11.** 10 **13.** 1,000,000 **15.** 32 **17.** 49 **19.** 2^2 **21.** 9^2 **23.** 12^2 **25.** 4^3 **27.** 5^3 **29.** 1 **31.** 1 **33.** 9 **35.** 6 **37.** 5 **39.** 9 **41.** 9 **43.** 2 **45.** 8 **47.** 6 **49.** $237

UNIT 8 **Pages 216–217** **1.** c **3.** c **5.** a **7.** 46×9 **9.** $q - 14$ **11.** $12n$ **13.** $w + 11$ **15.** $5x$ **17.** xy Answers may vary for Exercises 19, 21, 23, 25, 27, 29, 31. One possible solution is given. **19.** seventy-eight divided by thirteen **21.** three times fifty-one **23.** the product of thirty-one and a number v **25.** a number c subtracted from eighteen **27.** fifty-six plus a number y **29.** the sum of a number x and a number y **31.** the product of a number x and a number y **33.** $\frac{n}{5}$ **35.** $n - 20$ **37.** $12h$

Pages 218–219 **1.** 17 **3.** 12 **5.** 1 **7.** 6 **9.** 20 **11.** 3 **13.** 1 **15.** 1 **17.** 42 **19.** 20 **21.** 48 **23.** 21 **25.** 72 **27.** 8 **29.** 1 **31.** 6 **33.** 4 **35.** 42 **37.** 216 **39.** 1 **41.** 12 **43.** 16 **45.** 2 **47.** 15

Pages 220–221 **1.** Yes **3.** Yes **5.** No **7.** Yes **9.** No **11.** Yes **13.** Yes **15.** c **17.** c **19.** a **21.** b **23.** C **25.** A **27.** G **29.** E

Pages 222–223 **1.** 4 **3.** 24 **5.** 86 **7.** 66 **9.** 5 **11.** 84 **13.** 99 **15.** 38 **17.** 15, 7 **19.** 35, 35, 33 **21.** 14 **23.** 50 **25.** 69 **27.** 177 **29.** 177 **31.** 134 **33.** 8 **35.** 198 **37.** 138, 179, 260 **39.** $b = 101$; $i = 122$; $k = 136$; $e = 141$

Pages 224–225 **1.** b **3.** c **5.** $n + 14 = 72$; 58 **7.** $n - 29 = 41$; 70 **9.** $12 + n = 64$; 52 **11.** $n + 67 = 121$; 54 **13.** $1913 + n = 1956$; 43 years **15.** $x + 22 = 1835$; 1813 **17.** $s - 13 = 47$; 60 kinds CHECKPOINT A **1.** $57 - 9$ **2.** $q + 8$ **3.** $7x$ **4.** $\frac{a}{15}$ **5.** 25 **6.** 6 **7.** 10 **8.** 4 **9.** No **10.** No **11.** Yes **12.** No **13.** 43 **14.** 55 **15.** 98 **16.** 61 **17.** $n - 23 = 59$; 82 **18.** $n + 55 = 121$; 66

Pages 226–227 **1.** 4 **3.** 12 **5.** 2 **7.** 50 **9.** 4 **11.** 15 **13.** 12 **15.** 14 **17.** 6, 13 **19.** 5, 5, 25 **21.** 15 **23.** 32 **25.** 96 **27.** 102 **29.** 55 **31.** 13 **33.** 105 **35.** 150 **37.** 11 **39.** 228 **41.** E **43.** D **45.** B

Pages 228–229 **1.** b **3.** c **5.** $9n = 189$; 21 **7.** $\frac{n}{3} = 24$; 72 **9.** $6n = 96$; 16 **11.** $\frac{1}{2}n = 35$; 70 **13.** $14n = 126$; 9 planets **15.** $3n = 36$; 12 people **17.** $\frac{n}{10} = 50$; 500 sheets **19.** $45n = 585$; 13 colonies

Pages 230–231 **1.** Subtract 5. **3.** Divide by 4. **5.** Subtract 19. **7.** Add 34. **9.** Multiply by 18. **11.** Divide by 12 **13.** 50 **15.** 117 **17.** 21 **19.** 6 **21.** 26 **23.** 46 **25.** 22 **27.** 139 **29.** 51 **31.** 231 **33.** 88 **35.** 338 **37.** 219 **39.** 16 **41.** 8 **43.** 20 **45.** 32 **47.** 24

Pages 232–233 **1.** 2, 4; 8, 10 **3.** 6, 9, 15; 0, 12, 48 **5.** 3, 2, 4, 0 **7.** 7, 11, 6, 15, 10 **9.** 0, 1, 7, 4, 9 **11.** 4; 131, 134, 137, 140, 143, 146 **13.** 3; 30, 32, 34, 36, 38, 40

Pages 234–235 **1.** $(4, 7)$ **3.** $(2, 5)$ **5.** $(1, 0)$ **7.** A **9.** F **11.** J **13.** L **15.** Q **17.** P **19.** B **21.** $(5, 3)$ **23.** $(7, 4)$ **25.** $(6, 0)$ **27.** $(2, 2)$ **29.** $(4, 2)$ **31.** $(4, 4)$ **33.** rectangle **35.** square   CHECKPOINT B **1.** 13 **2.** 15 **3.** 82 **4.** 192 **5.** $\frac{n}{3} = 21$; 63 **6.** $7n = 154$; 22 **7.** 103 **8.** 19 **9.** 42 **10.** 27 **11.** 0 **12.** 1 **13.** 35 **14.** 9 **15.** $(3, 5)$ **16.** $(5, 3)$ **17.** $(3, 0)$ **18.** $(0, 4)$

Pages 236–237 **1.** B **3.** D **5.** C **7.** A **9.** B **11.** $4n = 20$; 5 packages **13.** $n - 4 = 20$; 24 students **15.** $\frac{n}{4} = 20$; $80   Answers may vary for Exercises 17 and 19. One possible solution is given. **17.** Raol has saved $5. If he needs $12 to buy a model, how much more must he save? $7 **19.** Maria has to buy 18 racquetballs. If each can contains 2 racquetballs, how many cans does she have to buy? 9 cans

Page 238 **1.** D **3.** B **5.** 27 **7.** 20 **9.** c **11.** 23 **13.** 80 **15.** 14 **17.** 161 **19.** 42 **21.** $\frac{n}{6} = 5$; 30 **23.** 6, 2 **25.** 0, 3; hexagon

Pages 240–241 **1.** Yes **3.** Yes **5.** No **7.** $y = 2x$ **9.** $y = 2x + 1$ **11.** $y = x - 1$ **13.** $y = x + 45$

Page 242 **1.** 34 **3.** 72 **5.** 50 square units **7.** 220 square units **9.** D **11.** C **13.** G **15.** A **17.** $\frac{1}{3}$ **19.** $\frac{3}{17}$ **21.** $\frac{5}{9}$ **23.** 150.72 m **25.** 62.8 m **27.** 1017.36 m² **29.** $130

UNIT 9   **Pages 244–245** **1.** $\frac{3}{7}$ **3.** $\frac{6}{5}$ **5.** $\frac{8}{7}$ **7.** $\frac{2}{4}$ **9.** $\frac{10}{1}$ **11.** $\frac{2}{9}$ **13.** $\frac{1}{3}$ **15.** $\frac{1}{39}$ **17.** $\frac{3}{110}$ **19.** $\frac{55}{73}$ **21.** $\frac{3}{146}$ **23.** $\frac{19}{15}$ **25.** $\frac{25}{1}$ **27.** $\frac{25}{6}$ **29.** $\frac{6}{55}$ **31.** $\frac{64}{55}$ **33.** 3:6.5

Pages 246–247 **1.** 4 **3.** 19 **5.** 37 **7.** 57 **9.** 25 **11.** 36 **13.** $18 **15.** $312 **17.** 50 pages per minute **19.** $.10 per package **21.** $7.50 per bouquet **23.** $8.65 per chair **25.** $.75 per subscription **27.** 65 words per minute **29.** 22.25¢ **31.** Yes

Pages 248–249 **1.** Yes **3.** No **5.** Yes **7.** No **9.** No **11.** No **13.** 1:2; 5:10; Yes **15.** 3:25; 4:30; No **17.** 85:100; 165:200 No **19.** $\frac{1}{2} = \frac{4}{8}$; 1:2 = 4:8 **21.** $\frac{5}{4} = \frac{1.25}{1}$; 5:4 = 1.25:1 **23.** A; 21:36 = 7:12; $\frac{21}{36} = \frac{7}{12}$ **25.** H; 30:1 = 90:3; $\frac{30}{1} = \frac{90}{3}$ **27.** C; 4:1 = 16:4; $\frac{4}{1} = \frac{16}{4}$ **29.** B; 12:20 = 3:5; $\frac{12}{20} = \frac{3}{5}$ **31.** J; 26:6 = 13:3; $\frac{26}{6} = \frac{13}{3}$ **33.** K; 300:45 = 20:3; $\frac{300}{45} = \frac{20}{3}$ **35.** $\frac{2}{3} = \frac{10}{15}$; $\frac{3}{2} = \frac{15}{10}$; $\frac{15}{3} = \frac{10}{2}$; $\frac{3}{15} = \frac{2}{10}$ **37.** $\frac{5}{6} = \frac{10}{12}$; $\frac{6}{5} = \frac{12}{10}$; $\frac{5}{10} = \frac{6}{12}$; $\frac{6}{10} = \frac{10}{5}$

Pages 250–251 **1.** 8 **3.** 4 **5.** 8 **7.** 4 **9.** 6 **11.** 2 **13.** 27 **15.** 5 **17.** 4 **19.** 36 **21.** 6 **23.** 60 **25.** 9 **27.** 50 **29.** $\frac{1}{3} = \frac{2}{x}$; 6 **31.** $\frac{1}{5} = \frac{p}{10}$; 2 **33.** $\frac{2}{4} = \frac{4}{j}$; 8 **35.** $\frac{4}{12} = \frac{20}{a}$; 60 **37.** $\frac{10}{15} = \frac{2}{b}$; 3 **39.** $\frac{5}{15} = \frac{x}{30}$; 10 **41.** $\frac{5}{7} = \frac{10}{x}$; 14 **43.** 900 cm **45.** 5 kg **47.** 31,000 m **49.** 1.3 kg

Pages 252–253 **1.** Yes **3.** No **5.** Yes **7.** Yes **9.** 7 **11.** 25 **13.** 7 **15.** 10 **17.** 150 **19.** 0.2 **21.** 1.2 **23.** 0.1 **25.** 348 km **27.** $16.80 CHECKPOINT A **1.** $\frac{1}{2}$ **2.** $\frac{5}{1}$ **3.** $\frac{3}{4}$ **4.** $\frac{2}{3}$ **5.** $1.69 per can **6.** $.025 per bag **7.** $.08 per clip **8.** $.02 per plate **9.** B; $\frac{13}{52} = \frac{1}{4}$; 13:52 = 1:4 **10.** A; $\frac{3}{5} = \frac{57}{95}$; 3:5 = 57:95 **11.** C; $\frac{13.5}{2.7} = \frac{5}{1}$; 13.5:2.7 = 5:1 **12.** D; $\frac{1.3}{15.6} = \frac{1}{12}$; 1.3:15.6 = 1:12 **13.** 15 **14.** 50 **15.** 3 **16.** 15 **17.** 9 **19.** 20 **20.** 0.6

Pages 254–255 **1.** 100 **3.** 88 **5.** 60 **7.** 3360 **9.** 116 cm **11.** 74 cm **13.** 480 mm **15.** 496 mm **17.** 64 mm **19.** 1 cm **21.** 3 cm **23.** 6 cm **25.** 2.7 cm **27.** 1.8 cm

Pages 256–257 Answers may vary for Exercises 1–10. One possible solution is given. **1.** 475 km **3.** 550 km **5.** 50 km **7.** 975 km **9.** 650 km **11.** a **13.** b **15.** 350 km **17.** 350 km **19.** 410 km **21.** 450 km **23.** Phoenix to Tucson is shorter.

Pages 258–259 **1.** True **3.** True **5.** $\angle Y$ **7.** $\overline{XY}$ **9.** $\overline{XZ}$ **11.** $\overline{XY}$ **13.** 14 **15.** 21 **17.** $\overline{TR}$ **19.** $\overline{RO}$ **21.** 20

Pages 260–261 **1.** 10 **3.** 25.5 m **5.** 56.25 m **7.** 2 m CHECKPOINT B **1.** 60 cm **2.** 27 m **3.** 2 km **4.** 2.75 km **5.** 9 cm **6.** 5 cm **7.** 5.1 m

Pages 262–263 Answers may vary for Exercises 1 and 3. One possible solution is given. **1.** $\frac{75}{2} = \frac{n}{12}$ **3.** $\frac{60}{15} = \frac{n}{25}$ **5.** 1435 students **7.** 144 students **9.** $204.40 **11.** 216 people **13.** 12 boys, 9 girls

Page 264 **1.** $\frac{5}{1}$ **3.** c **5.** Yes **7.** Yes **9.** 28 **11.** 72 **13.** 2.4 km **15.** 20 m

Pages 266–267 **1.** b

Pages 268–269 **1.** c **3.** a **5.** c **7.** a **9.** c **11.** a **13.** b **15.** a **17.** c **19.** a **21.** c **23.** c **25.** b **27.** c

APPLYING YOUR SKILLS **Pages 270–271** **1.** B **3.** A **5.** A **7.** B **9.** $.11 per bag **11.** $.06 per ounce **13.** $.02 per gram **15.** gallon; $.82 less per quart **17.** $3\frac{1}{2}$ gallon can **Pages 272–273** **1.** $1063 **3.** $64.62 **5.** $90.85 **7.** $218 **Pages 274–275** **1.** $420.45; $45.20 **3.** $9400; $1475 **5.** $2900; $346 **7.** No **9.** Yes **11.** No **13.** 3 payments of $160 **15.** $30.44 **Page 276** **1.** $4\frac{15}{16}'$ **3.** $3\frac{5}{8}'$ **5.** $1\frac{1}{8}'$ **7.** $6\frac{1}{2}'$ **9.** 3'

UNIT 10 **Pages 278–279** **1.** 99% **3.** 9% **5.** 27% **7.** 85% **9.** 42% **11.** 16% **13.** 98% **15.** 3% **17.** 9% **19.** 15% **21.** 70 **23.** 55 **25.** 15% **27.** 12%, 88% **29.** 50%, 50% **31.** $12\frac{1}{2}$%, $87\frac{1}{2}$% **33.** 78.5%, 21.5%

Pages 280–281 **1.** 9, 9 **3.** 125, 12.5, 12.5 **5.** 5, 5 **7.** 84, 8, 4 **9.** 20.5, 205, 2, 0, 5 **11.** 95, 9, 5 **13.** 37% **15.** 81% **17.** 40% **19.** 70% **21.** 21% **23.** 52% **25.** 74% **27.** 12.5% **29.** 6.5% **31.** 91.3% **33.** 0.25 **35.** 0.63 **37.** 0.75 **39.** 0.333 **41.** 0.2 **43.** 0.8 **45.** 0.015 **47.** 0.05 **49.** 75% **51.** 31.1%

Pages 282–283 **1.** $\frac{1}{10}$ **3.** $\frac{9}{10}$ **5.** $\frac{1}{20}$ **7.** $\frac{12}{25}$ **9.** $\frac{9}{25}$ **11.** 989 **13.** 69 **15.** $\frac{1}{100}$ **17.** $\frac{1}{2}$ **19.** $\frac{1}{5}$ **21.** $\frac{4}{5}$ **23.** $\frac{1}{50}$ **25.** $\frac{3}{25}$ **27.** $\frac{13}{20}$ **29.** $\frac{121}{1000}$ **31.** $\frac{7}{8}$ **33.** $\frac{157}{250}$ **35.** 0.125, $\frac{1}{8}$ **37.** 0.25, $\frac{1}{4}$ **39.** 0.4, $\frac{2}{5}$ **41.** 0.6, $\frac{3}{5}$ **43.** 0.75, $\frac{3}{4}$ **45.** 0.875, $\frac{7}{8}$ **47.** 1, 8 **49.** 100; 7, 400 **51.** $\frac{11}{200}$ **53.** $\frac{81}{400}$ **55.** $\frac{3}{40}$

Pages 284–285 **1.** 25, 25 **3.** 80, 80 **5.** 4, 4 **7.** 6, 0; 60 **9.** 6, 2, 5; 62.5 **11.** 1, 4; $14\frac{2}{7}$ **13.** 50%, 100% **15.** 25%, 50%, 75%, 100% **17.** 12.5%, 37.5%, 62.5%, 87.5%, 100% **19.** 4%, 8%, 12%, 16%, 36% **21.** 33% **23.** 38%, 37.5% **25.** 33%, 33.3% CHECKPOINT A **1.** 4% **2.** 82% **3.** 56% **4.** 6% **5.** 20% **6.** 69% **7.** 33% **8.** 12.5% **9.** 0.32 **10.** 0.07 **11.** 0.5 **12.** 0.955 **13.** $\frac{3}{4}$ **14.** $\frac{2}{25}$ **15.** $\frac{41}{500}$ **16.** $\frac{7}{8}$ **17.** 62.5% **18.** 44% **19.** 70% **20.** $83\frac{1}{3}$% **21.** $66\frac{2}{3}$% **22.** 37.5%

Pages 286–287 **1.** 60; 6 **3.** 2, 5, 200; 50 **5.** 2, 150; 75 **7.** 20 **9.** 10.5 **11.** 4 **13.** 44.1 **15.** 24 **17.** 24 **19.** 24 **21.** 4 **23.** 64 **25.** 42 **27.** 72 **29.** $33\frac{1}{3}$ **31.** 66.5 **33.** 2.25 **35.** 6, 3, 15 **37.** 500 **39.** 80 **41.** 600 **43.** 500 people

Pages 288–289 **1.** 9 **3.** 24 **5.** 75% **7.** 20% **9.** $66\frac{2}{3}$% **11.** 50% **13.** 80% **15.** 20% **17.** 75% **19.** 40% **21.** 25% **23.** 25% **25.** 5% **27.** 25% **29.** 20% **31.** 15% **33.** 12.5% **35.** 20% **37.** 80% **39.** 16%

Pages 290–291 **1.** n **3.** 0.25 **5.** a **7.** 30 **9.** 34 **11.** 25 **13.** 65 **15.** 25 **17.** 80,000 **19.** \$3 **21.** \$5,882,352.94 **23.** 400 **25.** 900 **27.** 6475 **29.** \$212 **31.** $0.6 \times 540 = 324$ **33.** $0.6 \times 324 = 194.4$ **35.** $540 \div 0.6 = 900$

Pages 292–293 **1.** C **3.** F **5.** A **7.** 15% **9.** 350 **11.** 550 **13.** 6500 **15.** 800 **17.** 60 **19.** 204 **21.** 700 **23.** $33\frac{1}{3}$% CHECKPOINT B **1.** 37 **2.** 42 **3.** 18 **4.** 11 **5.** 20% **6.** 6% **7.** 72% **8.** 25% **9.** 82 **10.** \$34 **11.** 30 **12.** 80 **13.** 18 **14.** 5% **15.** 25 **16.** 60

Pages 294–295 **1.** 150; 62.5% **3.** 24; 24; 75% **5.** 24 TV stations **7.** 10 stations **9.** 3 TV stations **11.** 125%

Page 296 **1.** B **3.** A **5.** F **7.** $0.33\frac{1}{3}$ **9.** 0.15 **11.** $\frac{4}{5}$ **13.** $\frac{9}{25}$ **15.** 12 **17.** 20% **19.** 87.5% **21.** 2.5 **23.** 800 **25.** 12 TV stations

Pages 298–299 **1.** 10, 20; $\frac{10}{100}$, 200, 20 **3.** 9, 60; $\frac{15}{100}$, 60, 9 **5.** 100, 350; $\frac{20}{100}$, 350, 70 **7.** $\frac{50}{100} = \frac{5}{10}$ **9.** $\frac{45}{100} = \frac{27}{60}$ **11.** $\frac{70}{100} = \frac{84}{120}$ **13.** 20, x; 15 **15.** 3; z; 25 **17.** $\frac{90}{100} = \frac{36}{n}$; 40 **19.** $\frac{30}{100} = \frac{n}{80}$; 24 **21.** $\frac{n}{100} = \frac{45}{300}$; 15% **23.** $\frac{20}{100} = \frac{25}{n}$; 125 **25.** $\frac{12}{100} = \frac{n}{475}$; 57 **27.** $\frac{45}{100} = \frac{36}{n}$; 80 runners

Page 300 **1.** $d + 6 = 15$ **3.** $\frac{p}{9} = 50$ **5.** $5m = 1.50$ **7.** 38 **9.** 12 **11.** 79 **13.** 12 **15.** 18 **17.** 8.8 **19.** $\frac{5}{7}$ **21.** $\frac{11}{12}$ **23.** $\frac{1}{2}$ **25.** $5\frac{7}{8}$ **27.** $7\frac{1}{12}$ **29.** $2\frac{1}{2}$ c

UNIT 11 **Pages 302–303** **1.** $n = 75\% \times 200$; 150 **3.** $9 = n\% \times 90$; 10% **5.** $4\% \times n = 2$; 50 **7.** 20% **9.** 83 **11.** 5.5 **13.** 80 **15.** 12% **17.** 20 **19.** 2.5% **21.** 20 players **23.** violin, 50%; viola, 16.2%; cello, 19.1%; bass, 13.2%; harp, 1.5%; Total, 68

Pages 304–305 **1.** \$.45 **3.** \$1.50 **5.** \$4.06 **7.** \$3.85 **9.** \$1.22 **11.** \$9.62 **13.** \$19.40 **15.** \$26.57 **17.** \$154.60 **19.** \$17.23 **21.** \$21.14 **23.** \$37.82 **25.** \$1.25 **27.** \$3.18 **29.** 6%

Pages 306–307 **1.** \$250; 8%; 1 y; \$20 **3.** \$650; 20%; 1 y; \$130 **5.** \$11 **7.** \$180 **9.** \$140.88 **11.** \$3200 **13.** \$2025 **15.** \$21.97 **17.** \$52.50 **19.** 12%

Pages 308–309 **1.** $12.50 **3.** $7.99 **5.** $15 **7.** $63 **9.** $115.21 **11.** $15.96 **13.** $56 **15.** $66 **17.** Hat World **19.** $23.16 **21.** 30% CHECKPOINT A **1.** 7.5 **2.** 25% **3.** 35 **4.** $18.46 **5.** $8244.01 **6.** $19.38 **7.** $58.75 **8.** $10,125 **9.** $71.80 **10.** $29.97 **11.** $148.75

Pages 310–311 **1.** 22% **3.** 20% **5.** 29% **7.** 31% **9.** 47.96 million **11.** 43.6 million **13.** 63.22 million **15.** 67.58 million **17.** 36 **19.** 12 **21.** 6.3% **23.** 3.1% **25.** 8.3% **27.** 45°

Pages 312–313 **1.** 4.7% **3.** 6.4% **5.** 41.9% **7.** $4380 **9.** $1760 **11.** $4769.78 **13.** 35% **15.** 5% **17.** $12\frac{1}{2}$% **19.** 15% **21.** $67.50; Neither **23.** $90; Less **25.** $210

Pages 314–315 **1.** 20, I **3.** 20, I **5.** 30, D **7.** 10, D **9.** 0.05, I **11.** 0.2, D **13.** 50%, I **15.** 60%, D **17.** 1.20 **19.** 2.40 **21.** 1.62 **23.** 200% **25.** 210% **27.** 50% Increase **29.** 50% Decrease **31.** 50% Decrease **33.** 6% Decrease **35.** 20% Increase **37.** 64% Decrease **39.** 12.5% Increase **41.** 37.5% Increase **43.** 100% Increase **45.** 10% Increase **47.** $33\frac{1}{3}$% **49.** 100% **51.** 70 m

Pages 316–317 **1.** $5.60 **3.** $175.60 **5.** $90 **7.** $240.15 **9.** $411.15 **11.** $35.75 **13.** $106.14 **15.** $405.64 **17.** 15% **19.** $6000 **21.** $1050 CHECKPOINT B **1.** 120 **2.** 105 **3.** 25% **4.** 20% **5.** 40% **6.** 30% **7.** 104 **8.** 50% **9.** $108.75 **10.** $211.26

Pages 318–319 **1.** 10% **3.** Protein, Vitamin B12 **5.** Niacin **7.** 45 g **9.** 1.8 mg **11.** 30 mg **13.** 0.72 mg, 4%

Page 320 **1.** $137.80 **3.** $162 **5.** $787.50 **7.** $161.46 **9.** 10% **11.** 33% **13.** 5% **15.** 210 **17.** $272.36

Pages 322–323 **1.** 9 **3.** 64 **5.** 1 **7.** 196 **9.** 400 **11.** 6 **13.** 9 **15.** 1 **17.** 13 **19.** 25 **21.** 8 cm **23.** 18 cm **25.** 1.41 **27.** 3.00 **29.** 3.87 **31.** 4.12 **33.** > **35.** < **37.** > **39.** < **41.** < **43.** F **45.** T **47.** F **49.** T

Page 324 **1.** A **3.** O **5.** O **7.** 109° **9.** 65° **11.** 45° **13.** 6000 **15.** 20 **17.** $1\frac{1}{7}$ **19.** $\frac{1}{5}$ **21.** $\frac{1}{16}$ **23.** $4\frac{7}{8}$ **25.** $2\frac{1}{10}$ **27.** $\frac{1}{2} = \frac{4}{8}$ **29.** $\frac{3}{5} = \frac{21}{35}$ **31.** $\frac{2}{3} = \frac{8}{12}$ **33.** $\frac{1}{4} = \frac{6}{24}$ **35.** $\frac{3}{8} = \frac{15}{40}$ **37.** 3 **39.** 11 **41.** $4.38

UNIT 12 **Pages 326–327** **1.** between 0 and 1 **3.** 1 **5.** 0 **7.** 1 **9.** 1 **11.** C **13.** A **15.** E Answers may vary for Exercises 17 and 19. One possible solution is given. **17.** Each candidate should get the same number of votes. **19.** It is certain that Bernie will not set a record.

Pages 328–329 **1.** 8 **3.** $\frac{1}{8}$ **5.** $\frac{3}{8}$ **7.** $\frac{4}{8}$ **9.** $\frac{6}{8}$ **11.** $\frac{2}{8}$ **13.** $\frac{1}{6}$ **15.** $\frac{1}{6}$ **17.** $\frac{3}{6}$ **19.** $\frac{3}{6}$ **21.** $\frac{2}{10}$ **23.** $\frac{4}{10}$ **25.** $\frac{5}{10}$ **27.** $\frac{1}{6}$ **29.** $\frac{3}{6}$ **31.** $\frac{1}{5}$

Pages 330–331 **1.** 1, A, A, 4, 5; 1, 2, B, B, B; C, 2, 3, C, 5 **3.** 5 **5.** $\frac{3}{15}$ **7.** 6; 6; 1 **9.** $\frac{1}{12}$ **11.** 676

Pages 332–333 **1.** 16 **3.** $\frac{4}{16}$ **5.** $\frac{12}{16}$ **7.** $\frac{1}{16}$ **9.** $\frac{7}{16}$ **11.** $\frac{2}{9}$ **13.** $\frac{4}{9}$ **15.** $\frac{1}{4}$ **17.** $\frac{5}{12}$ **19.** $\frac{1}{2}$ **21.** $\frac{1}{4}$ **23.** $\frac{1}{4}$ **25.** $\frac{2}{4}$ **27.** $\frac{1}{8}$ **29.** $\frac{1}{64}$

Pages 334–335 **1.** 7 **3.** $\frac{7}{20}$ **5.** 8 **7.** $\frac{11}{15}$ **9.** $\frac{2}{5}$ **11.** $\frac{1}{20}$ **13.** $\frac{1}{2}$; $\frac{3}{5}$; $\frac{11}{20}$ **15.** 25 games; 30 games; 28 games CHECKPOINT A **1.** B **2.** A **3.** $\frac{1}{8}$ **4.** $\frac{2}{8}$ **5.** 6 **6.** 9 **7.** $\frac{1}{64}$ **8.** $\frac{7}{64}$ **9.** $\frac{1}{5}$ **10.** $\frac{9}{10}$ **11.** $\frac{17}{20}$

Pages 336–337 **1.** 9 **3.** 18, 18 **5.** 4, 54, 13.5 **7.** 6, 22 **9.** 9; 6 **11.** 27; 28 **13.** 48; $53\frac{5}{6}$ **15.** 309; $366\frac{1}{2}$ **17.** 37; $98\frac{3}{5}$ **19.** 192; 2583 **21.** 0.250 **23.** 0.259 **25.** 0.033

Pages 338–339 **1.** 6, 7, 7, 7, 8, 11, 14 **3.** 56, 56, 56, 68, 72, 72, 72 **5.** 7 **7.** 68 **9.** 7 **11.** 56; 72 **13.** 15; 16 **15.** 23; 21 **17.** 50; 48 **19.** 135; 135 **21.** 226; 256 **23.** 62.5 min; 55 min, 70 min, and 75 min **25. a.** 17.5 **b.** 13 and 22 **c.** Answers will vary. One possible answer is that the modes may help the purchasing agent decide which popular colors to keep in stock.

Pages 340–341 **1.** June to September **3.** It is much shorter. **5.** None; no **7.** 68°F, 78°F, 82°F; no **9. a.** 363.$\overline{3}$ m **b.** 809.$\overline{6}$ m **c.** No

Pages 342–343 **1.** Rock **3.** 10; 200 **5.** 40 **7.** 260 **9.** 6000 **11.** 3500 **13.** 9500

Pages 344–345 **1.** About 400 m **3.** About 550 m **5.** South America **7.** About 5500 m **9.** About 8800 m **11.** About 7000 m **13.** About 3500 m **15.** About 3500 m **17.** About 6500 m **19.** South America

Pages 346–347 **1.** 19 days **3.** 4 days **5.** 18 days **7.** July **9.** 50°F **11.** 78°F **13.** 50°F **15.** November CHECKPOINT B **1.** 8; 6; none **2.** 8; 8; 7 **3.** 3 **4.** 2 **5.** 1 **6.** 30°F **7.** 40°F

Pages 348–349 **1.** 1100 red; 500 blue; 1700 silver; 880 yellow; 820 black **3.** 186,000 birthday; 204,000 get well; 228,000 Valentine; 132,000 Halloween

Page 350 **1.** $\frac{1}{3}$ **3.** $\frac{1}{6}$ **5.** (1, 1), (1, 2), (1, 3), (1, 4), (1, 5), (1, 5); (2, 1), (2, 2), (2, 3), (2, 4), (2, 5), (2, 5); (3, 1), (3, 2), (3, 3), (3, 4), (3, 5), (3, 5); (4, 1), (4, 2), (4, 3), (4, 4), (4, 5), (4, 5); (5, 1), (5, 2), (5, 3), (5, 4), (5, 5), (5, 5); (5, 1), (5, 2), (5, 3), (5, 4), (5, 5), (5, 5) **7.** $\frac{1}{36}$ **9.** 7 **11.** 8 **13.** 45,000 **15.** 14°C; 6:00 **17.** 6000

Pages 352–353 **1.** Yes **3.** Yes **5.** No **7.** Yes **9.** Yes **11.** Yes **13.** 5 **15.** 29 **17.** 30 **19.** 10 **21.** 50 **23.** 12 m

Page 354 **1.** Yes **3.** No **5.** No **7.** No **9.** 0.3 **11.** 0.625 **13.** $\frac{13}{25}$ **15.** 0.18 **17.** $\frac{5}{2}$ **19.** 0.45 **21.** 225 **23.** $1.17 **25.** 37.5% **27.** 28 pets

Unit 13 **Pages 356–357** **1.** $\angle P$ **3.** $\angle Q$ **5.** $\overline{QR}$ **7.** QFT **9.** XRM **11.** $\angle M$ **13.** $\angle R$ **15.** $\overline{SM}$ **17.** 6 **19.** 7 **21.** C **23.** CBD **25.** $\overline{MQ}$ **27.** $\overline{LM}$ **29.** MQN

Pages 362–363 **1.** $\overline{ED}$ **3.** ABC

Pages 364–365 **1.** Yes **3.** Yes **5.** Yes **7.** Yes **9.** line **11.** line **13.** point **15.** T **17.** T **19.** H, I, O, X, S, Z CHECKPOINT A **1.** $\angle P$ **2.** $\angle D$ **3.** $\overline{QR}$ **4.** $\overline{DC}$ **15.** line **16.** both

Pages 366–367 **1.** T **3.** F **5.** T **7.** T **9.** T **11.** F **13.** T **15.** F **17.** Rectangular prism **19.** Triangular prism **21.** Cone **23.** Rectangle **25.** Square

Pages 368–369 **1.** 112 cm² **3.** 184 cm² **5.** 6 m² **7.** 550 m² **9.** 60 cm² **11.** 30 m²

Pages 370–371   **1.** 10   **3.** 20   **5.** 314 cm²   **7.** 785 cm²   **9.** 4622.08 mm²   **11.** 163.28 cm²
13. 722.2 cm²   **15.** 244.92 cm²   **17.** 196.25 cm²

Pages 372–373   **1.** 162   **3.** 156 cm²   **5.** 300 mm³   **7.** 100 m²   **9.** 7000   **11.** 0.545
13. 100,000 mm³

Pages 374–375   **1.** 8; 400   **3.** 5; 90   **5.** 40 m³   **7.** 753.6 cm³   **9.** 461,580 mm³
11. 6358.5 m³   **13.** 6280 L   CHECKPOINT B   **1.** F   **2.** T   **3.** F   **4.** 792 cm²   **5.** 2198 mm²
6. 210 cm³   **7.** 125 mm³   **8.** 502.4 mm³   **9.** 628 cm³

Pages 376–377   **1.** 12 m²   **3.** 8 m²   **5.** \$44.82   **7.** Panthers   **9.** 36 posts

Page 378   **1.** $\angle M$ **3.** $\overline{MP}$ **7.** RSP **9.** both   **11.** B **13.** A **15.** SA = 628 cm²,
V = 1177.5 cm³   **17.** 1 m from the length, 0.2 m from the width

Pages 380–381   **1.** \$30.94   **3.** \$9.04   **5.** Robert

Page 382   **1.** $\frac{3}{8}, \frac{3}{4}, 3\frac{1}{8}$ **3.** $11\frac{3}{4}, 11\frac{7}{8}, 13\frac{1}{3}, 13\frac{3}{4}$ **5.** \$3.30   **7.** \$1920   **9.** 7, 3, 2; $7 \times 3 \times 2$
11. 36   **13.** 24   **15.** 1   **17.** 6   **19.** 7; 8; 8; 5   **21.** \$60.40

UNIT 14   **Pages 384–385**   **1.** Positive   **3.** Positive   **5.** Negative   **7.** 4   **9.** 25; ⁻25
11. Yes   **13.** No   **15.** No   **17.** 1   **19.** 5   **21.** ⁻5   **23.** ⁻7   **25.** 6   **27.** ⁻6   **29.** 8   **31.** 30
33. ⁻72   **35.** ⁻100   **37.** ⁻160   **39.** ⁻9999   **41.** 873   **43.** T   **45.** T   **47.** ⁻5   **49.** 1500
51. ⁻3   **53.** ⁻8   **55.** ⁻10   **57.** ⁻2

Pages 386–387   **1.** left; <   **3.** right; >   **5.** right; >   **7.** right; >   **9.** left; <   **11.** <
13. >   **15.** <   **17.** <   **19.** >   **21.** <   **23.** >   **25.** <   **27.** >   **29.** <   **31.** >   **33.** <
35. 2 < 4 < 6   **37.** ⁻7 < ⁻2 < 2   **39.** 1 < 4 < 7   **41.** ⁻4 < 3 < 4   **43.** ⁻7, ⁻4, ⁻1, 0, 3, 5
45. ⁻12, ⁻10, ⁻9, 0, 3, 4   **47.** Asia, Africa, North America, South America, Europe, Australia

Pages 388–389   **1.** 6; ⁻6   **3.** 8; ⁻8   **5.** 8; ⁻8   **7.** 13; ⁻13   **9.** 15; ⁻15   **11.** ⁻18   **13.** 10
15. 12   **17.** 15   **19.** 21   **21.** 24   **23.** 50   **25.** ⁻63   **27.** 17   **29.** ⁻17   **31.** ⁻29   **33.** 80
35. ⁻91   **37.** ⁻57   **39.** 103, 97, \$200   **41.** ⁻5, ⁻10, ⁻8, \$23

Pages 390–391   **1.** 0; ⁻1; ⁻2   **3.** 0; 1; 2   **5.** Positive, Negative   **7.** Positive, Negative   **9.** 4
11. 5   **13.** ⁻5   **15.** ⁻6   **17.** ⁻7   **19.** 8   **21.** 6   **23.** ⁻6   **25.** 22   **27.** 11; ⁻7; 4th floor   **29.** 9;
⁻10; 8; 7th floor   **31.** 12; ⁻9; 3; ⁻8; 2 floors below ground level

Pages 392–393   **1.** ⁻6   **3.** ⁻2   **5.** ⁻4; ⁻6   **7.** 4; 8   **9.** 4; 8; 12   **11.** ⁻14; ⁻4; 6   **13.** ⁻4
15. ⁻11   **17.** ⁻4   **19.** ⁻2   **21.** 19   **23.** ⁻21   **25.** ⁻25   **27.** 7; ⁻49; 56°   **29.** 31; 20; 11°
CHECKPOINT A   **1.** ⁻8   **2.** 12   **3.** 0   **4.** 5   **5.** >   **6.** >   **7.** <   **9.** <   **10.** >
11. 12   **12.** ⁻11   **13.** ⁻15   **14.** 12   **15.** ⁻24   **16.** 24   **17.** 5   **18.** ⁻2   **19.** ⁻7   **20.** 9   **21.** 0
22. 9   **23.** ⁻2   **24.** 12   **25.** ⁻13   **26.** 9   **27.** 16   **28.** ⁻8

Pages 394–395   **1.** 18; ⁻18   **3.** 48; 48   **5.** 32; ⁻32   **7.** 30; ⁻30   **9.** ⁻2   **11.** 12   **13.** ⁻24
15. 72   **17.** 40   **19.** 0   **21.** ⁻20   **23.** ⁻26   **25.** ⁻60   **27.** ⁻45   **29.** ⁻60   **31.** ⁻72   **33.** ⁻6°C;
⁻9°C; ⁻15°C   **35.** ⁻8°C; ⁻11°C; ⁻14°C; ⁻20°C

Pages 396–397   **1.** 2   **3.** ⁻2   **5.** 3   **7.** ⁻3   **9.** 5; ⁻5   **11.** 3; 3   **13.** 4; 4   **15.** 6; ⁻6   **17.** ⁻2
19. 6   **21.** 6   **23.** 7   **25.** ⁻9   **27.** 0   **29.** ⁻13   **31.** 23   **33.** ⁻12; 6; ⁻2 m/min   **35.** ⁻24; 12;
⁻2°/h   **37.** \$215/mo   **39.** \$80 profit/mo

Pages 398–399 **1.** 8, 8; $^-5$ **3.** 6, 6; $^-7$ **5.** $^-4$ **7.** $^-15$ **9.** $^-2$ **11.** $^-7$ **13.** 7 **15.** $^-63$ **17.** $^-43$ **19.** $^-43$ **21.** $^-60$ **23.** $^-15$ **25.** $^-45$ **27.** c; $^-128$ **29.** b; $^-3$

Pages 400–401 **1.** (2, 3) **3.** (4, $^-2$) **5.** (1, 0) **7.** (0, 1) **9.** B **11.** P **13.** S **15.** F **17.** (5, 3) **19.** (0, 9) **21.** ($^-3$, 3) **23.** ($^-10$, 3) **25.** ($^-6$, $^-2$) **27.** ($^-8$, $^-5$) **29.** ($^-3$, 5) **31.** ($^-2$, $^-4$) **33.** (3, 0) **35.** (4, 0), (8, $^-2$), (7, $^-8$)

Pages 402–403 **1.** (0, 4), (1, 3), (2, 2), (3, 1), (4, 0), (5, $^-1$), (6, $^-2$) **3.** (0, 2), (1, 3), (2, 4), (3, 5), (4, 6), (5, 7), (6, 8) **5.** 1, 0, $^-1$, $^-2$, $^-3$, $^-4$, $^-5$ **7.** $^-1$, 0, 1, 2, 3, 4, 5 **9.** 3, 2, 1, 0, $^-1$, $^-2$, $^-3$ **11.** $^-5$, $^-4$, $^-3$, $^-2$, $^-1$, 0, 1 CHECKPOINT B **1.** $^-24$ **2.** 42 **3.** $^-9$ **4.** 20 **5.** $^-4$ **6.** $^-5$ **7.** 8 **8.** 4 **9.** $^-3$ **10.** 8 **11.** $^-9$ **12.** $^-40$ **13.** ($^-1$, 4) **14.** ($^-5$, 0) **15.** ($^-3$, $^-2$) **16.** (2, $^-5$) **17.** 2, 1, 0, $^-1$, $^-2$, $^-3$, $^-4$

Pages 404–405 **1.** b **3.** a **5.** Anne

Page 406 **1.** $^-15$ **3.** 0 **5.** > **7.** > **9.** − **11.** − **13.** − **15.** ($^-1$, 4) **17.** ($^-4$, $^-3$) **19.** (3, $^-1$) **21.** $^-2$, $^-3$, $^-4$, $^-5$, $^-6$, $^-7$, $^-8$ **23.** Sara, T; Tara, L; Lara, S

Pages 408–409 Answers may vary for Exercises 1–23. One possible solution is given. **1.** $\frac{13}{3}$ **3.** $\frac{-13}{2}$ **5.** $\frac{76}{3}$ **7.** $\frac{6}{1}$ **9.** $\frac{-100}{1}$ **11.** $\frac{-1}{1}$ **13.** $\frac{3}{10}$ **15.** $\frac{-27}{100}$ **17.** $\frac{-19}{10}$ **19.** $\frac{2}{9}$ **21.** $\frac{-17}{99}$ **23.** $\frac{-7}{99}$ **25.** $\frac{-3}{5}$ **27.** $\frac{1}{3}$ **29.** $\frac{5}{9}$ **31.** $^-1$ **33.** $\frac{-2}{9}$ **35.** $\frac{-1}{7}$ **37.** $\frac{3}{10}$ **39.** $\frac{-1}{3}$ **41.** $\frac{-7}{8}$ **43.** $\frac{1}{5}$ **45.** T **47.** T

Pages 410–411 **1.** c **3.** b **5.** a **7.** c **9.** b **11.** a **13.** b **15.** a **17.** b **19.** d **21.** a

APPLYING YOUR SKILLS **Pages 412–413** **1.** $1725; $225 **3.** $4270.08; $770.08 **5.** $6920 **7.** $185 **9.** 12 mo **Pages 414–415** **1.** $1.24 **3.** $13.37 **5.** $950.61 **7.** $9.52 **9.** $2133.42 **Pages 416–417** **1.** $7\frac{3}{4}$ h; $7\frac{1}{2}$ h; 7 h **3.** $65.81 **5.** $81.07 **7.** $883.72 **9.** $75.00 **11.** $824.68 **13. a.** $1596 **b.** $106.93 **c.** $71.82 **d.** $1104.77 **Page 418** **1.** 2, 3, 4, 5, 9, 24; $p = l - 1$ or $l = p + 1$ **3.** Yes **5.** Yes

EXTRA PRACTICE **Unit 1 Page 420** CHECKPOINT A **1.** 307 **3.** 33,000,286 **5.** 209,065 **7.** 10.7 **9.** 0.291 **11.** 32.5008 **13.** < **15.** 2.63, 2.53, 1.69, 1.53, 1.06 CHECKPOINT B **1.** 390 **3.** 71,000 **5.** 6 **7.** 0.238 **9.** 3 cm **11.** 500 **13.** 17,000 **15.** 19 **Page 421** (pages 10–19) **1.** < **3.** > **5.** < **7.** > **9.** < (pages 20–23) **1.** 790 **3.** 4000 **5.** 65,000 **7.** 7500 **9.** 8 **11.** 1.2 **13.** 4.39 **15.** 1 (pages 24–25) **1.** 3 cm (pages 26–31) **1.** 400 **3.** 25,000 **5.** 17,000 **7.** 9000 (pages 32–33) **1.** Jane

Unit 2 Page 422 CHECKPOINT A **1.** 8 **3.** 13 **5.** Associative **7.** 12,705 **9.** 3.501 **11.** 242 **13.** 6888 **15.** 0.51 **17.** 4.286 CHECKPOINT B **1.** 54 **3.** 0.591 **5.** 854 **7.** 3500 **9.** 16 ft 1 in. **11.** 24 min 35 s **Page 423** (pages 40–43) **1.** 6 **3.** 5 **5.** 7 (pages 44–45) **1.** 987 **3.** 117 **5.** 6.26 **7.** 1.589 **9.** 0.537 (pages 56–57) **1.** 112 **3.** 2.5 (pages 58–59) **1.** 6 h 6 min **3.** 4 pt 1 c **5.** 32 h 17 min (pages 60–61) **1.** $288.75

Unit 3 Page 424 CHECKPOINT A **1.** 5 **3.** 9 **5.** 7 **7.** 22 **9.** 15,678 **11.** 2.72 **13.** 9 **15.** 125 CHECKPOINT B **1.** 4 R16 **3.** 12,765 R3 **5.** 13 R13 **7.** 45 R18 **9.** 0.3 **11.** 0.0288 **13.** 32 **15.** 0.02952 **17.** 2.5 **19.** 1000 **21.** 210 **Page 425** (pages 68–73) **1.** 3 **3.** 64 **5.** 8 (pages 74–79) **1.** 468 **3.** 7280 **5.** 0.72 **7.** 3.888 **9.** 49 **11.** 81 (pages 80–89) **1.** 122 R3 **3.** 634 R10 **5.** 0.37 **7.** 17.4 **9.** 304 (pages 90–91) **1.** 10 **3.** 200 **5.** 192 (pages 92–93) **1.** Answers may vary. One possible answer: How many tickets do they need to sell to raise enough money for costumes?

Unit 4 Page 426 CHECKPOINT A **1.** T **3.** F **5.** Acute **7.** Right **9.** Hexagon
11. Square **13.** Rectangle CHECKPOINT B **1.** 14 cm **3.** 8.0 cm **5.** 50.24 mm **7.** 300 cm^2
9. 51 m^2 **Page 427** (pages 100–105) **1.** line AB **3.** angle JIH; right (pages 106–111)
1. Isosceles triangle **3.** Square (pages 112–115) **1.** 18 cm **3.** 19.782 cm (pages 116–121)
1. 54 m^2 **3.** 19.625 cm^2 (pages 122–123) **1.** 391 cm^2

Unit 5 Page 428 CHECKPOINT A **1.** 8; 4 **3.** 24; 2 **5.** Yes **7.** Yes **9.** $2 \times 5 \times 5$
11. $5 \times 5 \times 7$ CHECKPOINT B **1.** 12 **3.** 3 **5.** $\frac{3}{5}$ **7.** $\frac{4}{5}$ **9.** $\frac{7}{9}$ **11.** $>$ **13.** $>$ **15.** $5\frac{2}{3}$
17. 4 **19.** 0.8 **21.** $0.\overline{7}$ **23.** 0.75 **25.** $\frac{9}{40}$ **27.** $\frac{1}{8}$ **Page 429** (pages 138–145) **1.** 20; 2
3. 30; 3 **5.** 63; 1 **7.** 27; 9 **9.** 36; 2 **11.** $2 \times 2 \times 5$ **13.** $2 \times 3 \times 7$
15. $2 \times 2 \times 2 \times 3 \times 3$ (pages 146–155) **1.** $>$ **3.** $<$ **5.** $<$ **7.** $<$ **9.** $<$ **11.** $5\frac{1}{4}$ (pages
156–159) **1.** 0.2 **3.** $0.8\overline{3}$ **5.** $\frac{3}{4}$ (pages 160–161) **1.** \$7.53

Unit 6 Page 430 CHECKPOINT A **1.** $\frac{4}{5}$ **3.** $\frac{1}{3}$ **5.** $\frac{2}{3}$ **7.** $1\frac{1}{2}$ **9.** $\frac{8}{15}$ **11.** $7\frac{3}{7}$ **13.** $4\frac{11}{12}$ **15.** $5\frac{39}{40}$
CHECKPOINT B **1.** $\frac{1}{2}$ **3.** $\frac{1}{6}$ **5.** $\frac{11}{18}$ **7.** $3\frac{1}{12}$ **9.** $6\frac{7}{12}$ **11.** $4\frac{2}{3}$ **13.** $5\frac{1}{5}$ **15.** $1\frac{2}{9}$ **17.** $2\frac{1}{2}$ **19.** $\frac{5}{12}$
Page 431 (pages 168–175) **1.** $1\frac{3}{10}$ **3.** $1\frac{1}{9}$ **5.** $10\frac{11}{24}$ **7.** $13\frac{11}{30}$ (pages 176–183) **1.** $\frac{1}{2}$ **3.** $3\frac{2}{3}$
5. $2\frac{5}{12}$ **7.** $2\frac{1}{15}$ **9.** $2\frac{1}{7}$ **11.** $1\frac{3}{4}$ (pages 184–185) **1.** 120 ft^2

Unit 7 Page 432 CHECKPOINT A **1.** 18 **3.** $7\frac{7}{8}$ **5.** $\frac{6}{25}$ **7.** $\frac{5}{36}$ **9.** $\frac{1}{8}$ **11.** $\frac{5}{14}$ **13.** $\frac{1}{3}$ **15.** $\frac{1}{2}$
17. 3 **19.** $53\frac{1}{12}$ **21.** $8\frac{22}{27}$ **23.** $28\frac{1}{8}$ CHECKPOINT B **1.** $\frac{4}{3}$ **3.** $\frac{5}{49}$ **5.** $\frac{9}{119}$ **7.** $\frac{1}{60}$ **9.** $\frac{3}{88}$ **11.** $1\frac{1}{2}$
13. $\frac{7}{9}$ **15.** $1\frac{17}{27}$ **17.** $1\frac{3}{11}$ **19.** $27\frac{1}{5}$ **21.** 28 **23.** $3\frac{21}{85}$ **25.** $1\frac{47}{49}$ **27.** 6 **29.** 16 **Page 433**
(pages 192–199) **1.** 9 **3.** $5\frac{1}{3}$ **5.** $\frac{5}{48}$ **7.** $\frac{2}{15}$ **9.** $\frac{2}{3}$ **11.** 21 **13.** $11\frac{7}{10}$ **15.** $8\frac{16}{21}$ (pages 200–207)
1. 10 **3.** $17\frac{1}{2}$ **5.** $\frac{7}{9}$ **7.** $1\frac{1}{2}$ **9.** $\frac{7}{12}$ **11.** $8\frac{2}{5}$ **13.** $3\frac{9}{13}$ **15.** $\frac{6}{7}$ (pages 208–209) **1.** \$19.96

Unit 8 Page 434 CHECKPOINT A **1.** $b + 6$ **3.** 16 **5.** 24 **7.** Yes **9.** Yes **11.** $n - 7 = 11$;
18 **13.** $n - 35 = 14$; 49 CHECKPOINT B **1.** $\frac{n}{4} = 5$; 20 **3.** 13 **5.** 125 **7.** 6 **9.** (1, 3)
11. (0, 1) **13.** (4, 1) **Page 435** (pages 216–219) **1.** 15 **3.** 2 **5.** 3 (pages 220–225)
1. 22 **3.** 68 **5.** 68 **7.** 18 **9.** 131 (pages 226–231) **1.** 48 **3.** 45 **5.** 100 **7.** 112
9. 264 (pages 232–235) **1.** 6 **3.** 4 **5.** 9 (pages 236–237) **1.** $m - 5 = 15$; 20 nuts

Unit 9 Page 436 CHECKPOINT A **1.** $\frac{1}{4}$ **3.** $\frac{2}{3}$ **5.** \$.26/can **7.** B **9.** A **11.** 78 **13.** 19
15. 4 **17.** 2.5 CHECKPOINT B **1.** 24 cm **3.** 6 km **5.** 2.4 km **7.** 8.4 m **Page 437** (pages
244–247) **1.** $\frac{1}{4}$ **3.** $\frac{1}{5}$ **5.** $\frac{2}{9}$ (pages 248–253) **1.** 14 **3.** 9 **5.** 144 **7.** 2.8 **9.** 0.1 (pages
254–261) **1.** 450 km **3.** 1500 km **5.** 20 m (pages 262–263) **1.** 36 students

Unit 10 Page 438 CHECKPOINT A **1.** 18% **3.** 16% **5.** 48% **7.** 0.21 **9.** 0.162 **11.** $\frac{9}{10}$
13. $\frac{33}{200}$ **15.** 80% **17.** $16\frac{2}{3}$% CHECKPOINT B **1.** 27 **3.** 3.3 **5.** 35% **7.** 75% **9.** 120
11. 45.5 **13.** 5% **15.** 75 **Page 439** (pages 278–285) **1.** 0.08 **3.** 0.95 **5.** $\frac{9}{10}$ **7.** $\frac{13}{25}$
9. 19% **11.** 75% **13.** 9% **15.** 70% (pages 286–293) **1.** 31 **3.** 75% **5.** 51 **7.** 75 (pages
294–295) **1.** 254 stations **5.** 75%

Unit 11 Page 440 CHECKPOINT A **1.** 40% **3.** \$20.95 **5.** \$10.77 CHECKPOINT B **1.** 220
3. 5% **5.** \$5600 **7.** \$787.50 **9.** 85% **11.** \$11.23 **Page 441** (pages 302–309) **1.** \$68.90
3. \$131.25 (pages 310–313) **1.** \$704 **3.** \$264 **5.** \$220 (pages 314–317) **1.** 18%
3. \$62.84 (pages 318–319) **1.** 60 g

Unit 12 **Page 442** CHECKPOINT A **1.** 1 **3.** $\frac{1}{6}$ **5.** $\frac{1}{6}$ **7.** 12 **9.** $\frac{1}{36}$ **11.** $\frac{1}{36}$ **13.** $\frac{4}{5}$
CHECKPOINT B **1.** 12; 75; 75; 75 **3.** 40; 26; 40; mode and median **5.** 37°C **7.** 39°C
Page 443 (pages 326–335) **1.** $\frac{1}{8}$ **3.** $\frac{1}{4}$ **5.** 2 **7.** $\frac{1}{64}$ **9.** $\frac{1}{16}$ (pages 336–341) **1.** 88; 55.8; 45;
32 **3.** Median (pages 342–347) **1.** 400 **3.** 200 (pages 348–349) **1.** 2000 birds

Unit 13 **Page 444** CHECKPOINT A **1.** $\angle$E **3.** $\angle$A **5.** $\overline{BI}$ **11.** line CHECKPOINT B **1.** T
3. 158 m^2 **5.** 189 cm^3 **Page 445** (pages 356–357) **1.** $\angle Q$ **3.** $\angle P$ **5.** $\overline{LM}$ (pages
366–371) **1.** 812 cm^2 **3.** 408.2 m^2 (pages 372–375) **1.** 160 m^3 (pages 376–377) **1.** 400 tiles

Unit 14 **Page 446** CHECKPOINT A **1.** $^-$14 **3.** 25 **5.** $^-$9 **7.** > **9.** < **11.** $^-$33 **13.** $^-$31
15. 23 **17.** 10 CHECKPOINT B **1.** 126 **3.** $^-$26 **5.** $^-$7 **7.** 8 **9.** $^-$5 **11.** $^-$12 **13.** ($^-$2, 3)
15. ($^-$2, $^-$2) **17.** 5, 4, 3, 2, 1, 0, $^-$1 **Page 447** (pages 384–387) **1.** $^-$3, $^-$1, 0, 3
3. $^-$3, $^-$1, 0, 3 **5.** $^-$3, $^-$2, 0, 1 **7.** $^-$5, $^-$2, 3, 7 **9.** $^-$6, $^-$1, 0, 5 (pages 388–393) **1.** $^-$2 **3.** $^-$27
5. 33 (pages 394–397) **7.** 36 **9.** $^-$160 **11.** $^-$4 (pages 398–403) **1.** 4, 3, 2, 1, 0, $^-$1 (pages
404–405) **1.** Yellow: 16, Blue: 11, Green: 7